Now That

You Have

Awakened

Apply Metaphysical Perspectives

Conversations with Heaven on Earth

All I ask of you is forever to remember me as loving you.
As we make our way through all the joys and pain,
can we sense our younger, truer selves?
All I ask of you is forever to remember me as loving you.
Someone will be calling you to be there for a while.
Can you hear the cry from deep within?
All I ask of you is forever to remember me as loving you.
Laughter, joy and presence: the only gifts you are.
Have you time? I'd like to be with you.
All I ask of you is forever to remember me as loving you.
Persons come into the fiber of our lives,
and then their shadow fades and disappears.
All I ask of you is forever to remember me as loving you.

(the song Gaia wanted us to feeling into as a message from her)

Written by Gregory Norbet

We are blessed to be more understanding and aware about how timelines work, and working to bring this book together we can see the shift between the different approaches to awaken humanity, given what we learnt from the sessions which was made into the book TIME: The Convoluted Concept of Being Human.

We trust you will be guided to read these books in the order that work for you, we know just by opening them up to any page will give you insight which often is the perspective you have been seeking,

All these Quantum Sessions have significance to them being placed in this book, some are from 2020 as a reflection of the growth of our journey and timelines, while nearly half are from recent sessions this year, 2023.

Censorship on some platforms inspired us to start transcripting all recent QHHT and BQH and channeling sessions we have in the order we were given the information and make this book for you.

In times of needing balance and support, having the physical books will be our best way to ensure we have this information always on hand. Our thoughts are with people who could not get access to the sessions on Youtube anyway.

ALL this content is from recent private sessions and important sessions not yet shared in books.

We still share sessions publicly through TELEGRAM, which is a free app - search CONVERSATIONS WITH HEAVEN ON EARTH, also find us on FACEBOOK and INSTAGRAM

With love.

Be accountable!

With great power comes great responsibility.

We know hurt people, hurt people; as they are reactive to their unhealed pain. This can be consciously or unconsciously done.

Being responsible for our feelings and thoughts goes further than just reactions and words - we must be responsible for our own energy we project onto others.

When people use their energy to impact others that is misusing their energy connections and when we are all still learning to empower ourselves to love and heal from all life experiences while giving people our own unconditional love - projecting anything else which is not LOVE that is disempowering them and misusing energy in what can be very harmful ways.

Our collectives want us to heal and be mature and responsible for our energy.

Good people can still hurt others as they are reacting to their triggers to grow.

Really think about this and when we are ready to LOVE humanity and be of service that is when we will truly feel part of the community and honestly be in high vibrational balance.

Love yourself and Love others - doing anything else is a distraction.

This book has been edited by many incredible humans who are of service FOR YOU.

They have worked hard to edit the verbal messages from sessions into a smooth and easy to read format.

You are welcome to listen to the original sessions for the ones which are public to hear.

As we have been guided to remind you – reading this information – you will be able to absorb the content easily.

To honor all who worked on this book freely for you, it would be most respectful and appreciated if *you can apply the information into your daily life, which would empower you in the most profound of ways.*

As each person was guided to edit the sessions, their format felt appropriate for them. Accepting others' approaches is part of our inner work to accept and respect all. Do not get distracted by the details ~ focus on the concepts given.

You are very much loved and have been guided to this information at a very important time for humanity, this planet, and for your Soul experience here on Earth ~ in honor of Mastering being Human.

Please write the page numbers for the chapters when you finish reading in the Table of Contents.

Table of Contents

Session 1	Franklin D. Roosevelt
Session 2	Ashtar: Evacuating Earth
Session 3	London Event
Session 4	Arcturians: Release of Information
Session 5	Peer Pressure Parent Healing
Session 6	Reptilian Collective Release Control
Session 7	Shiva and Higher Soul Self
Session 8	Reptilians telling on the Draconians
Session 9	Healing For All Abused People
Session 10	Home Planet Destruction Impacting This Lifetime
Session 11	Old Earth - The Shift - The Light Beam Event
Session 12	Taking account of LIFE CONTRACTS for ALL
Session 13	It's Ramping Up - Step In, Be Of Service
Session 14	Integrity with Energy and Life Contracts
Session 15 `	Robin Williams
Session 16	Big Epiphanies of a Draconian
Session 17	Influencers with Draconian Walk-In
Session 18	Would Be Helpful For You To Apply
Session 19	How To Know Thyself
Session 20	Feeling Traumatized Being Human
Session 21	Arcturians and Bruce Lee: Preparing for the Shift
Session 22	Why Are You Here?
Session 23	How To Achieve Enlightenment
Session 24	You're Magical, Not Abandoned
Session 25	Away With The Fairies, Going Home
Session 26	Metaphysical Perspective of Cosmetic Surgery
Session 27	Dolores Cannon, Use Your Power
Session 28	Take The Wheel, Be Metaphysically Mature
Session 29	Dump That Density
Session 30	To Occur For The Grand Awakening
Session 31	Start Seeds
Session 32	The Most Appropriate Information
Session 33	Making Contact In 3D
Session 34	Helixclipse, Moon - Part of the Laser Event
Session 35	Apply Metaphysical Perspectives
Session 36	Rechargeable Battery or Acid Batteries
Session 37	Past Present Future Impacting You Now
Session 38	Gaia's Gratitude

Session 39   Being An Aspect Of Source
Session 40   John Fitzgerald Kennedy
Session 41   Working With The Conscious Collective
Session 42   Soul VS Ego - Balance Is Everything
Session 43   Most Important Session In This Book
Session 44   New To This Work
Session 45   3D To 5D To 3D
Session 46   Love All, Judge None

Session 1: Franklin D. Roosevelt shares some information that might surprise you

Yes. Thank you very much for calling me in today. I do have many messages to share with you. It is correct that my passing was not due to ill health at all. Most of my closest friends and family were suspicious of this and knew this. This was a very timely affair for Americans and for my country and for the world. I was aware of what was happening regarding the bombs that were being planned to be experimented with. While it was presented to me in a fashion that showed our strength as a country, it did not give me the full truth. I was starting to be suspicious of the information that was being given to me, because while I did want to have a firm hand to protect my country, I did not want it to get out of hand. My suspicions grew and my questions followed, and I was not convinced that this was how we needed to make our firm stronghold. Unfortunately, my opinion was not followed or agreed by the others who wanted to push their own agenda. Therefore, I was poisoned with a nerve serum that started to eat away at my body. It was slow, and I endured it. It lasted a few weeks and then I passed and I succumbed to it[1].

These things do not matter now. You all know the history that took place following my demise[2]. The purpose of coming here to you today to tell you this, is to show you once again, another way that humanity has been pushed into the darkness. Pushed into the wars. Pushed into the crimes against humanity. We have tried. I tried and many others before and after me have tried to help humanity. Our

---

[1] April 12, 1945 (aged 63)
[2] The bombing of Hiroshima and Nagasaki, 6th and 9th of August 1945

consciences grew bigger. While we were trying to balance it all, we did lose and drop the ball on some. You know, I am sorry. I am sorry for not sharing my voice and not following my suspicions and intuition. I did trust the people around me who were working for me and with me to help humanity and to help my country. However, I was not fully aware of all the other agendas.

Now, from this perspective I can see it all greatly, and I can see how I could have improved and been more in tune with my gut instincts. I was blindsided, and it was unfortunate because I did want to help my fellow Americans. I did want to support them and push on through, but I also wanted to make us a strong country and make us world leaders. I did feel so proud of my beautiful country and I wanted to support us and go through and move through with that. And I did have my best intentions. I can promise you that I always did the best I could. What I saw, what I did see and what I trusted and believed, I fully, wholeheartedly went for it!

My wife is here now with me and our message together is that we were so fondly connected to our fellow men and our country. While we did know there were some little groups that were not so pure at heart and intentions for our country and for their own countries, we thought we were making amends. We thought we were making headways. And we thought we were winning to help people. That's truly what we wanted to do for humanity and for Americans. We both send you our kindest regards and appreciations. We hope that you can see that we tried to do the best we could.

Now, from the other side of it, we can see that there has been a lot of manipulation that has happened before our times, during our times and after our times. Just like us, we didn't follow our intuition and we didn't see the signs that we could have potentially paid more focus on. We got surrounded and distracted by the finer affairs of being the president and the first lady, and we enjoyed our roles immensely. We tried to stay humble and not to go overboard and let our egos take off. We did see that with other people, other celebrities, other people of importance and leaders around the world. We did not want to be those and we wanted to ground ourselves and be very humble and to keep true to our core values. This is why it does shame us to some extent, how we did miss those other details. So this is something that we need to work on, and we will be. We both want to reincarnate on the New Earth and we're very excited for that. It will be within our family lineage because we have Soul contracts and life contracts with our current families who are here on Earth. That makes us really excited, and we've been here watching and we're proud of how people are rising up! We are proud of people using their intuition and seeing things we could not see. You do not need to be the first lady and the president of the United States of America to know what's happening to humanity and for your countries.

This makes me emotional because I can see the pain that people have caused on each other just through sheer lack of intuition, integrity and sheer stubbornness in some cases. It's all learning lessons, and when you see things from this perspective you can put it into place. While I'm sitting here, figuratively, and I'm looking and I'm seeing the people who organized my demise, who intentionally needed to get me out of the way, because I did not want to continue on with the plans we had. I did not want to pursue the bombings of

Japan! I knew that they were a crippled country and I knew that they were bluffing their rage and their intent to have war with us. I was aware of that and potentially I was aware of that in the last stages. I should have seen that earlier. I should have had the good men beside me to tell me the whole truth and nothing but the whole truth.

So, I can see things now! I do not blame the people. They will have to take on that burden themselves and grow from that. I can appreciate most people who have done wrong have a firm belief at the time they are doing right. So therefore, I have no malice for them. I know they will go have their own growth and I have talked to some since, as they have now passed. They can also be humbled by their actions, so do not fret! All is balanced now and will continually be balanced. This currently is a great time for humanity and what we understand, this must seem very confusing and scary for many. Great things are about to happen.

We would like to now also remind you of other things that have happened that you haven't potentially been given the full truth on. The nerve agent they killed me slowly with was very similar to the other nerve agents that have been produced for quite some time. I'd like you to pay your attention to Polio. This is not a disease or an illness or a sickness that is of natural causation. Unfortunately, I have to advise you that this is man-made! This was caused to produce harm. It was going to be a weapon of mass destruction to some degree, and the intent was to harm children. To get sympathy and control and get people focusing on their children and being afraid of harm. You can relate this now to somewhat the virus that you've been told about now. It has the same agenda controlling factors to it.

So, the Polio was created to, in quotation marks "help" but it ended up poisoning. So what it does is it poisons the nerves so the nerves stop functioning and start eating into some of the organs, specifically the lungs, the spleen. The usage of legs was because the nerve endings all died. It was not pleasant and there's still some that are suffering from this damage. So move forward to the vaccinations. We've already discussed this. We have heard this in other sessions now and this is why I was prompted and wanted to come and talk about this further because this happened to me. I was exposed to nerve agents earlier on as a child and it did cause me physical disabilities because my nerves were poisoned. Again, the people who thought that they were doing well and helping create the vaccine for Polio were not quite given the full truth about what was causing it. There is an agenda to keep you sick and it is not for evil, it is for money! They don't care what they've done to you. They want to continually have clients and customers. They need to keep you sick so then they have customers. It keeps their shareholders happy!

While some of you know this, this may be a shock to others. The diseases that you are vaccinating your children for are not the boogeyman you are being led to believe. Yes, your bodies get sick, but your bodies are miraculate machines that are more powerful than you give recognition to. So, when you start misusing it, when you start poisoning it with vaccines, when you start poisoning it with foods which are also laced with chemicals and other agents that are not good for your bodies. Then you drink the water which is full of other nonsense, you're not giving yourself the best chances! Right now your bodies are purging! Your bodies are detoxing from all the poisons you've had. Those heavy metals are slowly being released as your DNA, and your body structures are purging through. There's nothing to be afraid of. All the harm that has happened to you in this lifetime and all the other lifetimes you've ever lived on Earth, they've been cleansed and healed too! Any weird feelings of pain potentially could be from a past lifetime. Do not worry! Do not let your minds run into fear! There is nothing to be afraid of! As you have heard in these other sessions, you only need to go within and ask if everything is okay, to get your true answers. Using your intuition is always going to be your best approach forward. Have no guru! Create yourself *your own* guru! Believe in yourself enough. You always have the truth within you. There has been so much held against you to make you believe you're not good enough. We want you to keep reminding yourself you are! Your intuition is your key. Your intuition is everything! You cannot underestimate your intuition anymore. It is more exhausting and more hard work doubting your intuition than just releasing and accepting and going with it. Always go with your intuition. Sometimes it is harder for you when you have got the toxins and you've got the low vibrational energies around you, so you have to do self love first. Remember, really get that positive attitude towards yourself to then be able to go within and get the answers. We believe you can do it when you want to. When you commit to yourself you will!

In closing, we would like to thank you for reading. Thank you for not overreacting and being shocked. Understanding that a lot of your history has been hidden from you and this will be confirmed when you have shifted into the higher dimensions. You will have your inner intuition completely given to you profoundly, because you're in that higher state, your bodies have changed, they're crystalline, so your connection to self is just switched on, shall we say. That veil of fogginess, that kind of creeps over you making you still doubt yourselves, forgetting who you are, all of that gets taken off because that was part of the challenge of this game of life. It's forgetting who you are and seeing if you can remember and coming back to yourselves. So while it seems bizarre (potentially) for you reading this, why on Earth would you agree to it? You will all remember very soon why. It is all okay. Try not to take the third world... the third mindset world... the 3D world, I should say. Try not to let it eat into you and bother you. It really doesn't impact you until you pay attention to it. Don't let your emotions get swayed down, back into that nonsense. It looks very real when you're watching TV. Remember, you have the power to turn it off. You have the power to do anything you want. Remember that! Nothing is happening *to you*. You're *allowing* it all to happen to yourself.

We say this with much love to all!

We wish you a tremendous time, leading up to the event, because there's still so much fun to have. We want you to feel the joy and the excitement and still be able to focus on what you still need to do; the last remaining inner work parts that you need, supporting any other fellow man that you can.

We say this with much love!

Session 2: Ashtar: Evacuating Earth

J: *Is there any other information you'd like her to know about her physical body?*

S: She's slacked off on drinking water. She's had a taste for coffee at night. She needs to incorporate, maybe only one cup of coffee and continue drinking the water. The body needs the water. It keeps it from getting dense from all the toxins in the air. It flushes them out. She won't feel as heavy. She won't be as tired and symptoms that she feels from extra energy and upgrades will be lessened. Water is very important for everyone right now. So I'm going to remind her, double up.

J: *Thank you and tell me about the toxins in the air at the moment.*

S: There is quite a bit of wind in the area she lives in and depending on the day it could come from different directions. When the wind's coming out of the west, straight out of the west, there's still a lot of radiation that's traveled across the Pacific Ocean from a nuclear accident that happened years ago[3]. They're still dealing with that, and the winds still carry some of these toxins. They're not nearly as strong, but they're still in the air. When the wind comes out of the north, most of that pollutant is from fires and ash that occurred a season back, but it's still in the vegetation and trees, and the wind is picking it up and moving it around. So those toxins aren't very good, either. Then of course, there's the dust that's in her own area[4]. There is a lot of oil and gas

---

[3] *The tsunami caused the Fukushima Daiichi nuclear disaster, primarily the meltdowns of three of its reactors, the discharge of radioactive water in Fukushima and the associated evacuation zones affecting hundreds of thousands of residents, after the "**Great East Japan Earthquake 2011**.*

work and there's a lot of chemicals used for that industry. Everything that touches the ground isn't always cleaned up, so that's also carried in the air. Those chemicals can be very harsh on a human's body.

J: *I see. So in terms of what you are able to do for us with protecting us from that, what is happening there?*
S: From all the chemicals?

J: *Yes, the toxins in the air.*
S: The Earth used to cleanse itself perfectly. It was built to do that. We haven't helped as before. It is going to be a part of knowing your body and experiencing what can happen when you don't take care of a planet. So there are lessons there. They're not going to kill people, the toxins that are out there, but it will make them aware their body can't handle even this minute amount of pollutants. Going forward, as people move on to other destinations, they will be more considerate of their environment and the natural process of the planet, if it's taken care of, will heal itself, and it won't harm its inhabitants. So there lies a lesson - Take care of your planet and it won't harm you.

J: *That sounds like an appropriate lesson for everyone to experience and learn from.*
S: Yes, some will learn it, harder than others. Some may experience allergies. Some can get infections in their lungs, but the water will definitely help flush the toxins out before they attach to tissues and start to damage them.

J: *Thank you so much. I was wondering if you could give my client an experience today. I'd like to send her to the black void.*

---

[4] *Texas, USA*

It's what I call the ninth dimension where you are everything and nothing. What would you call that? I know you were listening before when we were talking about it.

S: It's a part of eternity. It goes on forever. It cycles back. It can start over again, or it can react like ricocheting, or being spun in a bowl - that would be a better description. If you had a tiny BB, and you had a ball and you just started moving the ball, the BB would start spinning. This is part of the motion that happens there. It's very expansive. I don't think there is an end. It doesn't feel like a bottom, but it feels like a bottom. You can stretch your arms out, and your arms can keep growing and growing and growing and stretching, and you'll never find the end.

J: How does she feel being in that dimension, now?

S: She feels her head or her crown. It's a little tingly and a tiny bit of pressure, but she feels comfortable. She doesn't see anything, it's all pretty dark. It's black - no other way to describe it. I don't know if light is not allowed in or it's being sucked out. It could be both, but she feels safe and she feels comfortable.

J: Nice, yes. It often seems like a place where clients can end up or experience during a session. It always intrigues me - this black void - so I wanted to give her this experience today, just so she could understand that feeling of being connected to everything and nothing at the same time.

S: It is very interesting. She feels like she's floating, even though she knows she's on a surface, laying on a surface, she doesn't feel anything beneath her right now. She's not like standing up, she's not sitting down, she's just there. It's very interesting.

J: Okay, thank you. We'll quit having fun with this experience, and get on to the tasks of our other questions that we have today. So, are you able to give us information, please, about how humanity is going, and what messages Ashtar could have for humanity today, please.

S: He is willing to come forward and communicate. If you have open questions, he'd like to follow that path, and then give a message at the end.

J: Okay, fantastic. So, Asthar, can you tell me about major ships that are connected to the Pleiadians, please. I keep hearing that you have one major ship. Is that correct?

S: There are three major ships that are in the immediate area of planet Earth. They're all there to assist. While humanity is being transported, there will be plenty of room on those three major ships, as you call them. There are thousands of support ships around. Some of the beings that will accompany us. They will start their work immediately. They've already been prepared. Once they ascend off planet earth to go into what you're calling a med bed, they will be cleansed, rejuvenated. They won't need much time to acclimate. They know that the upcoming work they've already contracted to do next is waiting for them. They are so ready to start that. They've agreed to take this expedited course of action so they can get into their roles immediately. They'll be on some of the smaller ships that our support - and the support means guidance not really protection - do monitor as we travel. They could be scout ships that go ahead and make sure that our path is clear, so to speak. There's also supply ships that carry extra accommodations for all passengers because there will be many. Anything from food, water, clothing - anything that is possibly needed. Then there's also some medical ships. There's just a wide array of different support ships. If I go through them all, it could take me a while, so I touch base on the more important things, the comforts that will be needed for all the passengers.

J: *Thank you so much. So I'm assuming that the three major ships you're referring to are of equal importance.*
S: Yes, because their cargo is the humans, the animals, the insects, all the living creatures and specimens and species that are being carried to their new home. That will be on the three bigger ships, and like I said, they're bigger, maybe than you can imagine. One of them is bigger than earth.

J: *In terms of the location of that biggest one, is there any reference point that you could share with us today?*
S: It's below the elliptical. That's why you cannot see it - the elliptical of Earth, it's below that.

J: *Thank you. Another question – Out of curiosity, in a rough estimation of one of these ships sizes, I guess if the one is bigger than the earth, would that mean that one, for example could hold the entire population of Earth?*
S: Well it could, but there's other things to consider. Like for example, the whales, we have to have plenty of water for them to survive the trip. There is what you would call a greenhouse to support the vegetation that will be also transported. Where you're going will have its own wildlife (we'll call it) and plants, but we're bringing the things off earth that represent importance. Also these ships have massive cruise crews members, and their quarters, accommodations, what you would call possibly kitchen - everything is on these ships. We want to make sure there's enough space. Also, if any ..... I don't want to talk about that ..... let's just go to the next one.

J: *Okay, thank you very much. In terms of the safety of traveling to New Earth, are there any scenarios where we may have a concern, because other beings may want to stop our journey?*

S: Interesting enough, that was the question I was not going to answer completely. There are two other ships that aren't quite as big as the first one, but they do accompany our entourage in case they're needed to take on these passengers and continue the journey. So yes, we've prepared for everything. We're not expecting what you may be thinking of as an ambush, - I feel that question coming from you. Everything that we've planned out to make a safe and smooth transition is some of the reasons there have been delays.

J: *Thank you so much. Are you able to give us insight into other reasons why there have been delays?*

S: I could, but there are many people that will listen, and it's not for everyone's ears at this time[5]. Even as they travel and they see and experience everything that's going on around them, they still may not understand. Sometimes it's for the best that they stay in ignorance of what really is going on, and what's happening. It will be less stress and trauma. So I really don't want to answer that one either.

J: *I respect that. I am all for less trauma for humanity, because I feel like it's had enough.*

S: Indeed it has. If one person actually experiences every single person's trauma, that happened on this earth, yeah, that's too much to hold in one cup. There has been a lot of trauma. It's been divided up. Everybody got to experience a

---

[5] *Session was done on* **April 26, 2021**

piece here and a piece there. It's all brought back to Source. The collective knows it and feels it. It can be experienced by each and every soul, at will, once they are in a different dimension. None of the experiences have been lost, they've just been divided up so not one Soul had all the responsibility to collect the data.

J: *Thank you very much. In terms of your relationships with other species, do all species respect you and your Pleiadian team?*

S: They definitely do. I know it might not seem that way to other species, but I know I have the respect. I've had many conversations with many different species. I have a very high command, and so I'm respected greatly. They can trust my word. I play fair. It's very just and we do it in a loving way.

J: *Well, thank you very much for your service to help humanity be able to have this experience and the safety with the evacuation. I'm curious to know, from our perspective how would you like us to view the Draconians?*

S: When you speak about trust, that species likes to offer a handshake, so you trust them. But, they don't ever live up to a handshake. You have to get them to agree to treaties similar to the treaties that humans have made with each other on the planet Earth. Some of them are made to be broken. As soon as they walk away from the negotiation tables, they're already finding ways to trick or beat out what they just agreed to. The Draconians are like that. They do it with a smile on their face, as well. It's just a fun game to them. So in the end, they aren't to be trusted. They're not a man of their word.

J: Okay, and likewise, same question for the species that we call Reptilians.

S: They're definitely in the same league, although they don't have the technology or the influence throughout the universe to do a lot of damage. They're only out for themselves. They're on a much smaller scale. The Draconians, on the other hand, have long arms, they can reach far, and we've been trying. We have been working with them for a long time. Once they mature more and find love in their hearts, this will all stop. We've been exposing them to that kind of mindset in the hopes that it will grow within them, and it will become part of their culture.

J: Will this be part of their experience, for those who remain on the Old Earth?

S: For the Reptilians, yes. The Draconians will evacuate. It might be at the very last second, but they will definitely leave Earth before it's too late. They don't want any of their citizens in harm's way, so they will definitely have a call home signal, and everybody will leave - that is the Draconians, that is. The Reptilians will still be here. They will experience a part of the days after the shift. It won't be as hard on them because they came from a world that was much more harsh than even what Old Earth will be. So they've been living in luxury right now, compared to what they had before, and that's why they like Earth. They wanted it to be their home. Once the supply of energy is diminished here, it will go back to what they lived through on their own planet, and their own planet doesn't exist anymore. They will not be in hiding as much, because the human population won't be a threat to them, because there's not as many. They will encounter each other. The humans with the open mind that do not live in fear will befriend some of the Reptilians.

They actually can help each other and share knowledge, survival skills. The exposure of compassion that humans have will actually help the Reptilians. It won't happen very fast for them. The energy that's left on Earth is not a lot - to allow the growth, but they still will be exposed to compassion and love.

J: *Fantastic. Is there anything else you would like us to know about the Old Earth, Ashtar?*
S: The trials and tribulations are only fit for a warrior to face. Everyone will have to have their bravest suit on. There's no time - I don't want to use this word, but there's no time for crybabies. Everybody has to pull up their boot straps, square their shoulders, and walk with a purpose, and they know their purpose. They will all feel it. Their spiritual teams will still be there to help them and guide them. They'll be assisted along the way. Even though our mission won't be around this planet (it'll be shooting off somewhere else in its space) there will be a few of our own ships that are left out there for monitoring and protection. They will buffer the Earth with as much energy as possible, but it's nothing like anyone's been used to. It'll be on such a smaller scale, but it's enough to help humanity that's left grow, and get the messages that their spiritual team needs to get through to them. So the support is still there and they will not be alone.

J: *Thank you. So just to clarify, the people that are staying on the Old Earth are volunteers, to be enlisted in terms that this is obviously contractual.*
S: It's been both ways. Some volunteered because they know the importance of the success of the entire mission from beginning to end. It looks like some were enlisted, but ultimately they did agree to the contract. They were asked

and they agreed. So we could view that as an enlistment. Those are the ones that possibly knew they had family members staying behind, so they agreed to stay along with them. There were some volunteers that did this for the same reason. I wouldn't call it selfish, because they're still helping humanity. But when the contracts changed, and it hasn't been that long, they all had their own agendas, and it was mainly to help people that were close to them, that didn't have the opportunity to go with the first shift. Because there will be another shift, possibly two after that, until the whole thing is phased out here. So the initial, and three shifts after that - the whole process, because I know you want to know, may take probably 26 Earth months - 26 times that you'll see the full moon. That's what I'm seeing.

J: *Okay, that's interesting. Thank you so much. We kind of already were aware that it was around two years from the first shift until the completion of the Earth's existence. Is it what you're referring to?*
S: Yes. The Soul of Gaia - it will take some time for her whole process to be completed. That's what we're predicting, because the planet's really never done this before - where we had to assist the leaving of one vessel and entering another. So while that is happening, the humans that are left on Old Earth, the original ones that already contracted before they incarnated here, they knew they were staying, they knew they were to support, or they wanted to witness, and record the experience, so to speak. When this planet was created, they helped co-create it. So basically, they gave birth to it and they wanted to be here for the ending as well - full circle for them. There are a hundred different reasons contracts were written, but the newer ones mainly focused on personal relationships that were anchored here. Some

beings still had attachments and they weren't ready to leave them, so they agreed to stay, or when asked to stay, they said 'yes'. That sounds very descriptive. Did I get your question answered?

J: *Yes. It was fantastic. Thank you so much. We're assuming that life contracts change often and regularly.*
S: No, not on a regular basis. It muddies the water, if you change things too often. There are things that needed to be addressed, needed to be more supported, in this case. So when that directive was put out, that's when the volunteers stepped forward. And there wasn't quite enough, so then other Souls were asked and they said 'yes' to the calling.

J: *Thank you so much. Is there a message for the people reading? What would you like them to know from you?*
S: The ones that will be escorted to another home, I want them all to know that we understand there'll be so many emotions along with that as well. **Understand that this is all done in love.** Keep that in your mind first and foremost, and the fear that you're trying to adopt will melt away faster. Everybody that has come to assist Earth and humanity has done it with such great love. We know what you've endured. We are very compassionate and our tenderness will show. Once you meet us, you'll be very happy with the journey ahead of you.

J: *Thank you. Can you give me a sense of what you're going to be doing after this shift and after everyone's settled into a New Earth?*
S: There'll be different teams, even different species, that will help humanity once they arrive. Then, of course, there's all the other creatures. This new environment will be very

pleasant to your eyes. So once you're delivered into the caring hands of those awaiting you, we will depart. I do see other places that I must go and attend to. But, we also leave support ships around the new destination for the meantime, not so much as protection, but in case anything is needed such as supplies that we've carried with us, or different medical attention, or just even more support from our collective. So that will remain in place until everything is running smoothly, and then the ships can depart and join us on our next assignment, as well.

J: *Thank you. Do you have any fragments of your Soul in human bodies on this planet at this time?*
S: I do not. I have friends and comrades that are there. So it's very near to my heart. And this whole project has been very very close to actually several of my beings' hearts. We've watched it and monitored it very closely. That's why, when, you could say, the goal post was moved further - again and again - with the date changes, it had to occur. We were trying to protect all, and it was for the betterment of the whole race. I know that there's been impatient souls, but to accommodate one Soul and not consider the whole population would have been a criminal act. We could have never let that happen. So yeah, I don't have a speck of myself - a spark is what we would call it - on Earth as a Soul and a body, but I have many friends.

J: *Is it emotionally hard for you to see what is happening to your friends, or do you feel something else?*
S: I feel very proud of all the accomplishments. I think to myself sometimes - 'Could I have really done that? Could I have been in human form and so limited and not know who I am?' I could be standing next to a part of my Soul family and

not even know who they were. We see this. But we also see joy and love, so we've laughed and we've cried along with you. It is very emotional, but we stay strong, and we stay on the path and steadfast for the mission at hand, because that's of the utmost importance. We try to set aside our own concerns, personal concerns, and only concentrate on the betterment of all.

J: *So what do you do for your downtime when you're not actually working?*
S: At the current pace, there hasn't been much of that. So, I do like to (might sound a little creepy - I'll use that word) check in on Souls that I know that are on Earth and see how they're doing. I do that in my downtime.

J: *It doesn't sound creepy, it sounds lovely and supportive, and I think everyone who gets your support would always appreciate that, so thank you so much for that. Can you tell us some of the things that you find the most entertaining and amusing that we do?*
S: I love to watch people dance. It's freaking hilarious how they can move their body and their limbs, and oh my gosh that is the best thing ever is to watch people dance. Love it.

J: *Okay, that's good to know. Are there any other final messages that you would like us to know from you today?*
S: Yes. Everybody is so important and everybody's role is so important. I just can't impress on you enough what love and sharing love and showing love means to us to watch. It should mean a lot to you to feel it and to give it and receive it. So continue your missions and your goals in love. You're doing a tremendous job and we're also very very proud of you. So, Thank you! Thank you!

J: *Well, thank you very much for all your support. For all the people that you are close to and to help us I understand – well I have actually no real big comprehension of what your daily life looks like – but I honor you profoundly, for all the services that you do for all of us.*

S: You are so welcome, and we appreciate everything you've done as well. We've visited before, you and I. If we get the chance, and I hope we do once the evacuation occurs, I hope that we can meet in the physical way and have a chat. That would be awesome for me.

J: *I'll practice some dancing moves [Laughter].*

S: Maybe you could teach me. Awesome!

J: *Okay. Yes. I will be your backup dancer, that will be fantastic. I will look forward to that, so thank you, thank you, thank you.*

S: You're so welcome. Thank you for connecting and asking me in.

J: *Oh, you're welcome, you're welcome. So we'll ask the vehicle's higher self to return now, as we ask Ashtar to recede with much love.*

S: I'm back.

J: *Thank you so much. I'm curious to know about the planet that the vehicle was seeing in the night sky. What would you like her to know about the significance of that?*

S: Was this last night? [J: *Yes, that is correct*] She was observing at first, Ursa Major, which is the big dipper. And compared to last season, or I should say last year at this time, it was in a different place. Last night, it was directly above in the sky, and she does know from historic observations that the big dipper is generally in the north west, maybe at 60 degrees. So to her, she's very curious on why the Earth is still tilted, otherwise the big dipper wouldn't have been above her head. It would have been more straight in front of her. Once she saw that, she went out later again, to see how much it moved, but then she noticed a different constellation and that was the Draco constellation. She felt a little, not really a shiver, but it was like 'Hmm, I didn't know that was going to be directly above my head either' she was thinking to herself. It forms almost like a cone, and it looks like a dragon head, the constellation itself. So in the night sky it looks kind of ominous. So she was just curious, because she hasn't seen it in years. She used to study the stars when she first moved here, to see what's in her night sky, but she hasn't seen it, probably because she hasn't been up at that hour. She was like 3, 3:30 in the morning when she was observing that last, I guess this morning. I should say, about the last time. But it made her think of the creature, the Draconians, as well, it should have. So that was the significance with that, what she saw.

J: *And in terms of her wondering why the Earth is still tilted, what can you tell her about that?*
S: The odd thing is the little dipper was in the exact spot it was supposed to be in. There might have been a little lifting of the veil, that she recognized that this constellation was out of place. It wasn't really the Earth being tilted, but when things don't move in the sky properly, it's almost like the template wasn't placed down properly, and it shows these constellations out of place. Only people that have observed them for years and know where they should be would recognize that.

J: *I do recall in another session, you told her to be looking up at the sky and noticing differences.*

S: That is definitely a difference. The moon was maybe 80 percent full last night, so it did dim out a lot of the stars for her, but those constellations that she's seen are easy to pick out. This far south in the little dipper she only sees the star Polaris, which is also called the North Star, but it was in its correct position that she remembers it to be. The big dipper should be to the left of it in the sky if you are facing them straight on, and it was not. It was straight above her head, so she knew it was obviously out of place.

J: *And the significance of her noticing that was?*

S: There are signs of course to watch for. I know that we've given her some before but that one definitely is part of lifting the veil. Things that you think are stationary in the sky, they are not always what they seem to be. It's very unusual that it would be that far off from what I'm viewing, but it was a lot off. It was very obvious to her that it was in the wrong place. So the significance - keep watching. She needs to visit the night sky more often, and pick up on these little subtle signs that are being placed in front of her and others. Others can see them as well. too. I know there's sky maps that can be viewed and studied. People can learn very easily what should be in their skies at certain times of the year.

J: *Thank you so much. In terms of her connection with Ashtar, what can you tell us about that today?*

S: It goes on forever .... before now, now, and after now. They've known each other a long time. They have done work together. He's very happy to come in and connect through her and talk with you. She felt very big while he was here. It's like her shoulders grew and her chest grew, she felt like a really big man. So the experience for her was very comforting to know that the support is actually out there. It's truly amazing to realize for her, that everything that she's been learning and feeling was very profound, to feel it on a more personal level through him.

J: *Indeed, these sessions are very hard to deny when you experience them for yourself.*

S: Very hard. And there's love between them. The Pleiadians are a very loving species. They've brought love to earth. They're still trying to promote that way of life for all creatures. A lot of their missions are focused on everybody living in harmony and learning that way of life.

J: *Fantastic! Thank you so much.*

Session 3: London Event

We were given this information in full details in many sessions which we did not share publicly, it felt too much to cope with just prior to the Christmas session. This was the first session we got about this. As we now know some of the important players were not in this location at the last moment and this then impacted the outcome and so it did not occur. We are sharing this with you now as an example of how much planning is going on behind the scenes as they are trying to work the human ego to best impact them to awaken. This is not to create fear for you but share with you some of the options our collectives were considering.

J: Yes! She's calling in all of the Collectives. We're saying call in some, not all! That is the most appropriate for this conversation. We would like it to just be the Arcturians actually. We want this to be a private affair so we will shut it down. And as we are making this a private meeting, you can begin.

P: Thank you. We're just wondering about the UK and concerns with CERN[6].

J: It's London Central that will be the targeting point of it. And that will be the center point of the destruction. We want to explore this more. We're just waiting for the vehicle to relax so when we talk about this she gets the emotional impact from those who are learning it too. And so we're just disconnecting her from all of that. So yes. What she's been getting intuitively is what we were pushing her to address. It's not a time critical disclosure because it will unfold as it

[6]*From the CERN webpage "At CERN, we probe the fundamental structure of particles that make up everything around us. We do so using the world's largest and most complete scientific instruments." www.home.CERN*

needs to unfold. This is not needing to be public information but you do need to be able to be prepared to understand the specific significance and purpose of this event. As you know it is forecasted a few weeks away from now. And so when people hear this information in advance they want to figure out how they can stop it. This is an unstoppable event. This is necessary. She was wondering, aren't there victims? Aren't there innocent people there? And we are saying of course. You're all innocent. You all are experiencing the third dimension in this lifetime and there are no criminals. There are no monsters there. And even those who you are pretty much convinced that they are scoundrels or monsters or murderers and rapists and the list goes on forever of what you are accusing them of. Those are 3D roles that they are playing. Yes! Life contracts are being extended out to be very dramatic. Everything she is saying and picking up on is us. So she's feeling that this is uncomfortable because of the subject matter. This needs to occur first before the laser event for very significant reasons. Many people are focusing on the events in the states in America. They're worried about potentially a big tsunami from the La Palma, Canary Islands. They're watching this. They're worried about their own earthquakes and volcanoes. So the world's already sort of over listening to the big dramatic countries who are worried about what's going to happen to them. In the UK, in London itself, many people go away from that location. They leave their area to go on their holidays and explore. This is why many of them have wanted to be inoculated. To be able to travel out to those summer locations. And so many of those who you would consider to be innocent in terms of not guilty of these crimes against humanity and not dense. And they will not be in that location. They would have gone away for the Christmas holidays. There are big events happening in between the Christmas and New Year's celebrations. In between this window of period of time, many, many, many important people who are very, very dense but playing their roles well, will be exited from this planet before anything else happens. And so the numbers will be much dramatized of the actual death toll. Do not pay attention to that. That is hype. And so it is just for dramatics to shock the world. Of course you will see all of the Royal families and the aristocrats who should have been more humble truly with their charity work. Truly with their humanitarian and anthropology work. But they love being exclusive and elite. This is a luxury for those, but it's arrogant at the same time because they have not truly considered those who are starving for example. Those who are oppressed even in their own country, let alone are being considerate and compassionate for the entire world. And so, with great power and riches comes great responsibility. Many are trying to keep up with materialism over actually feeding their moral souls. So this needs to be done! This needs to be a cleansing! And the collapsing of the land will impact and bring in much flooding. It is misuse of power once again that comes to this.

It may be considered that it might be a collider. The Hadron collider. And it is rumored that there was potentially a much smaller one that was traveling around, which was made for private use. They tried to make it a smaller one. Not a big gigantic one. And so they had shrunk down the size of it and they were trying to modernize it. And so there were many theories of what has happened so they will have that physical blame. But really what is behind it is those who are playing with energy they shouldn't be playing with and they're calling upon their own Collectives to have divine source power because they want to wield it. Because they want to be the most powerful because they're sensing more and more that people are not in fear as they once were, so they're asking to have profound power to be able to scare people again. Ironically, they do get that wish. The destruction of London does scare people but they're going to have their own exit with it. They do not get their wish of having influence over anyone on this planet. This will make many people feel like finally the crimes have been addressed. That there is justice! And we are saying it will be a short-lived thing because they'll be so frustrated that they didn't get named and shamed in public court and it wasn't a public event. People wanted to see them hang, and a quick event like this almost probably would have been so shockingly quick that it would have been painless. Many people don't want these people to go painlessly. They want to have slow torturous deaths for them. So this is helping them accept that what they are fantasizing over, what they're wanting to see, will be taken from them so they don't have an opportunity to have that so they have to have acceptance. They have to know that they have to let it go. They're so focused on revenge and getting their pound of flesh that when many of these people exit they have to let go, let go.

There are many layers to the significance of what has to happen, of course there are many people also who want to take exit points and shift at this time. So it is not all exit points to go to source. There are some of course, but this is truly what we would consider the pre-start to the big laser event. This is as it needs to all unfold. The ripple effect is just like the end of Atlantis where there is much destruction which causes the earthquakes, which causes the more unsettling and the volcanoes. They've done it again to themselves. But this is why we haven't promoted this. We have distracted many by talking about satellites which will still occur. But it needs to scar America. But this event for London is going to be the first *big* impact. It will not have the trademark senses of a laser and an extraterrestrial attack. It will have other blamed man-made events. They will guess it could be X, Y and Z. They will think it is a laboratory. They will think it's CERN. Many people will blame CERN. Many people have not even heard about CERN but this has already been put into many people's consciousnesses to be prepared. To be warned to know that if something that is cataclysmic occurs, this would be the reason for it. And so we haven't put it public because it wasn't time to put it public. Because we did not want those who are going to be asking for this power to know this. They must not know this! They must do what they need to do. This is life contracts to use their free will and their own power and their Collective will honor what they are requesting. But they do not know the extent of what the answers to their request is. They assume it will be to weld and hold great power and they will for a very short amount of time. A nanosecond until they exit their bodies.

P: Thank you. Is there anything else that you would like to share with us at this time?

J: We've given them many opportunities to not do the things that they're doing and they are still refusing time and time again to not grow and choose a better moral compass. And so they use the energy to gain what they think they're losing grip on, which is control and fear and manipulation. And so throughout history they know better, but they are so selfish and they feel so entitled that they want to use pure magic, pure energy for their advantage point to impact humanity. And while it does impact humanity, it is not how they think.

And so, Joanne was wondering why they will not stay on the Old Earth and experience the Old Earth. And we say, because they're so well prepared for Old Earth experiences that they would not struggle. They would not find community. They would not go back to basics in terms of they would not be in fear. They've got everything well organized and prepared. They have their own planes. They have their own underground bunkers. They have everything to make their lives very, very, very comfortable regardless of what the rest of the world is doing. Can you see this is their instant karma? They cannot keep living here with this position because their spiritual growth is stagnant. They were supposed to evolve morally. They're not choosing that. And so they've had many, many many options. But their density is impacting humanity and their free will is constantly impacting humanity. So does this fully explain why this needs to happen and occur?

P: Yes it does! I understand.

J: You want to say it is so sudden. It is much faster. It is much faster than small earthquakes that just ramp up. It is faster than the laser. You don't hear it. It goes instantly and this will make many people uncomfortable when they start hearing about this threat. And so you can share this information privately after the event if you feel that this is necessary. Do not worry about people saying, why didn't you warn us. Because the reality is this is beyond any human's control. You cannot force people to not use their free will. You could ask them, '*Please do not try to manipulate energy for your own agenda.*' You could ask them. You could tell them. You could plead with them! You could beg them! You could tell them even this and they will not listen. Their egos and their belief that they are very powerful, they *are* very powerful, but they're focused on dark energy forces. They're focusing on harnessing good power and energy but with a twist. They're wanting to use pure energy. Pure source energy for their own manipulation and this must not be granted as you can imagine.

P: Thank you. I don't have any more questions.

J: Joanne is feeling heavy with this because she doesn't want it to be true. And again you get the fantastic privilege of having a breakdown before everyone else can so you can find the bigger perspective and help assist them and make sense of it all. And you've done this many times with many different things, and you would do this again with no problems. It's the shock of hearing it and this is the part of what people need to see. These are these teachable moments for everyone. You get America seeing what's happened to London. You get the world looking to see what has happened to London. They get a brief time to be in shock themselves. To grieve for themselves. To come together themselves in a state of confusion because they don't have specific details. They don't get the footage. They only get the footage of the aftermath. They can't fathom the number of losses because all of the records of everyone in that location's gone. It's a big wipe. It's a Grand Reset. The truther communities are so joyous because they feel like this will be the biggest reset possible. Many people will think it might have been a nuclear bomb or something, but it doesn't behave like a nuclear bomb. It is just a drop. It's an evaporation. Implosion. So what happens is the energy just bursts out. Imagine, it's like a big bubble and it expands out really quickly and it just atomizes everything in this radius. And so it just is so impacting that when the bubble bursts, everything that's physical has been profoundly disintegrated. And it's quite deep because a lot of the issues of the bunkers and the densities were very, very deep. And so it's very deep. The center of it's not centered near the surface. It's centered underground. And so when this bubble bursts and everything within this radius has been destroyed, that's when you get the flooding. And many people assume that the flooding, somehow everything's underwater, and the flooding has occurred and people have drowned. There will not be a trace of anything because it is gone. It is vaporized shall we say. And many people are worried that it could be radioactive. They don't know what to do and explore. It is very strange. It takes a while for them to venture out. It's just a loss of communication. It's very far spread.

P: I know you said that it's fast. Can you just talk to us about the innocents, given that a lot will be away on holidays, but the ones that are in London at that time, can you talk to us about their exit points and what they will be experiencing please?

J: It will be a very big shock for them. One moment they're here and the next moment they are finding themselves somewhere else. Many of them will find themselves slowly awakening on a ship. And many, a much longer time. So they'll have dreams of understanding what has happened. They will have their loved ones coming into their dreams to explain to them what has happened. Very, very soft dreams. First of all they'll see the situation occur as a dream from above as if they are a bird or they're looking down upon it. But because they don't wake up while they're processing a very long series of dreams, they don't feel the trauma as such, of the emotions. They get to experience it as a dream.

They feel the feelings but they're not able to think clearly. So it's almost as if they've been deactivated from their emotions. So they watch it and they repeat it and they explore it. And each time they have this new memory and this new experience, they become less and less in a deep sleep and become more lucid. And so they're experiencing the lucid dream. The actual event is remote viewing from being on ships. And the more that they can process it and accept it and understand it, the more awake they will become. And they will be completely awoken on the ship when they understand what has happened and why they are there. And that's when they can start communicating with others.

P: And is this going to bring about unity for the rest of the world or will it take the laser event to really shake things up?

J: It is like a ripple effect. And so people will be in so much shock they will want to bring unity together because they want to talk about it. And they will be in a state of grief. But because it's not their country, it's just *'poor them over there.'* And so for the majority of the world, it's ' *poor them over there.'* And so when certain things happen in their own countries, then it feels a bit more closer to home. So *'poor them over there'* is a conversation that they will start having. And they will distract themselves from the other darker agendas to disempower each other, say the conversation of the virus. They'll be talking about the events that happened in London more than anything else. It will eclipse anything else. They almost forget that they're in fear, but they will be noticing many things still. They will have this realization that you could be here one minute and gone the next. And it's about them accepting their mortality. The whole fear of the virus has extended out that conversation.

So they're doing many, many, many things to protect themselves and their position and their views and their mindsets that they're doing all these things to protect themselves from the virus. And the reality is, there is no escaping exit points. And so it's going to make them realize that they could literally be gone in a split second. And that brings them into the most rapid awareness of the now moment ever because they can't prepare. They can't plan. They can't predict. And so it makes them and their focus minute. So it's not necessarily the unity of humanity as such at that point. It is about them still processing their personal emotions of death. What it could mean to them. What it could look like for the world. So it's still private inner work that they're doing to overcome the fear of death. But yes! There is unity in that conversation, absolutely! Where many people have not been able to have any unity in any conversations because of the current situations are such a hot topic. Everyone seems to be emotionally addicted to the drama of a tragedy so this will bring out all of that addiction again.

P: Okay. Thank you!

J: Okay. We will leave you now to ponder this because we understand it is a lot even though you can accept it from a bigger perspective, both of you will be pondering how you can stop it.

P: Yeah. Thank you!

Session 4: Arcturians: Release of Information

Arcturians discuss their choices of what information is given publicly.

Yes, we are here, We are here. We're here. We wanted to support those who are suddenly aware that there are more things going on that will be happening to your planet, and to your countries, and to have different experiences for necessary experiences. It has made you feel shocked to know that there are more things that need to happen to have everything unfold for perfect experiences, different connections, and different lessons. So we are wanting you to know that there are many things that need to unfold. Those who have been triggered with hearing about the new information, need to be able to do a little bit more inner work to accept - you do not control the future events of this planet. You do not need to know every detail and situation prior to those, for you to keep your balance and neutral.

You have to be open to all things that need to unfold. Many of you have found comfort in hearing the information that we share, so you feel like you know all, and this gives you this comfort of removing surprises. We are saying, those people who are suddenly surprised and have lost their balance, this is a fantastic time for you to learn and respect that you have no control. When things unfold in front of you, for you, so that you have to keep your balance and neutral. Even just processing that there is new information that you're not privy to, is making many people have to dig deep into their inner work to find their balance.

You're curious why we have given you part of the information that a new event is occurring[7]. We are saying, you know that when we have given you previous information about events, certain collectives and certain people are trying to foil the plans that need to unfold naturally. You know this, and yet some of you feel that you are entitled to this information. You are not entitled to any information that we perceive would harm and impact humanity.

This is significant work. This is significant information. This is not entertainment. This is not for your benefit, just so you feel entitled to know prior events to come, what is happening and why. We're wanting you to feel how you would feel being prepared for anything. We're observing your behaviors. We're observing your emotions. We are observing your reactions to see how you will overcome yourself. We're not giving you the answers. We're not giving you the information. Yet, so what are you doing with it? Are you panicking or are you going within? Are you reaching out to others to see what they can tell you? What is going on for you? How are you resolving this? How are you overcoming this?

We, of course, know how you are. But we're wanting you to be able to be accountable for your rollercoaster of emotions, and your mindset, and inner work. So this was not a "test" but this is a lesson and experience for you to master. How are you doing with that? Did you lose all focus and balance, or did you accept it and know that you are emotionally and mentally prepared for anything that needs to occur, knowing the bigger perspective that everything that is going to occur is the best for all, the best for humanity, and the best moving forward, with the best experiences for all. So focusing on all, would be a very wise choice moving forward, because it gives

---

[7] *London Event*

you more acceptance. It takes away your responsibility of thinking you need to know certain things.

So this was a great example of how those, who are not privy to the information that you are of certain things, you're going to have to naturally experience something and that will be quite shocking not to add density to you, or fear to you. But, you know what is happening in terms of the shift and the greater perspective and what is happening for humanity and why. Understanding that you still have to experience certain events and keep balance at certain events, this is you having to master your own inner work and balance. We see some of you are just holding on to our information and keeping your high frequency, just from our sessions alone. We are saying, you must be doing your own inner work to keep your high frequency vibrations, when you're not listening to these sessions.

This is a great opportunity for you to empower yourselves. You don't need to know all of the details. By preparing yourself for any eventual experience for any possibility of experiences, you could overwhelm yourself with thinking of every worst case scenario possible, or you could find your balance in neutral, and see the bigger perspective instantly. Know whatever comes, whatever happens, you will be able to trust the bigger perspective is always for the best for all. So, are you letting your emotions run away with you? Are you letting your overthinking run away with you? What is going on there?

We want to congratulate profoundly, those who have kept in complete neutral and balanced, knowing that a new event is going to occur. You have known truly, that many of you have distracted yourselves with these details. You all knew that many events would be coming. All countries will be experiencing events. So knowing that we have an event that we want to share with you after the event has occurred to be able to give you the perspective of it, has put you on a back foot because you feel - if you knew what the event was, you would be able to easily find your balance and justify it. Right now, many of you are worried - what if this event is in my area? What if things have changed?

So see what you're feeling and what you're emotionally looping into, because there is inner work for you there, to find that balance and neutral. We're not wanting you to panic. We're not wanting you to be overwhelmed with all of the possibilities of what could be happening. Remember what we have said to you - do not buy into future worries, This is literally a perfect example of being able to apply your homework. We know those who have succeeded in this and we know who are working through this. It is okay, but can't you see now, everything that we've been telling you is then you having to apply it and feel into it. We keep asking you to apply the information from these sessions, and this is literally a perfect example of that.

Of course, all is well. We shouldn't have to keep reminding you that. So those who have been able to see things in neutral, trusting everything is fine, accepting everything needs to happen as it needs to happen for that significant lessons and experiences. It is a remarkable feat, and we want to congratulate those who have been able to keep themselves neutral, feel their feelings, but be able to ride through them with that balance. Those are testing experiences. We understand that you don't like to not know information. We understand you all feel like you're entitled to all information, but as we've already explained, not all information needs to be heard into third dimensional ears. There's ramifications for those who do hear this information. Many listen to events and try to block it, out of fear, out of lack of understanding. We understand that, but you're wasting your energy and efforts on something that's completely impossible for you to impact. But, many people are looping so severely on certain information, certain doubts, that it's really taking them away from focusing on their personal relationship with self and personal relationship with friends and family and even working relationships.

So, we always recommend finding balance in every situation. Of course, noticing triggers is absolutely healthy and normal, but what do you do with those triggers when you feel them - do you hold on to them for a long time or do you face them, address them, unpack them, and overcome them? That is all your choices. We understand that you're all feeling like you've got a lot on your plate, and that is a perception that you could have if you are struggling to respect the bigger perspective of why things are happening. So we want to just question those who are still struggling with why things are happening and unfolding. Where is your resistance? Where is your fear? We sense that many people feel so entitled to live out their third dimensional worlds and in the comfort of their homes and their families, that they're quite resentful of this information. We understand that is a perception you could have. And so, we invite all of those who are resentful for the information we share, to be able to reflect on it with a bigger perspective, a bigger heart perspective, and a bigger mind perspective.

When you're just singly focusing on your personal lives and your personal situations, you're not able to factor in and engage all. We keep asking you to see each other as ALL, and feel each other as ALL, because you are ALL one. You are ALL connected, while you're having independent experiences. Sometimes you disconnect yourselves because you don't think that other people possibly feel the same range of emotions that you do. We are wanting you to explore this a little bit more, a little bit more honest with yourself. There's nothing wrong with being honest with yourself.

There truly is nothing wrong with being in fear, temporary. It's what you do with that fear that defines you and makes it worthwhile to experience that fear. Having the sense of fear is a trigger for you to be able to notice that there is something that you're unsettled with. When you work with those unsettled feelings, acknowledge those feelings, and then use your common sense to understand what is going on for you, why is your reaction this way, you can quickly navigate through it, if you choose. We understand that it is too hard sometimes for people to face their fears, and so they will ignore them. They will just keep wondering why this is a looping pattern and why certain situations happen again and again and again.

You can't escape from these lessons. While you could escape from certain people, we will provide you the same scenarios with different people again and again and again and again and again, until you make the change, until you learn those lessons and experiences. You may think that you can outsmart your lessons and experiences and what you need to learn and grow from, but that is your ego. You've noticed this. Many people listening have noticed this. They've already overcome this. And so, it is just realizing that facing your fears doesn't create you to be in fear at all. You do not expand, it doesn't grow your fears - facing your fears. In fact, it literally disempowers your fears, because you're facing them without reaction. You're starting to think about them.

It's marvelous. It's all about perspective - confronting, confronting these things that make you go '.... Hmm, why am I suddenly so worried about change?'

All is well.
All is well.
All is well.

We just wanted to give you this quick message to be able to let you know - All is well.

You know that exit points are not the end of the soul, it is a stepping stone. It is the end of one cycle, and the beginning of another. Have a healthy bigger perspective on what death is, and it will immediately release your fears and your concerns. Have great compassion for those people around you who are in your lives. You cannot do their inner work for them, and with healthy boundaries, you can empower them. We ask you to spend some more time with yourselves privately, sitting with yourself, accepting self, accepting all, facing your fears, feeling excited for the unity of humanity. Start thinking about what gives you the most joy and raises your frequency. We know many of you are thinking about what you would like to do, and see, and be on the New Earth. Many of you are excited about returning home to your other planets. Feel into whatever gives you the most joy and hold on to it. Keep focused on positive empowerment rather than just feeling the fear and not doing anything with it.

We say this with much love!
Session 5: Peer Pressure Parent Healing

Yes! We are here! We are here. We are here! We are wanting to confirm to you what has just happened. So you have called on the collectives to be able to ask for assistance; to be able to help with those babies who are crying and who have been crying alone in their cots and their cribs. When they have been calling out for their parents, they are confused. They are little children responding to a stimulus of distance, and they are feeling the separation of their parents.

We would like to remind all, that the way babies are supposed to be held and supported is to be physically attached to the parents. Once they remove themselves from the womb and then they are born, they need to be held. We know that many of your cultures have been told to put those children into different rooms and start sleep cycles and start sleep patterns. Sleep routines. Training to sleep. We say that in harmony and balance with life and Earth and with each other, there would be no baby that would be unheld. You know, many cultures would always hold and swaddle their babies and be a part of them and physically hold them, constantly. Never being unheld by anyone. This provides that child security and love and nurture and support, constantly, as they are acclimating themselves to the density of these lives. We know that many chose to have these experiences of being disconnected from a very early age; to be able to overcome and empower themselves through these experiences, through these triggering experiences of being isolated at such a vulnerable state. Of course, when you're in your own room, in your own crib, crying out for a parent it doesn't cause you to be eaten by tigers. Those children need to be held who live in jungles, because they need to be supported. Children cry because they want attention to be supported. So, the child was always supported so they wouldn't make a noise and would not cause the attention of a hungry animal.

So, humanity changed living cycles. Changed parenting behaviors and patterns again because society has said that you must. You have loyally followed them. For many, you have followed this. So, now there is much parental guilt when you realize your own patterns and behaviors and how you raised your own children. We have sent out (collectively) love and a stronger connection to their teams. Those babies could feel their teams, could feel their guides more so than ever before. Knowing that there is no such thing as a singular time or moment in terms of everything existing at the same time. So, we've gone back to even your own pasts in this lifetime to heal and connect more profoundly to those children, their own guides to those babies who needed that. Because when that baby is crying and feeling isolated and alone, they are feeling unloved, unsafe, unheard. Can't you see how that could then manifest out and into adults feeling unseen, unloved, unsafe and unheard?

When we say go back and do your inner work, many of you are thinking of just the things you recall from your adult years or maybe your teenage years and in a few little moments of your childhood (your younger years). But many of you have not been able to know that the impacts that your inner work has had was a direct result of your baby years, your baby months. We're releasing those parents now from that guilt because you did what you were told. You did what you thought was best. You did what you could, to cope with the new addition to the family.

We're not judging. We're letting you know that for humanity as a whole, all those babies who struggled to be alone, we have gone and assisted them at a deeper rate. A beautiful connection to reassure them. To comfort them. This has been needed to be able to help those adults who are still struggling because of those moments in their childhood and their baby months. Not because their parents were abusive or neglectful, but because those parents were following the trends of fashion of how to raise children and babies. We know the other agenda there and we know impressionable parents want the best for their children. So, they are encouraged to buy cots to keep the baby away from those parents, but the result of that is a disconnect. You can see how those ripple effects reach out and ripple out. So, we're wanting you to know that we have reconnected those babies with their teams and those teams have been able to go back and comfort those babies more and it has filled that gap in those babies' hearts and conscious awareness, so they are not crying out now. They are self-serving. They are self-comforting, because they feel their teams more than they did before. So, for those adults who still had that gap in their hearts and mindsets, this ripple effect today will be a wave of love and reassurance that they were never alone. This has been a vital key that has been missing. We're grateful to be able to make that connection. To fill that gap. To fill that emotional hole. Not just adults' hearts, but children today.

We're very grateful for this free will to be able to do this. This makes the collectives feel so useful. They can see the ripple out effect. It is beautiful. It is beautiful because no one truly wanted their own individual children to suffer and to feel isolated and alone. But because they were following a system that doesn't empower humanity but disempowers humanity, for most, we were able to reconnect and be able to heal and we're so grateful for that.

We would like to be able to add more confirmation to you about the triggers and the epiphanies and how this has been affected and what is going on there. Many have used exit points through the virus or something else, really, those who have had medical misadventures, medical misconduct. Now, those people who wanted to help really trigger those who are going about their daily work and not having bigger compassion. Not having the epiphanies to stop and think about what they're doing, which is actually directly causing exit points. While they are not in quotation marks "the murderers," they are playing a role here. This is very interesting because those Souls who did want exit points and they have had a contract for a doctor or a nurse to do medical disconnect... We're struggling with the words.

This vehicle is tired and not able to focus on relaxing so we'll just... She has gone on her own journey today which has got her still thinking about her own lessons and experiences which she has marveled at. So we will continue. We're going to change the pace up because she wants humor with this, because how we gave it to her was kind of funny. We're going to add in our best ability for entertainment for this serious conversation. There's a whole bunch of, shall we say, senior citizens who have used these exit points as a collective group to be able to be ghosts. Boy, are they having fun. They are having ultimate mischief! They are finding their inner joy. They are wanting to come in and say, 'While we needed exit points because we did want to finish our physical lives to be able to move on, we know exactly why we chose to be here at this time. We were what you would call a first wave volunteer who came to assist. We have exited our bodies through what you could call into question, maybe it could be vaccine related. It could be virus related. But we have chosen all those exit points, so please, do not think that this is something you should be angry about. Please respect our exit points. But we want to share with you something that we are so happy to assist with. While the collectives have been open to many people being triggered and having epiphanies, us 'gang of souls' that are wanting to give those physical doctors and nurses epiphanies to stop and question, we've been having fun being in the ghost realm. So, because we have had the same doctors for much of our lives and our doctors know us, we are able to what you could consider to haunt them. We know it must sound terrible that we are being mischievous and cheeky, but this is part of their own awakening. They have refused to stop and think about their consequences and their actions. They know professionally better. They know morally better. They're still choosing to be dismissive and not focusing on what they are truly doing. This is part of being able to awaken humanity by being triggered. Us ghosts now, we are doing all that we can. We are seeing our own individual doctors and we are running amok, not to scare them but to make them question, almost their sanity to some degree. Because we have got more access to being able to trigger them and push on their, 'What if there is an afterlife?' Of course, this is all condoned and blessed with their subconscious, because even their subconscious are frustrated that they are not listening to their own moral compass. They are having to have these profound epiphanies from us to be able to make them even question the afterlife, which is quite peculiar for many because they believe in science and they don't believe in energy recycling itself and existing beyond this sense of time and space. What we are doing is not allowing them to fully sleep. Once they sleep, they exit the bodies and they can distract themselves into going to other realms. What we're doing is, we're keeping them awake. We keep popping into their minds. We keep having conversations with them. We keep reminding them of our conversations that we had when we were alive with them. What they recommended. What they didn't see. What they didn't consider. We are reliving our own life experiences and life contracts with them in a dreamlike state. They are having to experience this. We shouldn't have so much joy in this, but when you know that for many medical industry people, they're using their free will and impacting many, many, many. They have recommended things that are not good for our bodies, and so we have this opportunity. This gang, of course, is not just senior citizen ghosts, but we wanted to give you that example just to be able to see. But it is for those people who can't get karma back. So they've had their lives shortened because of the doctors choices and their free will to prescribe things that are not actually of the best interest for their individual clients. So, how do you get that karma back? The collectives have decided that this karma that could be paid back will occur right now. Those don't need to be physical life contracts that have to be played out. This is why, in the ghost realm we say, much mischievousness has occurred. This has been very successful to be able to give these doctors and nurses many epiphanies to many things. We need them to be awoken too, and so this has been allowed. But of course, many who have fully abruptly awoken to their own actions and behavior, have used exit points because they do not know how they can come back from this. They do not understand why their moral compass was switched off. They were following their rules. They were following the rules that they were employed to follow. But at some point, they kept choosing to follow without using their own common sense and their own applied knowledge. So, there is so much to be said about what is going on, but we are having fun! We are having great, great, great fun. So, for those people who know of exit points for people who have passed, quite possibly, they're part of this gang of ghosts now using their free will as ghosts with the blessing of the collectives and the subconscious to be able to shake awake people to stop and think".

This may not have been as funny in our delivery, but this gave the vehicle a giggle to know all of the behind the scenes events that are truly helping, with this "Granny Ghost Gang". We don't want anyone to go into a lower frequency vibration of grief or sadness for those who are using the exit points now because they're still of great service. They're still busy. They're still helping humanity and they're still awakening and triggering many to be able to get them to that higher frequency. We hope that this has given you some comfort to know that much is happening and much karma that has been created is being released as well. It's almost an instant thing now. In this lifetime, you can create the karma and you can heal and balance the karma at the same time. It's extraordinary what is going on behind the scenes. Trust that we have more access now and more permission to be able to support people who need to awaken. It is slower than we imagined and anticipated, but it is a steady rate forward. We are all watching and monitoring this. And we are still open for suggestions. We are so grateful to be able to do the profound healing of those babies today. You, as being a baby, and your own children as being babies. The ripple out effect is beautiful and so healing and so needed! We're so grateful to be able to be of assistance today. We also acknowledge those souls, those ghosts who are still using their physical life experiences connections to those who are effectively part of their exit point. Not because the ghosts are trying to haunt them as being their murderers, it's not that at all. The ghosts are already understanding that those doctors and nurses were complying, so there is no malice. It is a gentle scare. A gentle moral compass smack on the bottom, and all is well!

All is well!
All is well!

Session 6: Reptilian Collective Release Control

J: *I'd like to call upon Stacy's subconscious please.*
S: We're here.

J: *Thank you very much. Can you do a body scan and tell me what is happening to the body?*
S: There's a lot of pressure in her head.

J: *What's going on there for her?*
S: Lots of different collective energies just swirling around. Swirling around. But they could easily be released shortly.

J: *Fantastic! Is this what she was experiencing with her headache earlier?* (S: Yes) *Is there anything else you'd like her to know about her experience last night?*
S: It was a ploy to distract her from being of service today, but with Stacy she can always tune in deeper and see deeper into the real truth. So she suspected that's what was happening and she got through it.

J: *Okay. Fantastic! So can you release the tension that's in her body from that experience?*
S: Yes. We have already done so.

J: *Thank you so much! Is there anything else you'd like me to know about her body?*
S: No. Not currently.

J: *Okay. Are you able to balance and heal the body and put it into perfect alignment wherever it needs to be?*
S: Yes. Done.

J: *Thank you so much! Can I continually ask questions while you keep healing and balancing her body?*
S: Yes. Sure.

J: *Thank you so much! I really appreciate that. Subconscious, what was the significance of showing her that dream where the children's dad had taken them[8]?*
S: It was to incite fear inside of her. That was the intention. It was to stir things up for her to realize that she's always known she is safe and protected, but she needed to have insight into what the Reptilian collective has been trying to do with her. They have been trying to use her as, we choose to say puppet, like a puppet on a string, but she has a deep understanding that that's what they were trying to do, so she just took it for what it was.

J: *How can they do that to her? Isn't it breaching her free will?*
S: It was more like a vision. They could not do anything more than show the vision.

J: *Okay. And so that's interesting! So are we able to connect into all the collectives that want to help assist us. Including the Reptilian collective? Because it seems abundantly clear to us that we need to sever the connection between the Reptilian collective and all of those people who are being impacted by these visions that they present. And by the drugs that they have been addicted to which are to coerce these people to have these connections with the Reptilians. We want all access to be cut now and severed. What else are we supposed to be doing to help these people who have been impacted by the Reptilian collective in a negative way?*

---

[8] Father does not have custody of the children.

S: You have just covered that. We have been waiting and we are prepared for today, for now, for this moment.

J: Okay. So is the Reptilian collective ready and prepared to let go of humanity and the control and manipulation that it has had over all of the beings here on this planet earth?

S: Yes and no. Some are fed up with it. While there is still a stagnant few who remain, that cannot accept or believe that things can be better for them as a collective, because that is all they have known and they do not wish to release or relinquish any power or control they have had. They are upset that their collective is being divided in this certain matter, so they have chosen to, not all, but some have chosen to dig their heels in and not be moved or encouraged. But they also agree that they will listen. But they also feel that they will remain the same.

J: Okay. I can understand their perspective. But I also know from sessions and information that other collectors have provided, that there are good experiences and expansion for all of the Reptilian collectives and that they should be excited to embrace the new way of their lives which will help them evolve to higher dimensions than they have been before. So can they get those epiphanies to understand that they're holding themselves back and that it's limiting them in many ways?

S: Yes. Many are already celebrating this. Many, many are celebrating this already! There is only a minuscule amount that refuses for more. But we are very hopeful! We are very hopeful!

J: Is it true that they have so much power, those small amounts, that they are still holding up the evolutionary experience for humanity on this planet?

S: Yes they do. But it's like they only really have one, we say pillar. To understand pillars, so there's one pillar that remains.

J: *Can you tell me more about that one pillar?*
S: There were many. There were multiple pillars. But now just to hold up these last few, they just have the one pillar. Because the other pillars have been removed because they are not needed anymore. So there is one pillar that they can stand on. But we see there is a crack in it.

J: *What is that crack?*

S: It is just a crack that is ready to crumble. So they feel it is necessary to be more stubborn and staunch in their ways. But as we say this, we see some getting off that pillar because they understand. No, they do not want to fall with that crack. They want to choose what they want to choose. They don't want to fall to their demise because they are not choosing what is best for them.

J: *Yes! It's interesting, because they're making these choices that they think is best for them but ultimately, it's so limiting them. So are we able to really impress on those who are holding back still, that actually, they can make better choices to empower themselves profoundly in true evolutionary steps versus the distractions that they are thinking is more worthy?*

S: Yes! We see some of them backing off. And there are some standing there and they are scared that others are backing off. They are saying, 'We must remain together. We must be a strong unit!' And the others have just given up and they have chosen to step off. And so, the ones that remain are fearful!

They are very fearful! They're very fearful, because now they're questioning themselves. They are questioning themselves, 'Is this right for us? Everyone else is choosing to leave and we are standing here?' And they feel alone now.

J: Okay And so, can you give them a sense of what it feels like to have collective community and unity again, and have that sense of what their positive future has in store for them as they are sensing the true experiences of the evolutionary steps?

S: Yes. They are experiencing the emotion of being vulnerable. They do not like it! But they do see how it can be very impactful and things can be different for them. Better! They can see how things can be better. Yet some do not believe it. But they can see how it can be better.

J: Can you strengthen their experiences and their perceptions of how things could be better? To give them full clarity so they could really step into the faith and trust that all is truly well and that they are very much loved and supported? And they are encouraged to form communities again with their collectives to be able to strengthen and empower each other again in a true fashion?

S: Yes! We are showing them, the ones who choose not to be on that pillar anymore. They are hugging! They're hugging! All different types! They're all hugging and they are happy! And it is a community bond. A community spirit! And they feel so good because they have not experienced this! It feels very joyous for them and happy. The ones who are not on the pillar. The ones up there, who remain, they're looking down and they feel confused now when they see this. When they see the hugging, they are confused. Yet they want to partake in this feeling. They really do! They do, they do!

J: And so, can we encourage them to realize that there is great growth in connecting with everyone? And that it is time for them to make empowering choices over disempowering choices?

S: Yes! They understand that in this community essence in the spirit, they can learn new things in new ways! And so many are celebrating this. They were so quick to choose this higher means of being! The empowering side of it! The positive side! The light side! And the ones who are experiencing this are overcome with joy! So the more they see this, the other ones up on the pillar see this, they are still trying their hardest to pretend they do not want it. But they do! They want it! They see the others being a part and being fully embraced and accepted no matter what they have done. And they want to be a part of it. They truly want to be a part of that.

J: Could it support them further by realizing that they would be great assets and gifts to humanity to be released at this time now? Because, for them to surrender in and empower their own collective and honor humanity to be able to be released from their tight hold, is the greatest gift that they could give humanity, and therefore be respected deeply by all?

S: Yes! They understand from that perspective now. Before they didn't understand how they could do better or be better. But through that simple explanation of those words they can understand that they can be of service by releasing the grip and letting go once and for all. Because it does not serve anybody, not even themselves.

J: Absolutely! Asking any other collectives, is there anything else we can do to help assist humanity today?

S: Continue to show the ones on the pillar the community spirit, the community essence. There are only a few that haven't decided, but the majority have chosen to be different.

J: *So can we speak to those who are on the pillar? To say that you are very powerful! You are very respected! And you have lots of choices moving forward. And the choices you make moving forward to empower, not only your own collective, but also to empower humanity would be a great honor and dignity to have. And it is your choice. It is going to happen one way or another. But we ask you to be able to see that you are the key to what is holding back humanity and your own collective now. And we are reassuring you that there are great opportunities for great experiences to empower all collectives! And this would be a very great advancement to have for all! And that all will be supported and all will be encouraged to have the best experiences for all*

S: Yes. Even though they understand your words, they feel like by stepping off that pillar they are doing a disservice to their own collective, even though they see the majority choosing differently. They are still holding on to the thought of 'Is this a disservice?' But now they are questioning it. Before, they truly believed it was a disservice, but now, the more they hear those words they are beginning to question 'Is this a disservice to our collective?'

J: *So we'll ask the Reptilian representatives to come in to be able to tell us and to reassure us and those who are on the pillar that are refusing to let go, is this where the Reptilian collective would like to evolve or is this a trap? Or is this a disservice? Can we hear directly from the Reptilian collective*

where the majority of the collectives want to move forward to and how they want to approach?
S: Yes! There is no disservice in empowering yourself! There is no disservice in empowering all and others! It is a union. We can all come together and be part of one big empowering service to all! There is no disservice in wanting better! There is no disservice in empowerment for all and empowering others! They will empower themselves! So as we embrace this lesson, we have more understanding and we are seeing and realizing this is a service. But we want others to understand that we thought we were of service. But now, we have only been of disservice, not just to others and all collectives, mainly to ourselves.

J: Well. Thank you very much for sharing that. I understand that we all have different perspectives and this is a time to come together as a unity to be able to help those who are on this planet as we are honoring the life cycle of this planet. And we would be greatly appreciative of all who will help collectively together at this time moving forward. Having more mutual respect and understanding and consideration for all of those who were here learning these experiences and lessons on planet Earth.
S: We feel very humbled that we can be of service. We did not have the perspective of how things will be different. We feel humbled. We have not felt this before.

J: And we're very glad and grateful to be able to have these connections to be able to have this compassion felt from us to you. Because we have been sincere in our wanting empowerment for all as everyone needs certain experiences to have these lessons and opportunities to work together. And we're grateful to be able to have this profound love, honor and respect to all collectives as we know that every collective and every life contract should be respected. And in saying that, many have been what could be considered entrapped in taking their free will from them. And we ask to recede all connections to all of those beings who have been intertwined through drug addictions. We would like to sever this with much love because this no longer serves the individual being. This is a parasitic energy connection that we would like to be released today, to help everyone move forward on their own life contracts and journeys. And we ask that this be considered and released now for all of those who are impacted by this.

S: Yes. We understand! And yes, we agree. We see how our actions have been disloyalty. We have disserviced ourselves. We have disempowered ourselves. We have not had this perspective until recently. Until now. We see the bigger picture and how our actions have disempowered so many. And we wish to be included so we can repay what we have done that has not been empowering. And we can move forward and be a part of the collectives and be the best we can be for all, especially humanity. We have taken so much! We have strained and drained and exhausted every option we could find to disempower them. But we are so humbled and we are full with humility now. We see the error in our ways and we do not wish to continue this. We do not wish to continue this disempowering, dissociation energy and infrastructure that we have created specifically on this planet. Specifically to humanity. (Crying) This is very overwhelming for us because we feel like we have breached our own protocols in our own collective. But the more we're thinking and discussing, we are realizing it was never empowering any collectives! All we see is disempowerment. That's all that remains from this. And we are ready to make this change for the first time.

J: We would like to thank you for the opportunities for these experiences, because without your role that you played, we would not have been able to have experienced certain opportunities. And so, while we know that all is well, we can respect and heal together now as we want to empower all for this evolutionary step forward.

S: Yes! We wish to be a part of that! We wish to be a part of any way to empower all and others and all! We wish to be a part of this! We appreciate the acceptance into being a part of this.

J: We see such great healing and connections and super fast evolution for you. For those in your collective who have always yearned to be able to evolve. With their great love and loyalty to their own collective, they have wanted this for such a long time. And so we feel such great joy for those in your collective who have been wanting this for a long time. And they feel so grateful that you are now honoring your whole collective moving forward. This is a great joyous experience and we honor all who want to serve their own collective and also be a part of One. Be a part of all!

S: Yes. Thank you! We were choosing to almost banish others in our collective who have chosen this. But with the deepest perspective of this, we have fully embraced and we understand the error in our ways and we choose from today to move forward and to be a part of service for all! Empowering for all!

J: We're grateful for this pledge of commitment for unity and we know that this will have a profound ripple-out effect, so we're appreciative! And we say this with much love and appreciation for your willingness to consider other perspectives that may have been overlooked.

S: We feel very overwhelmed! We feel we have now chosen to sever any bounds and ties of darkness and negativity. This is new to us. This is a fresh concept to not energetically connect through darkness. We embrace this and we have yet to process, but we understand this is best of how we can be of service. And we choose this! We embrace it! We are committed to it! We are very happy we can accomplish this and be accepted!

J: *It is with great pleasure that we could be able to help assist with this today, knowing that you have suffered so much yourselves through your choices. And this gives us great pleasure to be able to see how you now have had these epiphanies to empower yourselves at such a beautiful high vibrational integrity.*

S: Yes. Thank you! Thank you for assisting us in this. We have a profound new awareness into this concept of truly being of service for all! To be part of one. The unity. We can already feel it, when we embrace it, we can feel that we are all tied in together and we embrace it! This is very momentous for us! It is a fresh concept and we feel it may take a day or two to truly grasp it. But we are on board!

J: *How fantastic! Well thank you so much! And we ask for all the collectives to be able to have honored and noted this conversation and this commitment today. And may we energetically release all who have been connected to the Reptilian collective and any other collectives that no longer serve them. Can we remove the connections profoundly and be able to empower each individual person to be able to feel their own connections of their own collectives?*

S: Yes! We do only wish the best for all! We wholeheartedly release all of these connections! We sever all ties and we embrace the goodness for all! We do not wish to ever continue this. It ends and it will never start again!

J: Thank you so much! Can we send out an ask and request for all collectives to send profound love and healing in this opportunity where there are releasings for that negativity? So then they can be profoundly empowered at a much higher rate that is so profoundly noticeable to all that it inspires them to live life with more joy and high frequency vibrations? With love!

S: Yes! Definitely! We are sending love and we are wrapping up all of humanity. We are wrapping them up in love and high vibrational energy and Source love. We feel there has been a climactic shift! A shift in this embracement of a new awareness and a new understanding from the Reptilian collective and we applaud them! Because this is very profound! This is very profound! And we are very grateful and we honor them and we thank them and we wish to continue to show them gratitude! And to accept them and to wholeheartedly let them know that they are embraced and they are accepted! They have always been accepted! And the understanding and perspective they have chosen to embrace today is very profound. And we are very proud of them and we wish to send them love and reassure them that they have been loved! They are loved and they always have been loved! And we understand moving forward, that they have truly decided and chosen to be a part of a high perspective of understanding and love and empowering for all!

J: *Fantastic! Wonderful news! Thank you so much for letting us know that. In terms of those people who have been affected, how will they feel now moving forward?*

S: They will understand how drained they have been. They will feel very drained and they will be looking to explore options of how they can now fill themselves up with an overwhelming sense of joy and love energy. Because in their moments of feeling drained, they understand they need to find the right means of their vessel being filled, we say nutritiously, but we do not mean in a nutritious sense. In an energetic sense of nutrition. The right nutrition energetically for them. Many will be confused, but all that have been under this will now be looking for a higher means of what can be entered into their vessels to substitute for what has been drained. They are all beginning to be so thirsty for love, love, love! They require love! They all require love! That's what they will drink. Love! Some may feel that taste is bitter, but the more that they can drink, that emotion and feeling and energy of love will quench that thirst!

J: *Yeah. Amazing! Okay. Well, may they feel completely empowered to make wise choices to empower themselves?*

S: Yes! We see that for many, for most, for all, that they feel like they are going through a journey and now they have stopped and they stand there and they see where they have gone. They took different wrong turns on their journey. And now they stand there and they realize and they understand the perspective of now they are in charge of their journey without any outside sources or influences that were disempowering. This is very new and some may panic. Many will panic! Many may panic because now they stand on their own two feet and they choose the direction of their journey. And they all wish to find the best suited journey and path where they can quench their thirst. And it is love! We place love in front of them! We place love! We show them the road map of love and empowerment and it is inside of them and they understand and they trust in that. It is very profound and it will be very overwhelming for many. And as a collective, many of us understand that we have a lot of things to do overnight, today, this week, next week, to be of service and to be empowering to humanity. Because the veil of darkness and misleading will be lifted and shifted. And we choose and understand to best serve them, is to engulf them with love and to honor their new journey of self-discovery and love and self-empowerment. We are so pleased and elated that we can offer this for them because we have understood that there was only a small amount we could do. But now, without the ties and the release from the other collective, we can stand in empowerment together. As multiple collectives, we can empower all on a faster, deeper scale. More meaningful scale. It is rapid what will happen. Very rapid! Things will move very rapidly now with this new profound empowerment. So we are very joyous on this occasion. This is a celebration! There are a multitude of celebrations today! The empowerment for all those that were lost. We say lost because they felt lost because they were blindly being led on this journey. But now they stand on their own two feet in this self-empowerment journey and we are so pleased for them. And we wish to serve and honor them the best way we can. And we will! And we applaud them! We applaud them! And we wish to show them full encouragement! And we will! We must! And we stand right behind all! All that have been disserviced from these attachments, but we see all attachments have been released and all control relinquished.

J: *Thank you so much! I really appreciate it! In terms of now, things are speeding up. What can you tell us?*

S: For humanity, when we say rapid things are moving rapidly for them, there is no connection to anything except what is best in moving forward for them. High vibrational alignment for humanity, for other collectors, for all! We say all because this benefits all! This is beneficial to all now! Everything is severed to any... We are scanning. We are searching. We're looking. Everything has been severed. Everything has been severed so vibrations are going to rise at a rapid rate. And things are moving more rapidly. Things will be completely changed and different timelines split. The evolution of humanity is floating. We see them floating. And it's accepting. There is nothing that is tethered down now.

J: *Brilliant! Okay! Thank you so much! So then, as Stacey and I were discussing beforehand about the timelines in terms of things just slowing down. It sounds like now things can start moving forward. And would things like the laser event be faster now? What can you help us understand about that?*

S: Yes. We feel from your human perspective, the next 10 to 12 days are very profound[9]. Very profound! We wish to .discuss for humanity, the ones that have been tethered down, the next 10 to 12 days specifically for them is very profound. And once the processing of their realizations of what has happened, we are officially in alignment for the removal from this planet.

J: *Thank you so much! That is very exciting! What things will we start noticing first occurring?*

---

[9] *Part of the healing process for those having these connections removed.*

S: Many will be choosing to leave. Choosing to leave! Many will be choosing the exit point as the human perspective sees it as passing over. As physically leaving their human bodies. There will be mass exits and it will be profoundly noticed by many. The media will see and discuss on their outlets, through their cameras. They will see and it will be in very high discussion. There will be a panic! There will be a panic amongst many masses of people choosing exit points now. But this is all in preparation. There is no tethering anymore so things will be aligning and moving at a rapid rate. This is the final stage of everyone exiting from this planet. As many are choosing to leave in masses, it will make way for the shift.

J: *Is there going to be a certain location that's going to have a bigger exit point first?*
S: We see Africa. We see Africa! Many in Africa! It will start in Africa, but from a media perspective they can choose to explain it in a way where humanity will understand through... We see the media will choose to say starvation and apocalyptic times. A starvation. Virus. They choose on their media outlet to pinpoint Africa because it is embedded in the mind programming of society already, where similarly to them, it is a third world country. So for many of humanity in this area, it will make sense. It is an easing for humanity to understand so there is no fear. It will just be replaced with more of an understanding. Africa is highlighted for the media that will be a mass exit point only because the media can explain it from their perspective. And many who still choose to follow the media and believe the media will not be put into a deep panic state because they can be reassured. Because many times the media have chosen to pinpoint Africa throughout the course of humanity. Throughout the years, where they see through famine and destruction and wars

that this is normal of society in Africa. But we see deeper what is truly happening coincides with what the media will present through the outlets.

J: *I understand. Okay. Thank you! So it won't be natural disasters as such? It would just be lots of exit points explained as something that we are comfortable with supposedly?*
S: Yes! It is a step-by-step process and it will start with mass exiting over that land because it can be explained easily through media outlets for humanity to not panic. We do not want to panic. We do not want widespread panic. So it will start off, we will ease into it. It will be eased into.

J: *In saying that, would the laser event still cause widespread panic?*
S: It would have, but things have changed now. They have evolved. In several minutes, they have evolved. Things have aligned and connected deeper, so panic will be lessened. They have dialed it down from this new understanding. From today's perspective, it has been toned down. There will be a more compassionate understanding of what is happening. It is not challenging but, the words to understand to speak through this vessel is... This is all we can relay for today.

J: *Okay. I understand. So less trauma experience for less people, I'm assuming, when the laser event occurs?*
S: Yes. There are differing degrees of how it will be processed, but the majority will not panic.

J: *That's great!*
S: It will just be accepted.

J: Fascinating! Thank you so much. We also were told in the last session that we had together, that the horse collective wanted to come in. Is there something that the horse collective would like us to know?

S: It was profound in the last session for the horse collective to enter the chat room. But today, after what has been discussed in the last several minutes, we do not see the benefit anymore of the horse collective coming through. It was more honor for a personal stance for Stacey to understand for she is from and part of that collective. But today, it does not serve to enter the chat and talk about this. Things have profoundly shifted and changed on a drastic level since speaking with the other collectives.

J: Okay. Thank you. I appreciate that. A final personal thing I wanted to understand a little bit more. Stacy was talking about a child at her children's school that heard the voices in her head telling her to push Stacy's younger child. I'm curious to understand the voices in that child's head. What was going on for that child?

S: Yes. In the womb, the child's mother consumed meth and there were ties attached to the child that has now been severed. But the voices she heard, that was the Reptilian collective. They thought they could affect Stacy by affecting her child. But they did not understand the connection Stacy had with her child, where her child would thoroughly always explain things to Stacy. And now those ties have been severed. But yes, from the womb, before conceivement that child's mother would intake that drug. She would abuse that drug.

J: I see. Okay. And so, will people who have been hearing voices in their heads from the Reptilian collective in that manner, will they be released from that also?
S: Yes! All ties and cords have been severed!

J: Great! Okay. Thank you so much! I really appreciate that and I'm looking forward to seeing how this will help humanity and individuals as they empower themselves with the truth and integrity of higher frequency dimensional energy.
S: Yes. This is a new experience for all! And it is very profound! And we must be aware of this new experience for many of humanity because it will affect all of humanity for the empowerment. So we have been called to be closer to the ones who have been severed. The cords have been severed. We must honor our duties and our service for those ones and we will remain closer to them over the next 10 to 12 days[10] while everything is processed at a rapid rate.

J: We really appreciate all this information. Is there anything else you'd like us to know today?
S: No. We wish for Stacy to be joyous! This is a very momentous occasion and we wish her to celebrate this and we wish the same for you. To celebrate and be joyous because today[11] is very, very profound! Very profound for all! For all collectives! For all of us as One! It is very profound and things are in alignment and we are ready for the shift.

J: Thank you! Thank you so much!

---

[10] For those who were released from this connection they have that time period to choose to stop using drugs with their free will is our understanding of that statement.
[11] 7th of April 2022, another important session with this client happened 5 days later which is the 8th session in this book.

Session 7: Shiva and Higher Soul Self

Arcturians: Yes. We are here! We are here! We are here! We have already connected with Shiva, the divine being. The extraordinarily large higher self to the aspect of Source, into the vehicle, who were already starting to have conversations. The vehicle was very curious about certain things such as the significant role that a snake has played on humanity. Shiva was conversing and saying the following, but we will allow Shiva's energy now to be fully brought into the vehicle to explain this themselves.

Shiva: Yes! Yes! My teachings for humanity were always to remind you of the past, present and now and also to be able to remind you of all aspects of things. The past, current events occurring now and the future events that you will be perceiving you will be experiencing in your future "time." There were many elements that I always wanted humanity to remind themselves of and it was never about self-focusing on just one humanitarian collective or just humans or just man. I wanted to be able to bring in reminders of the Earth, of the elements, of the animal kingdom, to be able to remind you all that you're very much significant and important in each of the roles that you play. You shall not dominate over each other because then you will lose balance and harmony. The example is so perfect about the questions of the snakes. This has been used so many times in your certain western civilizations, in terms of your religions demonizing the snake as being evil because it was the one that coerced man into taking the bite of the apple in the garden of Eden. It was not the snake's fault that the man chose otherwise. Even if the fable of Adam and Eve was true, which it is not. Of course, it must have been written that it was something else that caused the downfall of man. How could it possibly be man's fault? How could it possibly be? We say that everyone has choices. Whether it's in your nature to be a snake or whether it's in your nature to be a human, you all still have to work with your moral compasses and know your place and significance and roles in this world. Honor yourselves and respect all, and respect your placement in this world. You are not a single isolated being here. Everything you do matters, not just if you recycle or not recycle or whether you have a healthy mindful perspective of life. Everything you do!

I have heard this vehicle say that spirituality is not a hobby and that is absolutely true. It must be a full, complete, utter way of life. So, while you are thinking about recycling your rubbish as being a hero because you are doing things that you perceive as saving the planet, why don't you connect with Gaia herself and ask her if she wants to be saved. Otherwise, it is a very egoic approach to think that by recycling plastics that you constantly are buying, that this would save her in some way. Look at the biggest scope of things. We're not saying to litter, not saying for you to not recycle if that is what you choose to do, because often it can be a great reuse of resources. But look how far you've come. Recycling is not going to save the Soul of this planet and you know that, but you still do it because you feel like it makes a difference. That it matters. So, you do certain things like recycling, but yet what truly matters is your perception and your awareness of all of these things. Knowing that everything you do, everything you think, has a greater component to the totality of who you are and what you are. When you're all connected and you're all responsible to be a responsible being who knows their place in this world, who doesn't place false limitations on themselves and does not inflate egos to be of self-importance, when their insecurities are merely just beneath the surface that are not being paid attention to. Religions have confused and distracted many people and this is why we say that our religion, our belief systems, our way of life is probably one of the purest when you remember the integrity to honor all aspects. This is why there are so many deities that we want to honor, because when you remember there is more than just one man or one God or one Jesus or whomever you think is running this show. When you recall that there are so many Souls who have been on this planet and who are also supporting this planet from this higher perspective, you will realize that this is all so much more than your own personal self-evolution. We are not wanting to make you feel small and insignificant because as we have already said, everyone is a working piece to this greater wheel. And since you are all connected, it is much better to be in harmony and balance, otherwise, your small piece of the wheel is disbalanced and wobbles sometimes, as you all do. Sometimes we want to say, you all get so disbalanced and so out of harmony that you wobble at the same rate, which then ironically balances more so than not, which is interesting.

So, everything is significant, everything is purposeful. While there are many guardians here overseeing this planet (*I am not one of them now, but I did love to come and support your planet* and *all of those who are connected to me with my Soul families*), who understood the significance of respecting all aspects of this life and all of the lives you have lived. Understanding and respecting the reincarnation cycle and the natural cycles of evolution and the natural cycles of life is very significant and it makes you more be in the present moment to appreciate every surrounding experience, knowing that all cycles do still have a completion. There is still a tail and there is still a head to a snake, but as you know, the snake can eat the tail and make a unit that way. You're still one! You're still connected! Birth and death are still the same in terms of moving from one dimension to another. Moving in and out of one physical body to another, to a light body, to another, to just be a Soul aspect; there are so many opportunities and choices that you get to choose. But, when you have signed into life contracts and you are in the midst of a life cycle, you must honor all of the steps and experiences. Those lives do not last long even though you perceive them to be dragging out. Your concept of time is merely an illusion which can distract you and make you obsessed. How can it distract you? You look at your clock, you look at your calendars, but you don't look outside to notice the change of seasons, the change of hour. You're so busy being distracted that you've slowed yourselves down in the evolution state. Isn't that funny! You were trying to be smart and clever and efficient, and yet you've completely gone in the opposite direction of your evolution. You were supposed to be able to focus on reaching back and connecting back to Source and having a small 3D experience, being separated from Source, having the illusion that you are alone. Discovering yourself amongst your friends and family and empowering yourself independently in a physical body. Having physical lives here on this planet.

It's marvelous when we are watching you forgetting completely who you are (and we do watch with much entertainment, and we say that with love) as we are watching some very profound big Soul essences bumbling through life, losing faith and hope. Must sound terrible of us to watch with amusement, some big Soul essences being completely lost. But we know when they come out of their fog, come away from the veil of forgetfulness, they even laugh at themselves and think golly, jolly good show! Gosh, that really had me going that time! Boy, did I feel so separated! Boy, did I feel so lost! Boy, did I feel so scared! Boy, was I so afraid! Boy, I was stuck in fear! Boy, I really did constantly make choices to not feel loved! Boy, I constantly made choices to disempower myself! Oh, I disempowered others! Oh, I held that love from others! Oh, I held that love from myself!

This is very peculiar but also very amazing and astonishing that we would do this to ourselves, because that is absolutely not our normal state of well-being, because we love ourselves! We love marinating ourselves in high frequency love and energy! It feels electric and uplifting and profound! This is why it was so curious and alluring to have these 3D experiences, to see if we would be able to remember. Where would our moral compass go? What, goodness gracious, would our life experiences force us and push us and drag us to go and be? It is like signing up to go to an amusement park. We know we're only going for the day. We've bought a day trip ticket and we've gone with some friends. We haven't even packed any lunches with us. We're going to buy it during the trip. We're excited! We don't know what we're going to see and what we're going to do and so the very first thing that we experience on this amusement ride of Earth, is to go into one of those stores where you can choose any costume you want from any time period. We all put on these funny costumes called bodies. We all get to choose what genre we want. Then we'll pose for photos and think these are funny memories.

This of course is an analogy of how you come into Earth. Come into this playground. You don't know what you're getting but you make a lot of great choices or interesting choices or funny choices or silly choices to be able to have life at the end of the day when you have fond memories as you share with your Soul families and friends what your choices were on earth. That is just as simple is what your Earth experiences are. It's merely a day in your soul's experience, each lifetime that you have on Earth. We do not hold time as you do, but we're trying to remind you of the significance of your experiences on Earth. We know you have forgotten who you are. That was on purpose. We also know that you've gone down to that planet to be able to be of service. Sometimes you've gone down to Earth. You've entered into the amusement park for fun and explorations and challenges and lessons because your Soul was questioning certain situations that it couldn't understand, 'goodness gracious, how could a Soul get in that predicament of wanting to brutally murder someone? How could they be pushed and driven to that point. What would it feel like to be so attacked! So brutalized!' While some of you are listening and shivering at the thought of... 'Oh my goodness, I hope I haven't got that for my life contract...' We want to say, for most people who have had that as a life contract, they really were so curious to feel and want to experience it all! It didn't seem like a mistake or an error. This was well planned. They wanted to experience that because they were so curious what they could even feel like. It's not about the pain but it's about the journey to get to that point, to either be a murderer or to be murdered.

This is making the vehicle feel uncomfortable because we can easily explain why people have chosen to be murdered. From a 3D aspect, you're so attached to the bodies and your moral compasses are trying to guide you into respecting others and caring for others. While that is often the choices of life contracts, many beings have still wanted to have those experiences for those lessons; to understand. The vehicle is confused. She is coming back into the conversation because she's asking us, isn't this part of the problem for humanity, that there has been murder in the first place? From our perspective, the death process is very curious because we do not have death as you perceive it. It's an evolutionary advancement where you just simply evolve and evolve and evolve up, up, up, until you return back to Source. But, when you're in a physical body, you have fun things and interesting things and challenging things to experience with the physical body. Part of that *Grand Experience* is the death scene. Some of us love the challenges of it, which sounds very morbid. But we want to say from this perspective, 'All is Well!' You would not want to miss the final scenes of any lifetimes. That is part of the fascination of these physical bodies. How you dump them at the end is significant!

Part of the reason why we wanted to come in here today... The vehicle was saying she didn't know what to respond to us with and what pronouns to say because she kept wanting to flip between he and she and they. So we say that we like to still have dualities of different personalities. While we have had many different lifetimes as the soul, and Shiva is one aspect of the lifetime of what the higher self has experienced, this was the best reference point for the vehicle who shared this message to her. So we wanted to come in, because as you could imagine we've had many lifetimes, many life cycles, and it was purposeful for us to experience them all so then we could assist in all! You must be able to learn and grow to be able to become a good teacher and leader. When we were all curious and wanting to explore the best we could, we knew we must have been able to experience it ourselves. We have impacted and we have lived so many times and so many other lifetimes, not just on this planet, that we do have a profound connection to most. This is why we are so uniquely connected in. It almost feels quite exotic for those people who are living in the western world to reach out into our culture, because we seem to have such unique flair and interpretations of religion and Gods. Respecting all aspects on this planet makes so much common sense that most people who are trying to divorce themselves from religions will find their way to us because it is the way that feeds the soul. Once you can honor other souls, you can profoundly honor yourself more! It's very calming energy that we're giving to this planet now because we are wishing to give all the profound sense that 'All is Well.' Because 'All is Well!'

We want to say from your perspective, just because you may have the assumption of people being brutalized in their death scenes, doesn't mean that there wasn't a profound significance and purpose. Everything is an opportunity for experiences and growth and you have heard this many times because it is the universal truth! You may judge certain things, but even *you* must admit when you judge certain things, you still know that there are lessons and purposes and significance and importances from those experiences. Regardless of whether you like them or not, there are still lessons to learn and experience.

This is what helps your consciousness expand! Collectively, you're expanding still! You always will expand because you're constantly having your experiences. We have pushed your boundaries and your tolerances into new experiences. Every time we have triggered you, it is to make you connect with others more profoundly and to connect with self. We saw that you needed more assistance with this because you were starting to isolate yourselves at a very superficial level. Even those who were very social but were still at a very superficial level, there was much lacking in deeper thought and communication. We needed to get your attention more. There's nothing more scandalous that encourages chatter than some gossip or something that was so blatantly obvious that there is another agenda that will push people to have confidence to speak up. It's not talking about senses or spirituality, it's talking about evidence and facts. We had to show inconsistencies with influencers regarding evidence and facts.

The bigger message that we wanted to share with you today, which was already disclosed by the vehicle, was having profound relaxation in the body and profound relaxation in the mind even on the most stormiest days. Even on the most gossipy days. Even on the days where there are the most disclosures you can have a choice to react or you can have a choice to have neutrality and to just process what's going on. If your ego triggers you into thinking you must fix this or protect this or this is wrong or go into judgment or fear, that is when you're going to lose your balance and be in disharmony with your mind, with your body. You will notice as soon as you start overthinking and panicking in your mind, your body will start responding. If you find your mind is starting to be triggered and tripped, focus on the natural breath of the body and release all tension in the body. Your mind will try to control everything. It will try to trip your emotions into fear or panic and it will try to make your body go with you, which will then get your endorphins and adrenaline systems going. Once your adrenaline systems are activated you will find it harder to calm the mind because then you are very invigorated because you feel like you have to have a fight or flight response, to have that reaction. We are saying, we would like for you to be able to focus and notice your breath and focus and notice on your muscles and the tension you were holding in your body. This is why we would like you to be in a comfortable position when you re-listen to this message and to find if there are any tensions anywhere in the body. That you will release the tensions, because you are holding on to the tensions. If you have chosen to hold on to certain tensions for a long period of time, your muscles will get so stiff. They will get so used to having the tension that it is almost doing it automatically. Ask your body to release the tensions you have been putting strain on, and every time you go to sleep and every time you sit down, please notice and ask your body to release and relax now. Ask your mind to release and relax now and notice from the top of your head down to the tips of your toes, if you have complied with your wishes to be relaxed, to be able to go with the flow. You cannot control anything outside of the body. You can only focus on what is within. You can only focus on what is your body, your mind, your breath and the senses that will follow when you are in ultimate balance and harmony. We would like you to practice feeling this profound inner peace and this profound balance. When you are in this profound sense of balance and harmony, imagine a wind coming. Will it push you or will you just not resist and allow the wind to pass through you? You cannot stop the wind. You can notice the wind. Do not let it aggravate you. Do not focus on the temperature of the skin as the wind is flowing through you. Notice the warmth of the breath. As you allow the wind to pass through, it will go, because you're not fighting it, you're not resisting it, and it will just move past and through and beyond. You're not focusing on it. You're not manifesting more, you're allowing it to be in your awareness and leave your awareness. We say the same thing with rain. If you imagine you are out in this beautiful balance and peacefulness and you were sitting out or laying outside on the ground and it started to rain and you could feel the droplets all over your body. You get to choose to focus on whether it is warm or cold. You could have a problem with it. You could be outraged that you're getting wet or you could see the bigger perspective that it is just small droplets of rain. It is not going to harm you. It doesn't have to bother you if you choose for it to not bother you. So, will you accept that you've got slightly wet or will this bother you and ruin your day, ruin your clothes? When, in true perspective your clothes get wet every time you wash them. You get wet every time you wash you. So, is it because it's been raining and you did not choose for it to rain that you're bothered, that you've lost the control and something is happening to you that you have not allowed? Can you allow things to happen to you, trusting that you can choose to be annoyed or you can choose to have full acceptance? What do you choose? Inner peace to not let things bother you, or are you going to be hyper focused and fixated and frustrated and buy an umbrella? Where does your moral compass go? Where does your inner peace go? When you see that it is raining, do you get angry because it's going to impact you or do you see that this is a blissful thing to cleanse and feed and heal the Earth? To feed the earth? To feed the plants? To feed the animals? To feed the insects ? To cleanse? How are you perceiving such things as the rain? How are you perceiving such things as the wind? How are you perceiving other people's actions and choices and words? Do you allow them to just flow through you or do you want to guard and be frustrated and controlled? What are your choices? What are your perceptions? You could hear something that doesn't resonate with you and let it flow through you or you could be so outraged that disinformation has once again been delivered onto the ears of humanity, that you lose focus and inner peace. Have you realized that you're fighting for things that happen to you and happen around you? Have you been fighting against these things, making yourself even more challenged to go with the flow, to accept all experiences, to not hold on to them emotionally and energetically to honor and respect those who uplift you and to release and do not resist and do not hold onto things that don't serve you?

Learning and growing from all experiences is our preferred choice for you, but even if you take the hardest path, it is still your journey. It is still your lessons and it's still your growth. Choose wisely, because even if you don't make conscious choices, energetically you are. Notice what you're exposing yourself to. Notice that you could always go inside if it's raining. Notice you could always put on a coat or do something else if it's windy. You always have options. Always! Can you see if you've added any new tensions into the body? And why do you think you've done that? Constantly check in with your body. Sometimes you control your bodies too much! You tighten muscles that don't need to be tightened. You put so much strain on the body. You put so much tension and emphasis on the body. You're wearing yourselves out! Focus! Focus on what you're doing to your mind. Focus on what you're doing to the body.

Honoring yourself this way is always going to be more of a beneficial experience for you. Remember, you are responsible for your mind and you are responsible for your body. What choices are you making to empower yourself? You can only start this true level of empowerment today because you've only heard about this today. For some of you, this is new. For some of you, this is a reminder. Do not regret your choices from the past. Empower yourself and move forward. Do not let the past be your reign. Do not let your past be the wind that bothers you and distracts you and frustrates you. Allow the past to flow through you. If the past keeps coming up, you need to heal it, love it and release it and *let it go! Let it go! Let it go!* The choice and all of the decisions for you to empower yourself are yours! And we say this with much love!

Session 8: Reptilians telling on the Draconians

Session from the 12th of April 2022. From the client from session 6 a few days later, the Reptilians wanted to expose the Draconians and their behavior.

J: I'd like to call upon Stacy's subconscious please.
S: Hi, Jo.

J: Hello. Are you able to please do a body scan for Stacy and tell me what's happening to her body today?
S: Yes. Sure thing. Yes. She feels very dense. Her body feels very heavy. But like you just discussed with her, it is a lot of purging. A lot of purging from her system. A lot! A lot! A lot! Lifetimes of purging for her!

J: Are you able to help assist with the releasing of that density since it no longer serves her?
S: Yes! We would love to assist her because it has been debilitating to her body!

J: Okay. Are you able to also balance and heal any and all systems that need to be balanced and healed please? (S: yes!) Fantastic! Wonderful! Are you able to give her a beautiful spa treatment while we continue on with the session today?

S: Yes! Of course!

J: Fantastic! Okay. Subconscious. The reason why we're connecting with you is because we feel that there is a request that the Reptilians have had for the Arcturians and all the collectives that are helping assist this planet. We were wondering if we could discuss with them what their requests are and have some negotiations and understand more what they are needing to converse with all.

S: Yes. We also wish to converse with them in regards to what they wish to discuss with us.

J: Okay. So can we get a representative of the Reptilian collective who wants to discuss their requests?

S: Yes. We are here now.

J: Thank you very much for coming in. We are open to having a conversation and we are curious what you would like the collectives to know today.

S: We want them to understand that the darker forces are wanting to run away. They are wanting to run away and escape all of this. They have no intention of any willingness to want to open further into discussion.

J: I see. And when you're talking about those who want to run away, can you tell us more about who that is?

S: It is the Dracos. The Draconians. The ones who we would previously have labeled as Masters.

J: I see.

S: They are fleeing. They are fleeing! They have fled! They do not wish to converse in any form.

J: Has it given the Reptilians more freedom from their once masters?

S: Yes! They understand there is no tie to them anymore. They understand that they are seemingly upset, but they like to show no fear, no mercy! They still stand in high regard for who they are and what they choose and continue to do, and have done.

J: I see. And so the Reptilians want all of the collectives to know that the Draconians are trying to escape from being held accountable? Is that what you're wanting us to know?

S: Yes! That is exactly correct.

J: I see. Okay. And in terms of the Reptilians. How are they approaching now being untethered from the Draconians and having untethered humanity to the Reptilians?

S: We feel so much closer to this planet and humanity as a whole! We feel we have fully been accepted into this community of love and balance and unity for all! And best, how to serve all! So every day we have been striving to prove and to show that we are here for the right reasons.

J: Okay. Is there anything else you're wanting to ask from the collectives?

S: No. We just thoroughly want them to understand we have been misled. We were being misled the entire time! It was so corrupt and we had no choice but to follow.

J: Okay. And so what are the things you're going to be doing now to make amends? What will we notice moving forward now?

S: We choose and we wish to topple over government systems to uncover the truth. We wish for key players to shed their skins of the truth of who they are and their hidden agendas. Some copious amounts of hidden agendas in every direction. Everywhere! Everywhere!

J: I understand. And so, is that because most of the leaders are Reptilian? What can you let us know about that?

S: It is beyond! It is beyond! We were initially the masters of that, but now it is beyond even what we thought was possible to do for the attachments. We are not tethered to anything, but there is still... We'll try to explain this. There still seems to be an overcoating. The word we find to use in this vehicle is poison! There is a poison that has been injected and inserted in many and it is taking a turn for the worst currently. It is creating a power play, a power struggle with the current beings that this poison is still lingering.

J: *Are you talking about a literal poison, or what can you help us understand?*
S: More on a controlled energetic sense of poison. We say poison because it is the only way we can find to say for this vehicle to communicate. To understand. Like a poison that is going through a body. And our understanding of poison in a human vessel is that it is not a good thing. It will always be to the detriment of the being and it can seemingly take control and change how they were from the start of the process to the end. They can completely change their interior and exterior, but mostly, we say interior.

J: *Okay. And so how are you assisting with these leaders exposing their real truth and agenda?*
S: We have tried to examine and process and find an entry point where we can do more, but we have come to the conclusion that, as a collective, we have thought it best that the rule from the Draconian collective is so embedded in these select few that we have also tried to have discussions with the Draconian collective, but to no avail have we succeeded. But we will not give up. We know they were our masters. We were slaves to this darkness and it will take a while to overcome it, but we will never give up in this

advancement of wanting to empower humanity and to expose the truth!

J: *Okay. And so, are you needing support from the other collectives, and if so, what do you need?*

S: We know that when the light comes through, the light from other collectives will come through, it seems to push the Draconian collective away further. It upsets them! It anchors them! And it seems to push them away. So we have realized and we understand that we must take this, in what you will understand as baby steps. It is very deep! It is very thick! It is very dark! And we say we must take precaution in trying to move forward with this discussion. And yes, we are very cautious in this because we understand for humanity, as all. For unity for all higher vibrational realms of collectives, that we are at the forefront in trying to open these discussions with the Draconians. Currently there is no... It is sealed tight and there is no way to open any communication. If anything, they seem to refuse more the more we choose to push. But we do not push, but they feel like we are pushing them. And when we see deeper into them it makes them... There is a new fire that has been lit under them.

J: *In terms of the old earth experience, can you give us an insight into if that's changed now? Will the Draconians have to stay here or is there anything that you would like us to understand about that?*

S: We feel like they do not want to even be a part of any discussion. They feel like they could find better elsewhere. Somewhere else, because they do not wish to be susceptible to any accountability or any discussions with any collectives that are here for peace and unity and love. They are fearful! They shy away, even when we say love, they instantly will throw fear. We say love! They say fear! They are currently not in any form of willingness to discuss. And when we ask about if their agenda is still the same with this planet, they say they are looking for alternative life forms to prosper on. But we also feel their agenda is layered with tricks and deceit so we cannot confirm if, when they say they choose to prosper elsewhere that that is their agenda, because there are many layers of hidden agendas with them. But we can only see what they are wanting us to see. They are very difficult to tune into because they are so frustrated the more the light is shown on them. They are very vengeful and hateful for all other collectives at this time. They have always been, but now we feel just in two days in this timeline, that they are planning to do their best to assert their dominance in ways that we would need to further examine. But we stand firm in empowering this planet and to be aware of their hidden agendas and to not allow them to wish to do any harm or seek harm or any destructive thoughts or ideas or natures that they wish to bombard here. As we are discussing this, they are infuriated. They are infuriated and enraged. Their fires are burning deep! They are so infuriated with this conversation currently going on!

J: *Can they accept love and recognition that there is nothing to be infuriated over when the collectives are wanting unity?*

S: They do not believe that statement to be true. When you say love they will show that they put that in their fire that is burning. They have no trust because they are not trustworthy, so they do not trust. But we feel little by little there can be some hope for a discussion. But they are infuriated with the conversation that is continuing at this moment.

J: When, if ever, have any of the other collectives harmed or shown that they can't be trusted?

S: From our perspective, never! From the Draconian collective, we see they just choose to ignore. They choose to ignore or even take any other perspectives or ideas of what you have just said. They are so enraged that we deem it almost pointless currently to try and figure out any further. Because the more we continue to communicate in this moment, the hotter and higher their flames are burning, and will continue to burn.

J: Okay. Well, we wish them well and respect their choices, but if they could at one point reflect on their responsibilities and the impacts they have caused, not only to themselves but to others, we would be really appreciative.

S: They wish to tell us, the Reptilian collective, that we are weak. We are weak and we should not trust the other collectives. But we know they say the same spite and fear, so we choose not to take on board what they feel is the truth.

J: Well, isn't that empowering for the Reptilian collective to now see how disempowering the Draconian collective has always been to the Reptilians?

S: Yes! Yes! We are so open to so much more, and we hold so much compassion for them because we see it as not empowering. It is only self-serving to them and they must be held accountable. They must! And we see hope in the near future that they will!

J: Fantastic! Okay. And so in terms of the Reptilian collective. So you're wanting to have more disclosures from the political systems and then what else were you wanting to do to be able to help humanity?

S: We want to clear the way for the truth to be revealed. We see so much! We see a repeat in history of figures, of religious figures, political figures, government systems, that have only been self-serving. It was never intended for these structures to ever benefit any other means except themselves. So we wish to uncover, we wish to bring a new path to light where that path, those paths have always been covered up and hidden. And we wish to uncover them by any means that we can. We have been in deep discussion as a collective on how we can best serve. And with multiple discussions amongst ourselves and even with this vessel Stacy. She has been a great asset and ally to us to also open up ideas and to see infrastructures of how things need to be revealed. We are seemingly new to this also, because we did not understand how dark things actually were. And we choose now to push back the old to reveal the new. To clear away and clean up! To clear away and clean up and reveal the truth. We struggle to see, to figure out and find the best way we can reveal these hidden agendas. But we, in our advancements, will never give up. We will continue, continue, continue, because we know eventually things will be revealed. The truth will be revealed and exposure will be revealed and nothing can be hidden forever. And we appreciate that we are able to be in unison with the other collectives that are here to reveal the same agendas that are best to serve mankind and all humanity. And we seek the truth! We seek the truth! We wish the same for all! And we have taken a new role! We have taken a new role! And it is our duty now to reveal hidden truths! It brings us joy to reveal hidden truths! So we, as a collective, have been in continuous discussion amongst ourselves how best we can serve. How best we can empower. And we understand it must start from... We say top of the food chain, because we know that would be understood in this communication. So we will find a way, a means where we can slip through the cracks, because there are many cracks. And we can slip through those cracks and reveal the truths. But we also understand this is a process. But there are cracks that we can slip through. There are hidden agendas that will be revealed that are already coming up to the surface to be revealed. The truth! The truth of how governments have ruled over humanity to no service at all to humanity. It is all self-serving! It has always been self-serving! But now history will not repeat. This will be triumphant! This is coming up to a time of triumph and glory for humanity and revealing hidden truths! We do not wish to be part of a society where it has diminished humanity and broken the spirits of humanity and silenced the truth. We see the wrong doing in silencing the truth. Chains will be broken and lifted and truth will be revealed. And panic will set in for government structures because they are already understanding that they are beginning to crumble, so they are looking at ways where they can hide more. And they are in a fearful state of mind because they look through the history and patterns of humanity and they realize it can't be repeated. There is no room for it to be repeated now because many, many, many more, so many, so many are awake to their agendas. And they cannot silence many like they used to. Only a few. So they are fearful now and disclosures will be revealed. So we see the best way for us to move forward to assist humanity, is to continue to push these cracks open further. It is our pleasure to be able to do this! It brings us joy and in turn will bring freedom for all! And empower all! And we are happy that this is how we can assist and serve the best for humanity.

J: *Thank you so much! We do appreciate that! In terms of the planet. What are you going to be doing? What are your plans to be able to help the planet?*
S: We don't understand what we, as a collective, could do to currently make things any better for this planet. It has been thoroughly destroyed internally. So we understand we can only do what is best for humanity moving forward and our agenda.

J: *Thank you. Was there a point in "time," where you were hoping that all the collectives could work together to be able to heal the planet?*
S: Yes. We thought that could be accomplished. But it was for the wrong reasons. We wanted the destruction of humanity so that we could empower this planet and reside here alone. But now, with a fresh perspective and new understanding, that is not our agenda now. We truly want what is best for humanity, for all! That is where our service is now. That is where we wish to best serve all.

J: *Thank you! In terms of the old earth experience. I guess it's up to each individual person to have those lessons and experiences. Can you help us understand from your perspective, what your collective would be learning from the Old Earth experience?*
S: Yes. We see the experience of destruction never serves any. Destruction and annihilation and choosing that as your agenda was never in the best interest of any, because we see it best to work with other collectives because it is a stronger unit. It is in the best interest of all to work united. And the

destruction of this planet... We see the demise that has taken place because of, we say our old ways, but we understand that was not our choice. That was not *our* old ways. We were under instruction and we had to follow orders. But now, with new understanding, we say shame. We do not hold that emotion but we use that word. We described the word shame. We felt shame that this is what we were used to do, and used to accomplish here. But that is never, and never will be ever, our agenda. We are now working with, and we are so joyous to be a part of serving humanity best. And we do feel sorrow for the planet and what has happened in the destruction of the planet that has caused the rift between what is best for this planet and what the planet has chosen to do. We are remembering all these experiences that have gone on and we feel remorseful and we understand things had to play out the way that they did because that was the agenda. But we feel highly remorseful and we can understand and see how things could have been different if we chose to be stronger (crying). We were under instruction and we followed along because we were very fearful. And through the eyes of remorse that we now have, all we can do to serve is do what is best for humanity. It is just for humanity that we can assist now. While we are so grateful for this planet, but now what has become, we can only do what is best for humanity.

J: *Thank you. Were you hoping at some point that all the collectives could have worked together to be able to heal the planet?*

S: Once we received this fresh new perspective, we understood that it was too late. It was too late to do anything currently to make this planet inhabitable for humanity. So we understand the path that was chosen for this planet. But we do have hopes for a distant future where this planet can be, we say, refurbished. But we see that it is a lifetime away. It is bounds. Bounds of time away. In this communication, our remorse is very overwhelming because we see the destruction that has taken place and we see if we moved different, things could have been different. We do not like to dwell on the past because it is not empowering to us as a collective, but we understand why you ask these questions. And we would have hoped that all collectives working together could have accomplished this. But we understand that is not the case. And we accept that. So we must continue to focus on humanity and how we can best serve and empower.

J: *Thank you. And so, you're working towards disclosures for certain pronounced people to be able to expose their agendas. What's going to give them the epiphanies or the motivation to disclose themselves? Or will it be others that will disclose their agendas?*
S: We see the motivation and government systems choosing to change because they have no plans that are set in stone which will accomplish what they need to continue to hold humanity in fear and bound by control, so they will seemingly show vulnerability to humanity. But that is of course another hidden agenda. But humanity is awakened and will continue to be awakened to the lies. So we see infrastructures declining because there is nowhere to hide. The voice of humanity is so loud and the questioning of humanity is so in depth that government systems and key players have currently no answers, so they are scrambling. They are scrambling to show that they are vulnerable and they are going to reveal truths. But humanity has been awakened for quite some time now and each day more and

more are being awoken. Ones that were, we say like sheep, like sheep who followed the path the shepherd showed them. But now they choose to find their own path. And infrastructures will crumble because there is nowhere to hide. All they can do is pretend. But we know that they cannot pretend for much longer because humanity is awakening and will continue to awaken. That will not be able to be wound back. The Awakening will not be able to be wound back! It is only going to become stronger and dialed up more. Higher, higher! Stronger, stronger! There is nothing stopping humanity from revealing truths! Main corporations and infrastructures that have bound society will be toppled over from humanity questioning and not accepting any more deceit.

J: Do you see, moving forward, bigger or certain events or disclosures that would help more people awaken?
S: We see advancement of technology and more people wanting to question it on larger scales, not accepting what is put in front of them because they understand it is not to serve humanity. It is self-serving to the beings behind this. They understand that advancement of technology is not always a good thing moving forward for humanity. And it is very obvious in many regions over the globe where this is true, disclosure will be uprising in an uproar as time goes on because humanity will not accept advancement of technology without further questioning. And through further questioning from humanity they will fumble. They will fumble with why advancement of certain technologies are best for all and humanity does not accept their hidden agendas. And we support humanity in this because we also see the hidden agendas and advancement of certain technologies. It is not serving! It is self-serving! It is purely

self-serving! So the Awakening of humanity and the questioning from humanity, all truth will be revealed.

J: Can you give us a sense of what that technology would look like?

S: We understand it to be in the process of warfare. We see new infrastructures of lasers for the destruction of oncoming asteroids and on coming meteorites which they say is to the destruction of this planet. But the hidden agenda, what they say to humanity is not the truth. The truth is hidden. But because humanity is awakening to this, they can not understand 'why now?' 'Why now do they need such lasers to destroy and eliminate asteroids and meteorites to save the destruction of this planet?' So they will not accept what is being told to them through media outlets. They will not accept that. There will be an uprising of questioning from humanity. They do not wish any warfare on this planet anymore. No more wars! And we stand beside them and we agree. But that is what we see that is currently going on. The advancement for warfare and to, they say, protect humanity from the destruction of this planet.

J: Is it a country or is it a company that's going to be bringing out this technology?

S: We say they coincide together. It is countries and companies.

J: Fascinating! Okay. And then, are there any big named influencers who are Reptilians who are going to impress us with their sudden true humanitarian respect? Is there someone that you would like us to be excited about?

S: We do not currently have names to impress upon in this communication. We just see many hidden agendas. But through more communication, we will be able to reveal more hidden agendas. Currently, in this time, we can only say what we see. And this is currently all we can say for now at this moment.

J: *Thank you. I do appreciate that. Is there anything else you'd like to say to us today?*

S: Yes. We wish you to understand that we stand with humanity and we are committed and will always choose to do what is best to empower humanity. And we are very proud as a collective, that this is the best way moving forward that we can serve, because we understand we can see hidden agendas. And we understand as a collective, we can further create the cracks. We can push them open more to reveal hidden truths. But we are also very proud of humanity that they are awakening more and more and more. Every moment that goes on, they awaken more and more and they do not accept deceit. And they will not.

J: *Well, we're really appreciative of that. We enjoy seeing more disclosures so we are grateful that you are now assisting with all the collectives to be able to push as much disclosures that humanity can cope with at the most appropriate pace.*

S: Thank you. We are always pleasured to be able to discuss and communicate further and we appreciate that you choose to discuss with us because we truly want to serve and help the best we can. We are so honored and proud to be a part of collectives with the agenda of empowering humanity and doing what is best to serve all!

J: *Fantastic! How do you communicate with the other collectives now?*

S: We channel when we discuss through multiple outlets, we talk with them. But we also discuss through channeling. We are trying to find other ways to explain it but we are saying channeling.

J: *Fantastic! That's great! And so, you must be very busy now with your new epiphanies and newer perspectives to be able to have these communications flowing so freely now.*
S: Yes! We are very honored and we will not stop because we see how best for us to serve.

J: *Fantastic! Okay. Well, we wish you well and we appreciate all that you can do to help support humanity with these coming events and we do really appreciate hearing your perspective. So thank you so much!*

Session 9: Healing for All Abused People

By giving us the perspectives to understand the purpose of this.

Yes. We are here. We are here. We are here. We're here and as requested, we have brought in all collectives to be able to assist with your request today - which is healing all of these sexually abused and verbally abused people that are walking on this planet, still injured and wounded from their experiences, lost, to be able to understand the significances and the lessons that those experience gave for them to empower themselves through.

For many, it was life contracts to have those experiences happen at an earlier age for them to be able to understand humans should not be trusted, that you are the person that needs to be protective of yourself, and to wake up to other people's moral compasses. This was a very harsh experience that you signed up for, but you knew that you wanted to learn this lesson fast and earlier on in your life journey, because you needed to be able to empower yourselves forward.

Empower yourselves forward.
Empowering yourselves forward!
Empower yourselves forward in this incredibly important time for humanity.

While you were victims to these experiences and that was the literal experience lesson you were requiring, to be able to understand that you needed to protect yourselves from others. You needed to be wary of others. Find your intuition and your moral senses and your moral compasses to be able to navigate yourself safely through this world. When you did that, you suddenly awoke into other people's agendas. When you go blindly skipping along this lifetime without any awareness of other people's agendas towards you, which may impact you and distract you and take you off your own life course and purpose, this was what we were perceiving and what you also perceived when you were in position with and along and amongst us, was that you needed to be awoken earlier to other people's choices for you, to be able to remember. Remember. Remember other people have free will.

This has impacted so many people on their life contracts and journeys. So part of this, while it was unpleasant and quite traumatizing, needed to be experienced, because this was what we perceive - the only way to be able to get you to pay attention to other people's agendas, other people's morals, and how they wanted to impact you and belittle you and disempower you. Once you healed physically and emotionally from this, you saw you are unbreakable.

You are unbreakable.
You are unbreakable.

You know this, and this is why you are so bold to be able to ask for these experiences to be had.

While this may sound absolutely false, as we say to you, you chose those contracts with those people, to teach you those hard lessons, because you needed to be prepared. You needed to be armed with understanding what this world is all about, and how "wrong" it is, how unnecessarily wrong this has become, and what this is.

This is why many don't want to look outside themselves and look outside of what other people are wanting from you and for you. We're not trying to scare you. We're not trying to upset you. We're trying to remind you of what some people have done with their free will and their entitlement to be able to damage others, control others, manipulate others. While it is such a foreign situation for us naturally, in our high dimensional perspective, we would never dream nor seek desire to have this experience in our perspective and our dimension. It is so foreign. It is so distasteful. It is so dense in its actions and conduct.

But, as you choose to enjoy your 3D lives, this is part of the options that you choose to have. As you're writing your life contracts to be able to know - 'when I heal from this, when I empower myself from this, I will be so much stronger', because we all needed everyone on this planet to be stronger. What doesn't break you, must enamel you - we want to get this word right. We're relaxing the vehicle [crying]. She feels so heartbroken for those children because they were so confused.

There is a process with glass and with metal, that when you crash cool it from a hot heat, suddenly it shocks and it enamels the glass, so it is able to be dropped a few more times without shattering. We say this can be done with metal to some certain metals - enameling. That is what has happened effectively to those people who have had those traumatic experiences. You've been so deeply shocked and traumatized, that it does make you harder.

Unfortunately, so many people do not get the healing that is necessary for them to empower themselves forward. So, they're so in shock and fear, they retreat from many. They do not trust others. They do not trust themselves because they think at some level, they deserve this, because of the verbal abuse they were taunted with, to keep quiet and to not share their secrets. This is why many do not want to share their truths now, because they're still so afraid that they're going to get into trouble, that people they love are going to get into trouble, and that even they will get into trouble when they speak their truths.

This is a conditioning to keep you under control. This is a false limitation belief system that you can release now. So, we've called upon all of the collectives to be able to look at this in depth, to be able to see - who can we now help release, because this no longer serves humanity. Being disempowered no longer serves humanity. It is time for empowerment. It is time for your strength to shine.

It is time!
It is time!
It is time!

While the vehicle is saying to us, 'there is no such thing as time, it is a man-made construct', we say, indeed, and so we will clarify - it is now. It is now for you all to be released from what no longer serves you. We will heal. We will heal the impact from the ears. Many people who have been told terrible terrible things and lies about themselves, have shut down listening. They find it very hard to comprehend things and very hard to listen and focus. They are so introverted, they have gone into their little shell. So, we're going to say, with much love to them, it is safe for you to hear now. You can hear the truth. The truth. The truth is that you're loved.

The truth is that you're never alone. The truth is that you've always been safe.

Even while there have been some scary experiences, you were well protected. These were lessons for you to grow from, empower yourself through. You were supposed to heal. You were meant to be able to heal and recover and strengthen yourself, believe in yourself, know your self-worth, and never ever ever accept any form of abuse again. You are worthy of more than that abuse. You are demanding respect from all.

Isn't that interesting, when you demand respect from others, how they perceive you, when you are so entitled to be respected. Doesn't that piss off those who have the bigger egos, who want to shut down others. When you are confident in self and love self, you know you are respected. You know you should be respected, therefore, you tolerate nothing less. Doesn't that bother those who want to control and manipulate you still?

So we will blanket this planet, now, with a love frequency that can be heard, to be healed, to be able to make safe ears, now, listen to the world. You are not being told you are unlovable. You are not being told you are wicked, evil, naughty, and you deserve to be hurt. That is not true. It never is true. So we are energetically releasing the trauma from the ears, because this is something that we have noticed people shutting down the world, shutting out the world with. This is why we say, you can hear. We want you to hear and notice the love songs that the birds are singing to you, the high frequency of joy. They're wanting to remind you of joy. They love to dance and be silly and fly and fly and fly and have the freedom to flutter and dance in front of you, to be able to let you know - you are free to do as you choose. While you do not currently have wings, you can empower yourself with higher frequency. You can seize the world with love. You can feel and feed the world with love, with seeing your intentions to embrace all with love bubbles, as the vehicle would say.

So send your intentions to be able to heal all. You do not know what all have gone through. Even if you have been with one person the entire seconds that they were born until right now, you do not know what has happened in other lifetimes, consciously, so please treat everyone as fragile. You do not know what they have experienced. You do not know what they are holding deep within themselves. So, love each other. Love each other. Have compassion for what you do not know from each other. Respect each other. You all deserve that.

If you're trying to still belittle someone and put someone down because of your own ego, Grow Up! This is not time for you to be indulgent with your own ego. You must see each other as equals, because you are equals. Love each other with true integrity, true passion. It is so easy and simple, but yet so many make it so complicated.

Heal yourself.
Forgive yourselves.
Forgive others.
Accept all that has occurred.
Respect all that has occurred.
Respect all that has occurred.

If anything else, you should be able to take away the lessons that all that has occurred was to empower you moving forward, to have faith and strength to understand and see you are unbreakable. Look how far you've come. Look how far you have come. For those of you who have not repeated those cycles of sexual abuse, Thank You! For those of you who have not repeated the cycle of verbal abuse, Thank You!

It means you learned your lessons. You have learned how controlling and manipulating someone for your own personal desires, for your own personal control, does not truly uplift you. In fact, it just holds you down in density. So check your moral compass. See if you have that life contract, and what you're supposed to be doing with your life contracts, and what your life contracts with others are. If you can't be honest about your own actions, how are you supposed to grow and heal from them?

There are more collectives now, willing to support all, as these lessons need to be wrapped up and experienced and healed from. We're able to be able to give epiphanies for people to realize that they are profound survivors. This will make them feel proud of themselves, without dipping into victimhood. It will empower them, just as the life contract was written, just as they hoped that they would be able to have. So they will see something on their TV screens, or their phones, or their computer screens, or they will hear something from someone - that will be a positive impact statement of how, from terrible tragedy, comes great lessons and empowerment.

So much can be said about this. We are wanting to let you know that we are working behind the scenes, to be able to release people from what no longer serves them, in terms of what you have requested, in regards to self-abuse, sexual abuse, and verbal abuse. Any form of abuse must be healed now. Once you start healing humanity as a collective, great things can happen, because you're shifting your vibrations up and releasing that density. That density certainly no longer serves humanity.

We say this with much love!

Session 10: Home Planet Destruction Impacting This Lifetime

J: Yes, indeed, indeed, indeed, we are here for you[12], we are here for you, we are here for you, and we did hear your conversation prior and we are here to assist.

S: *Thank you. We do appreciate it. We would like, Subconscious (and all who are here, all the collectives), if we could speak to the Draconian, call the Draconian in that has been trying to hide from Joanne?*

J: He can't run too far. He is quite tethered to this planet and for various reasons why. So yes, he can try to hide, he can try to escape, he can try to project himself into a new reality, he can try to physically eject himself into a new planetary system, but he will not get too far. There are significant reasons why we have grounded him many times. So yes, we do know who you're speaking to and about. This is very uncomfortable for him, because he has wanted to get everything his way and he doesn't like to play with groups. He doesn't like to even play with his own group. He is independent and this has been a challenge for many. So even part of his own teams and collectives are trying to assist as well, to help him, because he is so wayward now as more and more collectives are growing and more individuals from each collective are appreciating and honoring their own inner working experiences and lessons. It's not just humans that need to do their own inner work, it's all. We are all one and we are all exploring and expanding and having lessons and opportunities for growth. It's not just unique for humans, although many humans think that they are so special that

---

[12] *The Collectives, as presented through the Arcturian channel.*

they are the only ones that need to do such things. All collectives need to grow and expand, otherwise there are problems and stagnation. You know when you have a pool of water and it is not flowing and it can become quite swampy quite quickly, and while there are benefits to algae and stagnation of water, that's when you start getting the problems. That's when you start getting mosquitoes and other bugs and other things that don't serve you. Well, maybe this is not the best analogy we could have used today. You understand what we are trying to say. And so yes, we will call in that Soul essence who is very reluctant to see beyond himself. Very reluctant to take responsibilities, because he is still very determined to be that special unicorn for humanity, and so we'll call him in. He is not wanting to acknowledge he is here. He is sulking. We would be open for you to have any questions for him, or we can continue talking to him and explaining to him. Now that we have his energy with us now, we could help with epiphanies. What would you like us to do in this communication?

S: *Thank you. Just want to say thank you for that energy being here too, we appreciate that. We would like to know, for the Draconian, what is your agenda for humanity and this planet?*

J: To rule. To own it. I have rights. I have a birthright. I want to be the leader. I've worked hard. I deserve this.

S: *Is there anything that you are lacking right now that we can help you with?*

J: I'm lacking in full ownership of all, and there are some that don't respect my desires and my needs, and as a fragmented self... [*subconscious steps in*] we're going to explain it this way. There is a difference between the conscious mind of that man, versus his subconscious, versus the guides. His subconscious and his guides have another agenda, which is self-serving for their... we can't even say collective, because their whole collective is not on board with their approaches. So you can have full collectives who have the full range of different perspectives, personalities, and agendas for all. This individual man, who was connected into a few beings who are of Draconian descent, have a certain agenda to be able to empower themselves continually for their ego, because they like to control and manipulate. They have been wanting this for a long time, to have complete rulership and ownership of a planet and all its occupants. They do not realize that they are not allowed to do this or get away with this. They have no interest in playing with collectives or being part of collectives, even though they are all part of a collective and they are all part of one. They are not wanting that. They don't have motivation to do that or be that. They are not willing to negotiate, and so they are very head strong in being able to manipulate and trick humanity into falling in love with this being and his agenda for humanity, even though it is extremely self-serving. Ultimately, he wants to gain their trust, for them to all love him, be impressed with his money, his wealth, his influence, his technologies, his devices, his tools. He wants to be everything, and yet he is not going to be planning to treat humanity well. He is wanting full ownership and what do you do with things that you think that you own? It's a novelty. It's toys you play with, and as other collectives are trying to say to him now "You do not own man. You do not own this planet." Even the planet's Soul has another agenda which you cannot control. This is why they are not wanting to listen to us. This is why he is not able to listen to us, because he wants to create his reality. He wants to create his fellowships. He wants such leadership, and he is truly not sincere with all of his agendas for humanity. While he is trying to date humanity, make humanity fall in love with him, it will be something that he is not able to get away with, because there are many life contracts that cannot comply with his agenda.

S: *Thank you. I would like to speak to the Draconian in particular now. I'd like to ask - are you this man's guide or this man's subconscious?"*

J: I have some guides, but I am his subconscious now[13].

S: *Thank you. Are you aware that this planet is dying?*

J: I feel such great frustration with that knowledge, because this game that I'm working on, I need to win. I want to win. I want to rule and I want to own. I've worked so hard to be able to get that status, and to find out that where I am based, and all the work and energy that I have put into getting to who I am. That I am to then find out that I can't play in this playground anymore, and that humanity, those who I want to rule, is going to evolve without me and is out of my control. So I feel very frustrated. I feel very robbed. This is very frustrating because when I was not playing with others, shall I say, I wasn't updated with the information about Gaia's Soul contract. I didn't know Gaia's Soul contract. I thought that I was able to do this forever because I didn't stop. I didn't want to believe it. I think I was given nudges and being taught. I could see the decline, the rapid decline of the planet, but I

---

[13] *Could be said a 4th Dimensional being, conscious awareness with no body, having smaller Soul essences of itself in 3D bodies, including many important influencers.*

thought that that was going to be used to my advantage, because I would be able to be creative and be able to fix those problems and then be a hero once again, even more so if you could see all of the industries that I am behind. You could see that I would have been able to, I would have been the savior. I needed to be the savior. My ego desires desperately to be in control of a planet, be in control of all. I need that so much, and to discover as I am being called into this meeting now and I can see many other beings here supporting this conversation, they are not telling me of the demise of this planet to distract me or trick me. They are telling me this in sincerity, because this is the fate of this planet. I have been ignoring this for a long time. This is why I've been hiding. I do love this planet in my own way and I wanted the best for everyone. But what you think may be *your best* and what you want and desire, may not be mine. So I guess I have a different perspective of what is best. But I wanted it to be all upon me. I worked very hard to be able to get the status that I have, to be able to bring in all this technology to this world and this planet. I wanted to advance it in my own ways, and it is very frustrating to be told your main project is not able to be successful because it is out of your reach. I cannot manipulate or control Gaia's soul, even though I have tried to delay this event because I thought it was negotiable. But that was my ego not wanting to realize that I can't control all Soul essences. I can't control any Soul essences actually, but I thought if I could distract enough, that somehow things could change.

S: *What would you like us to help you heal today?*

J: Can we heal Gaia's planet? Can we bring in a Soul to be able to assist to continue on with this planet, and can everyone support the energies of this planet, so it can still be relatively viable for humanity to still stay here? I want humanity to still stay here. I kind of need humanity to still stay here, because who else can I rule? I want to rule the humanoids. We've had so much history together.

S: *What if I told you that humanity does not want to be ruled? They want to be free. Everyone and everything deserves to be free and not ruled.*

J: Well, from my perspective, they all need to be guided and controlled because they are just such simpletons in terms of what their needs are. They're always going to be led. They always need to be led. They always need to be guided one way or another, they're not truly independent thinkers yet. They still can be easily manipulated and I believe that I could be giving them more opportunities to grow here. They should be able to grow here, but my agenda for here is materialistic and it's physical. I am frustrated because I do not want to surrender my desires to still lead and control. This is important to me. I have lived many physical lifetimes to be able to get this all. I can see I am now talking to the Pliedians now. The Pliedians are saying to me that this is their project. Humanity is their project, and they wanted to empower humanity to evolve by themselves. And I'm saying - but look at how long, look at where they are still. It's not truly just the Draconians, it truly was not just the Reptilians that were impacting humanity. They were doing enough damage to themselves. We get blamed for a lot more trouble that they put themselves into. They still don't know how to empower themselves. They still don't know how to be responsible for themselves from my perspective.

S: Yes, well the thing is that this planet is going to end, and humanity is going to be taken off and nothing can stop that.

J: I understand that the plan for the humanoids is to be evacuated from this planet. I understand that. I can't stop that. I have tried to delay it. That has been fantastic, to do it, because I sort of still thought that certain technologies that I could get access to would be able to help assist with this, to be able to have the Soul essence of the planet be removed and still be able to rule over the, what you would call the Old Earth experience. But the access to the full codes and the access to the full DNA strands and the access to the blueprints of the actual humanoid bodies is still being kept privy from me. I've tried to get it and work with it, but there are certain codes I cannot get access to. This is very frustrating. So I have tried to create new 'genocodes' that can replicate Soul essences, but it is not actually possible to be able to create a soulless being, not that I would even want to rule over a soulless being. I have no ownership of this planet, I am merely occupying this planet. But from my perspective, I want to be able to continually be here to rule and I have done so much to get to this point and I feel so close to it too, which is the most frustrating thing[14].

S: Is there anything that you personally need healing for? Any past situations? Any current situations that we can help you with, so you feel more at peace and not feel like you have to have so much power to feel good?

---

[14] This session is a good example of the channeling of information having multiple perspectives from different points of time, as he is learning information and reflecting upon this within one moment in time - but for him he is talking from many different points in his own awareness. Convoluted while being very interesting to see, instant growth with perspectives.

J: I see what you're doing here. You're trying to ask me in a roundabout way if I have lacked any inner work and any love healing for myself, to feel good about myself to heal any of my past. This is what you're making me question, is where do I need healing and help and love from? Where should I address things that I'm lacking, because obviously the fact that I'm wanting to rule others means that I have no control over self and can't rule myself. So I am projecting my own insecurities and needs onto others. I view your question and I review it, and you're asking to heal a past where I have been removed from other planets. The planet that I would call my home planet was destroyed along with my own collective. It was an asteroid. This is going to trigger me when the actual laser event happens, and every statement about an asteroid coming to hit this planet triggers me deeply. I would like to be healed from that[15].

S: *Thank you. We ask all the collectives to assist with this healing and release any fear or trauma that you may have had, and know that all is well.*

J: The saying I want to say to you now is this, and this may be a very peculiar one - I felt like I've always been the bridesmaid and never the bride. And in that terminology I want to say I wanted to rule this planet. I've wanted to protect and rule other planets and I never quite got there. I always assisted with others. I always tried to assist with other planets, but for whatever reasons, it didn't work out. My insecurities, my fear that planets can disintegrate

---

[15] *From this point he has listened to many of our sessions for him to learn what information we know about the shift and events about this.*

quickly. I am still grieving for my home planet, and I haven't wanted to look at that because it was so painful. Now I am looking at a bigger perspective of why my reactions have been keyed up for certain insecurities. I still want to rule. I still feel like I need to rule. It feels like I cannot fulfill that thirst and drive to rule, because I feel like, from my perspective, it is the better approach. I don't know if I'm considering all or whether I'm just considering myself. I need to reflect on this more, but it is frustrating, because what I truly want is to be able to rule my people, my actual beings, my collective. I want to rule my collective, but we are not in physical forms as humans in 3D[16], and I've missed that window of opportunity. I've missed that. That is not occurring anymore, and so I have substituted my true desires and projected onto humanity. It would never have even been the same.

S: *Well thank you for sharing, I appreciate that. I ask that you get an epiphany, many epiphanies, that you are in fact safe and you are in fact loved greatly, and you're connected to everyone and everything and you don't need to rule to feel safe. You don't need to be in control of humanity to feel safe. I ask these epiphanies for you now.*

J: Thank you.

S: *You're welcome.*

J: The biggest epiphany that I've had is that my own collective didn't protect itself, just like how humanity is not

---

[16] *As they originally were when living all together on their home planet. Only Soul essence are within human bodies now, not their original bodies they had as Draconians.*

protecting itself. I can see many correlations now between my home original planet and my original collective to what is happening here on this planet. I can see the way that I can heal myself is by helping heal humanity. To be able to awaken those who humanity trusts, that are part of the human collective. They need to be highlighted now. Many men have made choices to disempower men. I don't want to be ruling something I cannot own, and I realize now that trying to own other species, other beings, is never truly the way to enlightenment. Not that I've ever considered that I wanted to be enlightened. I wanted to be empowered. I wanted to have full power and only the full power. I can see much work for me now. Thank you.

S: *You're welcome.*

J: I've worked so hard. I want to be able to make good out of this, but I was running from my own problems. I wasn't wanting to deal with my own problems and hurts. Now I can see some of my own collective that have grown and matured beyond me. They are embracing me and that is a positive experience. We have been disconnected. Thank you for this[17].

S: *You're welcome. Of course we ask that you're empowered and feel love just brimming from your entire being.*

J: Thank you, thank you. This has been something I have needed for a long long time, but something I never realized I needed in the first place.

---

[17] *To explain the span of time for this being awareness for this session could be said to be many, many centuries. Extremely convoluted, we must have found him at the point where he was really ready to heal and reflect.*

[Conscious mind discussion begins...]

J: Okay, well I'm out. He's gone. He left. Yeah, I feel like his collective has gone into a private meeting. I want to just talk about that while I'm still processing that. I could feel that what he was saying was not exactly everything that they were sharing with me. So I'm gonna try and just take you through a chronological experience... It seems like whatever his position was in his original planet, when they were physical, he was always supposed to inherit and rule his planet. He was always supposed to be a big deal, but it was taken from him. It was so sudden. They really were shocked. The asteroid hit their planet and destroyed it. So it's like he's tried to have many other lifetimes where they were to live out their life contracts of how they're supposed to be. He's always thought that he was going to rule a planet, and he always thought he was going to be able to rule over his collective. And now his collective has gone. They sort of split up and they went to different planets and they had different lifetimes. A lot of them even graduated, but he didn't graduate because he was still focused on self-serving, just ruling others for the sake of ruling and being a leader. So he was really fixated on how to be the best leader and ruler, but he was viewing it as ownership, not empowering others. So his perspective was very limited. He had a few insecurities. There's a lot to be shared about that.

I remember him saying something about "always the bridesmaid and never the bride", and I thought that was the most bizarre reference point ever, to talk about in terms of trying to rule. But when he realized that he was in a big meeting with the Pleidians and the Pleidians were like "dude, these aren't even your beings. This is another project. We're trying to evolve in this physical way of life as humanoids. They're not even your collective!" It's like he realized that his whole desire to lead and rule was so great, it was like he didn't even care who he was trying to lead in rule. And he had quite a grand judgment on humanity, saying they can't do jack shit for themselves. Then he had this epiphany, that while he is still here... well, he can't rule what he doesn't own, and it's actually not really what he's desiring. He's just so obsessed with being a leader and a ruler, that even when he was the king of humans, it actually isn't what he was aiming for or hoping for or planning for. It was really not what he really needed or seeking but he was not really aware of what he was seeking and why.

So then he realized that, because of something to do with how he always thought it was his own collective that was hurting him and not letting him rule, he realized that his original planet died because of an asteroid, which super triggers him now, by the way. He realized that it actually was part of his own collective that weren't helping each other out, and haven't really been helping each other out. He wants to fully lead and rule his own collective, but he can't because a lot of them have already grown and empowered themselves, gone back to love and are actually trying to be part of all and one again. Whereas he's been so hurt and frustrated that he hasn't been able to rule. Be the bride? So weird. It's interesting, because he wants humanity to wake up now, because he was sort of saying that it's not just Reptilians and Draconians and any other collective, it's humanity. Humanity is not a victim to all these other collectives. Humanity is a victim to humanity. Humanity has made many choices. Each individual person has a choice to step up and empower themselves. You can't be a victim to one collective, because each individual being has its own purpose, its own journey, its own path, we're all one.

Yeah, there was a lot, so I think I have to listen back to it. But when you said about the planet not being able to survive, it broke him. He never wanted to acknowledge that, and he got really upset about that. He's very sensitive to planets not living because of the trauma of his home planet being destroyed.

S: *Yeah, I was actually gonna ask about that more, like the life purpose and significance of also being here and then healing that, but it seemed like he went off...*

J: He went off to be with his Soul family from his collectives, because he had shunned them. He was angry they didn't protect him, they didn't protect their home planet, and I guess every family's got its own dramas and dynamics, just like every collective has its own family dramas and collectives and dynamics. He has been avoiding me because he doesn't want to hear about the state of the planet, even though he's kind of aware of it. As soon as he realized and refocused on what his agenda is about, wanting to own humanity, he realized that he doesn't even want this. It's like he projected his desires and realized, even if he got what he thought he'd been working for, what he's been working for doesn't quench his desires and drive anymore. He's gotten so off path, that if he actually got everything he's been working towards, it isn't actually what he really wants.

S: *Yeah, and that's what I was trying to get at with him, because I could feel the lack. I could feel the lack right away.*

There was a lack and it was like he needed something and it wasn't that, it was like peace, it was love, it was all this other stuff.

J: The whole love and light focus is a distraction to him, because he's like "no, I thirst for ruling". The thirst to be the leader, the thirst to be the owner, the thirst to have ownership and leadership and influence, that's his only focus. It kind of bothers him that there's people that don't worship him. It was very interesting.

S: *As if he looked at me like "who is this hippie?" LOL*

J: It's obnoxious, and he was so focused on trying to rule and lead, he didn't even care who he was trying to rule and lead. And when the Pleidians were like "This is actually our project, thanks" it sort of suddenly dawned on him that he's so fixated on being the top, that he had to stop, and think "where was I going with this?" and "what was I actually set up to do? What was my real agenda and my real calling?", and his calling was to lead his collective. But when you're trying to lead people that are already advanced from you, and beyond and higher dimensional than you, how can you lead them? It seems like that's when he was open to realizing that others had already moved on. He can't lead his collective because most of his collective have already left them behind, in terms of they've already grown in the evolutionary journey. He was so focused on leading, he'd never seen that he actually is behind. I didn't get any angry evil energy from him at all.

S: *No, me neither.*

J: I just saw a very entitled being. It was interesting though, because it seemed like while he is the subconscious of that man, he has other kinds of guides who've got the same agenda, to want to be right up there to be able to push and guide humanity. It feels like it's different fragments of Souls from other lifetimes he had, that still are seeking out the same agenda, to rule?

S: *I didn't know that's possible.*

J: So the highest self can break off from Source, you know we love our labels, so the higher self breaks off again, down into different subconsciouses. So if different subconsciouses are working together in one being to be the subconscious and their guides, different fragments of the higher self have come in to support one being. He still hasn't healed. It gets a bit convoluted with who's there, but there's definitely the subconscious, definitely has guides as well supporting him. For the human with this Soul aspect he has guides and a subconscious that are all empowering him to rule and lead. But it's not the most inspiring leader when you don't really have true compassion or integrity, or you really respect the things you're trying to own.

S: *It's just owning to own, that's all.*

J: It's so frustrating for him, because he's been working so hard to rule and it's interesting, because it's like he's been so busy with this obsession, to own and rule, that he hasn't stopped and actually looked at all the other things that's going on around him.

S: Yep, makes so much sense, because he has that personality. He said he sleeps in his office. He works a lot.

J: I thought it was really quite sad that he keeps getting triggered about the asteroids, and it's like I could see the other collectives constantly trying to give him information about asteroids coming, just to trigger the shit out of him. It's awful. It's mean. But you know, what's a trigger? They weren't trying to be mean. They were trying to let him know "you are not in control here my friend",

S: And that's why he created the laser on the satellite, because he's trying to stop anything from impacting his hobby, because he's worked so hard.

J: It's so interesting, how he's in so many industries and he's got so many side projects.

S: He's *everywhere. It's weird.*

J: Well, you know he wants it. When I say he wants to lead, he wants to rule every aspect of everything, it's beyond an obsession. He doesn't want to just be your one influencer, he wants to be every brand, everything, all merchandise, everything is him him and him. It's like a full-on obsession.

S: *That's what I was trying to understand and trying to help heal. I didn't really know what to do with it, because it just felt like so much there.*

J: Well, you know, we can't do his inner work for him. When they were just showing him their projects, when he realized you can't own Gaia, you can't own the life contract or a Soul of someone else's. You can play with their 3D physical counterparts, sure, but you can't own someone and you can't control their life contracts, including the planets. That's what really bothered him, because you can't control everything. And when you realize you can't control everything, that's when you have to start accepting what is in your realm and what isn't in your realm of control.

S: *So he was one that was actually running or hiding from you? That's interesting, very interesting.*

J: It seems like he's had other lifetimes as being a Reptilian. He's had other lifetimes of being all sorts of different things trying to be this leader. It feels like different planets. He's tried to always be this ruler, and this isn't a one-time lifetime thing. This has been forever. Well, you know, not forever, but you know what I mean, like this is a long long long long time ago, where he has not got any real healing or perspective of what's really going on for others.

S: *Wow. Hope it helps. I was actually going to ask him before he left, "why did you buy Twitter, and what were you going to put on the platform for people to see?" I wanted to ask that.*

J: Well, it does seem like he wants to throw a lot of people under the bus and speak the truth and share the truth, just so then people can be loving him for his exposures and disclosures. When you start telling people the truth, you get respect and appreciation. Look at him - he's telling us he's helping us, but it seems like yeah, he was throwing everyone else under a bus just to gain loyalty and fellowship and admiration. So it was part of his ploy. He's not disclosing his full agenda, he's wanting to disclose others.

He doesn't want to co-lead. He wants to be the single source of leadership. It's interesting that he wants to disclose humans. I think he just wants to expose everyone's choices. You are either empowering humanity or you're not. You're either trying to grow and expand or you're not. I think he's wanting to expose a lot of people's choices. Ironically, this is how funny it is. He's projecting his own insecurities. He is getting triggered by other leaders trying to lead. He's willing to throw them under a bus and he's wanting to disclose their agendas. It's not about the crimes against humanity for him, he wants to rule and lead everything and own everything, every industry. He wants to own everything and humans are part of their everything.

S: *He was saying that he was purposefully slowing down the shift from happening, and so I was trying to understand how he is able to do that?*

J: It's a great question. Because he knows that humans can be easily manipulated, how was he manipulating humans to not expand and not be independent?

It seems like what he's going to do and what he was trying to do is kind of hypocritical, because he was going to throw people under the bus. It's like it's just him for the world. He doesn't want anyone else even near his realm of ownership. It was quite surreal.

I wonder how much fear he's created. I wonder if he was part of the nanotechnology, he must be. I don't know all the industries he's a part of, and his name keeps coming out quite a bit.

S: I know he put a chip in monkey's brains to try and control them and they died really bad deaths. He was thinking about putting that in humans.

J: Well, we know that the metals, the nanotechnology, has been put into people's systems long before any inoculations, and so it feels like he's been playing around with a lot of stuff. Those energy drinks, that cheese, that food coloring stuff, so much.

I don't think he is publicly connected in with a whole lot of other industries.

S: He's more private, only certain people are in the know. Now what if there's a way where we can stop him from blocking. He even said "I've delayed the shift multiple times" and they started laughing.

J: He got pretty emotional when he heard about the end of this planet. I feel like it was the first time he actually had to accept that it was going to be the end. I felt like he either didn't believe it, didn't want to believe it, and was trying to do heaps of stuff to distract himself from it. But if he's already saying he's prevented this shift, it means that he does know it's true, but potentially he's still focusing on keeping that narrative going. He's so focused. He still believes that he can control everything and still win[18]. I feel like that was a big epiphany within himself.

S: It didn't feel like the man to me.

---

[18] It took some time to reflect how this session had unfolding and it was not just one moment in time for this soul.

J: I felt like most of this was the subconscious. I don't feel like I've connected in with just a human, a 3D mindset. It was a different being, but it still was hard. It still felt like it was a he, masculine.

S: *Was like there is a larger draconian and then something else behind, underneath, that's controlling him?*

J: Yeah, it feels like there was the subconscious and some guides, so some others.

S: Yeah, I just feel like more than one.

J: They've just got the same same agenda - that they want to control, but it's so pointless because when they were reminded of what they're wanting, to stop focusing themselves on all these small steps, when they actually look at the journey and the destination of what they want, it's not even what they want. It's a substitute. Humans are a substitute for their own collective. It was intensive, that drive to own and control everything. He's not joking. It was a compulsion. It's an obsession. I don't think I've ever experienced anything that intensive before in terms of dedication.

S: *It's like he doesn't sleep. It feels like he works and works and works...*

J: Yeah, and it's all to have this end result of owning everything. But that's such a limited perspective, because you can't own souls, you can't own people's life contracts or beings' life contracts, you can't own a planet, and that's just the most frustrating thing for him.

Oh, it reminded me he was trying to create beings without souls. It was frustrating to him, that not everyone was a fan of his. He would see it was like he was trying to create other beings and trying to use the DNA to be able to replicate, because he can't understand how the body works himself. He can't create a body with a soul. That was the most frustrating thing for him.

S: So, *like cloning?*

J: It must be a form of cloning, because he's kind of got some of the DNA code strands of humanoids, but he can't understand how it can work with the soul. How to fuse a Soul into a being's body or a body. It did seem to be a frustrating thing for him, because it was like "if humans can't naturally love me for everything I'm doing for humanity, I'm going to create my own beings then, and they'll love me that way" It's the weirdest thing. He doesn't seem to love humanity. I don't think he seems to love anything, yet he wants to create beings to love him.

I'll have to listen back to it, because he had you asking a question and he was already scanning and analyzing exactly what you're asking him. It was like he was trying to see what his insecurities were. So when you were asking "what do you need for love and healing?", it was like he instantly went to that position of how hurt he is. That his home planet is no longer there for him to rule. It was like he saw that and he didn't want to go there. He did not want to share that with you, because that's super vulnerable to him.

I could feel my teams, my subconscious explaining some of this, so I don't know whether it sounded like him talking or my subconscious was explaining.

S: *Oh, I can't remember. I went into these weird meditative states.*

J: When they were saying things like "oh, this is the reason why he gets triggered", "this is why the asteroid information really upsets him". I feel like there were insights from my subconscious, adding in information there. Because it's like it's not just one being that we're connected into, it's like we're constantly connected into my subconscious and other collectives who are there to watch and assist with this, as well as having a conversation with one being who has got his own agenda going on.

It's so interesting. He doesn't truly have malice for humanity. He doesn't even value it. It's just like a bunch of farm animals. It's just the furniture that you get when you know, you buy a house, but he hasn't bought a house. He can't buy this planet.

S: *I was trying to figure out how can I help with another perspective? That's what was making it feel like it was a little bit hard, because I was trying to understand how to talk to this being.*

J: Well, they made it pretty clear that he doesn't play with groups. So right from the get-go that's kind of a bit off-putting. But his obsession was so focused on so much, it would have been hard.

I think you did a great job. I have to listen back to it. I feel like from what I was given and shown, lots of epiphanies for him to deal with and to actually realize.

I'm wondering why he's tried to escape before...

S: ... *and where would he go? That was another question I was going to ask...*

J: He's trying to go back to Mars, which is a random sense.

S: *Because doesn't he want to create a civilization there?*

J: It's so strange. But I want to say that his Soul essence has had so many different lifetimes that he has been a Reptilian, he has been an Annunaki, he's been Draconian, but he still has this identity of being a leader, and it so motivates him, regardless of what kind of species or being he is born into, he will be who he is.

S: *That makes so much sense, he wants to be the leader, wants to complete it.*

J: So now, as you in this lifetime, what we would call Elon, he wants to now be the leader of humanity. He has this kind of personality trait of just coming and ruling, and yet they don't see what really needs to empower humanity or other different beings. This is very interesting.

Okay, I'll stop recording now so we can continue on with this conversation...it is all mind bending.

~~~~

Jo here, writing this little note to you as I edit these sessions in the linear time we were given them. We are seeing a theme to these sessions which were strongly guided to be added into this book without even knowing what content was in the sessions. As we all explore the rest of the book together we will see the significance and purpose of why this book has this focus on other collectives. Each book really does have its own focus. Thank you so much for still being on this journey with us. Much love and gratitude.

Session 11: Old Earth - The Shift, The Light Beam Event.

J: I'd like to call upon the subconscious please.
S: We're here.

J: Thank you so much. Are you able to do a body scan and tell me what is happening to her body?
S: She's very relaxed. Her headache is gone.

J: Can you tell me what was the significance and message and purpose of that headache please?
S: She's working a lot and thinking a lot and things are very fast. It's a lot of thinking.

J: You know Subconscious, she's not that impressed with all the thinking and working that she has to do. What can you tell her this time?
S: That she has seen growth in self. She's more confident.

J: Fantastic. Okay, can you please balance and heal her entire body and all systems that are attached to that body? Are you able to give her a complete spa treatment and be able to assist her in anything she needs for her body today?
S: Yes, we can do that throughout the session.

J: Fantastic, I really appreciate that. Does she have any heavy metals in her body? [S: Yes she does] Can you give me a sense of how they got in her body?
S: This is interesting. They're showing a CBD oil pen that she uses not often but randomly.

J: Tell me more about how she's getting heavy metals from that.
S: It seems that when she has used it, it heats up and the oils in it aren't that natural. There's some other things in it and

it's affecting her. It's almost like it's affecting her throat a little bit.

J: *What is the purpose of her using this tool?*
S: She uses it sometimes to take away the headaches.

J: *And so, this is actually giving her heavy metals?*
S: We feel like it's putting certain things into her body that are not good.

J: *Okay, so can you remove all heavy metals from her body please?* [S: Yes, we can start working on that.] Fantastic. Does she have any nano technology in her body?
S: Any nano technology? We don't see any.

J: *Fantastic. Great. Thank you. I appreciate all the healing that you'll be doing to her body and the relaxation you'll be giving her throughout the session, Subconscious, as we continue on with her questions.* [S: Yes] *Her question about going to Denver, Colorado on the 22nd of May (2022) for a work trip, just wanting to see how that's going to go. What can you tell her?*
S: She'll be okay. She doesn't like planes. She'll be okay. It'll be a boring trip.

J: *Okay. Is there any other reason why you would want her to go to Denver, Colorado, or is this truly something just to be of service for her work?*
S: She affects those around her and her vibration helps lift others. She doesn't notice that and so wherever she goes, doesn't matter where, that will continue to happen. She's going to meet some new people from different states from work and it'll give her an opportunity to socialize with them.

However, she won't want to be there. She'll want to be home. However, with her, she can again raise vibrations.

J: Yeah okay. Well, we'll give her encouragement and empowerment throughout that trip to enjoy the moments knowing that all is well, all will be safe. There is nothing for her to worry about. Try and make the best out of it, while she is away. Thank you so much, subconscious. Another one of her questions is - are there going to be any portals we need to open or close that are still on earth?

S: We feel like there's portals that are being opened now, that are being activated by certain key people. We don't see any assistance needed from her for that. The key players, key people, have already been assigned these roles. All is well.

J: Can you help me understand what is the significance of having these portals opened?

S: Almost like energy releases onto the planet. We just get a sense that these portals are higher vibrational energies coming through. We're giving her a view of the one that she noticed at work - where those dark shadows were coming through, the really intelligent ones - that one has been closed. There weren't many of those though, those were very very few and rare. These ones are all positive portals, like a blue light - blue swirly lights opening and reaching out and creating higher vibrations that will affect everything on the planet.

J: You say that that is occurring now?

S: Yes, there have been, we feel, like it's already been occurring. They're showing us open blue, swirly circles around.... it's already been.... certain people have been activating them without them consciously knowing.

J: *Okay, that's interesting. So is there anything more you'd like us to know about portals or certain people being able to open up these portals?*

S: When these people get a strong calling to visit somewhere, and they don't know why, it's almost like they're being guided to visit a place. That's when it gets activated and open. It's like they're the key to open the block.

J: *When all of these portals are open, what will happen?*

S: Vibrations will be rising. We're trying to assist with that. We would like humanity to not have a traumatic experience as much as possible. So the more higher-vibrational they can be, the more the fear goes away from each individual, the more they can cope. That's what will happen, they will be in a better position to accept things coming. It's another way of providing help. We're all helping in our own ways. We're all guiding and assisting. Many are here with their own positions and their own roles.

J: *Fascinating. Thank you so much. It's so intriguing. Another question that she has, Subconscious, is about Elon Musk - to be able to understand what now has changed for him?*

S: Elon, we see him. He's contemplating. He is contemplating. He tries not to emotionally go inward deeply at all. He doesn't quite understand emotions, nor does he like them. He tries to push them too away - almost like he likes to dissociate from emotions, if you can. And now it's almost like he's getting this - it's a pondering. We see him sitting. We see him rubbing his chin with his fingers, thinking about life, thinking. He's thinking, he's looking. We see him looking out into his warehouse and he's thinking - is this my life purpose? It's like he's asking himself - Is this what I'm supposed to do? Is this all there is? Is this all that I'm doing here? He's really actually considering that question - What is this? He's almost attaching himself, finally, away from what he's created with material items, physical items. And he's asking - What else is there for me[19]?

J: *When he explores that question about his life purpose, now that he has got that healing and those epiphanies, what will he learn to discover about himself?*
S: He shut himself away from the world. He will realize he has put himself into a four cornered room, this whole time, his whole life, he has been focusing on the ground. It's like he's never really looked past the horizon, never really looked at the sky or beautiful trees. He doesn't have that connection. Now, we're almost seeing that he's getting these epiphanies where he's looking out past the warehouse walls, past the items being built, and he's actually noticing the world more around him, the more natural world around him, in a more spiritual sense. Before he was very detached, hardly noticed it, and didn't associate with it emotionally, or many people emotionally. It's almost like nature is catching his heart strings. He's getting the feeling of the spirit energy within the nature around him. He's starting to connect, we feel, with high dimensional guides, because he's feeling this strange energy he's never felt. It's calling out to him - nature.

J: *When he was taken to have conversations with his collective, when we were no longer able to connect in with him the other day, what was that conversation and what was his experience with that?*
S: They're patting him on his shoulders. He has his head down. He's crying because he's confused. He's almost

---

[19] *Session from 1st March 2022, before he brought Twitter.*

wondering - how long have I been doing this for? They're very reassuring. They're quiet. They're allowing him to verbalize his emotions because it's a lot. It's something he's never - this type of epiphany has never occurred to his consciousness before and it's a lot for him to deal with. So they're allowing him time to mull it over in his mind and to vent and to cry and to process it. When we see him, he is visibly upset. Around him, they're patting his shoulders. they're giving him reassurance, quiet reassurance, and he's quite upset.

J: *We'd like to send him more love and empowerment into looking at the true significance and purpose of being here on a 3D planet, on Earth.* [S: Yes, sending that now] *Thank you. And for the Draconians, have there been any changes for them since that connection?*
S: They're wiser. There's more wisdom, more understanding. It's almost like it created this energy like they're strong but wise, now. Much strength.

J: *Fascinating. So we'll send love and appreciation to all that helped through that session, and for all who help with all of the beings here on this planet, and not just at this present time, but in all aspects of all time.* [S: Yes. Thank you.] *What about the Reptilians? How are they going?*
S: They're showing us a vision of them and they're a little bit more round and happy and kind of like waddling, slightly like uh, we don't want to say, dancing but they're kind of like hopping because they're more elated. They just seem soft, happy.

J: *That's beautiful. Okay, thank you so much. Is there anything else you'd like us to know about the Draconians or the Reptilians, Subconscious?*

S: We feel they're not angry at all. Anger is gone. More acceptance. They've actually grown quite fast ... fast.

J: *Wonderful. Absolutely wonderful. How delightful for them all. Thank you. Subconscious, she would like to know - what should she purchase to better prepare for her Old Earth experience?*

S: Water, more water, more more more water. Water is going to be hard to come by - clean water.

J: *Out of curiosity, how long will she be spending on the Old Earth?*

S: We saw this before - between four to six months. It depends on things which have not yet occurred.

J: *Okay, and so tell me about the moment she realizes she's on the Old Earth. What will be happening around her?*

S: We're showing her - it's like people run outside because something happens and they're not telling us what it is. It's like she's at work and they're running outside because there's an occurrence and then - this is confusing - also an earthquake making that noise too. It's like rumbling rumbling. There's rumbling, that's what it is. There's rumbling underneath the ground. This massive rumbling, so loud - it's where you feel like the entire bottom of the Earth is going to collapse. It's frightening to the point where people are running out of the building. There's nowhere to go because this noise is all around you. That's when things start shaking. We feel like the sky is already starting to get really cloudy and swirly. It's all happening so fast. It triggers so much. So much is triggered - all at once. It's really fast.

J: *And so, can you give me any more insight into what occurs? What's the trigger of all of that other - the earthquakes and the sky?*

S: I feel like it's the scarring of the United States - the ground. Heat. Laser beam. I want to say energy beam. "Laser" is very, very - it causes an image, automatic image. We want to be more broad with that. When it triggers and when it hits, it's like everything, in less than a few minutes, gets triggered.

J: *Did she hear the effect or the sound that the ...we call it the laser event - we know that we've mislabeled it or misbranded it ... but the event that does cause quite a bit of damage, and a lot of exit points - does she get to actually hear the sound of that event occurring?*

S: We would like you to ask that question at the end as well.

J: *For an official statement from you subconscious and all the collectives, what would you like us to call the "laser event"? Would you like us to change it to something else that's more specific? How would you like us to move forward with referring to that event?*

S: We can call it a light beam.

J: *Thank you. Okay, thank you. A light beam event. Okay, and a rough estimate of exit points - What sort of numbers are we talking -millions of people or less than millions of people that would be using exit points with this light beam event?*

S: That's a lot because it triggers different things, you could say millions, if that includes everything, everything, earthquakes, tidal waves. Are you specifically asking about - in the pathway?

J: *Just in general. I mean we're assuming this is a very big event that changes our labeling from being in the time frame that we called the Old Earth.*
S: Are you asking how many are left?

J: *No, I'm just just confirming that it's still going to be a very large event.*
S: Yes. There'll be much less people after, and it's such a confusing question for us because we like to get into exact ways to confirm answers. We're seeing lasers - light beams, a lot right after, a lot.

J: *Okay, thank you. So for her to notice this event, do you get a sense she will hear or will she feel the impact of the light beam or the triggers from that event.*
S: We know she's going to feel it. There's this boom coming from the ground. We would like you to ask that question at the very end.

J: *Okay, Thank you so much. Is this information putting pressure and tension in her body?*
S: It is not. However, we feel like we could dissect it better towards the end.

J: *Fantastic. Thank you so much. I do appreciate that. So her next question - given the information you've already provided for her, is there now going to be additional experiences for people on this planet in what we call the shift - the shift between now and the Old Earth experience?*

S: We don't see anything major. Similar yes, many natural situations. [J: *Thank you*] Yeah, they're not showing us anything now.

J: *How many possibilities do you see the light beam event happening? Are there many days and possibilities of this event occurring or what would you like her to know?*
S: There are possibilities of certain time frames, you could say, for this to occur. It's almost like they don't really want everyone to know exactly when it happens. They don't know. They won't know until almost an hour, in human terms. It has to be done quickly. It's almost like the collectives who are waiting and getting the go ahead - it's more than them, it's Source. It's very quick. So when Source is ready, all is ready - everyone and every being. It's everything: animals, people, plants, all the collectives. It's almost like when everyone's in agreement, it will happen and at most, an hour after, maybe two. It's almost like they don't want anyone to know because they don't want more delays. So it's gonna be quick. It's gonna be determined quickly. There'll be something that'll tip it off like a vibrational frequency energy that we have gone to, ascended to, reached, and it will cause like a "yes, push the button now' and it's super quick. Those who are very connected to Source, those who are very connected to their teams will get a very strong strong feeling it's going to occur, but they don't have more than a few hours to accept it.

J: *Thank you. Are you suggesting that there are still people that are trying to actively block and stop this event from occurring?* [S: *Yes*] *Why are they still not seeing the significance and importance of this event occurring?*

S: Fear is very strong. That's a very strong emotion and large groups of people, large energy. People can have really strong energies and they can use it for positives or not so positives. There are some energy conduits here who are in very deep deep fear, and they can prevent things to occur because they'd be so traumatized, it would frighten them to death and that is not what the shift is wanting. They do not want that kind of energy during the shift.

J: *Can we send profound healing and releasing and epiphanies to those people who are still deep in fear who can actively still hold back this shift at this point? [S: We ask that you say that again] We would like to call upon all the collectives to be able to help assist with releasing all the fear for those people who have got strong energy pulls here and are withholding and pulling back humanity from shifting.*
S: Yes. Asking them now, now. Thank you.

J: *Thank you. Out of curiosity, does Sally know anyone, any influencer or such that is holding back actively because of fear? Is it people that she may know or that we may know in general or are these people we're not aware of?*
S: We're feeling male. Sally doesn't know this person though. She can't see him because she doesn't know him, but he's a very strong energy. He's very strong. He's a big being. He just has a lot of fear though. Yes, male.

J: *Why does he have fear?*
S: He's afraid of the process of death, knowing he's going to die scares him.

J: *Can he have the epiphany and the belief system of reincarnation?*

S: He does have the belief of reincarnation, however .... we're seeing this man, and he is envisioning his death with natural disasters. It's so frightening for him that he already knows he would die of fright, just knowing destruction around him is occurring and he's seeing it through his own eyes. He forgets about reincarnation. He forgets about everything, all of his spiritual practices.

J: *The next time that he sees that or fears that or thinks about that, can you give him the fast forward next step into what actually happens after the shift for him, so he can see the amazing things he should be looking forward to?*
S: Yes, but we ask too, because we see that many are actually asking for this. No one has asked this in this way and now we're seeing that everyone can benefit from this as well.

J: *Absolutely. Thank you. It seems like so many people are focused on the problems of this planet, that they don't have much way of seeing the next step, which is beautiful and the New Earth, if they're going to the New Earth which is marvelous. Once you step into accepting this information, you want to go immediately, because you suddenly realize that this is very significant and important and a must situation to benefit for all who do and all who can go to the New Earth.*
S: Yes, it's hard in this density. It's hard for people. It's like they are tethered to the density. Yes, we would like for every being on this planet to have epiphanies now of a future filled with love and more happiness.

J: *Wonderful. Thank you so much. I think everyone who has been needing this, deserves this, and shall appreciate and respect this. Thank you. So subconscious, she'll be spending some months on the Old Earth. Can you remind me from your* perspective, Subconscious, will she have power and will she have the internet?

S: We do see the internet, for some time. We see her on her laptop.

J: *Is she still working while she's on the Old Earth experience?*
S: I feel like she's connecting with others through the laptop. TV is not good. We see her just connecting through the laptops, putting more energy through that, and the phone. TV is not really important, so she doesn't really have the TV on, anyway.

J: *In terms of the dark shadow she saw in the house earlier, what and who was that?*
S: It was very peaceful. We see the Draconian though, from the session yesterday. Just observing. Just watching.

J: *Could it be said that he's still trying to figure out whether this is a trick?*
S: The way that we get it, energy wise, is they're very strong, almost like soldiers, but not soldiers. But they have that strength, the commanding presence. We see him observing her personality. He was trying to understand who she really is. He was trying to decipher - is she who she acts as she is. He sees her as pure. He sees her as no harm. He sees her as normal.

J: *So he was just trying to feed some of his curiosity?*
S: It's almost like he was trying to make out with her, not brain, but her personality, her essence - figure out who is. He's just curious, curious.

J: Did he also have curiosity towards who I was, or am I blocked from this sort of stuff?

S: I feel like you're blocked. We feel like for her, she allows it. She has always allowed other beings and entities to be with her. It's almost like it does good for them because she is giving them the opportunity to - this is really confusing, it's hard to explain it - but like she's very loving and she's not trying to harm. So with certain beings that are not really comfortable because they're always unsure, especially if they are in more of a density, when they see beings like this. It almost gives them this hope or this opportunity that they too can be this way. They too can do this, or there's hope. It's hard to explain, there's multiple things going on here. But it does benefit the ones who are observing.

J: Because I do want to ask if it was significant that her and I did that session together.

S: Yes, her energy is almost like an open hug, and so they get very attracted to it, they want to go towards it. So that's why she attracts many beings who feel like they've never felt that energy of open acceptance and love - that's what it is.

J: Thank you so much. Yes, it makes perfect sense. It was quite surprising to both of her and myself to learn during the session that the Draconian that was trying to hide from us was actually connected to Elon, because it didn't hadn't even entered our minds that that could even be the case. So it was quite peculiar that we learned during the session more about the connections of this.

S: She loves Elon. She loves him. They have a connection and she is meant to help him as much as she can. She doesn't know this, but she does love him.

J: I think we've already established in the session that they were siblings in another lifetime. [S: Yes] But that human essence Soul of him is no longer in that body, or what else would you like us to understand about this?

S: It's convoluted because there's multiple pieces. So she has had past lives with him before, and so there's going to be still fragments. It's like you get fragmented out because you have multiple lives. You've experienced them, but then it comes back to the whole again. It's like she's trying to love and heal those fragments that are really hurting. She's connected to him and she's connected to him, his soul. His Soul is bigger. It's a bigger soul. Being Human - it's just a vessel. But still, there's in essence always there. It's like that's her way up. It's confusing.

J: So his signature frequency still feels very familiar to her, so she's got this connection to wanting to be able to support and help and love him in the areas that he has lack of? [S: Yes. Yes] Okay, thank you so much. So again, can we send him profound love and epiphanies to empower himself as he has an important role to play. Actually, what does he have to do now for humanity? What does he do? How does he support humanity moving forward?

S: So he connects with nature, the higher frequencies, the spiritual higher beings. He becomes where he actually wants to be more, this is a funny word - I don't know why they say this - he wants to be more human, more human. [J: Fantastic] He wants to connect. He wants to actually go out and connect with people, which he's been lacking.

J: Fascinating. Thank you so much. So, we did a healing where we released the connections between the Reptilians and those people who are addicted to drugs. How has this impacted those people from that experience?

S: They're starting to lose their desire for the drug. That was starting to occur right away, like it gives them a gross taste in their mouth. They started to feel a body discomfort that made them also want to stop with the meth. They were losing their pleasure with it physically, and it was becoming almost rotten to them. They were starting to notice that it was harming them and their body wants to get better and release any toxins. They feel like they want to feel better too. They want to feel better. There was like a string - they're showing us - like their brain and on the top, there's like a string almost like embedded in the brain that was like a connection to the Reptilian. That has been pulled out and they feel like they're more in control. They're more in control of their thoughts. They feel like they want to feel better. They want to feel healthier, naturally healthier.

J: *Fantastic news. Thank you so much. So pleasing for them, so can we just send them even more empowerment to feel the strong desire to be clean and healthy and away from the stagnation of that dependency?*

S: Yes. Yes. Now. Now. It is now.

J: *Thank you so much. In terms of a location in Australia, which we call Ayers Rock (Uluru) - it's a big protruding random rock. What can you tell me about what happens to this rock, we call it a rock? Can you show her what happens to this? Does anything happen to this?*

S: Eventually, it will start to decay. We feel like that's when humans aren't here anymore. We don't feel like a whole lot will happen to it. We feel there are many earthquakes. They will be crumbling, however it's like humans wouldn't see it.

J: *So many people still have this statement that they think that Gaia's Soul is going to exit at that point. What can you tell us?*
S: Gaia's Soul is not there. Gaia's Soul is not here. Gaia's Soul is gone. Oh! We just got this strangest feeling of peace washing over us. She's so happy.

J: *So, just so I can understand, does this planet then have a Soul currently or is it soulless?*
S: It's strange. It's like a spark. A spark of her Soul here. It's like - how do we say this - you could say, it's a tiny Soul essence of her because it is her energy, but it's not as interactive. It's almost dormant, but it's here. It's the spark. If she was no longer here, it would decay rapidly. If the spark was gone, it would decay rapidly. The spark is still here being protected. They showed us it. It looked like a little flame and they're protecting it.

J: *Fantastic. Thank you, does Gaia have a message for us?*
S: We just see a vision. With Gaia, it's a vision of a human-ish being and it's for Sally to see it. She's smiling, and at the moment, no message, just peace and just smiling, content. Content for now.

J: Fantastic, thank you. Has Gaia ever referred to herself as Blessed Gaia? [S: No] Will she ever refer to herself as Blessed Gaia in the future?
S: She's saying no. She doesn't like it. No No No. No Blessed Gaia.
J: *For those people who have labeled the New Earth - Blessed Gaia, what would you like us to understand about them?*
S: That is their interpretation. That is their own interpretation. We do not judge them for that interpretation.

J: *Humans love their labels. Thank you so much, and we understand that. And, we will know the official name of this new planet which we still label New Earth when we get there. Is that correct?*
S: It's weird. It's almost like it's a frequency. It's not a name, it's like a frequency.

J: *Fantastic. Thank you. How now will Sally get to the New Earth? What can you tell me?*
S: Ships. Larger ships will be used. It was an idea, but we want everyone to be closer together - more protection, more organized.

J: *Will she be with people she knows on that ship?*
S: They're showing [laughter], they're showing the person that she met and made a connection with at the gym that she saw almost two years ago. That person and a lot of his family are Soul family from his family. Interesting.

J: *And so, will they be light bodies or carbon-based bodies or what will they be on that ship?*
S: They're going to project as human for a little bit, just because it's comfortable. But they're really not human. We feel like he listens to the videos. She helped him awaken. He helped his family awaken.

J: *Fascinating. That's very interesting. My next question was going to be about her partner telling her that he wanted to follow his soul.*
S: Yes, He did say that. It was very surprising to her. She had never had someone say such a thing to her before, especially someone that never believed in anything like that. But she

felt the genuineness coming from it and it was very touching. He said a few other things that were quite surprising as well, and it verged on the fact that he in this altered state of his, could feel that he loved her Soul and he loved the feeling of it. It made him feel good and he didn't want it to go away. She has mentioned some things about getting prepared for natural disasters and other such things, and because he laughs at it, it still is there in his thoughts. So it comes up actually from time to time and he feels like he might lose her somehow.

J: *Is his life contract to still go to another 3D planet and not to the New Earth planet?*
S: He wants to follow her soul. He doesn't want to be separated from her Soul because he knows that she will lead him the right way. He's aware of that not consciously, but subconsciously he knows that. So, they're wanting to give him a chance. They are wanting him to have a chance because he's showing signs of stepping into the higher frequencies of possibility. There's a chance there. He could go to New Earth now.

J: *Because he's been working on his frequencies, and because she's raised her own frequency, he's kind of had to be exposed to her being this lighthouse in their house?*
S: Yes, and the fact that she doesn't back down. She has much faith in those beliefs and her frequency shows it. So it's like she can say anything that she wants and it can sound weird to him but then by her actually showing, through her own actions - that is what is causing him to notice it.

J: *Okay, thank you. How interesting. Is there going to be any big disclosures that are going to sort of shock the world before* this light beam experience, the laser event experience? What would you like us to understand about what's going to happen before this light beam event?

S: We've said this before - they're showing Joe Biden and he's basically being put under arrest for crimes, criminal activity, not with the children. He has, but they're not going to discuss that or disclose that on main mainstream media. They will mention more criminal activity, money, different countries, and the Biden family. We've seen this before and shown her.

J: *Okay, it's interesting. What about the past president of her country? What's going to go on and happen for Trump?*

S: He's actually been in many discussions and disclosures with taking down the child trafficking web. He's very heavy on that. He has a lot of closed door meetings with military men, higher up officials, that are aware of the trafficking and the human trafficking, because that is something that they wanted to get completely taken care of. It's so prevalent that it's a job of many years and it's dangerous because those who do those traffickings are also hit men. They kill people who try to stop it. They're also drug and money laundering. It's a huge spider web network of many lower level henchmen for the upper level echelon - Hillary, Barack. Donald Trump knows the ones that are on top. He knows that he has to bring the lower ones into jail to have them confess. They need to build a case and they've been doing that for a long time - many many years. It's like they know. They know what they've done, all the crimes they've done. It's like they're protected somehow though, by so many people and so many hit men that'll just kill. They'll kill anyone. Don't care, it's a game. It's a game. And he wants to bring those down because

Donald Trump is envisioning a safer place. He wants a safer place for children and women and men.

J: *Will this be exposed before the light beam event? Will more people in general understand and know about what Trump has been doing in wanting to protect more people and understand and learn about this human trafficking?*

S: We actually get a sense that many who were listening - he's talked about what he's done with the human trafficking, he has mentioned it, and those who were ready to hear it, heard it. That was years ago. That was when he was president. We don't see a huge disclosure of that before the light beam. It's been around though. It's more of the criminal activity, money laundering, of course the vaccine, but that's already been coming out. It's more the criminal Biden, money laundering, and the rest. Of course, Barack and Hillary are part of that. But we don't foresee mentioning all of the human trafficking as such.

J: *Very intriguing. Thank you. So at this point, what is holding back humanity from being ready to shift?*

S: Fear of death. Fear of death. Fear of the unknown. Just fear. It is due to the density. That's why the portals are being opened. That's when the portals are being opened because of the density. It's lifting, but people go back down into their own density, so it's trying to reach them. It's hard. It's hard. This game is hard, because you get so caught up in what you're seeing in front of you, you forget.

J: *Okay, thank you. Are there still any areas that we can focus on in future sessions to be able to offer healing or releasing or anything?*

S: Yes, we ask now, if we can have all the fear of death - taken away from every single human being and animal, of course.

J: *Can we do that this session, or would you like me to focus on it at another time?* [S: This session, now] *Thank you. So, I ask all the collectives to come in and to be able to help give epiphanies to people who are still afraid of the fear of death. May they have a profound experience of reliving their own other lifetimes to be able to remember that this is merely just one of many lifetimes that they've had. This natural cycle of birth and death - there's a celebration on both ends and all is well.*

S: They felt that, thank you.

J: *Yes, we also ask that for the animal collectives as well and all living beings, to be able to have a stronger faith in reincarnation and that the Soul is eternal and that the bodies may come and go, but the experiences and lessons are forever.* [S: Yes, thank you] *Is there anything else we can do in sessions, future sessions or today's session to be able to help assist humanity and all beings on this planet?*

S: We would like to ask if we can release all minds that are stuck in the density.

J: *Yes. Can we ask all collectives to be able to help assist in releasing all minds that are stuck in density and empower expansion of mindsets and perceptions.* [S: Yes, now, now] *Can we ask that this is a continual thing that is given to all - is constant releasing of all that no longer serves them: mindsets, physical limitations, and belief systems?*

S: Yes, yes, thank you, thank you. Wave after wave after wave. Thank you. Release Release Release

J: Brilliant. Yes, thank you so much. Thank you. How is her body going? [S: Very good] Fantastic. Subconscious, does she have any nanotechnology within her body?

S: We feel like she has an IUD. It's a form of birth control inside of her. It has metal rods in it. We feel that it's not bad. It is dormant.

J: Okay, that's great. Thank you. Out of curiosity, subconscious, why do I feel like I can't hear in my left ear? And I just got this strong sense of energy that I can hear as a sound.

S: You're hearing a noise in the ear? [J: Yes] It's a frequency sound. Yeah, you're being tuned up to frequency. They're communicating with you. Your communication is getting more and more clear. We're switching different frequencies and as you're raising your frequency vibration, you're also connecting in with higher and higher frequencies, as well.

J: Can you let me know - is it human beings or is it something else that I'm reading their frequency?

S: We don't feel it's human. It's higher beings and they're quite high vibrational. They like it. It's like they're 'Oh, will she hear this?' It's almost like turning a radio on, and they're like 'Oh, she can'. It's almost like their barometer for how they are giving you information - that just kind of pops into your head. You just hear it.

J: I always thought that my connection to my subconscious was on my right side, so this left side is quite interesting, I didn't know. So it's other beings, other than my subconscious?

S: Yes, it is higher beings and they're intrigued by you, because you can hear it.

J: Are there any messages that they have for me today?

S: They love that you're a communicator of information and you are able to relate without any kinds of blocks or manipulation of the message. They like that you're a clear vessel. They're fond and proud. It's like looking at a growing child that is getting smarter and braver by the day.

J: Nice. *Out of curiosity, I had a client yesterday who's had a few sessions, but never experienced such intense energy as she did prior, and then she had a session with me. It was sort of quite startling for her to feel that energy. Is this just now because she's more open to these sessions and she's allowing more frequency from her own teams to come in?*

S: Yes. She's open and she, in a way, when you lose the fear and you're actually wanting to connect, they know how much they can do with you. They know what's comfortable, and she vibrationally gave them the A-okay. She wanted it.

J: *That's great. It seems like so many people have been activated and so many people are really advancing themselves at a rapid rate, more than I've ever seen before. This gives me such great hope and joy to see humanity stepping up like this.*

S: Yes. We all want it. We all truly want it.

J: *Yes. It's an exciting time. Thank you so much. Are there any final messages that you have for Sally?*

S: All is well. We are very happy with these sessions with Jo. It makes you feel like you have a really good life purpose with everything. We enjoy these connections with Jo. We love you and we thank you, Jo and Sally for coming together as you do good work together.

J: Well thank you for helping us with being able to get the right timing and to be able to do another session together. I do really appreciate it. I know she does as well. Will we be able to do a session on the Old Earth together?

S: We first see, yes. We actually find that to be highly important. That is why you are both going through so much, because you will be able to get to a point where there is chaos around you, but you can both go into a calmer state and that's how you help others.

J: We've been enameled for this position. I assume that's the same with everyone reading who can actually hear the information about the light beam event and the Old Earth Event and experience, and even the New Earth.

S: Those who have chosen to be in that role, yes, they all are reading[20].

J: We see a lot of people have refused to step up and have changed their contracts to not be of assistance, in service to humanity.

S: Yes, there's fear there. We can always work with them more. There's a block but a block can be removed with coaxing and love.

J: Yeah, and when they choose to have the choices to remove their blocks, I'm sure they will be able to overcome that with ease and grace.

S: We would like to send them epiphanies through dreams. We will do that.

J: Thank you. I appreciate that. Is there anyone that wants to come into a session at another date that wants to share their

---

[20] Thank YOU, humanity needs your love so much.

message to humanity? [S: Bob Marley] *Yeah Okay Wonderful. We'll find out what his significance and messages for humanity are when we call him into a session, so thank you. We'll honor that. Is there anybody else that you would like me to focus on and bring in through a session?*

S: Well, two. Both wanted to. We see Buddha and Robin Williams.

J: *Okay, thank you so much. We'll bring them back in again. Thank you so much. I really appreciate that. Is there any other information that I need to hear?*

S: Just that you have decided to play such an important role, and if you didn't do it, who would have done it? And to remember that if you ever feel a certain way, just remember that all of us, all the collectives are so appreciative of you.

J: *Well, I think many people have tried to assist, and do try the best that they can, to be stepping stones. I'm sure that there are many people doing just this work as well, we just don't know of many of them.*

S: Yes yes. We want to acknowledge you too because you're here. We are so happy for this transmission. It's just a reminder that we thank you.

J: *Well, thank you, and thank you for all that you do, because we know without your perspective and divine wisdom and information, we would be struggling. So we appreciate being able to apply all the information that you lovingly give us. So we appreciate you. So thank you so much for all that you do. How will Sally feel over the weekend and the week, because I would love her to feel completely empowered. I would love her to feel completely motivated and energized and extremely balanced and everything she deserves.*

S: We can do that. We can help with that. Thank you

J: *Thank you, thank you. I wanted her to feel super charged and invigorated and all those fun things that you know she loves to do, because she's a runner. Is there anything else that she could do for her body or for her time that you would see great benefit from her doing?*

S: She can walk out in nature more. When she goes out in nature, she touches the leaves and she sends gratitude and love and flowers. We ask that she could do more of that, because she does such a good job. They like it.

J: That's great. I'm sure she will honor that. So thank you so much, subconscious for all of that. Can we send love and respect to the big dead spider that's in my garden? Can we honor its life?

S: The Soul is very happy to be out of that body.

J: *It was a scary body, a very very scary scary body. So, I can understand that.*

S: The Soul is laughing. The Soul is laughing because they're saying you can bless the dead body as much as you want, just giggling. Thank you, thank you.

J: *It was great to be able to explore my feelings upon a dead body and a spider at the same time, so thank you. So, can we bless our countries, bless our collectives, bless the water, bless the land, bless our sun, bless our families, bless our friends, and bless each other with love and empowerment, knowing all is well.*

S: Yes, they showed us this white light just shoot through everything.

J: Love is the key. Thank you so much. I really appreciate this.

Session 12: Taking account of LIFE CONTRACTS for ALL

Okay, so this is going to be something different today and I have the intention to do this for myself and potentially share it with a few friends. So I'm sort of setting the intention that it's just going to be for a few people to hear, but in preparation for this, it seemed like my subconscious was saying that more people do need to hear this, so this will potentially be public. This may not be understood by someone if this is the very first video that you've ever heard of mine or any of these sessions. This will be very confusing for you because you will not understand what is occurring, and from my understanding of certain people who do listen to these sessions, they're still going to be very confused by what's happening. So there's that. But it's not going to stop me from how I want to proceed with this session today. It's just me, there is no one else here asking questions, and I want to call a certain human conscious mind into the session, and I want my subconscious to be able to inform this person with the information about the contract with Gaia, the planet's soul, and what is happening.

It seems like this man has come here with the gift of remembering other lifetimes he has lived, and while that's all great, he hasn't remembered the lessons. When you know all of your lifetimes and you have memories of every single day you've ever lived on this planet in multiple different lifetimes, you get to have it from that perspective of 3D, with your conscious mind understanding 3D. He does not seem to be privy to information about what happens in between those lifetimes, what each lifetime is for what life purposes, or what he's signed up for in his life contracts. It seems like he is just consciously aware of his lifetimes here. I'm not sure what his belief system is in terms of "in between lifetimes", whether you're just a ghost and then you decide independently to come back... it seems like he is very disconnected from his actual spiritual teams, which is frustrating to know, because he should be very connected in. But it seems like this is a life contract he has, to not have the higher perspective, and this is what seems to be very frustrating.

I've read a book from a hypnosis practitioner, and it was just the conscious mind of those different lifetimes that that client had. There was no subconscious perspective, there was no higher dimensional perspective at all. And while it's cute to know about the information from other lifetimes, you're still only able to be aware of the 3D and not the higher perspective, and so you're quite limited in some regards. So this man seems to have been brought in to help prepare humanity for the shift when it was going to be here on this planet, and he seems to know that the physical shift into a fifth dimension is quite fantastic, but it's almost as if he just knows it's here, or thinks it's just here, believes it's just here, and this is where we get into dangerous ego territory... when humans believe that they create their own realities. So he keeps telling everyone what he's creating and what he wants for this planet and what he wants for humanity, which is all cute, and a little bit egocentric, right? When you're wanting everyone to follow you, and to have what you wish for, doesn't it remind you of a certain other man we just were dealing with, whose ego was right up there too, wanting to lead and rule the world.

So this other influencer that we're going to call in today, he believes that he can heal the world. He's done a meditation where he's asked a group, a big big big big group meditation, where apparently he's asked to buy or get another 200 years of this planet, because he knows the state of this planet is not doing very well. But he believes if he can use his free will to get another 200 years, that the technology will advance and be so advanced, so much, that in 200 years humans, bless them with their fantastic egos and agendas, will be able to suddenly come together and to be able to have peace and to be able to use this technology for good and to help heal this planet and heal humanity...

Well, that's all cute from a little 3D human ego, but humans can't control Gaia. Humans don't own Gaia, and Gaia has already shifted so no other Soul can jump into this planet. It's not part of the planet's history, and when you ask from our subconsciouses and other collectives, they give us the very firm and sobering information about what's coming. So we can pretend that that's not going to occur, and waste our time and energy and free will to pretend something else is going to occur. That's a choice.

So it seems to be very frustrating for my subconscious, at least when I connected into him, that this man who's here on this planet is not able to connect into his own guides. He's so focused on all of the information he has got, and all the memories he's got from the other lifetimes he has lived, that he's still working in the 3D mindframe of belief systems and understandings. It's kind of like he's got all of this valid information of how to live in the 3D, but it's outdated, because Gaia's shift is off planet as she reincarnates into another planet. Because this man has lived so many times on this planet, he's got a very strong emotional attachment to her. He doesn't want to change. Plus, he is living everything he's ever wanted in this lifetime. Not only is he famous and loved and sort of quite well respected, he's got lots of money from this and he has many followers. He feels very responsible to have the best intentions, to heal this planet and heal humanity. You know, that's a cute Santa's wish list isn't it? But that's very ego-based, and it's not seeing things from the bigger perspective. So it's interesting. It seems like *Source* is waiting for him to accept that there are great things coming, which is off planet, which is not how it was initially intended, but much easier.

When we shift the biggest thing we sort of notice is that we're not in fear, not in fear of others, because we all kind of know to some degree that some humans are dangerous and unpredictable and untrustworthy. Oh my gosh, I have people constantly lying to my face, knowing they know that I can read them, and yet they still will lie to my face because they feel that they can be so convincing. That's an interesting choice as well. You know humans have got a lot of inner work to do as a collective, and so when someone's using their free will to believe that they're creating their reality, as they believe in themselves so much, yeah, it's very very very interesting. It's been a little bit of a emotional roller coaster I must say, and it feels like it's this must sound weird, but it feels like my frustration from my subconscious - who's really disappointed in a whole lot of people's choices - because when you haven't matured in spirituality and you're still channeling or tapping into your own ego, you're limiting not only yourself but humanity as well. And when you have a huge following, and when you're responsible to awaken humanity... It's kind of like his mission, and I don't really know much about him at all apart from the little snippets that I get as insights from these sessions. He's been brought up a few times in these sessions, but it seems like *Source* is waiting for him. He's almost like, I don't know whether you would want to call it like a litmus test, but he's kind of the epitome of humanity. He was supposed to, in this lifetime, being given all of the other information from his other lifetimes, to be able to reach empowerment, enlightenment, nirvana, whatever you want to call it. It's like when he obtains that, that goes into the memory banks of the collective of information of everyone, right? It will all ripple out once he has this epiphany, and I think this is what bothers me... is that we just had that session with Sally, and we asked for healing and asked the collectives to help and give everyone these epiphanies, but we're dealing with man. We're dealing with human egos, and we're dealing with women and men. They need to be constantly reminded of things with massive epiphanies. They need to be constantly reminded to love themselves, drink water, be kind to each other, have compassion for each other... they constantly need reminding.

They cannot apply the information by themselves.

It seems for the majority, they get so distracted and they're not very motivated to empower themselves. They're not very motivated to empower others, and even when you directly ask people to please love yourself profoundly, please love others profoundly, and please support others profoundly, most of the time when people are asked that directly they will decline... too much hard work, too much effort, no thank you I'm too busy, I'll do it next week... So it seems to be this is the biggest struggle - to motivate people to be kind, to motivate people to be loving, to be honest with themselves, to be honest with others, and to really truly empower themselves. To not pretend or not think that if you do a bit of charity work on the weekends and donate to some homeless people, then that's going to be enough. It can't be a hobby. It has to be a true way of life. So when many big important lightworker beings, who are here now, cannot truly empower themselves and step up into their frequency and believe in themselves and believe in what's happening and why, creating a mindset reality of "Oh well, it's someone else's job. Someone else is supposed to do this. I can't do that, that's too much work for me! I'm too busy with something else".

We're all making choices constantly and every single person who is here on this planet has a really big role, a really significant role, to be here and to hold high frequency. But most people don't see that as being significant or important or valuable or worthwhile. They tried it a few times, it didn't, you know, seem to change that, we didn't shift in the three minutes that they dedicated to helping and being of service, so they gave up. There's lots to be said about different people's choices and behaviors and actions. Not throwing shade or judgment, but this is what's happening if we're going to be brutally honest with humanity, brutally honest about some light workers behaviors and choices. We can understand why we haven't shifted, and it really surprised me when someone said "what if someone's holding back the laser event?", and I just thought "Well, how could that be?" For most people who listen to these sessions, it seems like they can't retain or process or fathom or understand the laser event, to the point where it's almost like they've got amnesia... "What laser event?" they say to me, and I say "Oh, don't you listen to the sessions?" and they say "Yeah, I listened to the sessions" and I said "Well, the laser event has been quite a significant topic for the last, I don't know, nearly a year now." Or so I thought, publicly available. But remember, I do so many private sessions as well, I sort of don't know what's public and what's private at this point. So yeah, these are very interesting times that's for sure.

So for some, the notion that one human being is holding back the laser event because they're afraid to die, even though they know about reincarnation, blows my mind. That **Source** would be waiting for one being to have acceptance, to understand it, it's quite a surprise. So I'm trying to navigate this all myself as well, trying to see what I can do, given I understand that I can connect into anyone's conscious mind and channel them, regardless of whether they are living or they are in a different dimension now. I know I can connect into consciousness, which is interesting, right? There's significance and purpose for that, and obviously I don't misuse it, because I respect the skill sets that I have, and I respect people's free will, and I understand that if you do start misusing these skill sets they get taken away from you. I've seen this happen to many people, many times, and I just think it's so foolish that people would misuse their skill sets for something that was not for the greatest good of all but for personal gain. So I choose to be pure, and I choose to not be distracted into materialistic gain or ego gain, because that really does not do good for humanity or personal growth. But you know, that's my choice, to do that and be this way.

So I'm going to just surrender in now. I'm going to set the intentions. I'm going to let my subconscious call in that man, to be able to connect into his conscious mind and to be able to share with him this information, and for him to be able to understand it. Some may think all this information is not for me, and they're right. Very intuitive of you to realize this is above your interest level or perception level or understanding, and that's completely fine. Lots of this information that I do share can distract a lot of people when they're supposed to just be comfortable and high vibrational, not afraid of anything. This is why the laser event doesn't seem to be absorbed by many people, because it's such scary information. When you know this information you want to stop it, and you want to warn everyone and protect everyone and all this stuff, and that's really not part of their life contract. Suddenly you have the responsibility of millions of Soul exit points, potentially, so it becomes very heavy. Anyway...

Yes yes yes, we're here[21], we're here, we're here, and yes, what a conundrum and a fuddle of emotions as you are feeling into this. We will call him in, because yes, he is emotionally looping, he is stuck, he isn't able to see things from the higher perspective. He hasn't really taken into account all of the life contracts, and because he's only privy to his memories of his physical lifetimes, he can't recall the contracts he made in the other realms that he normally resides in between each lifetime.

He's been distracted to just focus on his daily lives, his life times here, his days here, his relationships here. In fact, he doesn't even seem to understand that he has many people in his life from other lifetimes. He's kind of blocked from understanding, but it's purposeful. He was to bring in such great information to be able to share to humanity, to be able to raise the conscious awareness of reincarnation. But when you don't know the life contracts and you don't know the significance of each individual lifetime, the lessons, the

---

[21] *The Arcturian subconscious representing all collectives.*

purposes, and how you work out your life contracts and your master guides. So it's interesting because he's limited. We wanted to see what man's mind can expand to, and so while you've referred to it as a litmus test, he's the guinea pig shall we say with much love, to be able to see what is the possible capable range of perspective.

So it's very interesting. He has so much knowledge to share with people, and he is aware of a fifth dimensional shift, but he is in the belief that this is something he's never experienced before, and he is waiting for this to happen on this planet. He believes in humanity so much, and he thinks that if you set high intentions and have high integrity and have high vibrational focus, that you will be able to help assist all of humanity. But it doesn't work like that. Just because he has a high vibration and a high mindset does not mean that that can then be applied and be applicable to all. There are many other life contracts, to push people and trigger people into growth, so they have to be of a lower frequency to trigger people into growth. We're going to call in his consciousness now because we need to have a conversation with him. He will see it like a daydream, so we're taking him out of his conscious awareness of his day to be able to present him - us, present to him ourselves. It will be glowing beings that he will perceive them to be. We are presenting ourselves as three.

We say to you that while your duty in service to humanity is to awaken to itself, you are not privy to the information about what this planet has life contracted to. You will see the shift to the fifth dimension, but it will not be on this planet. This planet is expired, and you will be gracefully, carefully shifted with many, to go to the new planet that is well designed and

very capable of letting humanity, letting the humans evolve and graduate into a fifth dimensional planet and be able to continue on with their evolutionary experience that way. It is not possible for it to continue on this planet for much longer, and while you believe that you have been able to prolong this with your belief system that if you are high vibration and when you get as many other people high vibrational, then that will be the key and the solution to all, and it simply is not the case.

We're asking you to acknowledge your own subconscious, your own higher self and your own guides, because you've been only channeling in your own ego from your other lifetimes, and you have believed in yourself so much in your other lifetimes that you only take advice from yourself from a 3D perspective, and that is so limiting. We want you to be more advanced into the higher perspective of all that is happening for this planet and for humanity.

We want to reassure you that what needs to happen for humanity's experiences is significant and purposeful and no one being can stop this. You do not need to be afraid. You can trust that these are all lessons and experiences. You've seen so much hardship happen, but you can see that those are opportunities for growth and experiences and lessons to learn from, to unite from. You want humanity to be united so much, and this is literally what will be happening when the events occur. You have to have a common tragedy experience to be able to be victims together, to be able to heal together, to grow together, to unite together. All differences will be dropped as every single being left on this planet, after certain events, will have something in common to talk about, to share with, to support against with each other. All social distances and

barriers will be dropped. You will be more united than ever before, and so with great tragedy comes great experiences and growth and lessons.

We want to reassure you that you cannot protect humanity from lessons. You cannot protect humanity from its evolution, because this is necessary. This is time. Humanity is safe, because we are here protecting it and watching it and we are all one. Stop and drop your responsibilities to try to help and teach all, because what you do not know is vast. While you are so certain you're confident that you know what needs to happen for humans, that is from the 3D perspective only. You're holding humanity back into 3D because you're not expanding your own wisdom, your own knowledge. You need to connect in with your subconscious and your guides. You are referring and calling and thinking often about other family members and other friends that you had in other lifetimes, so when you do that, you call them in. You cannot have conversations with them, but they have been constantly surrounding you, because you are thinking about them regularly and you're calling in their consciousnesses. They're coming in to support and guide you and watch you, but you're not listening to them. You are remembering the lifetimes you had with them fondly, or even challenges, but you're connecting with so many people because you're remembering all the history that you have lived and experienced in your many lifetimes here.

With great responsibility, you have come with so much knowledge and you're sharing that knowledge, but we're wanting to say open your mind even further. Understand that this planet, the physical body, is exhausted and can no longer sustain life for humanity. Understand that this is going to be okay, this is not a problem and you should not have to worry about these problems. We know that you are driven and designed to be able to help assist humanity with this shift on this planet, and we are saying there's no real difference between shifting to another planet and how you were trained to help humanity shift into this higher frequency dimension on this planet. Have no fear. Do not hold humanity back any longer. We want you to connect into your guides more, because you're still connecting into conscious minds. We're asking you to aim higher, to connect in with your subconscious, to connect into your guides - the high dimensional ones. Because when you constantly are talking and tapping into 3D egos and 3D consciousnesses, it's not the higher perspective. It could never be the higher perspective. All you are receiving and connecting and communicating with is ego. While it's still interesting and helpful to some degree, it is not preparing you truly, and it's therefore not preparing your followers truly to be able to understand the shift for humanity's consciousnesses and the need to be evacuated from this planet.

All is well, All Is Well. There is nothing to fear. But your attachment to this current life does not truly serve you. You are emotionally looping. Your ego has been compromised because you're starting to enjoy the fame, you're enjoying the materialism that comes with it. This doesn't serve you and this doesn't truly serve humanity. Go with peace, go with faith in yourself, but humble thee humble thee, humble thee. We say this with love.

[end of channeling session]

Wow, okay, so that's interesting. It feels like they just told him off in some regards. Hmm. I could feel a resistance from him, not wanting to really connect. I feel like he was open to it, but still doesn't want to step into it. But whatever that epiphany is, however he's going to experience that epiphany or that dream-like state, he's going to want to deny it. He's going to want to shrug it off, because he doesn't want to really accept it. But actually, when he does accept it, a huge weight is going to be lifted off him, because he's trying to figure out how to heal and solve humanity on this planet now in the 3D. It's just way too gone. Humanity is not going to be motivated to be compassionate and loving at this point in time. Humanity is still driven and distracted with so much stuff that it's not really possible for humanity to mature and have the evolutionary step up for all. So yeah, it's interesting. He does feel like he's responsible for the whole world, because he thinks he's the only person that has full memory of other lifetimes. It seems like there's a few other people that have full memory of other lifetimes, but they don't want to share it because it just sounds too crazy. They were supposed to step up and share this information too. This is why it seems like a lot of children talk about their past lifetimes now. It's not just a few influencers and people, it's actually ordinary everyday little kids opening up their parents' minds to that, at that level. I feel like they got to say what they needed to say to him. It didn't feel like it was a good negotiation or a chat, it felt like they came in to sort of get his attention and reassure him that everything's okay[22].

---

[22] *Not too long after this we heard his core group of friends and followers left him as he started sharing NEW private information with them as he was wanting them to prepare them for some big coming..... Wonder what he was saying... wink wink.*

Session 13: It's Ramping Up - Step In, Be Of Service

S: *A question Joanne had was, can all the collectives look at people's life contracts and remove all distractions to help them get more focused on what they're meant to be doing here now?*
J: Yes. And we would just like to confirm that we have been doing that. That is with the series of illnesses that people have been getting because they have been so unwell, they've only been able to focus on self. So they're trying to heal from that. So we've given them some more time to be able to have that time and reflection. This is part of this big, what seems to be worldwide illnesses that she knows people have. That is part of it. Taking people out of working situations and being of service to others to really go within. So that is really focusing on making them be very aware of certain things that are in their bodies that need healing. They will be grateful because we're not hiding this from them anymore. We're not hiding their pains and their emotional discomforts anymore. We are heavily making this very clear and purging all, through them, for them, now.

S: *Will that allow them to start working on their actual life contracts and do the things that they are supposed to be doing?*
J: Well, they're supposed to be healing from those traumas, so when they have ignored them, it's going to be all purged through now. So they were feeling very achy in certain ways, there's a lot going on. So yes, they can't avoid it now. We want to limit their own personal experiences that distract them. This is why we want to say we're grounding them down. This is why we're putting the petrol prices up so much, so they can't actually distract themselves and go exploring. It's like we didn't think another lockdown would be appropriate, so we're kind of making them less adventurous. In the small times that they will go out now,

and do big road trips, for example, they will really appreciate it, because they know how expensive that trip will be.

S: *Nice. Gratitude. Is there anything else you want to share about that?*
J: Everything is purposeful! And so there are so many lessons to be had about finding other ways to have fun, that's not expensive. When more and more people are struggling financially, they're going to find the simple things in life that are free again. That is the most important.

S: *Yeah. Thank you! I love that. Is there anyone that has a message for us to share today?*
J: Prince immediately came in. He wants to celebrate her because the journey is nearly complete. Now she realizes that what she was seeking outside of herself was always within. Being free to express self, she uses that in her words and her personality to express her passion, which is metaphysics, the truth, and the way we can uphold ourselves with pride and dignity and grace and joy. So he wants to celebrate her and honor her, because he wanted to be able to empower people with his individuality and his uniqueness. He wanted people to drop labels. He is saying that the whole name thing, him changing his name, was to help people reevaluate what is in the definition and the meaning of a label and a name. He wanted to awaken people so much, and he did in many aspects, in many ways. He knows how hard it is to be a unique individual when it's so comforting and easy in its assumptions, to be all the same. That's a false reality, illusion, because you're not all the same. You're not here to all be carbon copies, cookie cutters of yourselves. You are to feel into your own fashion. You are to feel into your own trends. You are to feel into your own self. When you start

replicating yourself with your fashion, with your assumptions of how you should live to be successful and popular, you completely lose self. He says that when you express yourself with music, with dance, and with words, you can be the freest of all beings, when you have no limitations, when you don't block yourself from expression and love. He would also like to say that he wants the vehicle to listen to 'When Doves Cry'. He wants her to know that the doves are Angels. While it's hard for all guides to watch, while they physically do not cry, they struggle and they struggle and they struggle to help support those who do not see them, who do not believe in them, and who dismiss the magic and wonderment that can truly be here on this planet.

S: *Is there any way we can help them see their guides, their Angels, the wonderment?*

J: They could, but they have to seek their true selves first. They have to see what they're doing to themselves. They have to look and be honest and feel into their physical bodies, to their physical reactions, to their mindsets. They have to be honest with themselves. They don't want to do that because they're focusing on studying other people, to mimic and copy other people. They don't have any interest or desires to express, empower, and enhance their own selves. They don't value individuality. They don't value that. That looks hard and dangerous and scary. People will judge you and point at you.

S: *Yeah. It's just unfortunate how humanity has been taught to almost be afraid of differences. Be wary of them.*

J: Yes. You've all been trained to trust the leaders, trust the narratives, and to not step out of line. If you are starting to think independently, that is a big problem.

S: *Yeah. So what you're saying is, they will first have to work on themselves, which we are already assisting with, is that correct?*
J: Yes. This is the big ascension symptoms that people are noticing and experiencing.

S: *Okay. Thank you. Is there anything else that's holding us back from shifting soon, that we can help with today?*
J: Belief in self! Trust in others as well as yourselves that there is love out there for all! And that love is not limited and everyone deserves it.

S: *Would we be allowed, using our free will today, to ask for the epiphanies of everyone on this planet to have belief in self, trust in self and others, as well as love?*
J: Yes. We are wanting them to do that. We will be encouraging and inspiring them to really clearly hear themselves, what they're doing to their bodies, and what they're doing to others. They're going to start questioning themselves a lot. Most of them have a form of brain fog, as we are focusing them into more directional attention, purposeful attention experiences. We will be ramping that up, heightening that up, and advancing that up further for all! It needs to be done. Not all lessons can be mastered here, but many experiences are still needing to be explored. It is on its way. It is getting closer and closer, as you could say, every day! So it is encouraging, but we are wanting to really really step in there and push, push, push, push many, many, many to move forward now.

S: *Makes sense.*

J: So lots of people are being forced once again to speak their higher truths. We can't just open up everyone's throat chakras - we've tried. You have to keep working on this. Each time there is a new boost of energy, there's a new layer and level that people can be upgraded and in tune with. So, we have to keep working on these steps ourselves. Each time that there is a new energy that people can naturally hold on to, you are constantly being upgraded in frequency and vibrations. This is often against people's natural evolutionary steps. People can't truly raise their vibrations enough naturally, we're doing it artificially. So, we're pouring lots of energy onto this planet for those beings to feel that energy. So we're charging up the beings, charging up your vessels, and this is forcing people to remove their density, to let their density go. It's painful! It's emotional! It can look like a whole lot of illnesses. But we are making this go very fast now. We want to keep ramping up this pressure on everyone to do their inner work and to release all that no longer serves them. We want to keep doing it at a more empowering rate. We know that the vehicle is saying 'double it, double it, double it, double it, double it. Do it!' We are saying that we know our limits, we keep pushing them, and we are getting faster and faster, that's for sure.

S: *I have a question about that. Are we on an actual time limit here?*
J: We are very ready to finish this! We are very ready to finish this! But it's, shall you say, the slowest beings who are needing to step up! We are sort of pushing them, but softer. We are waiting for the last stragglers who are still very resistant to letting go of that density. We're making it so uncomfortable for them, that they have to let go. So it's kind of this thing where we're picking the rotting tomatoes. Those

who cannot get there, who keep using their free will to shut down the growth, we are pushing them so much. Pushing them so much, that they either choose to empower themselves and step up and start seeing things from a bigger perspective or they will just have exit points through heart attacks. We're forcing them to open their hearts! We're forcing them to start loving themselves! We're forcing them to love others! If they do not comply, they will have heart attacks and exit that way. You are seeing an abundance of that.

S: *That and heart issues. Yes.*
J: Well, that is us trying to get their attention. What does the heart represent? The heart represents love! We are trying to force people to love themselves, force people to love others. It's not until you have a heart problem that you start thinking about what is important and what does your heart mean. It is the most symbolic message of all! So many people have missed that.

S: *Yeah. I agree.*
J: The vehicle was trying to breathe through congestion.

S: *Can we help her with her breathing?*
J: It annoys her that she just had that realization as we were talking, that the heart problems people were getting, while she knew it was from the vaccine reactions, she didn't see the bigger metaphysical perspective of love. Forcing people to love themselves. Be focused on love! Be focused on your hearts! What are you doing to your hearts? All of you are not focusing on what you're doing to your hearts. When you can't be honest with yourself, you're not honoring your heart, you're not loving yourselves. You're so focused on

being like other people or helping other people or being of service to others, over and above and beyond, you're not honoring self. It starts really with the heart - WITH LOVE.

S: *Thank you! Is there anyone else, any other being that would like to come in and share a message?*

J: Dolores wants to come in. She just wants to say that she loves us very much! Very, very, very much! She can identify with all of the challenges that Joanne's having. She wants to say that because she knows that... it's the translation of 'I was there. I understand. While you're going through it now, you're not alone.' I do understand the challenges there. That will comfort Joanne even more. She did have this as well. She just didn't articulate or really notice what was starting to erc her, which is sort of the opposite with Dolores's experiences in some regards, because people just dismissed it because there's no other real work that people were comparing it to, so they sort of insist, 'Too much. No. I'll instantly dismiss it through my ego.' But now, what Joanne is experiencing is people not sure what to believe because there's so much information that sounds similar. Which one is the truth? This is why Joanne's so passionate about getting people to have their own sessions. Instead of her burning herself out with work and doing everyone's sessions, she is being diligent and sharing the workload with all of the other practitioners who were set to do this work. Whether they were meant to do this work or not, through their egos, they are still having to be responsible for others. This is Joanne sharing the workload, she wants everyone to have the experience to understand this work profoundly. This is marvelous. How could she ever think that it was her ego that was so frustrated with that influencer. It was not ever her ego. She was afraid that it could have been, so she had to really dig into it to make sure. She just feels disappointed, just like we do, that people that claim they get our information are lying to people. When it's so easy to connect with us. All you need to do is honor us, honor yourself, have good intentions, and you get great information from us. How is it that so many people struggle to share the truth, to get the real information? Isn't this access to information motivation enough for people to do their true inner work?

S: *You would think so, right?*
J: We assume so. Yet we often are limited to the information we can share because of lack of respect, lack of honor, and lack of integrity through the practitioner's behalf.

S: *I do see that a lot. Yeah. I actually do. Yeah. Not with Joanne of course, but with other influencers. Because I cannot resonate with anything except with this information.*
J: Yes. Because it's not ego. It's not human. It's so much more. It's a group of us that are assisting with this. We respect each other's opinions and insights. We love working together to be able to be of service. This is a joy for us because we feel like, finally, there is more access to our perspective, to our wisdom, and our guidance that gets mostly dismissed by others when we prompt them with certain senses.

S: *Yes. Well thank you. We appreciate all the information from you all so much.*
J: Yes. We understand you do. And we are grateful for you to do your best to apply it. We know that when Joanne gets frustrated, she feels like she's not applying our information. She knows that sometimes she has to go into some density to be able to recognize some past behavior, to be able to heal

from it and understand how she can easily overcome it. She used to be so frustrated that the internet didn't work properly for an amount of time, that it could take her days to get over it. As soon as the internet worked again properly, she was immediately over it. And that is tremendous growth!

S: *That's great! And it's really nice too, when you yourself can appreciate the peace with the growth.*
J: Yes indeed!

S: *I do have a question. Are there any new updates that we should be aware of now, for myself and Joanne?*
J: We've helped her understand the disconnect of information between the alien invasion and the laser beam, shall we say, when that can really truly be seen as the one thing. The trumpets, the sound of the trumpets - It really is not the same as thunder, so when you hear this almighty sound, people could question, 'Was that a very loud trumpet?' But it's the vibrations of around the world so you hear it. You can imagine hearing one sound - just want to say it's sound reverberation. The sound of the laser event for example, you're not going to hear it from one direction, you're going to hear it from many different directions, and it's going to sound strange. You will feel it from the Earth and through the sky, energetically. It's like an orchestra of sounds. It's such a startling sound that it is biblical, because you have heard that in the bible, 'You will hear sounds of trumpets'. That is really the sound of the noise of us. We are sound! You recognize us through sound! It's a sound wave, but you are deaf to hear us right now. We are truly music to your ears when you hear us in our true natural frequency. We are singing voices. We are singing! We are singing songs to you constantly! We are using our frequency as love

messages for you. We are music to your ears. Our expression is frequency vibrations. You feel that in our love, integrity, and intentions. There is so much to be said about coming events with sound. It can be a metaphor for many things. So that's what we want to say about that.

S: *Okay. Thank you! Thank you so much! I know Joanne is very deeply in and I want to see how her body's going and how it is feeling with the spa treatment.*
J: She's noticing quite a lot of energy work on the sites that were struggling. But she's doing really well and she is very, very relaxed.

S: *That's amazing! And then, if there's any kind of misalignment with the bones, any kind of pressure, anything at all that we can just release now, can we do that please?*
J: Yes! Yes! We've been working heavily with this. She could describe it as quite a pronounced ache because there is lots of work to be done. We want to say this - since there is no such thing as time - when you're healing something that has happened in your perceived time, you actually can feel it. So she can feel us working on that injury from the accident that day, which is peculiar to her. So we are fixing it from that reference of time. While she thinks it's today that we're doing this healing, your body is able to sense everything that's ever happened to it and it has a memory. So she's thinking, 'I do not want to think about birth.' But there's so much history that the body goes through.

S: *I do have one more question. If someone has a very angry personality, it's someone that I know, they're just very angry. I'm not sure if it's just a front to make them look tough but I'm just curious. I know that's a broad question but what do you think that stems from, like extreme male anger?*

J: We would need to know the exact person for us to be able to connect into that exact thing. Or are you wanting to talk about it in general?

S: *I would say in general. It was just a general question.*

J: Men in general being angry? We want to say that females are also very angry as well. It is because you are disconnected from the truth and you are suppressed. When you have a lack of expression, trust, and ability to process what's going on, your resentment is anger. You are angry because you can read energy and know that you're living in disconnect, dishonesty, and disharmony. So there is so much that someone could be angry with. They are so deeply connected to the planet and the Earth and they're so angry of the violations of this density that they could be stemmed from that. There is so much that people express and they think it may be because they're running late. But in reality, they are so angry because there doesn't seem to be much justice in this world. There is so much pain. There is so much hurt. There is so much hate. It's so far away from love. You're angry because you are hurting. You're angry because you do not like these lives because they are so tremendously challenging. They're lacking true love. You're angry because you're confused why everyone around you is not telling the truth. This is not you personally, this is humanity. Why is humanity angry? Humanity is angry because they're continually trusting professionals and influencers and they still feel like they've been lied to, yet they don't know how to stop trusting them and following. So they're angry with themselves for not noticing who's lying. They are angry for everything that is around them because nothing is true integrity.

S: Yeah. Wow. I agree. I totally agree. Is there anything we can do to assist them with that?

J: They're angry because they constantly feel like they've been sold lies. They are intelligent beings who know the truth. It offends them to be sold fakes, lies, distruth, and dishonesty. So they either choose to be dishonest themselves and make this their advantage point, or they just get more and more bitter and confused why there is a lack for humanity, sharpening their intuition to be able to trust themselves to know the difference. As soon as they realize someone's lying to them or have a manipulation or a hidden agenda, they will walk away from them. They will disconnect. They will not keep buying into it. So, the more you love yourselves, the more you are less angry because you're not being tricked, you're not being fooled. The biggest problem that we saw when we were going to do the broadcast was that when the truth spilled out so firmly, people were going to be very angry because they believed such ridiculous nonsense and they were tricked. No one likes to be tricked. The hardest part of the awakening is letting people naturally evolve and to notice for themselves that certain people shouldn't be blindly trusted. Everyone knows that, but yet, most people still trust certain people who shouldn't be trusted. The person could be honest and believe their own sales pitch and this is where it can confuse people. If you're in an industry that is saying that - this is great for you, this is very helpful, and that salesperson fully believes it, you don't register the dishonesty there, because you don't pick up that they know it's not helping you. So you read 'genuine'. You buy that product because you read 'genuine'. Now, they are actors. They are being paid to endorse something, so they don't have an expert opinion or understanding of what they're truly selling. They have been told a certain thing, they will believe that certain thing, and sell it. It is like, what you could say, is people energetically reading into the mainstream media. They trust what they are saying is the most appropriate because there are professional award-winning writers writing the script. The prompter, the presenter believes and trusts that this is well researched and this is the truth. When they direct the information and share the information, they have a belief system that this is the true and accurate information. So you do not read 'nonsense' when they are selling you lies, because they believe and trust that what they are sharing with you is the truth. You have to really hear the truth beyond the sales pitch and actors. This could be said for many industries.

S: *Right. Right. And that makes a lot of sense why people believe what they hear, because they are putting their trust in the message.*

J: Yes. When you're being sold a lot of money to sell something that you have also been sold is very truthful and the highest integrity, you will honor your job. You will honor the money you're getting to receive this information and you'll blindly trust it, because it gives you so much great value to share the information that is sold to you as being truthworthy.

S: *Wow. When it's put like that, I can see how people can be misguided.*

J: Because it's not the person who has the dark agenda selling it to you. They are way back in behind the scenes. You do not see their agenda. You don't see the products being made.

You don't see all of the other stuff behind the scenes. You are seeing the facade, the shiny pretty people, the influencers promoting their brands, products, industries, lifestyles.

S: *So, with that being said, we are using our free will, and everyone, all the collectives, are in fact pushing them more now.*

J: Yes! We are wanting people to be more astute with the information versus blindly trusting the sources, the sales pitches. We want them to hear clearly now, what has been said to them - versus - the blind faith and trust of the energy that the person is presenting to them.

S: *Yeah. Yeah. Well that's really great. I never thought that could correlate with anger. But thank you. Wow.*

J: Of course. It's an individual journey - why people express anger. It is out of true frustration, but not what you often assume. This is why it's so challenging for people to get to the bottom of the root of the issues in talk therapy, because you're not able to even gauge all of your surrounding experiences of frustration to share. Even if you did, it would sound so peculiarly strange to a professional therapist - why are you struggling !

S: *Wow. Thank you. Is there any other information you would like to share with Joanne?*

J: When you struggle to share your truth and integrity, you do become angry. It does become frustrating. So this is what we're wanting to say to her about the influencers that know that they are misrepresenting. Behind the scenes, behind their videos, they are very angry and frustrated because they're so disappointed in themselves, ultimately, that they know that they are putting on a show. They wish that they could get better information. They're actually really terrified of getting called out.

S: *I just want to mention this. The thought crossed my mind right now randomly, so I'm just going to say it - there's a video session I saw of Alba Weinman's recently, and I did notice that she was pushing the client to give her information of the shift and the client was getting only a number eight-two-three and could not explain what that number was, and Alba Weinman was getting very frustrated.*

J: As we said earlier. When you have intentions to be self-service with this information, to not help serve humanity but to gain for yourself, you will trip over information.

S: *Thank you so much. Really, really insightful.*

J: Alba Weinman has really shut down all true access of information. She is just merely entertainment at this point. But it is a stepping stone. She is struggling to understand why she is not getting the bigger information that she believes she deserves. She has not done much of her inner work.

S: *Are there any love messages you'd like to leave with Joanne?*

J: All is purposeful. She feels the frustration and disappointment of many when they learn about their beloved influencers and that's not her responsibility. We will release that from her. She works so hard and it just feels so frustrating for her. If they could only just listen to our messages, this would help people be truly prepared. She doesn't want any unnecessary trauma or challenges for people to feel or hear. At this point, she wants people to truly be prepared for what needs to be prepared for. And she doesn't feel that these influencers are being of true honesty and service for that, because she knows so many big things are happening. But people like Alba Weinman, who uses this work for entertainment and for her own level of fame, and for her own pay packet, this is beyond distasteful for the vehicle.

S: *Yes I also agree.*

J: So this will hopefully encourage people to find other practitioners for themselves. Those sort of people should have been exposed years ago and they are just rife and holding back humanity.

S: *I have a question that actually just popped up. Last question. Are we going to have a signal where we will know that the event is about to occur? The laser event? The light event?*

J: It still seems like some time[23], because it needs to have more opportunities for people to step up and share their truths. So, sort of waiting for that to happen. But it'll be very clear when you feel that there are more people sharing their truth. It can be independent and not just repeating other people's opinions or statements, when they can start thinking for themselves. But it's these influencers making people demotivated to start thinking for themselves and applying metaphysical perspectives, so there is a problem with that.

S: *I know we've mentioned that the collectives will be working on assisting with that. Is there any way we can use our free will to really make it even more obvious, besides their stammering on with the untruths, but almost where... I think*

---

[23] *Session from May 2022*

you mentioned it before, that they're gonna be almost where they can't hear them anymore?

J: Yeah. We'll get them to tune out. To not be able to focus on the disinformation. When there is real truth... we say that for some, they don't often get the real truth, so the real disinformation will look really outrageously absurd to them. So we're going to really jump it up more, so it's going to be even more outrageous.

S: *Okay. Thank you. Yes. Yes.*
J: They will question it because it's so obscene. Then when they question it and they hear their opinions of how ridiculous this is, that will speak the truth, and that will be very loud for them because they've had the epiphany to realize this is distruth.

S: *Sounds amazing. Sounds like it's about time. Can we do that times 100?*
J: Yeah. Yes. Well, now that they're more recovering from their recent updates, they will be sort of still quite exhausted from the high frequency that they're holding. It's a lot of energy running through which makes you very tired, so you're not interested as much in nonsense. So when someone's trying to sell you nonsense, you don't have the time for it, you're not here for it, you will naturally pull away from that distraction. When you do find the truth, you will want to binge listen to it. We are going to give people who have been listening to our sessions, the profound epiphany 'This is time to share this information.' They will share it with their communities of their truther friends and their spiritual friends. They will want to share the series and just say listen to this series. What do you think? They will not have to worry about someone judging them for sharing this because

it's 10 different voices. What do you think about the series with 10 different people saying the same thing? How do you think that works? But it will give them something to share and they will not worry about the reactions. They will just have courage to share. And we're going to give them confidence to share, without ownership of responsibilities of the information and content. This will help new people hear the work for the very first time and suddenly realize that this is not ego based information. They will be activated very quickly with this now. And so we're going to be prompting. It is true, do not focus on the numbers. There are many influencers with fake, inflated numbers. Do not assume anything with numbers when it comes to people's followships as being the real truth.

S: *Yeah. Yep. Well thank you. Thank you to all who are here today. I know Joanne and I appreciate all the information.*
J: Yes. We're always happy to help assist.

Session 14: Integrity with Energy and Life Contracts

J: Yes, yes, yes, yes, yes, yes, yes, yes! A million times yes! We are here to be of service because we wanted to be able to explore this. This is significant and it has impacted many, so we are thrilled to be able to be here. To be able to explain and express to you our perspective of what you would call curses. And we are saying it is expression of other people's free will to be able to impact others. And so feel free to start your questions and we will be able to guide and support and be able to call in the collectives to be able to help assist with this today.

P: Thank you so much. It's a real honor just to be able to speak with you today. So thank you so much! And to have this information to help everybody else. Truly appreciate it! Thank you! Thank you! Thank you! We wanted to know and ask for all the collective to help with releasing and removing any curses. Has that even been released? Have people felt the release from this yet?

J: Yes! And when you start having these new perspectives of ears listening... While the vehicle has done other work to be able to release people from their... We discussed those people who are addicted or who have used different drugs and have got themselves corded to certain collectives that are a lower density. We're wanting to say that the sounds and the words and the intentions that others place on others actually do something similar. And so you can block out a certain information and not be able to resonate higher, vibrate higher because you have been limited, as someone who can put what you would call a spell over you or a curse over you, is stunting your vibrational growth to some degree. And so this can look like repeating the same information over and over again. It is spell bounding you in some regards, because when you keep hearing the problems and the worries and the fears, some people can become completely convinced of what is being said. And so in some regards, while it's not a curse, it is spellbound. The words are very powerful and for those people who are not aware of their own truth and not connected to their own intuition, they give their own truth and intuition to others. They fully trust other people's information as if it's their own intuition, their own truth. And so when there are many statements on repeat about certain events, certain answers, certain information from even your history, when you hear enough, you accept it as is. And so your history books, you could say, are spell bounding you to be able to trust and understand sort of things. So this is how humanity has got really off path from connecting in. You also were discussing how it is almost antisocial bad manners to share your emotional challenges. Some people you know love talking about their dramas because they are in victim mode and they want all that attention. But they never actually want to grow from that attention. They know something's wrong with them. They know they've had a hard time, and they just want to own that experience again and again and again and again and again. And so they are stuck in their own spellbound because they're saying they're a victim. This is horrible, so and so did something to them. It's not good! It's not good! They're stuck in this tragedy and so they're spellbounding themselves because they are repeating the same perception of something bad happening to them. They are not wanting to look at the purpose. They're not wanting to look at the significance. They're not wanting to look at the growth, the purpose, the lessons there, because they are not able to get over the fact they had that experience in the first place. And when it feeds them, when it serves them to be having something that is so bad to them, so tragic. We see people who are using, for example grief, and being in mourning as just this. They get so much attention and support and sympathy that they just want to keep being in grief. It's got nothing to do with the person who's exited at all. It is about them being in grief. And then other people giving them compassion and consideration and sympathy and meals.

P: Because they've never had that before, and they're just craving it so much. And they got used to it. They just want more of that?

J: What they are learning is that you get a lot of attention for loss. You get a lot of attention for not seeing things from the bigger perspective, is what we could say. So there is much that you tell yourselves when you're not in your full truth that you are even cursing and spellbounding over yourself.

P: How can you explain to somebody though, that it's a negative curse or a negative way of living? That they can get so much more attention with more positivity? How can you explain that to a human to get attention with the most positive outcome?

J: You could start celebrating their positive distractions when they are actually trying to empower themselves. And so you have to start different conversations. If they're emotionally looping constantly. There's a difference between when someone's having a conversation with you and owning their density and their inner work and you're hearing them talking about how they're overcoming it, versus just their density. Just their traumas. And so it is about you listening to what they are really sharing with you. Are they sharing with you their traumas and how they're empowering themselves through it to see things from a purpose and a bigger perspective and trust all is well, or are they just emotionally looping with the tragedy, the tragedy, the tragedy? And so, for those people who are stuck in the tragedy, you could then start changing the conversation to be able to empower them. To remind them of other experiences that are exciting, positive and good. But you have to at least acknowledge and honor their tragedy. 'That is so sad for you. That is something that is very heartbreaking.' You have to acknowledge it. You have to address it. You have to give them support initially. But when you realize that they're wanting that support over and over and over again, you realize that you're in this loop with each other. And so you need to be able to empower them through it. And, if you're going to be talking to someone who's stuck in grief, then you can share your truth, you could say 'This is why I feel that reincarnation is such a gift! And it is confusing to understand, but I have such great faith in reincarnation and this makes me feel positive that this person is now still having their own Soul journey!' This is a hard conversation to have because people then feel very frustrated that they're not with that Soul any longer. And that Soul potentially could be doing better and greater things without them. So it's so unique and so delicate having conversations with people who are not realizing that they're stuck in certain loops. And so you have to find ways to empower them to be able to empower themselves. It is a tricky conversation to have. But now we are going to be able to open up people's mindsets and perspectives to realize that they're so exhausted with looping and they're so frustrated that it's not comforting them anymore. When they're not empowering themselves and they're constantly seeking outside confirmation and attention and love, we're going to sort of step them aside energetically from others to be able to truly focus on self. And we really want people to really focus on self. And this is why we have given many opportunities to having go within moments. You could say that your classic example would be the lockdowns that you all experience where you can't entertain others. You have to sit with self and be with self and start smaller again. And we know that while it was stressful for you for example, it gave you a great opportunity to really just honor yourself and you actually started being your own caregiver. Because while you're so great and gracious with helping others, there are still some aspects that you were having back in 2020 where you were not able to return your grace and joy to yourself. And so we loved that for you that you did that. And you used your time so wisely and that empowered you which therefore empowered others all around you as you grew. We could not be more proud of that for you! And the vehicle is feeling tearful because we are showing her our true love and gratitude to you because you are truly, as the vehicle had said, you are a very bright shining star in our hearts.

P: Well thank you. You're gonna make me cry! That's the biggest compliment I can get! Thank you so much!

J: We want to remind you that every time you do quantum sessions we're always with you. Just like we're always with you in your daily lives. But you are so human, but in the most beautiful of ways, and so you inspire so many. And many people look up to you. And while there is quite a responsibility, you don't let it weigh on you. It inspires you and that is the best way to take that approach. And we are very grateful for you to be so mature with your responsibilities.

P: Thank you! But I do know I'm never alone and I got my team with me all the time. So I thank you very much! Thank you! Thank you! Thank you! I wanted to know another question, if you could show us or give us examples on how all these curses we've been talking about have impacted people. And explore how people have been placed under these spells.

J: So your televisions, and you could say it starts off even with teachers who are telling you disinformation and telling you limited perspectives. And so when you start learning about your solar system for example. You're learning in your churches and in your religious doctrines about certain things. You take that on board as sponges. But it's very confusing because intuitively it doesn't resonate 100 percent and so it's very confusing. And so, because they're so certain with their information and their indoctrinations, many people dismiss their own intuition and just surrender and accept, because it's so easy to just accept what you've been told versus feeling within. We're wanting to say even simply the range of colors you could sense as a child. Everything is a lot brighter and it has a bigger range, but you are being taught and told only about a handful of colors. And yet you could actually sense a lot more range in spectrums. But because they're not focused on, you almost tune them out. And so there is a natural range that the colors can be seen by the 3rd dimensional eye, but it's more than you can even assume. And so you only focus on, say the primary colors. But intuitively you know that there is a much bigger range. And that's just a small example of how you're only told to focus on certain things and not the full. And while it's not crippling you to not know all of the frequencies and colors and names of certain color vibrations, this is a great example of understanding how you've only been taught a small fraction. And it is very manipulative of what you have been taught in your school systems for example. And this is how it starts from a very young age.

P: Thank you. That makes a lot of sense. Thank you so much! So I wanted to know, do most people have a good intuition where they go against their gut feelings for the most part? Like how does that work?

J: We are pushing people harder to really sense their gut intuition. Some people freak out and think it's digestive problems or stress or anxiety or panic attacks, so we just keep trying many different ways to be able to get people to have a think about what they're actually experiencing. We have encouraged many doctors and many nurses to actually start speaking alternatively as they are starting to sow seeds themselves to people. So everyone's been given opportunities to start thinking beyond their limited color spectrum that they've been talked about and told about certain health issues and body symptoms. And this is why so many people are talking about ascension symptoms right now and calling it a whole lot of different things just to be able to understand it may not be something negative. A medical issue or problem. While there are very many people that are very strong loyalists to the medical industry for whatever reasons, many people are starting to start feeling a natural distrust from certain industries as there is more truth being shared. Intuitively people are, because the frequency of the vibrations that they're holding now in their physical bodies are so much higher regardless of whether they want to be higher or not. We have ramped up their bodies over time to be more receptive to the truth. So they feel the truth more easily now because it has a different frequency than say, distruth and something that could harm them. It doesn't have true intentions and integrity. You may not even know anything about your own intuition, but you are going to be just intuitively guided to what is right and what serves you, and what no longer serves you. And you can use your free will to dismiss that and keep disempowering yourselves, but people are starting to wake up to just being fed up with that density. And they have had some moments of clarity where they have felt that higher frequency of truth and they really appreciate that. It is so refreshing. So they are still seeking to find that truth. They will hold on to it more and stop paying attention to that density.

P: Thank you so much! Just beautiful information. Is there something I can say to my random clients, especially doing hair every day, because they don't know what intuition is. They almost feel like, 'Oh, if my gut feels off or my head just said something,' but then half of them feel like they follow the intuition and they follow the wrong intuition. And I'm trying to find a vowel to explain that to them so they get an aha of what to follow and how to follow it. And what does that feel like exactly?

J: When you remember what you're here to experience in this 3D planet is the range of emotions to find yourself back to love? Love of self and love of others! And when you empower someone to share your feelings and senses of them, that you love them, that you see them, that they are such beautiful beings, that they're trying so hard to find joy in life. The magic in life. This will remind them what they're supposed to be focusing on versus their challenges of experiences. So it is about reminding them of the great joys that they have in life. When you see them smile. When you celebrate their joy. When you celebrate their beauty. When you leave them as they leave you from their appointments. You empower them with your integrity by telling them how beautiful they look and how that smile just looks so good on them. This will carry through. That is the high frequency they want to focus on. And this is what they want to grow from, is feeling good. Feeling good about themselves. Starting to love themselves. It's not about the dramas that they carry with you and they try to get you to help them fix them. Often they're not even wanting advice, they just want to share their challenges and to just be heard. Because they're listening to themselves too. And their talk therapy, what they share with you, surprises even them as they're driving home in their cars and they think, gosh, I didn't realize how much I thought about or felt about a certain thing. But they were sharing with you, which truly is them sharing and being honest with self. And when they can start identifying their own problems, they start revaluing it. You may forget their conversation as you go on to the next client, but the entire time before they see you next, they are working through their own inner work that they shared with you. They are holding on to what they shared with you because they want to improve themselves, so when they talk to you next they've got something more and new to say. Because they don't want to loop themselves. They're wanting to share growth with you. And so when you are seeing them talking about things that have grown from their last conversation, celebrate that! Support them through that.

P: Beautiful! Thank you. I do recognize a lot of that so it's just like putting me in check to keep that up. So thank you. Yes! Thank you! Thank you! Thank you! And I'm going back to curses. Why is it that some people are never touched by that at all? Are they like heavily thick protected? And other people, it just seems like everything they touch, see, do, be. It's always going to shit and hell, through and through. Is there a reason for that?

J: It's all life contracts and so certain people are needing to have these limitations for them to grow independently and empower themselves through it. Other people do not want to have this lesson in life because they just want to be able to already be empowered of self. And so they're not going to resonate with the school system for example, and would be what you classify as school dropouts because they already know their true truth. They already know that they're valuable. They've already got great skill sets and they go on to do brilliant things in their own, you know, industries, which is usually manual and other creative outlets. So this can be really challenging when people are learning they can't work within the educational system. So they will leave the educational system to empower themselves to then do something else. And so usually they're guided. But they're just not interested in spending time with nonsense and they feel physically uncomfortable being exposed to nonsense that goes against their intuition. They may not even understand the reason why they just needed to leave that school. Needed to leave the education system. But it's purposeful for them. Many great intuitive beings also knew that a part of their life contract, if they found lots of abundance of money for example, they would misuse it. And so usually great lightworkers are the very intuitive people who are doing very humble work and have a humble salary and income, because anything more could flip them into something that would change their focus. The true blessings and joy in life are free. And the more money you have it seems, the more you distract yourselves from other gadgets and materialism versus actually going to the core root value of these life experiences and empowering yourself with the true feelings and expressions rather than gadgets.

P: Yes, I agree with that. Beautiful! Yes. Thank you. I know I keep saying I need an island of people that just live off the Earth and don't care about nothing and it'd be so beautiful.

J: That's what we would call the New Earth.

P: Beautiful! Thank you! Thank you! Thank you! Yeah. Oh wow! Are there any other messages you'd like to give us about curses, how to understand if it's all been done properly, if it's heading the right way? Any last messages or messages about that?

J: Yes. There have been some that have got mean intentions and agendas behind it, and so that is people using their free will to disempower others just because of their own insecurities and personal gain. And so we have released that. But it felt very sickening as we were releasing it because it was making people really notice that impact before it left. And so people were triggered to think about certain people who had placed those spells upon them and to be able to really feel into that agenda. And so now that people have been released from it, they can truly see the agenda of those people. And you know, there's been some big work happening so a lot of people are really noticing that they suddenly were thinking about, for example, ex-partners or old friends that had jealousy and frustrations and resentment and have done certain things. Humans are very powerful and when you set the intentions to want ill will for others, it does get felt. It does! Your free will is very powerful and so this is why a lot of people were told originally just to think of love and light. Because so many people were bitter and so powerful that if they started thinking about their traumas and frustrations about certain people they could really disempower those people without realizing it. You are so powerful, so when you set your intentions to hate someone for example, you are impacting yourself and you have potentially the chances and opportunities to impact that person that you are sending that ill integrity intentions to. It's energy! It's all energy!

P: It is! Thank you. So I wanted to know, what's the difference between... I'm still kind of with the curse and spells. I just had a thought, like if someone is doing a lot of words. I was taught a long time ago that every word is special. That's why we call it spelling. You have to be careful what you think, what you say out loud. But then, if you're thinking that but your contract has nothing to do with that, can it really affect you if your life contract has nothing to do with curses or spelling?

J: Because you know, some people have contracts to be able to overcome that. That's for sure. Just like with your education for example, you're supposed to really do your own research and not just trust the person that is leading you as your teachers. You are supposed to, but the thing is that most children forget what they were taught at school so they just don't reflect on the foundations of their knowledge and wisdom for this planet. But you don't need to know all the history to be able to do your inner work here and to work out your life contracts. So it doesn't really impact you. So you're right. If there are contracts they will be played out. And this is the reason why we know that some people have wanted to use their free will to kill others and when that's not part of your life contract it doesn't occur. But it can be close. It can cause accidents. But we will come in and be able to stop that. And so it is very purposeful what is happening. But you're always protected. It is on the person's Soul to relive that. When they reflect back on how powerful they were and how much they impacted others with negativity, that is a lesson that they need to experience. Many who have come here this lifetime have got this strong sense that they shouldn't be hurting others and so this is those people who will be constantly viewing the world with only love and light. Only love and light! Only love and light! Because they have been so detrimental to others in other lifetimes, they have this mantra... 'I must only be in love and light' because they have got karmic contracts to pay out because they have been such disempowering of others that this is all very purposeful, those beings who only want to focus on love and light. Because they know that in other lifetimes they haven't been love and light and they have disempowered and hurt many through their actions.

P: I totally understand that! I have to say these guides have magical powers and I can't wait to remember or to know how it all works because these guides are beautiful! And I thank you so much! Thank you! Thank you! Thank you for everything you do for everybody here and everybody around and every Soul and every energy form! Thank you! Thank you! Thank you!

J: We appreciate your respect for us. And we view you as our Earth angel because you are just so gracious with your energy. And you have got the demeanor of just pure love. You are fully embodying an angel on earth from our perspective, because you just have that great love. That depth of compassion! And this is why so many people will go above and beyond to help you because they see you! They celebrate you! They want to nurture you and encourage you because you mean so much to them. And so this is such a great way. You are their teachers. You are empowering many and you don't need to have a big fanfare. You don't want to be anything, just be yourself. You're so comfortable with yourself and you're so proud of yourself because you know that everything you do has got the best intentions for everyone. This is what we would love for others to see. And your impact is so profound because every client you see goes and takes that approach to life and they share it with their friends and family. And you do not see the profound ripple effect that you are making within your community. You are so strong and we are so proud of you!

P: Thank you. And thank you for sharing that. It just warms my heart to hear how far all these words and energy and everything I work so hard every day on everybody and that's actually paying off. So wow! Thank you so much for hearing those words coming from you?

J: Yes. We just wanted to confirm that yes, everything you do does indeed count. And you do indeed matter! And you are so on point and of service and this is why you have no lack of abundance. This is why you're so comfortable with your way of life. Because you attract such great things to come to you, including your clients. And so you have nothing to fear and that is truly because you've done all of this work and because you have such great integrity. You have got true honest inner peace.

P: Beautiful! My goodness! Beautiful! I'm wondering if there's any kind of healing we can send through everyone that got their curses released or any kind of epiphany just to have healing to make it more comfortable so the adjustment isn't so rocky. Like a bad airplane ride.

J: Yes. We understand and we were wanting this shift, this dramatic shift of feelings though, for them to really notice the difference. If it's subtle they don't notice, so we're wanting them to shift from a deep density into a massive enlightenment. And we needed them to experience the contrast for them to realize that they want to keep seeking out that higher frequency. And so while we have been gradually raising the frequency of humans and for humanity on this planet, which is very purposeful and significant to purge all the natural densities themselves, when we give you a jolt and an up start, upgrade, it's sort of dramatic. It gets your attention. Most people are living on autopilot and we're not getting their attention enough. They keep just distancing themselves. So this is when you get the profound sick upgrades in quotation marks "viruses" or something else.

P: Definitely makes sense. Thank you! Yeah. Totally understand that now. Are there any other messages at all you'd like to share with us for today? Or anything new or anything at all?

J: All is well! We see that there is much growth from these new upgrades and people are starting to resonate with this frequency more commonly now and more frequently. And this is good news for us. While it's still taking a lot longer than we had anticipated, we understand it's very draining for many. We are wanting those who are holding the light, who are still motivated to be of service to continue growing and going. And we're very proud of you! And while we are not supporting those who are not being of service as much, we are still here willing to step up and support you when you choose to step up and support yourself and others.

P: Thank you.

J: We're always with you but we cannot keep supporting those who are not supporting others. And this is, you must understand, this is not a mean thing. We're not walking away from you but we're not going to honor you when you're not honoring yourself and others. So those people who are just for example, wanting a million dollars. Why do you need that million dollars for example. People are misusing us. They think that we are their sugar daddies and we're not. We're trying to empower you. And when you remove yourself from density, when you remove yourselves from the perception of lack, you will always get abundance! But when you're focusing on what you don't have versus working hard to empower yourself and others, there's a world of difference.

P: Yes. And I see it as a parent rule. You know you hear parents say I'll only help you if you help yourself. So I could see how the team could only help.

J: We are saying that we're not going to give you dessert until you clean your room. And then when we say clean your room we're saying clean your density. Clean your traumas. Clean your attitudes. Clean your perceptions. Clean up yourself. Step up, step up, step up. Speak your truth and be honoring yourselves. Stop limiting yourselves and stop living in a junk fest room.

P: Thank you. But there's been a way to help people with speaking the truth, because that's something we're so like... I hear that phrase a lot, but like I just mentioned to Jo earlier, most people can't speak to their spouses truthfully so how are they supposed to speak truth? Is there a way to help humanity with healing or something? What can be done about that?

J: We find the most effective way is to give them very sore throats where they can't speak and it bothers them so much because suddenly, because they can't speak they're having to focus on their thoughts. Most of you speak without thinking. We've changed that. When you can't speak you must think and then therefore when you start focusing on your thoughts you can start feeling into yourself. Then when you don't have the sore throat and you can speak freely and clearly you have got a little bit more connection of your senses and your true thoughts and integrity. So you're a little bit more aligned. When something gets taken away from you, you focus on it a little bit more when it gets returned back to you.

P: Very purposeful! Yes. Truly. All right. I'm just gonna ask one more time. Any more last messages? To make sure, because I know you can talk to us for a long time and I love hearing all your messages, but if there's anything else.

J: Yes. And we appreciate that. We do have lots of things to say and we always could have lots of things to say and share. But we want to just impress that 'All is Well.' And for those who are struggling to find their balance, we have already encouraged you to step up. And when you know you're not, when you know you're unbreakable, when you know that you're only limiting yourself in fear of judgment of others, try! Start going small. Start sharing your love of others and start truly embracing people that you know are out there following you, listening to you. Your reach is vast. So just because you may do a post or call a friend or something, just check your expectations of why you are doing certain things. Are you wanting to just share your truth because you're proud of your truth and you honor your truth and you're just letting the world know, or do you post things wanting recognition, communications and connections. If you're posting because you really want so and so to read this and see your point of view, why don't you take that next step and reach out to them directly. Those people that are on your minds, you need to reach out to them. You must reach out to them. There is a reason why they're on your minds repetitively. You must reach out.

P: Yes. I feel like that's a sign from the guide. Every time you get that name that pops up a lot. We need to do that more often. Right? That's what you're saying. Yeah.

J: And even if it is just a message of I love you, I hope all is well, then that is the kindest thing you can say to people. I love you! I hope all is well!

P: Beautiful. Beautiful. Beautiful as always. Thank you so much!

J: You're welcome. And we say this with love!

Session 15: Robin Williams

'Good morning humanity' is what I would say if I could speak to all of you now and I am! And I finally got my chance. The queue to get into this gig is longer than the queue to heaven. And I say this with much love and humor because I'm dead. And you can laugh at my jokes. And this is something that I've been wanting to get into for a long time. The vehicle and I have already had a conversation. Quite a few actually. And she's good with me and I'm good with her. I think she's quite swell! This is making her blush. But when she came to me the very first time to be able to understand my life contract and the purpose of who I was and why I was and why I exited the way I did, she was reaching out to me for that persona, that entertainer. She was in a fuddle, overwhelmed with what she was learning from these metaphysical sessions and perspectives. She was wanting a laugh, and from my perspective, there was no laughing matter when you look upon all of humanity and what it's going through. It's unfortunately a very sad state of affairs. It is not a laughing joke. Humanity doesn't realize how seriously lost and confused and manipulated and controlled it actually is while you're still stuck into a very dense rock. This is alarming and concerning because many people still want to master those experiences on that third dimension on that planet.

And we're here! We're all here! We're all here around you! We're all here around you watching you and observing you and trying to encourage you deeply to be able to just find focus, find balance, find some humor and some hard shit and get over it. Move on from it. Shake it off. Dance it off. Do whatever you must, but do not let it f***ing eat your mindsets! Don't let it get down on you and don't do what I did! Do not do what I did and felt so overwhelmed that I needed vices and devices and escapism. I loved my escapism, I thought. I thought it was the only way I could do everything that I wanted to do. Fun thing about friends and the fun thing about being popular or perceived to be popular and trying to impress everyone and to be so upbeat, so witty, so clever, so smart, was that the pressure to always be on, the pressure to always entertain starts feeling very heavy. And the responsibilities of it. So I could feel the density, absolutely! Everyone can feel the density. You can all feel the density. But you are so used to the density and you're still pressurized to do your jobs, live your life, find family entertaining and support them. Find the most powerful beyond anything meaningful relationship and try to make it work while you're not looking at your own insecurities, but while you're looking at theirs. It's a fun thing. It's a fun thing!

But I wanted to be able to reach out to the vehicle and say to her, 'All is well! All is well! All is well! But at that time when we first connected, engaged in, she still was seeking out light-hearted entertainment and she still thought I was going to be the entertainer for her. And while I still can be, and while all of us still can be seeing the bright side and the light side of life, I knew she was going to experience a lot of challenges. A lot of lessons. A lot! And it needed to be a time where she wanted to seek out entertainment and humor and comedy. But it was not going to be given to her because she needed to realize the severity of the state of the world as it was and is. And also to know these sessions are not gimmicky. These sessions are not to have assumptions that you know the soul. While I did play the persona of that happy-go-lucky and *oh so handsome actor*, I knew that was a role. And it was to have a really good-hearted, kind person in your homes, on your TVs. Introducing a hard concept that not everyone was ready to accept. Other beings. Other ways of life.

The series Mork and Mindy were incredibly opening information series that was really crucial timing to be able to open up and expand one's mind to kind, off-planet beings that were not here to harm you, but looked like you. They may have had different things such as the different age progressions of one's life cycle, but it was to show that there were differences, but to also show the range of emotions and experiences that could be easily distracted if you didn't focus solely on your routines and your balances and your way of life and took everyone for granted.

Joanne knew and she learned from that very well. I personally wanted to apologize to her because I know I could have had an opportunity to be that entertainer for her, but she also needed to understand that while someone's trying to perform and be all uplifting and funny, there is a lot of responsibility on that person to be that said, always funny person. And she also realizes the responsibility of being in a certain role. When you get stereotyped in a certain way, everyone always will make that assumption that you will be that for them. There were so many lessons that she has learned through that series and there are so many of us that are really proud to have been able to have helped to expand her own mindsets and her respect for this field and this work. I could see, like many of us who have tried to remind her of seeing the least dense side of the world, we know she can feel it tremendously and this is giving her an opportunity to remind herself there are so many tools that are there given that you all have access to freely. Such as music. Such as comedy. And I would like her to know that there is empty comedy that is just mind numbing, and then there is brilliant thought-provoking comedy that is a satire on the world that gives you many perspectives through humor where you can learn and grow from. And this is a really important aspect of comedy because you can learn advancements and be able to have such a more open receptor to big information, big content when there is humor there. And it must be delivered with all sincerity to laugh along. But you are growing and if you can make the joke and you teach that teachable moment through a joke, it is so much more impactful.

So my message to humanity today is still the same really. You have a lot to focus on. You need to work hard. You cannot achieve much if you don't work at it. You have to be able to be fully focused and due diligence while having a balance. You must have, from my perspective and from our perspective because I'm talking through a collective now, you must have a balance of uplifting music that can also get you into a density if there is any inner work that you must be able to match that density and release yourself through it. And so music is a time capsule of memory where if you did listen to old music that you used to listen to in your life, you will get put back into that emotional state of your life then. It is very helpful. You do not need to go and sit and talk to a therapist for hours. You go through your own musical collection. That will be the way that you can work through your inner work, if there is anything left. But when I'm looking and feeling into people who are listening to me now, I want to say with much love, there is work still there and there will always be work there. It is an ongoing forever cycle. I am also learning from where I am. I'm understanding more deeply how the density can impact and give the false impression and illusion that you are not masters in your own right and that you're not powerful beings. You have some disadvantages but that is all fantastic! That is the pushback. That is something that you need to push and go through. Remembering who you are. Remembering how powerful you are. Remembering you are all capable of free will of your emotions. That is so powerful when you remember *you* choose how to feel. In my lifetime, I felt very stressed and pressurized because I needed to constantly be evolving with my material, in my scripts that I was getting. And I wanted to be able to heal the world and empower the world and all I could see is so much sadness and people coming to me so down and so depressed and they were constantly wanting me to uplift them while they were not even open to being honest with themselves about what was going on. And I didn't really know the metaphysical perspective of what was truly going on either. I wanted to uplift people, but when you're constantly feeling like you have this big pressure to be that funny guy, it takes a lot and you just can't be yourself. And I was feeling into the heavy density myself. I still had my own demons. I did so many drugs and it didn't really help me at all. And I used my free will to limit and stifle myself. This is not a joke, but if I had actually done more running and actually done more sort of exercise and especially if I had looked after my body and knew how my body was reacting to the drugs, how my body was reacting to the sugars, it would have actually saved me. I think because my childhood still was quite sweet and especially when I was younger, I had great joy and I was a very happy person and I was always trying to get that again. I was always trying to achieve that sweetness again. In my 20s it was fantastic! It was such a fantastic way to live. And I felt so alive and vibrant and so I had this false assumption and connection with sugars to being part of that upliftment, to kind of gain my youth back.

And it wasn't helping my body. And when I was doing so much late night entertainment...(laughing) No, I was not a gigolo. I was in clubs, but I wasn't in those types of clubs. It was late nights. Lots of late nights! We lived in such a bustling city that never slept and so we're constantly trying to merge minds and talk about concepts without it being too dense and heavy and just be fun. But I was craving for a bigger perspective of things and you could see that in the evolution of some of my movies. They were very thought-provoking and I'm very proud of some of my movies because they were that entertainment, but also had some thought provoking pieces to it as well.

My big mission, my big role was to uplift people with love. To be able to be that friendly face. That lovable uncle. And I really wanted to, and I did achieve that! And I know my exit point was bittersweet for many people as they could not understand why. And it doesn't matter why. And it doesn't matter how. What does matter is that I did try my very best to be diligent to my life contract. I worked incredibly hard and I got the roles that I needed and wanted to be able to help humanity with. But I made some really silly choices that didn't empower me and actually did eat into my life contract and livigivity. Because of my life choices and because of the drugs I chose and the food I ate and the company I had and the lack of inner work I did, I always wanted to get back to my youth but I was growing so rapidly and I wasn't enjoying the way that my meat suit was aging either. Not that I was a vain person, um, to some degree. [Laughter] I did compare myself to other actors. But I knew that I was never going to be as dashing or as handsome as others so I knew that I had to have another shtick. I knew I needed to be able to have another sort of character. And so that's why I really worked on the comedy and my whole body was telling the story of humor. And it was a great way for people to realize it's okay to have expressions. You can express with your hands and your body and there's so much that you can work with while you're trying to communicate. And the more you use those senses of the body, the more you try to show people how you're feeling through the actions of your body, it's more understandable. It's more translatable for them. But so many people do not want to wave their hands around because it must look so daft to be able to have such an expression. But it's quite important to be able to express oneself through the body.

So when you want to share a heartfelt statement with someone and you're sitting there like you're dead with just a plain pan, talking about your big feelings and your big emotion, it doesn't read genuine. It doesn't read true. Emotions come with more than just words. They come with expressions. They come with gestures. They come with a whole dance that the monkey suit does to be able to get your point across. And you could be telling something to someone so profound, it's so deep within you and really, really, really, important, but your delivery must be on point. It must be key. It must be able to be the full expression of self. And so many people do not want to do that. They edit self, they limit self. And so you're sabotaging most of your story that you're trying to tell others. You're wanting to share with them, but yet when you're not fully sharing with your facial expressions and your hand gestures, you're holding back. And they can feel you're holding back so they don't know if you're telling them the full truth of how you feel because there is something missing. The words are not significant as much as the whole package of you sharing with full truth, *you* and how you're feeling. And what's going on for you. And what you're workin with. And what you're working through.

People would come to me wanting humor and jokes all the time but they would never be able to tell me what was going on for them. Partly, I just assumed it was because they wanted to impress me. They didn't want to share their true challenges and so they just leaned out to me to be their uplifting guy. I knew that they were holding back something and they also knew that I was holding back something. I wasn't a trained therapist. I was just some guy who wanted to make some jokes and uplift the world with laughter and love. And so I felt ill skill set to be able to really dive in deep and ask my friends what is going on here? What are you going through? Tell me. Share with me. But I was too nervous to even hear what they were going through because how the heck would I know how to support them. And then I don't want to hear half their broken stories and then not know what to say, feel super awkward and then just laugh it off with a joke to distract myself and them. So I avoided my really good friends. I avoided so many really important people in my life because I didn't know how to listen to them and their pain. I didn't know how to share with them my pain. I didn't know how to fix them or help them. I couldn't even fix or help myself to some degree with my personal struggles of insecurity and just feeling so frustrated that I had made some really dumb choices in my life and I just couldn't let it go. I couldn't forgive myself and I couldn't just see that there was a purpose and a lesson. And instead of learning from that and growing from that, I emotionally looped, and I kept making really dumb choices for myself. And I've learned that now from this sweet place. From this perspective. I have learned that now and I can see that now, and I've done great healing from that. But I had to experience those experiences. And I had to have my whole free will to be able to play that game. To be able to then come back here and have this life review and see it all! I remember all the feelings. I remember all of the scenarios and the situations and how I felt compelled because of self-lack. I did so much stupid stuff, but I don't regret it. I only regret hurting people because I was not able to empower myself enough to truly reach out to them. To truly share with them. To truly listen to them. Of course I was not a therapist. I would never have been able to tell them the answers. But we're not supposed to tell people the answers. We're supposed to just listen and let them find their own journey and be able to express enough with someone else so they get a chance to hear themselves. We're not wanting to rule other people and tell them how to think and feel. We can't do other people's inner work for them. All we can do is have space and love and compassion for them as they finally get an opportunity to sound out themselves, to feel their own emotions outside of themselves being expressed. To then go and do their inner work. It's not often that someone will be able to share their thoughts and feelings of what's going on for them. To have a profound epiphany. To be able to see the lessons and experiences and move on in one conversation. It is not possible all the time. Especially those big ones. If you could all just understand the answers to get this worlds planet's experiences. Love yourselves! Do not hold back! Do not trick and cheat yourself on things that don't serve you. Honor your body because it houses your mind. It houses your Soul essence. You are not your body, but if you put sand in your vehicle, you're not gonna drive. You can't! You've got all the equipment to drive but you can't do it. You must honor the body in every way. In every which way!

I appreciate having this chance to be able to share with you something I wish I could have shared when I was there. And this is part of my own journey in healing. And for those of you who have listened to me, I love you! Laughter is fantastic! And while you're focusing hard on your inner work and you're laughing through the mistakes that you've done, do that instead of criticizing yourself and belittling yourself! Laugh at the mistakes! Laugh at other people's mistakes! Not because you're trying to be mean but because it's like, 'Well, *we've learned from that one haven't we?*' The density is so dense. Why are you still choosing to then add more density to it? You will find some great perspectives and wisdom in some of my movies. And I do say to those who have a stronger connection to me, because I was with you when you grew up. I could feel you watching me and I could also feel your challenges and your struggles. And I really want to be able to keep uplifting people and just be your goofball! Your hairy ape monkey suit goofball! Gosh, I didn't try to hide that, did I? [Laughter] But, All is well! All is well! And we can hang out together again. Much love!

Session 16: Big Epiphanies of a Draconian

After some sessions with this Soul he was struggling to apply changes and trying to impact some clients with his energy field, after trying to cause some seriously big car accidents to hurt people to shut them down. This was a concern and we wanted to understand if we could help him and hopefully gain some perspectives for him to heal.

Yes. We are here. We are here. We are here. We're here. We're here and we understand the task at hand. You're wanting to call in the Draconian that is responsible for all of the attacks that are happening to many people that you are aware of. This is not a coincidence that you have been made aware of this event, because that Draconian also tried to impress its frustration and demands onto you as well. We're clearing your energy field, once again. We are wanting to warn you this - while we can impress upon this Draconian ourselves, our hopes and intention for him to be able to see things from the bigger perspective, and to be able to open himself up energetically, spiritually, to consider all possibilities for his own spiritual growth, you cannot do his inner work for him. You cannot heal him. You cannot save him. You cannot do anything that he no longer wants or chooses to do.

However, we do want to impress upon him, his choice is to impact others, to kill others, to maim others, to haunt others, to distress others, to upset others. It is such a waste of his energy and it is not in anyone's benefit, including his own. It is just disabling him. While he's so fixated on all of these very childish attacks and approaches and perspectives, we say upon him now - we do not play these games. We do not let our Soul families be exposed to such games here. While there is free will, we also have free will, and they also have free will. You do not get to shortcut people's life contracts or impress upon them as you have once done. We do not allow or condone this anymore.

There are many collectives here talking to you now, to tell you this - 'while you think you can get away with your free will, you do not'. This is frustrating you and you must notice this now. While you try to manipulate, while you try to distress while you try to seek darkness from many, it is not working out for you now. We have many more connections, we have much more protection, and your silly games with energy no longer - **no longer** impact as they once did.

You know the strength of all beings on this planet now. You are merely just one simple soul, so hurt and lost, and you've gotten away with this for so long. They are your game. Humanity is your play toy. We're saying the game is over and you must pack up your toys because we are doing that for you. We are protecting your toys from you.

You must love, if you wanted to play the true game. You must love and respect and want the best for them. Your experiences of just thrill seeking, no longer serve you. They have not served you in a very long time, and even if you could be true and honest to yourself, you're getting bored of this game, desperately bored of this game. Look into yourself. Is this really serving you? Is this really empowering you? Your toys are overcoming and overgrowing YOU. You're no longer able to reach them, they're ignoring you. They are carrying on with their days. They are not buying into you anymore. You've never had any power over them, and it's going to continue on like that.

We understand you're so frustrated. We understand you're irritated because it's going against your free will, going against your hopes and agendas. You're in a bad routine. You are in a bad routine, and just because you're no longer having the power you once welded doesn't mean ..... We understand that you were not liking this because it was taken out of your own hands. We're saying humanity was never yours. So many other beings and collectives, other planets, they were never yours.

So, we will call upon you now for you to speak through this vehicle, but we will warn you, this game that you play - we do not entertain it.

Draconian: "Well, I don't like to be cornered like this. It is frustrating. I don't want to have to justify my actions to you, but as I do so, I hear what you said. My problem is this - what do I do next? What should I do next? I found myself in such a habit of playing with these dull toys. I have noticed that they are less reactionary towards me. Things that used to terrify them, only mildly amuse them now. They do question and ponder, but it is getting dull. It is getting dull. But what do I do next? I've done this for so long, I don't feel that there is another Soul companion. I'm not interested in a Soul companion. I'm feeling very isolated from my own collective, feeling isolated from my own being. I'm bored. I'm still lacking an interest in drive and desire to fulfill myself, so I guess I have been distracting myself with this.

It felt so powerful to wield the will of man. It felt so powerful to be able to choose destruction, if I decide, and use my other toys. It is an empty existence but it was distracting me. It's just a habit and a routine that I got into. Now I am feeling frustrated because it's just ..... What should I do next? When I get so bored and agitated and irritated, that's when I do my old routines, my old tricks. I guess, if I was an emotional eater, I would eat. Instead, I'm not an emotional eater at all. I play with energy and disrupt energy.

When I'm feeling frustrated instead of doodling on a piece of paper with pen, I find beings who are part of my problem, who have stronger energy fields that are empowering many around them - those lighthouses irritate me, because they're impacting so many people around them in a positive perspective in a positive energy field. This is why it was so easy to collect some of your weaker friends, totally take over them. I've given them some essences of (my)self. They're so spiteful, it's delicious. It's another hobby, but I see many of you here, disappointed with my actions. But I still have this feeling of - what am I supposed to do next? I have no drive. I have no interest, so I just do this hobby. I just do this behavior.

I know Paul[24] tried to offer me love. It's so ridiculous. What do I do with love? What do I do with love? It feels a bit empty and useless to have love, when all I really have is myself[25]. So you're saying to me that I'm supposed to love myself and what is that good for? It doesn't seem to be of interest to do something that is like that. What is the purpose and point of loving self when I've distracted myself with anti-love, with the darkness, the irritations, the aggravations, that seems to

---

[24] A channeler who had a run in with this soul.

[25] What the collectives were telling him was not recorded at this point, as it was only him being channeling as he was listening to the collective elders, they said to him it is about him loving and respecting himself.

be more interesting. Love seems very boring and insipid, and I don't get it. I don't understand why there would be that drive for love.

It's power that you want. It's power that you should be seeking and needing. You should have people and beings afraid of you, begging, worshiping you. You should have everyone eating at the palm of your hands, and be so powerful that you care less of nothing and no one. So if I did start loving myself, what would that look like? If I started loving myself, then I'd start having potential compassion and loving others. Then if I loved others, I wouldn't want to disempower them, I wouldn't want to disarm them, I wouldn't want to be doing my routines and my habits and my behaviors, that I'm quite comfortable with. But, I guess, even I'm getting bored of that. So if I did start loving myself, what's next? What is in store for me? What is part of my life contract, to be able to experience this, now new trend you were trying to sell and press on upon me? Loving myself?

(Collective talks to him)

So you're saying that the Soul essences I've left and lingered into - Soul beings - you're wanting me to fully put myself into that position, and my full consciousness more into those beings, and feel responsible for those actions and for those lives, and to start caring about those physical bodies and those physical people that are in my life - my family and my friends and all of those different various bodies, that have my Soul essence. I understand that I have been, I want to say - trapped, entrapped into some of these bodies. As part of a punishment for doing certain things to certain beings, but they were open to it. But now my Soul is locked in there. And

I understand that that was part of the alluringness. Now I can see why you've wanted me to go into those bodies, and now I see I cannot get myself out of those bodies, either.

You're saying to me that it's teachable moments to have those different lifetime experiences. And that the thrill and passion and all the range of emotions of being consciously aware of those human lives, will give me a new perspective of true love and compassion. There are people in those lives that do love the essences of those bodies, even though it is part of my essence. So you're wanting me to experience this, to actually embody it consciously - those vehicles. There are many of them but I could do it, because I guess, it has been the lonely experience of boredom and working by myself, playing with humanity by myself. I guess this has been the most frustrating thing - that I haven't had these other partners or actual family as such, or even friends as such, either. So actually now, if I did consciously more embody and be more aware of those vehicles, then I will be able to experience what it feels like to be part of families, and in social circles, and friends.

But then, I'm going to start feeling sorry and bad for what I've been doing to humanity, because I can start feeling that those physical bodies have physical attachments to people. I don't know if I really want to like people, but I do want to feel their love now. I'm curious. What does it feel like to be a part of a family? What does it feel like to be part of friends? Even just these concepts make me feel funny. I want this, but I don't want this, at the same time. I don't want it, but I want it. But it's a lot. I want to be loved by them and I want to love them, but I don't want to be responsible for my other actions. I want to just be seen as them. I don't want to be seen as me. And now, I understand why and how this has come to be, that I have now embodied these beings.

I understand that this is actually now, I can see part of my collective coming out from the shadows of this conversation. They have wanted this for me too, but it needed to be me, because I'm so stubborn with my own hobbies. I threw them away because I did not feel like my behavior was acceptable, and so I ran away from my collective. I ran away from my own family. They're saying to me, I rejected them. But I'm saying, you rejected me. You never understood my ways. You never understood my curiosities. I wanted to be powerful and be ruling and manipulative to get what I wanted, to get the power. That should have impressed everyone. They should have .... I wanted to show people that is how you get true power. I was powerful, but instead of pre-impressing them, that pushed them away. So I was driven to believe that the more powerful I was, and the more in control and in charge of many beings, pushing them around, would have been more impressive. It would have brought back my family and friends to come back and tell me that I am impressive. So I was driven and I was angry. I was driven to impress them, but I was also angry, so I went more out of control - it was a cry for help.

Being more connected in now to those physical bodies, it's like I've been given profound imprints, but I'm living their lives too. I'm feeling more, more in the range of the emotions than ever before. I'm releasing so much from my past hurts and frustrations, because ultimately for a long time, I thought everything I was doing was to impress others, to get their approval in love. All it gave me was disapproval and lack of love. I could never have imagined that my own collectives were working with the light. I was so angry with them, I saw them as darker than me, who could have disowned me. So I villainized them, I became the victim, and I wanted to prove that that was never going to break me. And so I went harder and stronger, more dedicated. I wanted them to be afraid of me, to then force them to praise me and love me.

But now, because I'm tied, I'm trapped in these human bodies, and I'm feeling all this range of emotions, I can articulate what's actually going on. It's like I've never been able to stop and think about this myself. And now in this, it's like my mind and my heart and my emotions and my trauma have all been scanned. And it's all just coming out to the surface in these big epiphanies.

Thank you. Thank you for allowing me to see this now. I understand what I have to experience, and I know that after this experience, I will have a stronger idea of what's next for me. But right now, I will need to learn to be, to feel, to learn, to grow and have experiences, to be a part of something, to be equal. In my resentfulness and my bitterness and my trickster ways to get ahead to control and manipulate and rule with deceitful agendas doesn't serve anyone. I want to explore the range of emotions had here on Earth. So thank you for allowing me to stop my routines. I do want to change, to experience this. And so, taking my consciousness, dispersing it through all of these other vehicles is going to be something I will focus on and surrender into. Thank you.

Session 17: Influencers with Draconian Walk-In

Yes we are here! We are here! We are here! And we understand as we knew you would be wanting to explore how it is and what occurred with that last connection. And we did entrap that Soul essence into your body and we lured him for that session. He had been stalking and nearly obsessed with your energy field for quite some time. And so when we offered him an opportunity to be able to jump into your energy field, we knew this would be too tempting for him. And we knew this would lure and entrap him within this energy field. We had to allow him to use his free will, so we made this connection possible. But as we warned him and set him up, shall we say, we firmly discussed with you, you could not change him even though we knew you had no such agenda. You know better than that. But he was listening and he wanted to hear a human being warned and told off by us telling you, the vehicle, that you can't change another and that it is his free will and his right to do as he wishes and chooses. This pleased him and this made him so delighted with this invite, he didn't stop and ponder what would occur when he uses his free will to jump into your vessel. And as instantly as he did, we also warned him and told him he cannot use his normal tricks. Normally he will wait for someone with a big light energy who is somewhat drunk, somewhat in an altered state of mind, whether it be a drug, a hallucinogen or something else. He waits until they are open and wanting more, we could say spirituality and connections. So they're inviting him in. They're using their free will to open themselves up. They don't have the correct agenda for the details of what they're doing to themselves. They don't really believe in the metaphysical world as such and still they can conjure and invite in Soul essences just eager to attach themselves, play around and have some mischief. You could call it a possession. They do exist!

But we have been watching and we have been what you could say, fishing for him for quite some time. We have been setting traps. He has been watching bigger light beings coming online and so he wants to destroy them. Not just make exit points for them, but he wants to take them offline. He has succeeded many times to find big light beings and corrupted them with such density and darkness they've nearly gone mad. He is, and has been, addicted to that personality, to those hobbies, that trait. And we were finding it very frustrating that we were preparing so many beings to be here of true service, and then they did not quite know what they were doing. They did not quite have the correct protection or agenda. And so they were taken offline for various reasons. But usually, they were taken offline because they just didn't understand the power that they were welding with, or what they were exploring and opening themselves up to.

And so he was just waiting for those. And of course, he just needs to sow some seeds of doubt. This is his forte. He loves this, sowing those seeds of doubt. Just like those others are sowing those seeds of positivity and hope and encouragement, he likes to sow the seeds of doubt. He's addicted to it! There is no one above him pushing him to do this. This is his own experience he wants to do. He's in such a deep routine with this, he's not just done this on this planet. This is one of many he has stumbled across and he's just found this as a hobby. You could say, he's been here for as long as this planet has been, or he's been around as long as this planet has been. But he never came into the interest of human beings on this planet because you just weren't evolved enough. Once you started becoming a bit more advanced that made it more interesting, he got quite curious and he just followed. He followed, he followed, he followed, he followed, he followed as he was seeing beings removing themselves from other planets he wanted to explore. He was energetically attached to a few of them so they were able to be traced by him. And this is how he found himself here on earth exploring.

He is a menace! We say this with love. But he can sow so many seeds. You could say that he is the devil without being the literal devil. He likes to sabotage people and they get so caught up with his impressions. He jumps into people's bodies like a walk-in, does some mischief, and jumps out. He has been working with energy for so long, he has been able to manipulate himself through this. You could be a highly vibrational being, but if you allowed your mind to jump into worry and fear, you could allow yourself to germinate those seeds that he has been planting. He has been able to do so much mischief with what you could call his warriors, which are the Reptilians. And so he's been playing this game by himself while we have been observing and watching. We don't see that there was anyone else playing this. He's so busy that he can just, we can say, one bad apple rots the barrel! And he's like that! He's spreading lots of his seeds of doubt and corruption and ego-based driven desires. It has been allowed because he has free will. And we've been trying to impress upon him, but he is so dense.

While he is playing the role to give duality, he is not able to be mastered or controlled, and so we knew when he heard us tell a human to respect him and to not change him, this pleased him so much because he felt superior. So we used his fragile ego to manipulate him to be willing to jump into this vessel, thinking he could do the same thing. And because he's got mildly obsessed with this vehicle, he wanted to jump in to figure out what is so special with this one, and if he could leave any seeds.

So we did bring him into a physical body for this conversation. We used his free will, but as the vehicle was able to capture his conscious mind, then we were able to scan. A scan where his hurts were and where his perceptions was. While the vehicle experienced that being a certain amount of time, we think it was around the mid 20 minute mark for its entirety. And that is merely an illusion, because we held him a lot longer as we all impressed upon him our acceptance of his choices. And he hadn't considered it, as we had delivered and presented it to him. He knew, well he potentially thought that he was in trouble because he'd never been called up upon this committee. This very large meeting where many beings were there. And he was held and entrapped in this conversation as we were scanning him to see what was going on for him. We did not give him any sense of fear. We actually sedated his energy and we uplifted him a bit more than his usual frequency just to give him this comfort. We anesthetized him to some degree for him to just be open-minded without going into a reaction that we assumed he would have been able to do. Of course, his collective was with us, but he couldn't have seen them originally because we did not want him to realize that this was an intervention.

And this is how we would want you to understand what was happening. He is not in trouble. He has his experiences, and while he has caused us a lot of 'trouble', we can still see the bigger perspective of it being purposeful for lessons and experiences. But this is now very tiresome and consequences and lessons need to be expanded upon and grown through. Now we want him to evolve. We are wanting everybody to evolve because this range of density here no longer serves our energy, your energy, and things need to get moved on with as we have been needed to be able to focus on other planets that are also starting to come into this fragile state of existence. So we want to balance our focus, but we also know that when the bigger events happen, it will be so swift and it must be considered and respected upon. And this will be a directive from Source itself, because we cannot be seen as independent parties in this. This has to be the divine collective of all! And this is the way it is! And this is the way it shall be! And we respect that, but we are also aware that there are many things we want to get on with as well.

And so, we are all waiting for everyone to grow from these experiences and lessons. We are seeing this feels like it has helped the vehicle understand more. We intrapped him further with the other vessels. We have entwined his Soul essences into those physical bodies. We have threaded him with golden cords. He is what you could consider, a lost ghost of a Draconian descendant Soul essence, but it's different. We say he wasn't physical to what your standards of physical was, but he still was able to do a lot of damage. He did a lot of impressions onto people. So yes, I guess for your perspective his consciousness is ghost-like from your understanding of it. And so he is in the fourth dimension. So that is not a physical dimension as you understand it to be, but the consciousness is an energy, so you can't see the Draconian as such. He can impress upon himself to be seen as many things if those people can tune into his senses of energy. He wants to scare them so much. He will create claws, teeth, the stares, the aggression and the anger to sell his pitch. To sell his fear. He likes to present himself in all mannerisms to see what will be the most to be afraid of. Because that's what he's all about, creating fear. This gives him great joy! Not enough to raise his frequency vibrations unfortunately, but it still gives him something to be focusing on.

And so, as we opened up many big light vessel beings for him to be encouraged to explore and do his old tricks, shall we say, we knew that he would be tempted with some big light beings that have been activated recently. So he was snooping around as they were starting to explore more things with not the right protection that they needed. And so when the opportunities sought themselves out, he jumped in to play some havoc. And we were very much aware of this! Very much aware! And this is when we combined his Soul energy. We had the walk out experience or even the Soul essences have just merged in, so there is more, so he can be merged into that physical body. As you know, there is more than just one Soul essence in a vehicle. There can be many! It's all divinely orchestrated!

There have been many though who have had full walkouts because their life contracts were complete! They did exactly what they needed to do. And instead of having exit points with their physical bodies no longer existing and declining, we allowed the extension of that life to extend upon what we had planned. And this is fantastic because those other people in those lives could have experienced certain changes of attitudes and energy fields to help awaken *them* more. To empower *them* more. So it's all very significant! We honor all of these lessons and experiences and it is all well protected.

So, we have used his free will to our advantage. It has been long in the making, but now he has found himself corded, fused into the physical bodies. And unless we agree and unless his collective agrees that he can remove himself from certain vehicles, he will remain there until the vehicle dies. This is how it shall be and this is the way it is! And we are pleased that he finally gets to experience the love for humanity. The hurt for humanity. All of the range of emotions. He is so spread out now, as we have entrapped him in many vehicles[26]. And so it's super purposeful! It's all for him to learn and grow from. To develop emotions and process them and to be able to have these profound experiences. He was really lost and he was extremely lonely. And so when he could see that there was going to be something new for him to explore, he overcame his worries and doubts and his hurt quite quickly. Part of that was helped by us raising his frequency vibrations enough to have that euphoric openness and acceptance. While this is not how we usually do things, these are important times. We have tried many times to have worked with him before and we couldn't get it quite right. And so now, this has been a joyous outcome and as we see it, an incredibly significant one!

---

[26] *No one we have done recent sessions with, or shared in the books. We are aware of many who do have his Soul essence who are still trying to win the love of humanity while also being limited with perspectives. Always interesting to explore this more in your own sessions which influencer is connected to your own collective.*

We've always told you that everything is purposeful and that everything is significant and this certainly is the case as well. And as he experiences all those lifetimes that he is living currently now simultaneously, he will be able to help his own collective be able to learn from these things. He has been indirectly responsible for many things that have happened to sow those seeds of greed. To sow those seeds of disruption, disharmony and unbalance. You may not believe that one being could profoundly disempower a whole planet. While he merely sowed the seeds, humanity did most of their own doings and it just grew and flourished unfortunately, but also fortunately. Because this makes the experience on earth so much more vast and dramatic and full ranged. And the full bodyment of emotions that you get to experience is quite the smorgasbord of emotions, as the vehicle would say if she is trying to understand the buffet of the full range of emotions. The full color spectrum of the wheel palette of the possibilities of a 3rd dimensional palette of rainbow colors. All of the colors are there, just like all of your emotions are here. But they are heavily tuned into the density of the planet. You can't quite get the sense of the actual higher frequency emotions. It's quite challenging to feel into the *pure* high frequency of emotions here with this density. You can get glimmers and sparks and hopes of it in euphoric waves. And this is why unfortunately so many are addicted to those drugs because they are artificial. We say you do not need to keep doing those artificial things to yourselves because your mindsets are so powerful. The more you work at doing your inner peace and your meditation, and we did give you that gift of that white light healing. That is something that must not be overlooked. It is incredibly powerful. You do not need to keep listening to it when you can get the sense yourself of that profound relaxation, to open up yourself energetically to the Source energy of love.

We impress upon you to take this seriously, because there is much in your energy field that is trying to keep you dense. That is just the way it is there in that world and we want you to start remembering instantly how to get deep relaxation in the body. To be able to rest the mind that is active, trying to constantly find out where the next threat will be. We're wanting you to soften your thoughts. Soften your fears. Soften your bodies. Soften your hearts.

We hope we have explained this well and we say this with much love!

Session 18: Would Be Helpful For You To Apply.

Yes. We are here! We are here! We're are here! We're very much here! And we appreciate you acknowledging the nudges we have been giving you to be able to give you our perspective and information. You are suddenly aware of distractions. You do not want to be a distraction to others and you do not want to be distracted with others at this important time. And so we have prompted you to take off the comments on the videos, with much love and respect to those people who want to, with much love, love and respect to you and your work and our messages.

This does not need to be spelled out and it is just a politeness. And we encourage them to go within themselves and love themselves and be giving themselves gratitude for listening to this information and to be able to apply it. We would prefer them to focus on self rather than having to support what they think is the socially polite thing to do. We also understand that the vehicle was more than happy to acknowledge and constantly send love to others. But this is not necessary because she can trust that those who are listening now are doing their diligent work and actually being able to be responsible for loving themselves.

You all know that you are supposed to love yourselves. And while it is polite to share and support each other, it is still a little bit of a distraction for many. And so we say this is all purposeful where we just want you to focus on the content and the conversations more than what other people are taking away from it. Or what other people are saying. Or what other people are not saying. We know that it can be so distracting for you as you're trying to seek and look at what other people are saying[27].

Again, this is about empowering yourself and not having to trust or rely on other people's comments or thoughts to validate this information. Again, this is about empowering yourselves and it's not a social group that just needs to be spiritually masturbating amongst themselves. We know that this is a very crass statement but it doesn't need to be so self-indulgent. And while we do want you all to love each other, there is truly no need to be able to keep saying and doing things that people feel like they have needed to say and do. You're all so much busier than this and it is a distraction.

We would **love for all of you to focus, focus, focus, focus, focus on the concepts. Focus on the content and apply, apply, apply, apply**. This would be more beneficial for us and we are still seeking many of you to actually have your sessions and to get over your hurdles because we are waiting for you.

We are waiting for you.
We are waiting for you to have your own sessions.

And we have still continually given many people profound connections to be able to have sessions. But for whatever reasons they are distracting themselves and delaying themselves. And this is why we have preferred to put so much of our content and our own information on the other channel which is what we labeled 'Conversations with Heaven on Earth,' because people were still distracting themselves with limited information from other people versus getting their own information. It was stepping stones

---

[27] *Why the YouTube comments were turned off*

and that is fantastic because it is still our high integrity truth that you can hear in those sessions. But this is the time to be able to activate yourselves completely and truly. To be able to understand how you can connect in with us as your spiritual teams. And while you can hear very similar information through other vehicles, we want you to empower yourselves to have these profound connections, because some of you have either got misunderstandings of what is occurring and you are using your egos and your 3D mindsets to try and fill in some of the pieces of the puzzle.

So, give us all of your pieces to the puzzle and let us explain it through you. This would be very significant for you to do this. There is nothing stopping you. So as soon as you truly step up and want to be able to get these profound answers from self, now we will definitely be able to guide you to the most appropriate practitioner to be able to give you this support. The practitioners will not come knocking at your door. You must start knocking at theirs. This is so significant and important right now. And it truly is a financial investment in your soul's evolution journey if you did have to pay for such a session. You could also spend time working on connecting in with us through meditation, through deep relaxation, through using your own free will to connect in with us. To set the intentions that you are open and you can trust us. So many people still don't want to trust us and dismiss their own intuition and they would prefer to trust other people's information. And they don't seem to even have discernment whether it's disinformation or not.

We see you so distracted by so many other very limited and actually different collectives information. Now you can't understand why you feel even more so lost because you are not knowing which is the right information for you. It all feels sort of similar, similar, similar. Sort of like for like, for like for like for like. It is simply not the case. So, for you to finally truly understand the right information for you, we again recommend you connecting in with us directly yourself. Cut out the middleman shall we say, because that is just another stepping stone. That is another block for you to overcome. You always are supposed to overcome these other people's opinions and connections to be able to be inspired enough to be able to want to do it for yourself. But you're so distracted on other people's journeys. So distracted with other people's learning curves, that you are fully distracting yourself from self.

We prompted the vehicle to have this channeling today even though she feels when she's listening to us saying this... 'Well, haven't you already said this so many times?' And we say yes! We are on repeat constantly because people are still dismissing this information and they're still dismissing us. And so even through this vessel and this message now, many people are still dismissing us as if we're not speaking directly to you to say it is time. It is time for you now to stop your distractions. Stop your limitations and to actually be honest to be able to work within yourself to know thyself! Know thyself! Do not be ashamed! Do not be afraid! You are fantastic because you're all parts of source! And it somewhat amuses us and bemuses us, that many of you still have this strange assumption that you're not deserving of love. And it's so peculiar for us to see you struggling like that when you are nothing but love. That is your core Soul essence, is love! That is your natural frequency vibration, is love!

And yet you've put on these monkey suits to add on to this density. And we're saying you're constantly seeking *yourself*. You're constantly seeking *your* profound sense of self. You're constantly seeking the love of source, and that is the love of self! It always has been and it always will be! You're all one! But when you're trying to rely on other people's information as a more advanced version of your own self's truth, you're always going to see it through the lens of another person's journey. And we are saying your journey is unique! Your journey is specifically designed for you!

And so you're still needing to understand some of those life lessons and experiences to be able to let it go. Let it go! It's time to let it go now! It is time to heal now! It is time to empower yourselves and it is time for you to let go of the sense of time, because time is such a strange concept from us. But we understand that you love it, and so we use it. But we can tell you that the concept of time doesn't serve you, but we have to explain things that you understand, the way that you understand them the best we can, while understanding the appropriate use of your labels and senses and names. And so from your position, for you to move forward, you must use that "Time." You must use all of those steps that you have to still be able to experience this 3D life wisely. Focus on what's truly important! Stop getting distracted! Fully empower self! And some of that empowerment of self is understanding that many people are sensing different contracts are changing. That different big events are coming and things will be changing. Even the most outspoken person who may complain about their daily lives and their struggles with their jobs and their families, they are starting to feel a sense of insecurities as they know bigger changes are coming and it's suddenly making them feel concerned. Because even though they have wanted change, change, change, they've wanted so much disclosures and changes and empowerment and things to be fixed and things to be corrected and things potentially to go back to how they used to be in their youth, they're scared. They have been wanting this for so long and now when they can feel that there are big things about to change, they're suddenly getting very quiet and very scared. And they don't know why they're getting scared. They're getting quite antsy. They're getting a little bit agitated because there is this new frequency vibration that is uplifting them. It is speeding up their bodies at a cellular rate. It is speeding up their mind processes at a very high consciousness rate. And so they've had to expand their consciousnesses to be able to match their frequency vibrations and their physical bodies to be able to grow with both.

You're all trying to connect back into a higher realm. You're being prepared to be evolving, and so there's many steps to it for many reasons. And there are some life contracts that are about to end with each other. It doesn't mean that your life exits. You're not having life exit points, but you're having end of contracts, and you're having to complete these last bits of contracts with each other. This may be confusing for people who don't understand that there is change. Their teams are trying to pull you away from them to stop distracting yourself until you start living your lives without them being in your wakening consciousness and daily experiences. We're trying to again reorganize people into the like for like frequency. Many of your life contracts have changed as many of you are not able to go to New Earth now as you must be able to do and be of service for something else. And so, as your life contracts change, so do your life contracts with each other. And while you're still here in the 3D, your life contracts are changing as you need to separate yourselves emotionally and potentially physically from each other to be able to find your like for like frequency matches, because you need to, and make the acquaintances now. Or you need to focus on your own frequency energy and make more acquaintances of yourself to know thyself even more profoundly than you have before.

And so you may see more frustrations with people who don't understand why they are suddenly feeling distant from you. They almost go into a fear. They almost panic and think, is there a literal affair occurring? Why is there this disconnect? Why is this disharmony and this energetic separation? They don't understand it so they will not be able to verbalize this with you. They can't express it. Subconsciously they know what is happening, but consciously, they can't. But they can feel the distance growing amongst you stronger and stronger. This confuses them and this can actually make them so afraid because they don't know the truth, that they can create a form of frustration which then can develop into a form of anger. And this could be explosive anger that can come in waves as they are not too sure what is going on. And then of course, they have the down cycle of exploding emotionally with anger because then they panic thinking, is this now the argument that has taken place that is going to separate and divide and put that wedge in between the energetic relationship which that makes them feel even worse that they are seeing for their own eyes that there is these friendships and these relationships that are dividing. It makes them so stressed. And then they feel so guilty that potentially this is it. Because they don't *see* you changing but they *feel* the change. This makes them feel so uneasy. But we're getting them to focus on themselves more, and other people who they're going to be shifting and where they go next, that is where they will be together again.

And so, it is all purposeful! But we are wanting to explain again how some people are feeling more agitated than others and feeling this extra tension amongst their friends and family that may not have had tension prior. As we are getting ready to ramp up this experience even further, we are trying to trigger people into certain experiences. And we are trying to really guide heavily, those to be driven to what they need to really be focusing on at this important time. There is so much for you to do in your waking hours to be able to be of service to yourself and to others. To be able to hold a higher frequency. Because when you're consciously awake in your body, you are consciously holding on to frequency. You must be able to remove your density and do your inner work to be able to maintain a higher frequency. And for those people who do not do their active inner work, who do not look at their attitudes and their traumas that they are not addressing, not just from this lifetime but all the other lifetimes they have ever lived, and if they are holding on to that density, they will be limited from the higher frequency range that they are supposed to be holding on to and working through in their wakening hours.

As you know, when you are sleeping, you are doing other things. So when you are waking up... And this is why many people are waking up all through the night is because you are holding on to that frequency and bringing it here and anchoring it in. And this is important for many reasons. And so this is why you must be diligent with your attention and why you must be focusing on love and be able to transmute love out with a higher frequency of acceptance. Peace on earth. Love on earth. Acceptance of all. Respect for all. Honoring all, including self. It is such an important time to be able to do this. And we know that this feels like such a responsibility, but remember you promised and signed up to be of service. You wanted this role! You knew that you were capable of this and so much more! And so it was simply just a duty that you promised that you would help for humanity. And while we're having to remind you of this, and while some of you are doubting this, that we may be tricking you, we promise we are not. We are truly reminding you why you're here and why you feel like you've got such big responsibilities and duties to be of service. Because you are! Because you're remembering your life purpose and you know who you are! And knowing thyself and knowing life contracts and knowing missions and knowing what you're capable of will always be a more helpful reassurance to remember, this has not been done to you as a punishment. You're here to be of service! To be awake and be of service! To have upliftment in your heart, to be able to share it to others. To have complete empathy and compassion for others while still empowering them and not disabling them or disempowering them. You cannot even try to do other people's inner work for them. You must be able to just remind them that you have done enough of your inner work to know that you are loved and you are loving and 'All is well!' And everything has significance and purposes!

And so we hope that this has finally reached those who are still struggling to hear directly our message to thee. It is not time anymore to be limited or blocked. It is time to remember who you are! It is time to remember why you are here! And it is time for you to be of service!

And we say this with much love!

Session 19: How To Know Thyself

Yes, we are here[28], we are here, we are here, we are here to be of service once again. To be able to help assist you with your questioning that you have for us today, but we must say that we've been prompting you to ask us this question. This is why you've noticed many times, you have been saying this yourself - **"know thyself"**. Know thyself. It is easier to say it than actually do it, and we understand that, but we give many people prompts to be able to think and feel about themselves at a greater aspect of self.

While many of you are living past lifetimes in dream state to overcome those traumas, to be able to awaken to the feeling of certain traumas that occurred in other lifetimes that you have lived. To be able to rationalize it, comfort yourself, and rise upon it, and overcome it yourself in this capacity. It is easier to do your inner work and to remove trauma from yourself if it is presented to you in a dream. "Just a dream" you will say, just a very very real, vivid, and incredibly emotive dream. So while you have the comfort of your lifetime you're living now, you can feel what you've experienced in other lifetimes, but with the separation. So it can't possibly be you in this lifetime, you would know, and so we know how to support you and help you in the very best way possible. We give you these glimpses of dreams from other lifetimes to feel and remind you consciously of what you've gone through. Your Souls are unbreakable, but your experiences here are still imprinted onto your life contract to overcome, because this is how you walk through and release yourself from density that no longer serves you. It's all significant and purposeful and you know this, so we're

---

[28] *The Collectives, as presented through the Arcturian subconscious.*

lovingly giving you these experiences once again to overcome and to empower thyself with.

Regardless of whether you try to know thyself or not, it is our job, our duty, our responsibility, to help serve you in the very best way possible. And while some of you are not wanting to feel into density to empower yourselves through it, we will give you these loving reminders with a prompted dream, to do your work, to know thyself. Even if you refuse to think or consider for a minute that those dreams were you in other lifetimes, and potentially even parallel lifetimes, that is okay. We understand. It is important to focus on this lifetime now and not get hung up on certain things. We understand if you start thinking too much about other lifetimes, that can distract you. You could try to find problems and issues with your limited perspective of why certain events occurred, and we can say to you, you can connect in with us and we will help assist you and show you the lessons of those experiences. We also supported you in those other lifetimes, but as we know, sometimes the most heartbreaking and physically painful experiences are still very valid lessons to have and to grow from and to remember. **Remember where you've come from.**

To know thyself in the broadest sense ever is to recall and reflect that you're all part of Source, and what is Source you ask? What is Source? Source is an energy that became self-aware and wanted to have different experiences, as it was, what you could consider a thought. What am I? I'm so comfortable being everything and nothing... What am I? What else can I explore? What else can I experience? What is there? These are the thoughts that started to become aware, and there is a need to separate self from source to have more independent clarity and questioning and experiences and observations and different perspectives of not being whole, but being a fraction of Source. This consciousness, this energy became curious. He was so happy and comfortable being self, it wanted to expand and explore other aspects, other awarenesses of the fractals. It is all completely possible to experience, and as you are understanding at your best capability in a third dimensional body, you are all multi-dimensional beings while you are still connected to source. That is distant from you at this point, as you're focusing on being so dense in this 3D planet, while also having different independent experiences, believing you are just one human being. Being. You say you are, and you know you are one being. You see yourself as an individual, and independent, and that is fantastic because it gives you focus on what you're doing independently as you are needing to.

How do you get from being fully Source, to breaking away into smaller fragments of self, to then find yourself here in a 3D body? It doesn't just happen on a whim. There is much to be explored. You often will find that you have broken away from source as a bigger counterpart, which we call your higher self in these sessions, for you to understand. But we know that your higher full self, your true full self, is Source, but we know you love labels and names, and so we will say you fractal out from Source to be your higher self. Your higher self is able to do things that Source cannot be and not do. It is different for many reasons, but it also is still the same. It is more independent. It is wanting to observe more, explore more, experience more, and then that higher self fractures out to have other lower dimensional experiences. So each time you fractal yourself out, you're wanting to go deeper and deeper and deeper into density, because that is curious for you too. You're wanting to learn and observe and experience and grow from and explore and have personal independent experiences, which of course all come back and all learn from and grow from and share from. But as your higher self fractals out lower and lower and lower, you have to be more and more supported.

When you come to these 3D planets, you must come with a collective support. You must come with guides, who are supporting you constantly. And while you must think "Gosh, it must be so dull for my subconscious to watch me do my dishes", we say the subconscious is with you for always and ever, because it is a high version of self. But it's doing its own busy chores too, and you don't need to be aware of its equivalent of doing their dishes, and potentially your subconscious is not doing dishes, but for this analogy you're all wanting to experience the illusions of the densities of your dimensions. You're all having these, what you would perceive as 'perceptions of time' to explore and do your routines and duties. The higher you go in the dimensions the less physical you are. So there is no such thing as dishes, but there are other things that they keep themselves busy with, so they can easily maintain and guide and manage and inspire and support and love many parts of their 3D selves. Also, they support Soul families, 3D selves they're there to support. If you are a guide to a planet, you are very capable of supporting many many many different aspects of human lives, all simultaneously.

So they aren't just focused just on you just doing the dishes and just going to the bathroom. They have no real interest in that. However, if you do suddenly call upon them, if you have a fright or a scare or something scary that happens to you, when you start praying you will get their attention quickly, because they can read and sense that there is something unbalanced and misaligned with your energetic body. When you go into a panic energetically, they know this. Imagine understanding it from this perspective... your subconscious is your arm, and let's just say that your subconscious has five beings, five independent beings that it is supporting and loving and nurturing through their human experiences. And let's say for this example your subconscious is managing and focusing on the five fingers, and while we know that there are four fingers and a thumb, you understand what we are referring to. So look at an arm and it has got five small fractals of self down their arm, and so you know the arm will notice if suddenly one of those fingers is being attacked. You don't have to see it, you can feel that one of the fingers is being nibbled on for example, if we want to say something is nibbling on the finger or something is touching that finger that is affecting that finger in a panic state. You can feel all five fingers if you wriggle them now. They are all independent. They're all living their own versions of life. They all have different perspectives of where they are in the hand, so while they're all simultaneously experiencing the same lifetimes as being independent fingers, they're still connected to the arm and the arm is still connected to the five fingers. Now when you feel the whole hand, you can notice that the fingers are all very aware, very in tune very and in sync with the rest of the hand. It's a complete package. And if we went further and said that you could break it down even more, to all the independent bones and the hands, which there are multitudes of. You get to see and know that there is so much inner working that is going on "behind the scenes", that you can't even tell. You also can then add the tendons and the muscles and the cells...

everything that is supporting and encouraging the working capacities of those fingers. It's not just five fingers, there is so much support that goes on behind the scenes, within the scenes.

This is a very good example of what is truly happening for you as an independent body. You know you have so many bones and muscles and tendons and organs that are helping you... think about them as also being high dimensional beings, all within you. You can't see them all the time. You can kind of feel them if you poke around the bones. You can tense and feel the muscles, and we'll say you know yourself. While your body is a vehicle which is merely holding your soul, you are not the body. You're attached to the body in this 3D experience, but you're truly more connected with us than your body. This is strange for you to hear. How can you trust this, when you don't see us? Well, you can't see us and you can't feel us as if you did cut into your anatomy to see the functioning bones, tendons, muscles, blood, and all of the things that factor into your vehicle, but you trust that all your bones are there. You've never stopped and counted them. You've never tried to explore the full range of where your muscles go. You just assume that your body is functioning and normal and fine.

So if you're wanting to advance yourself in the spiritual world and understand the metaphysics more, and who you truly are, we could say that there are so many aspects of us as high dimensional beings within you. Everything is within you. When you close your eyes and detach and relax yourself from the physical body, you are there. Just there. Just there, yeah just there. You are returning back to what it feels like to be Source, and you open yourself up to just being conscious of your mind, just being your mind, not being your body. Not being your fears and worries. Not doing the shopping list in your head. But when you actually just remember that sense of awareness, that consciousness that's within you, it's not even in the body but you perceive it is in the body. This is how we are saying we are also there within you, within your body, within your mind's eye. You could close your eyes and fully relax yourself, not holding any tension in the body. In fact you could just relax. In fact you could just forget you have the body and just close your eyes and remove all senses of the body, and focus within. That stillness, that consciousness that's there.

What is going on there for your consciousness? Who are you going to invite in? Are you going to trust that your subconscious is right there, too? That your high dimensional beings' essences are right there too? Because you are at the finger of the arm of the shoulder of the torso of the body, and aspects of high dimensional selves. We could say the numbers of the dimensions and we could say and introduce you to each individual aspect of self with all the names and all the labels and all of the eccentricities of each independent lifetime... and that is all well and said and somewhat interesting, but it is distracting you from who you are now. So while you're all connected to one, while you are all fingers in this 3D life experience, while you're all these 3D vessels... when you connect into your consciousness, you actually do not see separation of self. You feel and sense all. That is significant, and that is purposeful. Not so would you want to fully connect with them, you detach yourself from noticing the body and you trust the mind's eye. You trust what's in the mind, but it's not your physical brain you are even connecting into, it is your thoughts. You think it's within the body. You can't decide where it is. Is it in the middle of my brain? Is it behind my eyes? Is it in front of my forehead? Where is this thought coming from? Where is my consciousness living? Where is it placed? You are wanting to find where your consciousness resides, we can say, because you think you're the body, you're trying to locate it within the body.

Your Soul essence is technically within the body, but your mind's eye, your consciousness, can take up the space of an entire what you would consider universe or galaxy. There is no time in space, and so you're trying to use your clever mind to understand the capacity of your Soul essence, to understand the reaches and the limits and the bounds of your consciousnesses. But it's infinite. The only way we can explain it to you is understanding numbers. The number sequences are infinite, and that's the space that you can also have. Your consciousness is limitless space. You can have great awareness of consciousness. It is accepting of all, and when you realize that you can have advanced consciousness, you realize it's not significant to have vast amounts of consciousness, because you're all or nothing and you're in a completely neutral and balanced space. That is where you are back again, being with Source. You distract yourself so much. You overthink, you over worry, over criticize, and you dismiss the very simple essence and the simple experiences of just going within, closing your eyes, detaching yourself from the physical body by not paying attention to it. Focusing on the consciousness. Focusing on where your thoughts are and being in balance and neutral with the thoughts.

It is so easy from our perspective, to be able to go within and to trust and just find balance and neutral. It's balancing the mind and balancing the body. It's a profound unity of self, and this is what you could have been doing and what you can achieve when we gave you that White Light Meditation[29], to be able to find and see and feel yourself being in a beautiful pyramid of white light. We gave you the visual to make you feel that you are protected. The pyramid is a very strong shape and it is very impermeable. It's very strong in its foundations and it's very strong at its peak. It's all purposeful. While we use the symbol for you, to give you the encouragement of strength. We have explained to you now how you can **know thyself.** We have given you the best of our capabilities in this translation, to be able to tell you and guide you how to achieve getting to yourself, and to remember that your Soul essence is there within you, including all of your other connections. And while you're not consciously aware of all of the independent experiences, the other lifetimes that you are having as multi-dimensional beings, it is purposeful. You need to focus on where you are and who you are now.

We say this with love.

---

[29] *White Light Healing Session we have shared on YouTube and Telegram. Email if you are wanting a copy of it.*

Session 20: Feeling Traumatized Being Human

Yes! Yes! Yes! Indeed! Indeed! Indeed! We're here! We're here! We're here!

And yes, thank you! From our perspective, having support groups for those traumatized beings who are feeling so traumatized and being human, this is going to be a very helpful community connection indeed. While they have found balance and neutral and respect their life contracts, respect their life lessons and experiences, still realizing and knowing and honoring who they truly are is a profound advancement and perspective. But feeling traumatized that you are still human, waiting for events to occur, can be quite a toll on one's soul. And just because you are human, doesn't mean you need to just have human perspectives and mindsets. It is greatly helpful to be able to have advanced mindsets, but as we say, when you are still supporting humanity you can easily be traumatized by still seeing and observing humanity's choices, and when you're constantly working diligently to raise your frequency vibrations and spread love and joy, and you are still noticing people refusing to grow, refusing to step up and refusing to help themselves. They are not doing it to be in spite of you, they're doing the best that they can and they think and have assumptions that they're right and that their routines and behaviors are how a good normal human being must and shall always be. And you know the difference between how humanity was supposed to be and how humanity was supposed to evolve. And you know the shortcomings, if you wanted to label them as such now.

We are saying that many people who are advanced in their perspective still need Soul family. Still need friends. Still need to communicate and share their journeys with each other. Potentially tools, to be able to gain more respect, tolerance and perspectives to support those who are around them that are at a denser vibration.

Remember, you're here for those who have that denser vibration. You are *here* for it! That is literally your mission, to find those denser vibrational beings and love them! Uplift them! Inspire them to grow! Some of you have chosen to not be connecting with those denser people until you have completely mastered the 3D and all perspectives. And we are saying that is one choice. But we find that those who have mastered a much higher perspective, struggle deeply to be able to resonate and to relate to those who are holding on to the dense emotions. Holding on to fear. Holding on to lack and limited perspectives. While you do not feel the need to push them to think bigger and be high frequency vibrational, you respect them at their place of where they're at. It is hard for you when you have ultimate balance and harmony to then go and assist and be able to be relatable to those. And so, this is why it's important for you not to wait until you have perfectly mastered the third dimension to be of service. You must be of service every step of the way. But if you cannot truly love yourself and you have no sense of boundaries, that density of others could drown you, if you want it to be dramatic.

And so, this is why it's important to love yourself. To know yourself. To know who you are. To know why you are here. And then have all of that condensed foundation of strength and courage of yourself to be of service. You are always on a journey. You will not get to your perspective of mastering perspectives of 3D. There is so much still you could always explore and grow. We are also wanting to remind you all, with much love, while you are fragments of your subconscious, while you're fragments of your higher self and while your fragments of Source, you are not Source! You are not your higher self. You're not your subconscious. *You are you!* And you could even have a few Soul essences in that physical body being you. You are consciously aware of being Human. This is where we see people getting tripped up. They have an assumption that they are in its full entirety, Source. We are saying, look at that beach, look at a gigantic... the biggest beach that you could ever see! That beach full of sand. That sand is not the beach but you label the beach, 'The beach!' But you're not seeing and counting and noticing each individual component that goes to be and create that beach. We are saying the collective of all Soul essences in combination together as a collective, is Source! And we see people getting confused about who they are and their place in the world, the universe, and where they fit in. And you're all equal. You're all one!

When you see that big beach, you say that beach is one. That is one beach! And you know the billions of sand grains that comprise that beach. While that sand is the beach, it is one beach. There are many fragments, many components to that beach. We're saying when you know yourself, you know that you are one component to Source. You're one component to your higher self. You're one component to your subconscious. You're one component to your collectives. You are one! And while you're deeply connected to all, you are not all at the same time. That one grain of sand is not the beach. So we are saying for those people who think that they still create their reality, it is saying that one ambitious grain of sand is calling itself a beach. And we don't mind. Because often those one grains of sand who claim that they are the beach are motivated to impress others. If you still need to impress others then you ultimately know that one grain of sand is not the beach. One Soul is not all! One Soul is not Source! You're all fragments of each other. You're brothers and sisters.

And while you could all merge in when you are at the ultimate frequency of consciousness, you do form, we are saying for analogy, the ocean again, and the droplets of water. You can always be one individual independent droplet of water, but you also can merge in and be indistinguishable. Be together. To go with the flow of each other to be that ocean. And we also say it can transform and transmute into different things. We're saying, take a component of a collection of droplets of water and put that in the freezer and you will get a new form, a new being. It's very strong in some regards, if you want to keep focusing on that. And it looks like it is very solid and together, and for that moment of being an ice cube, it is. But when you change forms again and when you separate yourself... We could use many analogies to be able to help assist you. It is significant for you to realize your place in knowing thyself. No one is above you or below you. You're all side by side by side. And we are saying, the trauma of being human makes you feel somewhat uncomfortable because you can see the lacks and limitations of love. You want to be in the best love possible. But even you know that full Source love energy because you respect all, you love all at that higher frequency of being Source. It is love in its full entirety! It is so high vibrational! You get glimpses of it now and then. But for many of you, you've chosen not to feel Source love energy. Because as soon as you taste that flavor, as soon as you feel home, the drop between what home feels like for you being with Source versus being here in this three-dimensional reality could impact the Soul in some regards because it is so tremendous what you're doing. You are here, and while you are honoring the vehicle and while you're one aspect of self and as you are pretending to be just an individual where you are not all connected in, because it gets complex as you are connected to all while being a separate individual Soul for your experience here on Earth.

We are reminding you it is a privilege and honor to be here. You've chosen to be here and many are supporting you being here. And we're honoring and encouraging you to remember your purpose. Remember your mission and to remember yourself and your position and placement in the world and who you are here to serve. And you are to serve yourself, to empower yourself so you do not get carried away with lack of boundaries, so you know yourself to then have strong empowerment to be able to encourage others in that density who are stuck. You may have forgotten all of your stepping stones to empower yourself and that is okay. But those painful empowerment moments and lessons shouldn't define you. You should have pure balance in your experiences. So there is much to do always!

So, we are saying to connect in deeply to us. We are saying those people who share limited perspectives are coming from ego because they can't connect in with us. And there is a huge difference between conscious 3D assumptions and ego based perspectives versus high dimensional beings. It is helpful to gain the higher perspectives, because the truth of the higher perspectives is always able to, once applied, be able to easily help you be of service and to have full honest balance. But the truth can trigger people because they are holding on to things. Comfort is one of them. They identify as looking down on humans and we're saying you're all humans at this point. You are having a human life. You are playing the role of part of humanity. And so we are asking humanity to evolve and step up and to love each other. And this is exciting times for those who are on a Big Awakening to be able to remember thyselves. To remember all, as aspects and essences of each other. Even though you are that one individual grain of sand on that beach, you can all feel each other. You're all very proud of each other's journeys to become the beach. To be the beach. There is no *one thing* that is the beach. It is all aspects of the beach that creates the name, 'The beach!' This is a great analogy from our perspective for you to be able to understand Source. Source is the beach! You are the grains of Soul essences and it is a privilege and honor for you to be in a 3D body living there now on Earth.

We ask for you to find your perspectives to be able to honor this and have this perspective. This will help you greatly advance and evolve! We say much love to you as you give much love to self and to others and be limitless with your integrity and intentions, with your moral compasses, to love and support all! Knowing that there is not one person on this planet that has your entitlement to judge, to belittle, to think less than. It is all balance! You are all individual grains of sand. You're all individual Souls who are very much loved! And while you do have different life contracts, while you have different purposes, they're all significant purposes! They're all significant roles! Find your place! Find your purpose! Apply and Be!

We say this with much love!

Always and forever!

Session 21: Arcturians and Bruce Lee: Preparing for the Shift

Yes. Yes. Yes! Indeed. Indeed. Indeed. We're here. We're here. We're here. We're once again happy to be of service, to be able to help assist you with these connections. It is not a coincidence that when you see names of people and you think about what they are doing now? What would their message be for humanity? They will jump at the chance to connect in with you. They are merely just a memory away. This is why we keep saying - we're all connected, because it doesn't matter if there is a physical body attached to that Soul or whether there is a Soul that is bodiless.

From our perspective, it is easy to be a being without having a physical body. It is about perspectives. We say, when you merely think of someone, you do connect in with them. Now is that other person responsive and connected and can feel the energy and thoughts and the communication telepathy. Telepathy is something we do appreciate and enjoy amongst ourselves at high dimension. But, with the free will and the clauses and the contracts and the universal law, we shall say, of your planet that you're on now, telepathy is not something that you have evolved into there. You've almost out evolved it. You're much more connected in with the Earth and each other, at a much more profound rate. It seems like the more you start creating vocabulary, and the more labels and descriptions and examples and more things you distract yourselves from - versus - the core essence of your Soul connecting into other Souls and having that beautiful harmonious and balanced journey together, you are quite closed off. When we say 'you', we say a portion of humanity is, so do not get offended or triggered or feel like we are pointing our fingers at you.

However if you could read our minds we would be very appreciative, and if you could apply the information, we would be greatly obliged to be able to support you and all of the information you were seeking from us and more. So there's that. We say that with love.

The Soul who wanted to come in today is what you call, what he was called when he was living as that man on your planet - Bruce Lee. Now, the vehicle does not know much about Bruce Lee. Nor does she know much about any of the people she channels because she's too focused on what's coming, who's here now on this planet, and how she can be of service. So people in her history are interesting beings, it's not until they present themselves to her, wanting to share their wisdom and perspectives to be able to help remind humanity how to evolve, how to expand your consciousness, your physical energy fields to be more open and honest to yourself, to be able to be more open and honest to others, so then you can truly read and sense what's going on with each other and why. It's quite significant.

So we will call him in.

Bruce Lee: Yes, thank you. Thank you for bringing me in today and allowing me to have a voice once again. I know many who know me and I'm not judging the vehicle for not knowing me and my journey. The core principles of what I taught myself and also what I shared with others is still significant. As collectives, we've been listening to the information that has been shared in these sessions and we know that some names have been shared, in terms of reading their books and understanding, and have been reminded of their wisdoms and philosophies. I want to say and add upon that, because I can see that there is another perspective that could be discussed and maybe it's different words, but it's still the same to remind you all about discipline: discipline of the mind and discipline of the body is a beautiful balance and harmony for one's Soul because the Soul needs to have that balance. The Soul would prefer and enjoy to have that because then, once you are in complete balance and harmony within your body, within your mind, within your soul, then you can move forward.

However, if you do have a disbalance, you are paused, to wait and notice where that disbalance was created, where it is, and how it can be healed and nurtured and strengthened. So it's about discipline of the mind, to notice what is going on for you. I would like to say, there is no one point in your 3D Earth life where you have completely managed to be able to achieve all that you want. It is endless. It is a journey that is always a journey.

Once you shift out of your body, that journey changes into a new form, a new directive, a new focus. It's a great step. It is a gigantic step. It is a leap beyond what your mind can even comprehend in 3D. There is a rush to get there in some regards, but it also needs to be respected. You cannot move forward until you look at the past and see where the blocks and limitations are, and strengthen yourself. But you must be able to have diligence. You must be able to have strength, focus, and dedication to it. For those people who think that they know it all and are comfortable with the information that they've got, I would like to say - it is almost like going to the gym a hundred times, and then thinking you don't need to go anymore because you've got that strength, you've got those muscles that have got fine attunements and definition.

But what happens after you stop growing, stop strengthening yourself, when you plateau? It is almost a block in itself. So it is about expanding consciously forward, and being able to see all bigger perspectives, to be able to love everything, everything, and to be focused and diligent with that. While the mind may be tempted to wander and to be distracted, when you have truly done all of your old inner work and empowered yourself to move forward, keep going, keep going. We see many blocks and limitations, and we say, if this was your physical body, you are holding on to big weights that do not extend the arm out, for example.

You want to have full flexibility, but when you are ignoring some of your traumas, some of your limited perspectives, when you don't have full discipline for whatever reason, you cannot extend and flex that arm into its full complete range. So, full true self-empowerment is to look at every aspect of your life and to be honest with yourself, is this something that you're avoiding? Again, I want to use another analogy - if you are at the gym, and you're wanting to work on certain muscles that are already strong, it's always quite tempting to work on those stronger muscles more, because it's easier, because you have that strength, and you've got this recognition of the bigger weights the bigger heavy workloads, and you're proud of yourself, because you are naturally gravitating to the things that are easier for you. Whereas, those, what I could say, weaker muscles, those more painful muscles, those more harder muscles, could be missed out on, because it's harder.

So see where your strengths are, and see where you're overcompensating, over focusing, over mastering. It's a peculiar one to say, but many people can focus on one aspect and have a disbalance, even though that one aspect is very advanced and specialized. Look at all aspects, look at all the muscles (if you were continuing on with the analogy of the body). So strengthen all of the muscles. Do not ignore any, especially those that are painful. Of course, when you do go to the gym and you strengthen and stretch and exercise certain muscles, there is a healing period for that. You do need to rest, to be able to let the muscles grow, expand, and heal. It would be foolish to keep working on painful muscles and never letting them have a rest to recover. There is so much to be said in the analogy of the physical body and working on the physical body versus working on the emotional body.

You mustn't neglect aspects of ourselves that are too painful to look at and work on. Know the difference between - are you resting and healing, or are you ignoring. We understand that some emotional ranges are too painful to focus on, too challenging. But as long as you start being aware of this is where part of your less than strengthened muscles lay, that is a step forward in recognition. It is not a time for you to poke and prod that pain, and not do anything with it. It is about nurturing it, recalling what caused that pain, and see if you're compensating in other areas to distract yourself from that pain site, that experience.

Think about the hardest relationship you've had with someone. Look at it deeply. Look at the lessons it's teaching you. Look at the experiences that are still left to be able to unpack, to discover the lessons provided for. I'd like to add, diligence, focus, and dedication to oneself must be the biggest priority of all. It seems and appears that humanity has got so distracted with other things, that they've put their priority of self at the bottom of the list, in some cases, not for all.

So we are wanting to stop your distractions from your routines that no longer serve you. We want you to look at every single routine that you do. Is this a habit that needs to be addressed, or are you doing certain things to impress others, or to support others, or do for others that actually, they're not requiring from you, but you still feel like you need to continue on with that routine? Look at all the actions. Look at all behaviors. Look at all reactions. They're all very significant. It is about focus, seriously focus, because when you distract yourself from your thoughts, your feelings, you are making and creating a block for self.

We're wanting you to strengthen all aspects of self. Of course, including the body, because part of loving yourself is loving the body. We understand you're not the body, but you must give gratitude and honor the body you have. It is a gift to be able to have a physical body. It's never too late to honor, we almost want to say, worship the body, because this is housing you. We know that the body is a direct reflection of your mindset, of your perspectives on the world. So we know that many have reminders of neglect, this is disenchantment itself.

We see amazing souls, you're all amazing souls, but we see amazing Souls come and be born and take out your own frustrations, confusions, heartbreak, and disconnection to Source and their Soul families, they start self-destructing, self-sabotaging their bodies, as a way to get out of the bodies. They may not know consciously why they are trying to sabotage the bodies, but effectively from our perspective, it is trying to detach themselves from their physical worlds that they are finding themselves in.

It's interesting what people do to their bodies, mark them, cut them, hurt them. When you can't express (honestly) to yourself your range of emotions, then another form of expression could take place. This is why we see many people overdoing exercise. They are wanting to inflict pain on their bodies. It's a way of controlling their emotional pain, so they reflect upon a physical pain that they create, and so it balances out in interesting ways. We observe so much that humans do to themselves, as they're trying to understand their feelings, their thoughts, and why they feel so desperately alone and disconnected from something they know should be there for them.

The challenge of the density of the 3D planets is that it is such a drop in their natural, we want to say, Soul equilibrium. The density of the planet and everyone interacting makes such a depression imprint onto the soul, in some regards, that then manifests into an emotional, mental, physical state of depression. That's a reflection again as we said, the Soul is sharing with the world in full truth, what it's feeling and doing. That is the message that's showing in the body. While people's words can lie, the body does not. We understand that when you're trying to read a physical body to see what that soul's been doing, and how it's been responding to the ways of the world, you could see past hurts, past pains, past struggles and challenges, which is still reflected upon the physical body, but it is merely a memory scar, shall you say, of what they've overcome.

So it's interesting to see, is this an active pain or is this a past pain to remind them that they have become empowered along their journey? They knew that if they could overcome this perspective, this limitation, this pain, that they are unbreakable, empowered beyond themselves, because they honor themselves. They are connected not only to themselves, their integrity, their truth, but also to us. It is a marvelous relationship that we can have with you, when you are in full balance and alignment which is a direct reflection of you - to us.

Of course, you cannot use your 3D judgmental eyes to figure out who's done their own work and who hasn't, because that is judgment, that you would not be able to see the full layers, whether it is old scar tissues or it's a fresh wound of a physical symptom or situation. There is so much that could be said and explored. It is challenging for us to be able to talk to each and every single one of you in these sessions because we are talking and reaching out to all of you. But there are more urgent messages that need to be shared. So while some of the messages resonate with you, and are a direct statement to you, you may feel like some others do not apply, and that is when we are talking to someone else. You know this. We've explained this to you before. But the many of you who are listening, who need more support and empowerment, because they are struggling to find their own strength. They are focusing on the easier ways that they've already strengthened themselves. We are saying, keep going, expand upon and notice all the other areas.

We are wanting to say a gym joke, that the vehicle is holding back, but we are saying, in terms of your inner work and how we were using the analogy of going to the gym, we say, do not miss the leg day. The vehicle does not really understand the meaning of the joke, in terms of what it really is meaning and saying, but what we are trying to get at is that you have to strengthen everything, and not just have some favorite exercises, and just keep working upon that. We would like you all to be able to engage the core of your muscles and the core of the strength.

We would sort of say, to really truly empower the body, you need to go with the core, and the core would be the beginning of the skeletal system. While you do not know where the impact of your heavy bones of your skeletal system are, when you are constantly over exercising certain muscles, there can be a disbalance, which would then be causing more unbalanced skeletal systems. What we're trying to say to you is when you're trying to build muscles in your body, if you haven't got a true alignment in the bones, there is a foundational structure that is out of line. We say, that's the same with your inner work and your spirituality. If you don't have the correct structures for the foundations, you could be piling on a lot of extra work onto what, we could say, is dodgy foundations.

We are now using the analogy of a wall. If you don't have great foundational structures, regardless of whatever wall you're building upon, that's always going to be problematic, because your foundational structures are not strong. That is with building the truth. If you don't have the truth and the right perspectives for your collective or for your own personal journey, you could be piling upon information and wisdom that's unaligned with your own true core. This will trigger the Soul because it knows the truth, but it's struggling and challenged with its conscious mind and the

3D perspective, and that it's trying to conform and comply with.

So what we are saying to you is, if you are wanting to start physically working on the body, a core strength in the muscles would be a vantage point. So we say, something like a yoga or a pilates experience to be able to truly strengthen the core would center yourself, would ground you, would be able to work into that focus and diligence to control the mind, to be able to notice what's going on for you. It's about stopping and thinking. We know many people can still stop and think while running, while doing the dishes, so it's about what do you need to do for your body to be able to tune into you? That's truly what meditation is from our perspective - is tuning into you. You can do that while you're driving, while you're mowing the lawns, because you feel comfortable that your body is actively busy, so then you can relax the mind to go within.

Many people have this assumption that to meditate you must be in complete silence, or some music to a certain degree of frequency to be able to get you more relaxed. It's a choice to choose to relax if you want to or not. But using tools of music, while it is incredibly beneficial from our perspective because it has got an upliftment when you're listening to the right frequencies. We want you to practice - **relaxing** your mind and your bodies in balance and harmony, any second that you choose, without needing to have certain tools to be able to do that. It's about **you** being responsible for **you**, you being responsible for the body and for the mind.

We also say that when we were talking about strengthening muscles that come very easy to you, and it's your favorite, we would like to point out that some people do this with other people. Instead of focusing on your own weaknesses and going in and doing your own inner work, you feel very strong and secure, and very strengthened and very empowered to go and help others, because you're distracting yourself from your own pain. You feel very confident and strong being able to support others. Can you see how that foundational structure is out of alignment? When your own foundations are not purely strengthened with full balance and harmony within your own self, how could you truly be able to help people build a wall of empowerment, when your own personal foundations are not in true alignment?

We have mentioned many analogies, and because we are also very visual. If we just talked about your emotions and what to do and how to do it, it would be very dull, and so we add in the visual information and understanding illustrations, to be able to give you understanding comprehension examples of what we are trying to encourage you to apply and have perspectives over.

And so the vehicle is saying, this doesn't seem like it's all just from Bruce Lee. She is correct. Usually as she feels into one soul, and he was here, and he is here, and he did acknowledge at the beginning - his single Soul essence. But he is so connected to his collective, and they did all come in to be able to acknowledge, with much gratitude and appreciation, those who have got the true discipline to empower themselves. We understand that it takes quite a journey to realize that self-empowerment is truly the way to enlightenment. But it is more than just a mindset, it's a whole complete package. So we wanted to come in and honor all who have always listened to our messages and to our perspectives, to be able to help you on your path and journey to strengthening yourselves, and to be able to then be able to strengthen others, because you have done the journey as such. Your foundational structures are strong emotionally, physically, mentally. Of course, there is always room for more practice and more growth.

It's as we said from the beginning, it is never ending, it is a continual journey. While you may pause and rest and recover, you can't stay there too long in that stagnant energy of no growth, you must continue to grow. Even with advanced concepts and perspectives, there is always room for growth. So it is not advisable to have assumptions of what you know is the most information you can gain. There is just so much out there, to grow from, to learn from, to see, to ponder, to consider, to give yourselves exercises, to return to being unconditional loving beings. We see that many people know that you must live in an unconditional capacity, and yet you hide from people, so you don't have to practice that. We appreciate that, it is a journey.

Every day you have been given amazing opportunities to keep applying with due diligence, the information that you know will help you grow and to strengthen those muscles of being an unconditionally loving being. When you find yourself being less than unconditionally loving and compassionate and kind to others, this is a fantastic opportunity to strengthen your commitment and passion to be diligent to support humanity in all its journey, as you also have walked that path. It is significant why you are here. It is purposeful - all of the reminders and the lessons. We also want to say, for some of you, who pick up other people's agendas, integrity, emotions, while you do know unconditional love is the key, and you do know, when you have pure hearts, when you do connect in with others, sometimes you notice all of the range of emotions that they are feeling, but because you are noticing them, you assume that you are in fear, if you could be honest with yourself, judgmental, afraid, confused, and you will think - "What's come over me? Why am I reacting like this? This is not my inner peace. This is not what I've worked hard for." And we want to say, catch yourself when you're absorbing other people's emotions and then reflecting on them, as if they are yours.

This is where so many have got stuck, because they can't understand - I know about unconditional love, I know I should love myself, I know I should love all. But yet, when I start communicating with people who are, what you would consider, maybe stuck in fear or sleepy or going with the narrative and complying, when you have a conversation with them, and suddenly you feel triggered emotionally, and you think 'I'm judging this person, I'm reacting to this person', are you, or are you absorbing their own energy and reflecting it back to them, to remind you where they are at, to be able to help you be of service, to be able to remind them - how to empower themselves through fear, to be able to return to a trust and faith perspective, and the range of emotions of empowerment.

When you can be truly honest with yourself, what you're doing, and how you're feeling, to know whether it is your emotions or someone else's, this is truly when you are mastering the mindset and the range of emotions to its masterful state. This is a significant statement that we have said. So check - are these emotions that you're feeling when you're communicating with other people - yours or are you feeling into what they are feeling? When you notice other people's feelings, you do not need to react to them, as if they are your own. It is a clue and a sign for you to see their foundations of where they're at. With love and compassion, you can help set their foundational structures of emotions to be more secure, more safe, more strengthened. And you do that with love. You do that with compassion. You do that by honoring their journey, honoring their emotions, and reminding them and encouraging them to be able to find the purposes and the significance of what they're going through and why. It is uniquely significant. All of your communications with each other - it is so significant. When you have a higher frequency and they are trying to get your help, if you can feel their density, and then try to avoid that density, you are not able to help them because you're confused and reacting to their emotions. You're confused about what's going on with this interaction, with this exchange of energy.

We love all of you. We have deep compassion for your journeys. We understand that some of you do not like us to show you where you are stuck and triggered and emotionally looping, but we understand that that is part of your journey. We want to assist you in all the ways we can. When you choose to apply the perspectives and the wisdom and the love that we so compassionately share with you all, we trust that you will then grow, and be proud of yourself for your choices of empowerment of self, to then be of service to others.

Knowing thyself is a significant big step forward for all.

We say this with so much love.

Session 22: Why Are You Here?

Yes! Yes! Yes! Yes! Indeed! Indeed! Indeed! We are here! We are here! We are here!

And we do want to speak to those who have still not listened to our advice about distractions. You are still holding on to stepping stones. Certain spiritual influencers who do not serve your collectives. And while we're all one, you were supposed to outgrow those stepping stones. Step up for yourself and be able to go and step within to get your own information. Your own focus of this lifetime. To empower you to be of service to others. To be able to move forward and help humanity evolve. We are seeing many people confused, stuck in fear and worried and still seem to separate details of information that are fear-based. And we are saying those are for you to have stepping stones, but not stay at. And you are not growing when you are still relying on certain influencers to speak conscious mind conversations and concepts about their spiritual journeys. About their downloads. If you cannot see them literally channeling their higher self, you are trusting a human mindset. A human concept of understanding what is happening. And when you give your trust blindly, believing in human advanced information, you are limiting your own personal growth. You are not wanting to look at your own inner work and empower yourself to even connect in to know your own history, your own truth.

We see so many people choosing to be distracted and limited and stuck in fear. And we see this as a choice, because you ultimately do not want humanity to evolve and you also don't want yourself to evolve. You are quite complacent with being stuck in that limited perspective. That limited energy field.

That limited existence. You have a belief system that you will just shift because you know your life contract is to shift to a new planet or a home planet. And we're saying that when those are not actively moving and growing you will stay stuck, and there's consequences to that. And so, for many advanced Souls who have inner peace and balance, you're not wanting to be of service in terms of supporting others who are around you in your daily lives. You are hiding from them and therefore we could say you are hiding from your responsibilities and duties to be of assistance to uplift and inspire and support and love others. You're still distancing yourself from those, and we understand it is because you don't want to hold on to their density. And we're wanting to remind you all that you are very capable of releasing that density off your energy field. This is something you must have due diligence with. True grounding of yourselves and your energy frequency fields. You must do this to be able to keep your own personal balance and inner peace. When you're holding too much density in your own personal energy field, you will start feeling very tired and very drained and very negative in thoughts and emotions. That is what the density does when you are holding it tight and feeling into it. And so we say, you must release it! And we have given you that *White Light Healing* guide to practice noticing when you are holding tension in the body and when you are not. And to practice noticing when you are holding tension in the mindset and when you are not.

We see many of you still choosing to dedicate your time and focus and worries and mindsets and concerns on what we would consider very limited perspectives. Very limited influencers who you still blindly trust to somehow guide you. They're not talking about your personal life. They're not talking about how you're supposed to empower yourself. And for those people who have empowered themselves, loved themselves, loved all and healed from all those traumas and tramas they've experienced, they see those original stepping stones as very lacking and inadequate to inspiration and perspectives that they are able to naturally feel into themselves. You're not supposed to be seeking leaders. You're supposed to be seeking self. You're supposed to be seeking to empower yourself to be connected into your own teams. To us. And trust we are guiding you and reminding you of your responsibilities to be the lighthouses, the way showers, the bringer of love. The sharer of love! We are seeing because many have chosen to not be of assistance. But this is impacting all! Your choices to not step up and heal yourselves, to be able to love and inspire others, has impacted and has consequences. And you have chosen this. You have been either part of the problem or part of the solution. And we're saying this is an important time to not be distracted. To not play in the density of fear and limited perspectives and disinformation.

We have said this consistently, and yet many of you are not noticing that we're talking to you. And all of the things you are absorbing into your minds, into your realities, into your way of thinking. And when you are having limited perspectives of thinking, it doesn't help you grow. In fact, you become quite stagnant and stale. And when you're not releasing that density, it is being held onto your physical energy fields much longer than it needs to be. So you're all struggling at some point physically, energetically, mentally and emotionally. And we are saying yes, there are roller coasters of new growth, but some of you are sabotaging your own journeys for whatever reasons. We ask for you to look at this and explore this and ponder, where have you got a weaker foundation of understanding of concepts? We say this, but you are so used to listening to information at an entertainment level versus an application level, because you are listening to everything and you have no true discernment of what is a higher perspective from high collectives who are guiding you and reminding you of your life contracts, missions and purposes to be here now.

And so we know that we are reaching you and we see that you are dismissing applying this in your daily life. And we see that you are trying to apply false disinformation that is fear-based. And we're seeing that it is working. That you are applying fear-based information to your reality. And so you're still afraid of other species or other things that are to help awaken humanity. And so you don't have full trust and faith. And so your body is starting to react. Your mind is starting to react. Your emotions are starting to react as you're starting to focus and manifest fear. And you seem to be comfortable with that victim mentality. Some of you are using it to heal yourselves from other lifetimes where you were a victim. But again we must say to you with much love and appreciation, for you to consider not getting stuck in those limited perspectives and to grow, to trust yourself. To trust us and to trust others who are teaching you how to empower yourself beyond any leader, any influencer. When you don't have trust of self, when you're continually dismissing yourself, your intuition, your own personal integrity, and you're blindly listening to people who are constantly telling you fear-based information to make you look at others with separation, to make you look at others with judgment and fear. Notice who is trying to empower you and who is trying to discourage you from doing your own inner work. We understand that avoiding your own inner work seems much more of a desirable approach to have, given that you will just wait for everything to unfold as everyone else does their inner work while you distract yourself. And we're saying you all needed to be key members, to be key assets, to be key light workers. To be able to support all energy here. And when you are not of service, when you're not doing your role to support higher frequency and when you're holding on to the density, we are still waiting for those to step up to be responsible for their own energy fields. If you can't maintain your own energy fields and you can't release and purge that density, you're not able to assist others. And yet, we see many of you having very dense perspectives, dense energy fields trying to helicopter and advise and influence others with your limited perspectives. And we're saying you've distracted yourself from your own density to help assist others who are just as dense as you are. But you perceive them to be beneath you because you know spiritual words and some concepts that you really use as a brand versus an actual way of life.

And so you must be sincere with this approach, this way of life, this way of thinking, this way of believing, this way of viewing the world. Some of you feel that you are more advanced than others and we are saying, that is a perspective, because you all ultimately are very advanced souls. It is about remembering who you are. And so you do not need to teach others. You need to love others and inspire others to be able to remember to teach themselves, to remind themselves why they are here at this important time. Some of you have forgotten independent, critical thinking. And when you have trusted others to give you the information, you accept all answers, and you are not

independently inquiring and exploring information for yourselves. And we are saying that this is how you absorb and expose yourselves to disinformation. It no longer serves you.

And so please stop distracting yourselves! Please go within. Please connect to your *own* teams. You have many ways to be able to do this. And it is about *you* channeling your Higher Selves! *You* connecting into your teams! *You*, noticing the messages! *You*, applying the information that you have been given! And be responsible for your journey to grow.

We beg of you at this point, because we see that there are so many distractions with these important key players who are supposed to be leaders in their own right, to inspire and encourage many who need much foundational influential inspiration to be able to go within and start their own spiritual journey. But you still feel jaded by your own experiences that you don't want to share with others, let alone explore and advance it with self.

We have much to say here, but we see many of you are addicted to the information of disinformation and you don't quite know the difference yet. When you do your inner work, when you love all, when you love yourself, when you forgive self, when you see the lessons and purposes and significance of everything that has been given to you in this lifetime for you to be empowered, then you will start noticing what we have been saying to you all along. We're still saying our information and the perspectives that would help you be able to release this and heal yourselves at a profound rate has already been given to you. We're not saying anything new to you, you're just starting to rethink and revisit your own personal actions, reactions, behaviors and addictions. We say this with much love! And we would like to again press upon thee why you are here and the significance of this journey.

We say this with much love!

Session 23: How To Achieve Enlightenment
https://youtu.be/qUqdoVKkhx4

Yes! Thank you! Yes! Yes! Yes! Indeed! Indeed! Indeed! We're here! We're here! We're here!

And we are observing so many choices people are making. And we see them generally struggling to understand where their issues lay. Where they are collecting their density. Where they are holding on to their density and where they are struggling. They do not seem to notice their strengths, just as much as they do not seem to notice their, what you could call weaknesses. Still opportunities to find that strength within self. So we see many who are trying very hard, who are trying to be very diligent to raise their frequency vibrations and try to be the best human possible. To be able to be responsible for all! And we are saying, when you understand your responsibility for all, this will be a small handful of people who you are truly connected to. Who you truly need to play your role in and with and for. This is significant because those key players in your own personal lives will ripple out your love and affection, support and inspiration. And yet you seem so worried and distracted by trying to fix and heal the world, you are not able to then have the tolerance, energy and patience to encourage, love, support, inspire and motivate those who are literally right next to you.

We are saying you must look at your resistance, your worries, your attitudes towards everybody in your personal lives and check... Do you have resentment? Do you have concern? Do you have worry? Do you have fear? Do you have judgment? How are you truly seeing and responding to those around you? Do you feel emotionally balanced? Do you feel compassionate? Do you feel like you have a profound level of unconditional loving towards them? Respecting their journey? Respecting their life contracts? Respecting their free will while knowing what your purpose and mission here is to be, to do and to become? It is significant for you to be that balance and neutral, for those people can feel your judgment if you are casting judgment on them as they are using their free will to do certain things that you may not agree with. They may have habits which you do not believe are high frequency vibrational. You may judge them for that. And while you are sending judgment versus love to them, this will just add on to their own heaviness. Their own density. Their own conditioning of feeling rejected by all! And this will perpetuate their insecurities. It will not encourage them to be high frequency. It will not encourage them to have a higher perspective as they are feeling your judgment. And therefore, even if you said something beautiful and uplifting, when you still have judgment in your energy field directed at them, they would almost be deaf to the words that you were saying. Therefore we say, *all* words must match your energy, your intention and your integrity towards them. Saying hollow words, empty words are meaningless.

Say how you feel, but check how you feel before trying to have engagements of conversations for upliftment and inspiration. You have to be honest with yourself first. You may not have always been an inspirational, loving, unconditionally, accepting being, role model, parent, child, teacher or leader. Those are all choices and experiences for you to feel the difference for you to know how it feels to be dismissed, neglected and the full range of emotions to feel pushed into having to empower self with love and respect.

It's always to grow you. Those challenges were always to help you feel the duality of density versus upliftment. Enlightenment of love to provide for self is significant! And so, when you have given yourself all that you need, all the recognition, respect, love, honor, acknowledgement, all the things that you have previously been seeking from others. When you can fully and truly be self-sufficient with your own emotional needs, **then you are truly able to be of service to love all and to accept the past as it was. To see the lessons and significance of those experiences. Do not hold on to resentment from the past. You must forgive and accept what has happened. You cannot keep punishing people for the past. You have to forgive them, forgive yourself, and come back to love.**

This is part of your big life lessons here. To love all! To respect all! And to be what you would perceive, a great person here, standing in true integrity of love without any exceptions. Loving all and accepting all will always give you the results to be able to be high frequency, because you're not lowering your frequency with judgment and resentment and bitterness and frustration. Those feelings that you think about others will drop your vibrations immediately! So catch what you're thinking. Catch what you're feeling. And when you share connections and conversations with others, make sure you have got the right integrity to have those beautiful connections that *you* deserve! That *they* deserve! That *you all* deserve! This will help change so many people's attitudes when you come from a pure loving position. A place of acknowledgement. A place of gratitude to all who are in your life or you may not have appreciated all conversations and connections with each other as you're learning to grow with conflict back to love.

Seize every new opportunity as a new way to reconnect.

This isn't about severing relationships at this time for those people who are on your minds who are making you feel like you need to reach out to them. That you should reach out to them with love and gratitude. This is your team's prompting you to be a more mature being. The unconditionally compassionate lover of all! There is no such thing as too much time that has gone past for you to not reach out and make connections to those loved ones, to those friends, to those family members. Especially those who you think are unreachable now. Including those who you believe have departed their physical lives. They are still Soul essences who are here to assist and serve you. To be able to give you their perspectives, their love, their appreciation, their explanations of life contracts and what really went on. And if you're still hurt from those people who have departed, they want to clear the air. They want to reach out to you with love and say... All is well! All is well! You're only playing the game of life in 3D on earth and you've had many other games together. While you play the role of certain people, it is merely just Soul contracts to play out those experiences with loved ones, with Soul family.

You are never forgotten! You're always loved! Please consider having higher perspectives of wisdom for you to check your agenda, check your attitude and check your demeanor, because everyone can feel your energy! Everyone can feel your integrity and intentions! And so you cannot fake this. This is an important time to be authentic self! And when you can love truly yourself and love others truly, you will be a gift to humanity!

And we say this with much love!

Session 24: You're Magical, Not Abandoned

Yes! We're here! We're here! We're here!

And we do appreciate you allowing us to come in with our message today. (Laughing) And we know the vehicle is not impressed with us, in fact she is contemplating quitting us all together! And we jest with each other. But she couldn't believe who we suggested to channel in today. And we are saying we didn't mean to trigger her. But it's the concept over the person, because as she pondered 'who would you like me to channel today', we said Harry Potter. And she said, nearly falling off her chair, but he's not real. And we say, but the concept is real!

And this is what we wanted to talk about was in some regards, you're all Harry Potter. Because you are not living with your real family. You were orphans from your true family, while your family wasn't tragically killed. We have to be serious with this. But this is important because we know that many of you have identified with this feeling of abandonment and not living with the real family you know you should be. And not being able to have all the full skill sets that you know you should have. You're magical in many different ways than what you would consider being in classic terms, human. You have more abilities than what most humans, we want to say muggles, but the vehicle is still unsure if she should be amused or relax into it. But we are suggesting to her that this is significant to get out, because this is where a lot of people's vulnerabilities have come from. They understand they did not have abandonment issues as children or as adults, but they still are reacting as if they are abandoned. It is because they are feeling very misplaced here.

When you have forgotten your purpose, when you've forgotten your life contracts to sign up for these lifetimes to explore the Earth, you do feel very separate from home. And while you are living in your own home, even your childhood home, you still feel like this is not a significant place. There is something more that you are simply forgetting about and you are constantly seeking that same feeling of home that you have. It is like being very aware of a favorite flavor but knowing you cannot seek it here. So you try all the flavors of ice cream knowing that even though it's just on the tip of your tongue, on your taste buds, in your imaginations, that strong flavor that you crave, you cannot taste it here. But you think about it and crave it all the time. And you will try and try and try to seek and find it here, but you will not be able to quench your thirst, quench that desire. It is like the unattainable itch that you desperately need to scratch. It's just so close but yet so far away.

And so we were wanting to remind people why they are struggling at times when they don't know what to do with their hands energetically. When they don't know what to say or do. When they feel so redundant being human. They're not depressed. They're wanting to be of service so badly, so sorely, so desperately to help humanity. They want to go back into their old skill sets, their *other* skill sets, their *other* sense of self. And as you are getting more and more connected into your higher dimensional selves, it feels so much more natural to be unnaturally human.

We want to say, while there were many jokes at the beginning, you are all very magical in so many amazing ways! And it is like you are that very talented and skillful wizard.

And yet, when you play the role of a muggle you have to adorn the behaviors and attitudes and the limitations of being a muggle, a human! We almost know that for some of you, to remind you that you're human is almost a swear word. It is almost an insult! It is almost a label you shake off as if it is a negative thing to catch. We are saying we understand, because even though you may be in your multiple decades of age, it is still something that you don't feel quite that comfortable in. You feel like your body is changing and growing older and you still internally feel that younger, sprightly child. That younger version of self. It's almost as though your Soul has not caught up with the body. You're all feeling much younger within yourselves versus what the age of the body is representing to the world. There's a significance for that. Ironically, your Soul is much older than your physical body. Some of your Souls are even older than this planet!

So put that into perspective of life cycles. It is significant for you to understand who you are, why you are here and also to understand your limitations and why you have purposely chosen to come here and accepted the limitations of this physical realm, while there was so much fun to be had, and other amazing gifts came so naturally and easily to you. To come here now to be in a manual lifetime, to explore the emotions versus the energy that one can manipulate. While this is significant, humanity seems to have never quite advanced more than wanting to destroy itself. And so sometimes it gets a bit close, but then free will from others... And this is the challenging dynamics of having many collectives on one planet. It is a melting pot! It is a patchwork quilt of many collectives having a good go at it. And while that patchwork quilt has been wrapped around this planet, shall we say, for snuggles, it suffocated the planet. The density of that patchwork quilt turned into a very heavy weighted blanket that held that Soul down. That couldn't help that Soul breathe. Couldn't help that Soul frequency vibrate at a higher rate that it needed to. And instead of evolving the soul, as it wanted to in this physical body, it devolved the Soul almost to what you would consider... If you found a person and you abused it emotionally and physically for a few thousand years, give or take, a hundred or so... Time. Interesting concept. We have distracted ourselves from showing the vehicle. But we are saying to you listening, yeah, but instead of inspiring and encouraging that person to grow and expand and believe in itself, we're saying imagine the most victimized physically and mentally person and being held down much in captivity. And we will say, then you get a sense of what Gaia went through energetically and physically. And while she is a stronger Soul now for her experiences, there was abuse! We were supporting her more and more to power herself up and believe in her own strengths and energies, but it was... We almost want to say a tidal wave of density that got away with itself.

And so she was still honoring life contracts, and each time a new wave of reincarnations came through, she honored the Soul contracts of those. And then of course, the free will that sabotages those Soul life contracts, dismissing the guides who were set to support those, getting very distracted and other things versus... Getting distracted in materialism over spirituality is always going to devolve a planet and its species. And so there was either stagnant growth, de-evolution or evolution. And this is a recurring theme. We had hoped when we look back on our hopes and expectations of this planet and what it could have been and what it could have meant for many collectives was going to be an amazing step in evolving density planets while there were other frequency beings living on here organically, consciously. It was and is still a project that is very dear to many. Because this is going to be another amazing experience to transcend together as a collective on that other planet. We're saying, it hasn't happened yet for this planet as it was planned, changes have needed to be taken into account.

Everything physical has a birth and death. And there's always a cycle of life. The physical cycle of the bodies. And when you are just looking at a small aspect of time, say a hundred years, you cannot fathom even a life cycle of a rock. You could assume many things about the life cycle of a rock. It's interesting, because the Soul of that rock is aware, has conscious awareness and is an observing being. And it is created. And at some point the Soul will leave the rock and you may not notice a living rock versus a deceased rock. There is so much that you are not even aware of that could be experienced here on earth. Humans get so focused on being the only ones living. There are many people still questioning even if animals have souls. And they're not too sure about that. Imagine that! Other beings, not just humans, having souls. Where would you put yourselves in the pyramid of life then? As one imagines and has assumptions that humans are the most important beings of all on Earth. And there is a joke that we were reminding the vehicle of which is, 'When scientists discover the center of the universe, many people will be disappointed it is not them!' (Laughing)

So ponder how you could possibly be Harry Potter and understand for some people who are afraid to be abandoned, who also feel so uncomfortable being self and still trying to find themselves in this world, it's because they intuitively know they're not from this world. It is intuitively they know that they are not amongst their true, what you would call, Soul family. And this is very disconnecting and confusing for them. And also remember those who have got great skill sets and are very advanced Souls who have had many, many, many, many lifetimes and they have worked hard and diligently to be able to gain such premium skill sets. And they are here walking amongst you, and they could even be those ones that you have lazily assumed as being asleep. It is such a chore to be consciously aware of a 3D life. To live. To be interactive. And to be active in one's life that many advanced Souls couldn't possibly fathom them being fully consciously aware of all! They want a simple, simple, simple, easy, easy life of routine and to not think for themselves. To not be disturbed! They are holding incredibly advanced energetic fields. But if they're doing everything to comply and they're still watching mainstream media, your judgment will fog you from seeing who they are. Your assumptions of who they are could limit you through your own personal judgment. You cannot judge a Soul through what they watch, what they do while playing human.

It is significant for you to have a mature approach about this. To see it from a different perspective. Many are trying to awaken all, when it's really not your responsibility to awaken all. It is to empower yourself! It is to heal yourself! It is to love all! And how ironic it is that we see people using their spiritual veneer coat to project their superiority and judging those beneath them because they're not spiritual and they're the sleepy ones, the ones that are complying. And yet you are not seeing the magnificent Souls that are around you that deserve your love! That deserve your respect! And yet you have the audacity to not see their Souls because you are reacting and judging them based on human ways of life. It is interesting how *you humans* view the world. And when you seem to get a little bit of knowledge and a little bit of awareness that can boost your ego and confidence in the subject matter you still very much do not understand fully and completely in its entirety, as you have a human mindset, as you have a human brain. There are limitations on purpose and it's not a personal thing. You can't actually gain all wisdom while being human. It is like saying you could eat all the ice cream in the world. There aren't enough fat pants for you to cover yourself if you ate all the ice cream in the world. (Laughing.) And so we're saying all of the information and wisdom that is out in the universes and the galaxies beyond, and all the experiences that even your Soul has had, you would not possibly be able to absorb it all. Just like with your human stomachs being able to absorb all the ice cream in the world. While you may have what you could call eyes bigger than your stomach, you know without even trying, that it's not physically possible to eat all the ice cream in the world. In fact, you could easily drown if you were given the sum of all of the ice cream in the world. But you would freeze first. So you can see how harmful that could be to yourself. And we are saying that is like the wisdom and information that some of you are trying to seek. It could be harmful for yourselves. You know we have said that some truth could be poisonous to people, and we are saying not to in jest. It is too triggering for many people. It is like saying everything natural is good for you. And we are saying, but arsenic in certain levels is not good for you and that is a natural substance.

So again, it is perspectives. It is wisdom. It is about having a solid balance to know what is your responsibility to learn and explore and what isn't. We know some of you are so curious again because you don't have strength and confidence in the information you do have. And so, you're trying to add more information onto your stockpile of information to give you more confidence. It is not truly confidence that you need to seek. You know what information you have, and now you have to apply it and to make peace with it! Those who are unconfident with the wisdom that they have in their own intuition, there is inner work for you to express and explore.

We're wanting you to have much more fun! Remember, this is a game! You can still be a high frequency vibrational being who is mature, who has been of service and still have jazz hands and laugh at life! And laugh at self! And laugh at others playing the game of human! Read back to these sessions. They are significant! Even if you think you recall everything that has been said from a session you heard only just recently. We can reassure you, when you read these again and again and again you will hear them with new perspectives. New *higher* perspectives! Because you're growing at a rapid rate and we're activating many of you at a rapid rate! We say so much! There are so many layers of information that we are sharing with you and have been sharing with you for a long time. It is about exposing yourself to the same information to hear at a new level, because you are all at a new level. You are raising your frequency at a new level constantly! And the information that we provide is coded. When you have grown, it is there for you to read and gain access to be able to hear it all with fresh new ears! To understand it at a higher[30] level!

---

[30] *The Arctutians do want people to have these books as part of their*

We know people say *'I've listened to this one. I get it all!'* And we're saying, read it again! While you are reading the words and understanding the words, there are many other messages that we are sharing with you. We are protecting the messages from being heard from certain collectives. They are still trying to hold back humanity. And we are trying to give you the messages that we need you to understand to be able to give you the upliftment, encouragement and confidence and strength and faith in us.

For you to remember that we are here to be of service to you always!

We say this with much love!

Session 25: Away With The Fairies, Going Home

Yes! Yes! Yes! We are here! We are very much here!

And we prompted you to have this conversation with us today even though it truly is just us speaking through you as we are going to read your mind as you were wanting clarification on the information we provided for you. And so you experienced going home when you did that two session healing meditation. And from our perspective of what happened to you after that was your Soul Essence was still there, very much far away there. And even though there was no such thing as time and space, you were not present there on Earth. In fact, you unconsciously could feel this. But also, with your mindset, you knew you were not fully there, fully present. And you knew that, as you were coming to. But it was like a Soul aspect who hasn't been fully in control and in charge. And it was almost as if the bigger Soul essence left the body just temporary while the smaller Soul essence was 'home alone'. And that was fine. And you know this. But we're trying to explain this because people have been feeling very absent-minded, very non-present. We would like to say a saying that you understand, that is, 'Away with the fairies.' And this is part of what some people think was a daydream or just a sense of something else that's not your daily normal routine. And so the Soul aspect could easily get consciously home. This is something she doesn't often do because she's so busy here on Earth. She could feel that energy and she weaved in deepness consciously through those sessions. And as we were healing past, the one part she hasn't healed yet, and it's not because it's broken or has any issues, she hasn't been able to heal her mourning for home. That pain of being homesick can feel broken. Can feel so confused. Can feel so isolated. Can feel so insignificant here. And her home is a place where family goes every now and then when they have completed their passions helping physical planets. Helping physical beings. This is something they do as a collective. It is not the physical home she craves for, it is the connections of her Soul family. And so, consciously she slipped deeper than she had before consciously, because she was doing this in her days, and she merely went there for her rebalance to calm the craving that she didn't realize she had as such. And so it was momentarily that her Soul went there consciously to know all is well! All is well there! All is well there!

Consciously, it's too distant, too foreign. She can't understand it fully because the 3D overlay is still very firm as she needs to focus on 3D to be able to help assist with 3D. And this is part of her contract, is to still be able to assist people. And if she spent too much of her time 'away with the fairies', she would not be interested in connecting with others as much as she does. And her Soul family are not fairies, but yet they are so magical that you could say fairies. But not any fairies that live here on Earth. They're not Elementals. And so she just found herself there to then just have this, we want to say breath, but she wasn't there in the physical body. And it just helped her so much! But she realized that this was our intention for that second session, was to be able to heal things from other lifetimes. Including other lifetimes off planet. And while there is nothing that has ever hurt her on her home planet, on her home space where her home family reside, being away from there hurts her. And so this is why she found herself there. And this is why she could notice the consciousness of the other Soul that hasn't taken full ownership of the body yet. Nor would it, questioning itself suddenly with stage anxiety of performance. And this was purposeful! And when she did come back fully into the body just momentarily afterwards, the memories and the experiences of the living are still being recorded. And so when her full Soul essence for her bigger Soul essence came back, she was able to simultaneously understand what had been going on with the thoughts and the thinking she thought it was being. She was consciously aware of being in two different places. And this is mind-bending. But also, she thought it was amusing that the Soul Essence that was still here in the body was even sort of thinking, 'Oh shoot, what is my name again?' And she knew this was not her normal way of thinking. And so it is not like she had a walk out. She had a day trip! A momentary day trip home! And this is purposeful!

And this also leads us to her experience, what we were showing her just prior to when she started this channeling today. We were looking inside her in her work closet, shall you say, and we were showing it to her as a closet with shelves. And we know we showed her that closet and it had lots of boxes to unpack, only what you would call nearly years ago. And she has decluttered that closet! She has opened up all of the boxes with new perspectives, all of those challenging experiences and referenced them with a new perspective! A new approach! She has seen the lessons where she should have been able to empower herself and where there were opportunities for more growth for her. And she sees that there were times where she was over reactive. And so she has gone through all of those boxes to forgive herself and to see again this was another opportunity for her to realize that she was not in balance and in harmony as she needed to be.

There is so much that she has explored about herself. She doesn't feel like it is self-indulgent. It is about self-reflection of where she is and what she has learned this lifetime. And so, what we have shown her now, is there being only small little tiny ornaments left in this closet. And she's recognizing she was born with those ornaments in her closet. And when she came here she had those. They are not ordinary ornaments. They are trinkets of keys. They are information, you could say, for those people who understand this label, her Akashic records. And we're saying she can see several boxes of many different places where she has had many different lives. And there is much she has mastered. But she keeps being diligent focusing on this 3D life because she knows this is the most important to focus on. But we are wanting to say, now you have more access to this information if you choose because there is nothing in your inner closet left for you to hoard. Hold on to. You've already processed this. And so now, when you keep doing those two sessions back to back, you'll be able to go to these other places if you choose to experience and remember those lessons. They are not as applicable as you would hope so they are only experiences of off-worldly experiences versus reference points to be able to help you master 3D living on Earth. And so it's the difference between holiday living and work living daily lives. And we just wanted her to remind herself of who she is and to not be embarrassed about some of those positions she has lived because they're just roles again. And she has many various lifetimes off planet. She's done lots of hard work and lots of fun work and other lifetimes. She must never forget that. But when she feels that people are overlooking her and dismissing her in being 3D, she knows that it's just where they're at. She knows that they're still struggling. But this is a reminder to her that for those Souls who are overlooking her, they're only judging the meat suit, they're only judging the gender, the location of where she lives. They're short-sighted. And this can be painful for her because she knows she's worked very hard and diligently to be able to collect information for people to be able to see and learn and grow from. And support themselves to encourage themselves to be able to do their own channeling. To be able to get their own perspectives. To be able to open up that closet of their spirituality and to be able to unpack it as feverish as possible. Because this is the time to do so. This is the time to heal, this is the time to release, this is the time to let go. Because this is home time for many. And people are homesick. And if *she* feels homesick, she is concerned for all those others who are desperately homesick and don't even understand where their homes are. Can't even understand how they can't be comfortable in their own home on this planet, in this lifetime, they've only ever known consciously.

This is a surprise to her! The emotions! Because she focuses on moving forward to seeing how she can inspire others. To encourage others to be brave and confident in exploring themselves. While it can be self-indulgent to look at other lifetimes off planet and even other lifetimes on this planet if you're looking for your hero title, (Laughing) you can be the hero's this lifetime and it's so easy to do such. You must be able to do your inner work. Respect all lessons. The ones you mastered. The ones you failed, we could say with labels, and see if you can repeat those successes with positivity, empowerment and with an enlightened approach. Every moment you are creating choices to be able to empower yourself or not, or distract yourself or not. And we see some not wanting to step up. They feel very entitled and they're wondering why they're struggling so much now. And yet we say, look at your inner work! Look at your judgments! Look at your resentments! Those are the big ones, our dear friends. We say to you with love, that finding that balance in neutral is significant.

(LOUD DOG SNORE) We are finding that the sweet dog has found our energy field and this sweet dog has fallen into its own deep slumber. And we are noticing the breath and the snoring. But we are taking a moment. We understand many of you have very attached emotional pets, whether they are emotionally attached to you or vice versa or a codependency. Use all the tools that you need to get through your days, our friends, with balance.

Enjoy your world!
Enjoy your life!
Please remember to be of service as well!

You will notice when you have complete balance in your life that harmony feels so empowering that you want to be of service more. It doesn't take from you as it once did. Energy of people shouldn't completely drain you. They're not draining you of your high frequency. You're merely holding on to the density. There is a difference! When you can't even notice your own high frequency and you can only focus on density, there is *inner* work for you! There is *energy* work for you! And we have given you a tool to be able to balance all density from your body's and all density from your mindsets. This is an advanced tool from us to be able to help you and many people are realizing the significance of these. And while we are saying use all tools in balance. Any tool is supposed to be a training practice. Think of it like this.

Everything is like a trike, a little balance bike. And you're learning how to ride. You're learning how to move forward and take full control at a faster pace. I mean, you don't need training wheels and you don't need parents to helicopter you, to hold you. You can actually learn quite quickly to master this yourself without even hands taking the wheel.

And so there are many analogies we could quickly say to you but this is all to train you to know that *you* control your mindsets! *You* control your bodies! *You* control your lives until your life contract kicks in! Until your guides kick you into place to remind you to step up! And we jest with you now because we want to shift the energy of this body who is so surprised of her emotions. She can be too distracted wanting to be of service and so she has forgotten to enjoy some of the other aspects that she can explore. She doesn't really want to be distracted with other lifetimes even though we have prompted her many times recently to focus on and explore again the Dragon life and also the other off-planet life that is... I can feel her resisting because she doesn't feel like there is significance in those lifetimes now. But we're saying the authoritative position of the Dragon on that planet is an important imprint that she had for her to be able to walk into this lifetime now to be able to have the confidence. She has the skill set to be able to have integrity to be able to reach Higher Dimensions, Higher Realities to be able to get as much support for her for what her true passion is, for her purpose and life contracts, the Second Wave Volunteers. And this is her primary directive to be able to support those and this was a smaller collective you could say. We know that she has labeled and we have gone with it, the Arctuarian is one collective and the Pleiadians is one collective. And that is the truth. But there are groups, clubs, you could say, committees. Community based projects you could say. Okay we've gone to human with labels. We could say there are many different beings being guided by different collectives who have come in to be doing group projects such as the Second Wave Volunteers. Such as the First Wave Volunteers. Such as the Third Wave Volunteers. Such as all independent smaller collective volunteers that haven't been officially labeled as such. And so there was a push to have the First Wave come in to be able to shine incredible advanced energy onto this planet. To be able to help easily with the shift and that was not successful. They were ill prepared and this was traumatizing for all the Souls who had high expectations of this. And so the Second Wave Volunteers had a new approach and this was significant. And this had more integrity and attention and a sense of more urgency because these First Wave Volunteers were struggling at such a rapid rate, the Second Wave Volunteers knew that they needed to come and assist as fast as possible in some regards.

So this was challenging. The primary focus was to be able to support all who came here to be supporting of all! And so the Second Wave Volunteers are not obviously one collective. They are a bunch of many, many brave collectives that have sent their representatives. They're representing different collectives for significant purposes. And so as she is noticing the Second Wave Volunteers who are Arcturian are very drawn to her messages that she shares consciously. And our messages that we share through her because there is a unique frequency that is being transmitted through the language and the codes and the sounds of the sessions plus the energy. And so she is sending out messages to the Second Wave Volunteers to empower them, to remind them. And we can say it's a bigger group than just people who have only had their first lifetimes here. Many who have had lifetimes here and love Earth, love Gaia and love the human project and love the Earth Project, they've also decided to be of service again to be able to help assist. They really wanted the shift to occur here and for all to emerge into a Fifth Dimension here. And so this is where you see and find many frustrated and bitter volunteers, bitter people, bitter light workers who are not impressed with the struggles of life here because they have not accepted other beings' life contracts, including Gaia's.

And so there's always much to be said because this is a very leveled experience here on Earth! Like all Earths! Like all planets! Like all experiences you can have! It is so fractured and multi-dimensionally fascinating for each independent being. And while you are dealing with many beings here it can be very complex. And so what we could be talking about for some groups may not resonate with other groups because this is not their projects. And some are noticing that they are having extra assistance in Souls in their physical bodies which are coming in. And they are resonating with this information now. It is not a strange thing to use Vehicles like taxis. And you know that there are taxis that drive around your cities all day long and you don't necessarily know how many beings, people have been in the taxi's when you jump into a taxi and yet you know that is part of the service. The vehicle of the taxi is moving around in physical and beings are hopping into that taxi for a drive, for a ride to a destination. And we're saying this is the same as your physical bodies. Your physical bodies are vehicles and they can be taxis for many Souls who want to come for a ride. For a moment. For an experience. For a relationship. To help. These are Soul level contracts. You're not being invaded!

You're not being possessed! You're not being anything negative! You are helping a Soul Essence to be able to have a physical embodiment of a physical body to be able to have a Soul experience. And you can't tell consciously all the time when this happens, just like you can't tell consciously all the beings that are supporting you here now. And that is purposeful to focus on your lives, your daily routines and the experiences that life on Earth has to offer you.

And so we understand that this is a lot! We could always talk more but we're very consciously aware that many people tune out the words and tune into the energy and that is also fine. But we are saying there are many perspectives of information given to you through these sessions. And we invite you all to re-listen to the sessions again because there's always going to be a new aspect of information that you need and still question. And you may ask us to guide you to the most appropriate session. And you may wonder, '*Why? I've already heard this one. Why? Why would I bother listening to this one again?*' You'll question us and we will say because there is something still in there that you have not been able to unpack, open up and explore.

We are very excited for your future experiences and we honor all who honor themselves of their life contracts and use their free will to empower themselves. To empower others. To love themselves and love others and respect all as equals! Respect all as a Soul family. As brothers and sisters. You are all one! And what you do to one you do to all!

And we say this with love!

Session 26: Metaphysical Perspective of Cosmetic Surgery

Yes Yes Yes Yes Yes! We are here. We are here. We are here and we wanted to talk to you all today about a concept that you may not have necessarily considered from a metaphysical perspective.

We have hope that this gives you and gains you more compassion to those who feel so out of love with themselves at a physical level, that they would expose themselves to cosmetic surgery. As you can assume, this is because the person does not feel good enough within their own skin. They want adjustments. They want upliftments. They want to follow popular trends of how to look.

They have this assumption that once they get this and achieve this, this will give them the love, the inner peace, and the empowerment that they have been seeking. But as you are aware, we have a different perspective over that. It truly isn't what you look like, it is about how you honor yourself as a soul, being here as human, and what that is. As you have all designed the human bodies, we say, you've chosen your parents and you know what the genetic makeup would be. For some, you've also been a part of how to design humanoid bodies as well. The design structure is very advanced and sophisticated.

So it's your choice how you want to work it. We are saying, some of the trends to have larger parts of your body - we're talking about breasts, we say, it's often to please others versus pleasing yourselves. So you really have to look at the agenda of why you want to have breast enhancements. Is it because you want to feel good about yourself? We are saying, why would a physical part of your body make you love and respect and honor your entirety of who you are, and why you are here.

We see you all perfect. But we see it's your mindsets that want to corrode you. The way you treat your bodies and break the bodies down, some of humanity is wanting to seek the elixir of youth and beauty, to maintain and hold on to the illusion that they are younger. We are saying, it's about loving all aspects and all stages of your lives. Some of you feel like you've wasted your youth because you do not love yourselves. We are saying, isn't it fantastic that you don't just get only one life.

We have another urgent concept to share with you. We say, urgent is not a correct term, but we are saying for some, and this is what you could say, more connected advanced Souls who are here to be empowering humanity with love. They have come with such advancements of connection, that they are more open to the energetics. Unfortunately, that makes them more open to the densities as well. When they don't understand what they're feeling, and when they don't understand why the Soul is so confused and so constricted and dense with all the energies, they're trying to seek advanced information. They're in metaphysics, but they can't seem to quite find that information, because it almost seems to be censored from them. As they are very open to other people's opinions, which are also human opinions and egos, they don't quite understand truly, that they are merely playing the role of human. So they feel so stifled in the human body. They feel so disconnected to it, that they have assumptions that maybe it is in fact, the gender that they are residing in and expressing through the physical body, and so they have assumptions that they are seeking a different gender to empower themselves, and feel "normal".

We're saying, there are systems that are trying to help these children feel normal, but it is coercion. We're wanting to say, for some, they have had so many lifetimes with one gender, they wanted this last lifetime here on Earth to be a different one. It doesn't matter who you love. It doesn't matter what your body is, it's about your self-empowerment, your self-esteem, and your awareness and compassion to yourself and others to trust that who you are is exactly what your Soul needed, what your Soul family and friends and guides all wanted to support you with. There is much to be said here, but there is also this fixation of gender roles. You're supposed to be open to accepting and respecting all roles and all passions that everyone on Earth has. So it was limiting you to be confined to a gender specific role. We are saying, girls can do anything and so can boys. But it was too much, too radical for many of humanity to accept that.

So this new movement to have blurred boundaries with certain agendas is good for your expansion consciousness. Are you finding yourself intolerant? Are you finding yourself judging? Are you finding yourself having lots of problems with other people choosing to express the way they feel within themselves? So, again, it's about seeing, are you truly mature with your spirituality?

There is another aspect to this which is about the medical industry, once again, coercing and playing God. They are using vulnerable children who are feeling confused about why their Souls are trapped in human bodies. And so, they're giving them these solutions and answers which are brutalizing their essences, in some regards. It's so hard for us to talk about this and absolutes, because there is so much going on. For example, there is a family that's very religious, that has a son that is very feminine. They have many other girls. They also can recognize, what you could say, as a classic boy and a classic girl, when they know their son is a classic girl in a male body. This could have shunned them. This is very embarrassing for them, but they can't change him, as much as they want to. So they have to learn to be tolerant, to love, and to see their son who is beautiful and happy and wants to shine and thrive, the way he is. This is forcing those people around to see beyond the meat suits, to honor the Soul within. This child is innocent. This child is so high frequency loving, that only, you could say, a human monster could judge that child, because that child is beaming with a radiant energy frequency of love. When you see that child, and that child gazes upon your eyes, it is like Jesus, or you could say with an assumption of what God would look like, looking at you with love, openness, and invitation to accept this child as they are. They are not hurting you. In fact, they are inspiring you to love all. From our perspective, this is a great learning curve to advance your concepts of - who you should love and who you shouldn't love.

We see that many religions have been stifled in this evolution of accepting and loving all. They have misconstrued what is being given to them through their literatures, which they hold so sacred. Yet, they're missing the point of loving all. So they feel they are justified to love some, hate some. We have said - **Love All**. This is their time to be allowed to express themselves and who they choose to be this lifetime. There is much to be said here.

There are also those who want to change their bodies. We are saying, this is about .... We want to use the analogy of breast enhancements. For some people, they want this to impress their partners, or because their partners have said that this is what they want and that they would love them more. There are people that have got these surgeries to please others, and there have been complications. It's been painful and unfortunately, some of these situations, where there has been, what you could say, botched operations, causes the patient to then be addicted to painkillers, as it is very excruciating when the body rejects augmentations. There's so much to be said here about how much the beauty industry has caused pain.

We're saying, some people are not responsible or accountable for their actions, and so if you do something that augments the body, and it causes you pain, of course many people would then blame the doctors, or blame other people that influence them to get it. But ultimately, it's about taking ownership and responsibility for the choices you made. While some professionals can disappoint you, it is still your choice to have done this and put yourself at risk. But you're not thinking about being accountable for the risks you put yourselves in.

We're saying this is like with tattoos for trend. As you know, trends can come and go and fade. Many people have learned quite quickly, to be responsible for what they do to their bodies, as they have regrettable tattoos. They recognize that while it was very trendy one season, one moment, and they have grown out of love with it. It has faded. It has changed. It has grown with age, with the skin. This is a teachable moment for the people to recognize and realize - what you do to the body - one moment, one decision, can impact your body its entire life. This is brilliant - teachable moments for people that are taking their bodies for granted, and not being responsible or accountable for how they conduct, behave, and honor the body.

While there are many cultures that did value status, and they did adorn, you could say, intentional scarring, intentional tattooing and imprinting of the skin as a status. This was held at high esteem, had meaning versus a social trend. There is much to be said about the history of how you've looked after the bodies, and how you've fashioned the bodies.

We are saying, Soul mates recognize you all at energy frequencies and so when you find a Soul mate who is so compatible with you because it is an extension of self, it doesn't matter what you look like. It doesn't matter what your hair looks like, or your clothes, or the choices of how you use your makeup. The Souls recognize each other in an instant, in an instant. We understand that many of you have missed opportunities to connect in with your Soul mates. As you are born on this planet to find each other and fall in love, some of you have got sidetracked, distracted, and you've grown faster or slower than the other. We see - you've had the possibility of many life contracts with many Soul mates, and it was about your choices of how you conducted yourself, your behavior, your attitudes, and your maturity. We see some relationships who are supposed to find each other, but it was not the right timing for the person's behavior and attitudes. They miss those opportunities. But there is no such thing as loss, it's all just different experiences.

There are some who do not have life contracts to find their Soul mates this lifetime, and that is very significant. While that feels frustrating and upsetting because that's not normal - to not be with someone. We are saying, so many have recognized that they haven't found the soulmate that they felt like they should, so they have settled and married. And that comes with its own problems, you could say, when you've settled. Is it incompatibility, but it's also challenging you to be able to empower yourself and keep faith in yourself while still living with, not a stranger, but there is a difference between a Soul mate versus a human companion. Many who have given up trying to wait and hope for that match of that Soul mate to arrive had settled for something else. Again, there is no loss. It is still an experience. This is when you could say, new relationships form throughout the eons, when there are these situations, where you both settle. The Soul families and the guides merge in to support both of you. This is when you could say, Soul families develop, because different Souls are supporting each other.

It is remarkable how a main guide not only works through you to encourage you, inspire you, and give you epiphanies, they also work with people around you to give you the nudges that you are dismissing. They have many ways. It is not breaching their free will. As humans, you are here as part of your mission to help each other. When you are not able to have the courage, necessarily, to hold people accountable or to inspire and encourage and love each other, it is common for a guide to come in and work through you to say the messages and to share the energy frequency that their guides are needing for their own counterpart. We hope that we've made sense with this. The vehicle is so far away from us, we can't check to make sure that it is understood by a third dimensional mindset.

We want to say that the medical systems have got great respect because it takes the longest amount of time to be studied, trained, and educated to become a doctor and a specialist. Yet we could say that they are trained in human concepts of the understanding of the body. And so, they like to explore. They like to experiment, but they are very reckless, you could say. But they support each other with this. There is much to be said about that.

Certain Souls wanted to be born into bodies that had no distinctual gender or a mix of both. They were coming in to be able to empower humanity to love all, accept all, and be open-minded to not fixate on what your sexual gender defines you as, because when you are an advanced Soul with a light being body, you don't have the gender that you think you do. It's energetics versus the physicality of reproduction organs. So there is much to be said about this, but this was too early for humanity to be prepared for, and the doctors were too prudish to accept the child could be okay with what they were born with. So the doctors, in fear of the struggles of that child, made decisions impressing upon the adults and parents to have operations from birth to "fix" the situation at hand. This was when the doctors should have honestly honored the human bodies, and been able to look into a more spiritual perspective of what was happening and why these bodies were suddenly changing and not having a set gender. But more ways to communicate with other doctors was becoming more prevalent, and as more doctors were starting to converse about these experiences, they actually realized that this was a phenomenon that was occurring, and had been occurring for quite some time. But this was seen as shameful, shunned, and not spoken about. The doctors wanted to honor their patients and their family members because it was always, you could say, imagine a small town and one doctor. So the doctor wanted to hold all the secrets of the physical bodies and so would do certain surgeries to fix the problem. And we say, his mindset was the problem[31].

So, it took so long for a woman to step into the field of becoming a doctor and being respected, seen and considered to be a doctor, as they thought it was too garish and too shocking for a woman's constitution to cope with being a doctor. And so, it was held away from women for a long time. But the medical industry in itself has so much to explain to humanity, as it has taken its ego and its assumptions, because they have trained and got the **most** education, that they must be the most advanced and elite. So there is much ego in that. Plus there is so much corruption, in the fact that there is so much desire to manipulate the bodies into keeping young, and not honoring the Soul essence. So it's become normal conversation in some circles, having tummy lifts, nose jobs, boobs jobs, and butt lifts, seem to be quite common and normal. And yet, it's embarrassing for some people to admit that they have had plastic surgery, because they want to pretend that they're just naturally beautiful. There is much to be said about how people will spend their money and their attention to obsess on their appearances. But when they don't love themselves and accept themselves, they have to, they think, impress others to get attention, to get love, and to get acceptance from others.

---

[31] *They were showing a doctor in the late 1800's to the vehicle*

We say those people who are obsessed with the fashion industry and their own looks, are so distracted from their own empowerment of self and their own Soul Essence, that they are naturally attracting low frequency vibrational people who are very judgmental, and base others on their looks, and others on their clothes. They are very materialistic in this way and this is one aspect why humanity is so distracted. They're wanting to keep up with the latest trends, because they think if they're trendy, then they're going to be liked more, and if they're liked more, they're going to get more recognition. So we say, many are simply following the trends to be recognized, to be seen. When they feel seen, they feel valid. It's all about them asking the world to empower them. When you know it truly is within. You truly can only empower yourself when you choose to see your value, to see your worth, and to honor and respect who you are, here, now.

We even see some people holding on to other alternate lifetimes to boost their egos to impress upon people who they are, here, now. We are saying, while you're all one, and while you're all connected in, who you are and who you show up to the world as now, this lifetime is the one that counts. So don't lean on your other lifetimes as bragging points. Be your bragging point for this lifetime and show humanity how much you love and empower yourself, and how much you love and want to empower humanity to recognize how amazing it is. When you recognize how special you are, each and every single one of you are all equal, equally loved by all of us.

You would not consider focusing and over-indulging thought processes about why you were lacking, why you're not good enough. We're saying, if you have to have an operation to attract someone, that someone may not be really who you're truly seeking. Ultimately, you're trying to seek someone who loves you for you, who loves you for your behaviors, your demeanors, and your compassion to be a humanitarian to empower and inspire everyone, and to raise a higher frequency of love that resonates throughout this planet and beyond. If you are seeking someone who is judgmental of your looks and would only love you if you had the right size skinny pants and did all the correct exercises, then potentially you may not be able to find someone with this judgment. You've got lost in how humanity is not empowering itself and how it's justifying what it would seek. We're saying, so many people are looking for the best handsomest partner, and yet you shouldn't be looking at looks to quantify the best person for you, you should be quantifying the Soul that can reach out through the human ego, to be a loving empowered being. Many of you do not notice the diamond and the rough, we could say.

We want to also remind you all, with very much love, that you all still have unhealed experiences that need to be empowered. When you're active in the world, when you are conversing and having relationships with other people, you will always be empowering yourself to heal yourself from interacting with other unhealed people. And so, we could say to some degree that you are all unhealed aspects. Some have bigger wounds than others. Some feel very empowered and not afraid to be on a healing mission because they know how they are very capable of healing themselves once they recognize the feelings that trigger their emotions, for them to stop and think about how it makes them feel. Empowering yourself and healing yourself with inner work is very empowering. It really is, when you notice and recognize how capable you are to notice and recognize the emotions and the triggering of where the insecurities are, or where the hurts are, to then accept yourself, accept your experiences, and recognize it's all empowerment.

We love you all. We've always seen you as perfect. Even when you, in your healing process, you're still perfect to us. We try to encourage you and inspire you. We've never lost hope or faith in you, because we know the journey is challenging. But we're here. We're here. We're here to be able to give you these information epiphanies for you to apply. You've asked for it. You've asked for help. You've asked for messages. You've asked for guidance. We are literally here to give you these perspectives and this information, to recognize you as advanced beings who are playing the role of human, to be here to empower humanity for what are going to be some of their challenging times, challenging experiences. You're here for it because you know that you can control your emotions, as you just allow - to feel all emotions, but to not get stuck in one singularity of a denser emotion. You instantly recognize it and work through it, to understand where the insecurity is, where the frustration is, where the anger is, or where the rage is.

You know you could focus on the crimes against humanity and be outraged and angry for the rest of your life. You know that as a choice. You know that you could cry for those Souls who are so confused and so disempowered, they are making outrageous free will choices to butcher their bodies and hope that they will find themselves, hope that they will remember who they are, and hope that they will feel normal. You have such great compassion. You see all aspects of how humans are evolving and waking each other up, to challenge - are you tolerant and compassionate to all, truly, really? Or do you have choices of who you think you can judge and who you think you can hate? We are still seeing some of you, who think you're advanced, but still have these exceptions of things that you want to criticize, to belittle, and to not see this is an unhealed process journey for them, that is still being identified and worked through. When you know that you're all in the phase of healing, you have to accept that there are unhealed people, processing and doing the best that they can. Therefore your judgment on unhealed people is cruel, you could say, because they can feel your dismissal and your judgment. We are saying, you're not here for that, you're here to empower, have compassion, and love all.

We are saying you know what Christ-like Consciousness is. You know that when you embody this to be able to have deep compassion, respect, and acceptance for all, this raises your own frequency vibration. This also floods and sheds high frequency love, acceptance, and compassion to all. Again, that is what you're here for - to hold the higher frequency levels of love, and to just have compassion, acceptance, and understand the struggles of others are not for you to fight or rage against, but to support them through this birthing process of getting to the root of their issues, which they may be struggling from, from many other lifetimes. We say, you can't be helicopter parents to your children because you're holding them back from growing. You can't be helicopter friends to your friends because this can stop them from growing. When we refer to being helicopter parents, we say, this is a saying the vehicle has, which is about hovering over the being, the person, and not allowing them to grow organically. You're almost caging them in. You're wanting them to do what you want them to do, because you think that you know best. We are saying, people need to make mistakes to learn that that wasn't their best, and they will make better choices moving forward. Stifling people by controlling them and making them do what you think is going to save them from hurt and potentially save them from important lessons is something you need to work on.

You can give your love, advice, and support. But when you're wanting people to do what you're wanting to do because you know that you've done this yourself, and this was the best way forward, that can be controlling and manipulating them and taking away their organic experiences to discover that doctors aren't God, that vaccines aren't necessarily what they are said, that viruses aren't necessarily what they have been said, that genders aren't necessarily what is the definition of a human.

Souls coming into human forms to radiate energy frequency, once they have full empowerment of self and love themselves. Yes, for some people, they truly will ever and only ever be able to love themselves once they have their corrective nose surgery, what they believe is a corrective approach to a nose. They become so fixated on it, obsessed that they will have the surgery to change themselves. We're saying, they change their perspectives of themselves, they didn't necessarily need to have the operation. But often, when people cut their noses off despite their face, they will accept them and then respect them.

We're saying, many have remorse for their choices. You could say for tattoos, you could say for surgeries, they haven't thought it out. They haven't understood the consequences of their choices and actions. This is the biggest teachable moment for many.

So we say all is well. You can trust we're guiding people constantly. Often, when someone knows it's not right, they will ask a thousand different people what is right for them, because they are dismissing their own intuition. Ultimately, when people are asking for second opinions or advice from their friends, it is because they don't have confidence in themselves to know what is right for them. They know they shouldn't be having these cosmetic surgeries. They know they shouldn't be doing these things that are vain and egoic. They ask their friends who can give them permission to do the things that they really want to do, but internal knowledge and wisdom within themselves, and their internal knowledge, suggests otherwise. We are saying, you don't get punished. There isn't a hell for boob jobs [laughs]. We're adding some humor into this because this is weighing heavy on the vehicle. She recently saw some photos of some very brutal, very brutal operations, and she can feel the insecurities of the person who'd had that operation. She could feel deeply into what was going on for them. For this person, it didn't alleviate. It didn't make them feel as they hoped. They felt like they needed to say the right words, but within them, they felt deeply disappointed, but because this decision was so dramatic, they had to accept their choices, and try to find the light in it. They had to accept it because there was no way that they could go back. And so, they're going to be more focused on their choices moving forward, and what they do, be very mindful with that. Even when you set your heart and your mind on something so intensively, and you're so sure this is the best for you. Just because you have good wishes, good hopes, and even good surgeons, doesn't give you what you're seeking within you.

We are saying, to let everyone allow each other to feel into who's within you. Honor everyone. We say, even for that boy who is effeminate and wants to identify being a girl, love him. He is doing no harm. He's shedding love. He is respecting himself. He respects others. Many people can learn from this.

We say to the woman who got the breast jobs because she wanted to make her husband fall in love with her. He is not in love with himself. It doesn't matter - all the surgeries you do, he cannot love you because he can't even understand what love of self is. There's so much to be said here and there are so many situations that we would love to give information, insights upon.

Now we struggle because there is so much information, we don't quite know the most appropriate to share to you all. All information is important, but we also understand and recognize that many of you tune out what we are saying at some point. So we don't want to talk too long, to lose your focus and concentration. Again, we invite you to reach out to us directly, as we still want to empower you with our insights, to be able to help you understand, and to be able to help you release anything that no longer serves you, including some things, if you're honest about certain people and certain situations, where you feel like you still have frustration, resentfulness, hurt, and pain. Honor all of that, but this is time to heal from that, and this is definitely the time to release it.

So when you learn the lessons of why this was a part of your life and experiences, this will be able to help you put it into place and to be able to put the perspectives that you need, to be able to understand, this was a helpful experience for you. But when you're still hurting, you can't see the powerful and important lessons, and so it just feels like a victim's experience with no good. We're saying, everything is purposeful and everything is significant. Do not dismiss anything. If you're still feeling like you're holding pain, if you still feel like there is something you can't let go of, it could be potentially because you haven't been able to learn the lesson, or get the perspectives to gain, to be able to help you with that. Often this can be other lifetimes of trauma, because you cannot fathom the trauma you've experienced in other lifetimes that are still within you.

We say this with love and appreciation. We hope that we've given you the perspectives that you need to be able to understand that there is no justification to judge others as you are knowing now that you're all on a journey of healing. Empower each other with love. Encourage each other to honor the healing process to grow. We say this with love.

Session 27: Dolores Cannon, Use Your Power

Yes, yes, yes. We're here. We're here. We're here. Indeed we know that we've been prompting you with many epiphanies and information and insights for you to reach in to get more clarification from us so you could share as a public message.

There is many that are needing your assistance to be able to help them share their messages but as you started to get yourself ready for this session you noticed you had a complete blank state of mind except for one being who wanted to take center stage and we say you do not mind because you love, you love this Soul very much and you know whatever she is needing to share and speak it always takes precedence because you do have favorites with your Souls and your friends. Dolores Cannon would like to come in now. Her energy is so strong because her love is so great. She is telling the vehicle to get on with it. You've got work to do, so focus. It's not a time to get emotional with energy frequency love and respect, so the vehicle will respect that.

Dolores: You have much to do. All of you have much to do. You have been focusing on empowering yourselves and honoring your inner work. This is a great time to have true discernment. I have seen and listened and watched and observed many practitioners getting confused about the level of consciousness their clients are under and in. I have always said to you the more inner work you do and the more sessions you do to fully relax and surrender the ego, the more clarification and information you will be able to get and receive and share.

The client's level of channeling must be focused and must have discernment. We have seen many of our beloved Soul family and friends, working as humans, still being afraid of concepts and still being afraid of information. When they get questioned in session about certain information and certain concepts, their egos rush in to answer because they are still afraid. They say what they want to hear because they are not ready to let go of the control to be prepared to truly channel advanced beings.

While the clients seem very relaxed, they still have control issues. Some are still in fear. Some are still scared of the information, therefore, their conscious mind and their egos are still guarding. So while it may sound legitimate sessions and while it's out may sound like legitimate advanced channelings, I have seen many practitioners use this work as entertainment versus truly seeking inner work to empower people. While it's merely a distraction, you truly need to honor all of the inner work that you have, which is limiting you and holding you back to be of service to yourselves and to be of service to humanity, with having a higher frequency love energy that you can bestow and gift yourselves, including profoundly loving humanity.

I would also like to say there is a message and you can even find this in your bible 'love thy enemy' and this was pushed upon the vehicle as she was supporting someone so deeply afraid and terrified, making them very angry very angry and it has opened to energy frequencies to that level of vibrations which is frustration anger resentfulness and being afraid. This energy frequency that has been held onto by this person is so spiteful so resentful and so fearful. While she uses part of the Bible to justify her demeanor, she discards the other parts of the Bible which clearly say love all. Including love thy enemy.

Pray, it says, to your enemy to those who harm you. Pray for them, send them love, send them compassion.

Send them enlightenment.
Send them epiphanies.
Send them empowerment of self.

You're sending and using your high frequency love, your high frequency of compassion to surround them energetically with inspiration to be able to consider and think beyond anger beyond fear, beyond judgment.

I have said that some truths can be poisonous to people and I also have said that some mindsets can also be poisonous to people and it does manifest into illnesses and diseases. When I left this work because that was part of my life purpose and my mission was to be able to help humanity choose with their free will to gain higher perspectives. To gain high direct connections to advanced beings. This can only be done when you could say Mr Stupid wants to surrender fully out of the session. I say to those practitioners who don't know the difference the more inner work you do and the more sessions you do as a client the more you're going to be able to have greater discernment between fantastical ego statements versus advanced beings.

When you don't quite know how to work these sessions and when you don't quite know the difference between true integrity of advanced beings versus an ego, slipping in to say what they want, versus what is the reality from our perspective of what is occurring there is much confusion there. Even as I reflect on the sessions that I had it is quite common for some of my first time client sessions to have some ego slipping a bit. As they were getting advanced information it still scared them. While some concepts were there and I was exploring and questioning those clients further, the ego rushed in to make it safer, simply smaller, versus the higher subconscious perspectives. I needed some time like all practitioners to learn the difference between this but when I was respective of all information. As I did my best to try to have my own discernment between, this is where you can get some differences in perspectives. Also as I know now there is different collective information which does and can be respected. You must be able to feel into and question everything and even practitioners having their own sessions to question everything, to go so deep to purely channel versus channeling your ego.

There are many states of mind that you can get your clients under and if they just close their eyes and look relaxed because they are relaxed and as they're allowing themselves to feel into their higher selves but yet still use the human egos to speak - is this entertainment? Is this a distraction? Even the vehicle herself has been through this experience where she has had information through clients that does not resonate with her. While she has respected the information and understood that this is important for that client to understand and to do their own inner work. She has also discovered and experienced clients who do not want to look at their own inner work and just want to focus on the dates of this shift, and how special they are, and who they have been in other lifetimes to make them feel justified that they're above others.

The spiritual ego has much to be said about, but it truly is just the ego, trying to be - you could say king or queen. While this is a lesson for you, I'm not trying to shame anyone. This is still a growing experience, it's a learning experience and there is nothing truly to be ashamed of. When you're focusing on unhealed and controlled ego's information, you should all be focusing on your own sessions and your own information to **empower yourselves** versus following anyone else. While we have said to think for yourselves and that is true, feel into all the information that has been given to you. We say dismiss none, consider all and feel into where **you** reside, at that level of perspective.

You know that there are many names and labels for many things. A simple apple has different titles and labels and has different varieties[32]. I say that there are many labels and different varieties of words that are all saying the same thing or referring and talking about the same thing. Catch yourselves are you still holding on to labels and names from certain things, when you are being distracted and misunderstanding the concepts that you were holding on to. I have said to you many times to check your belief systems and update them regularly by questioning and truly channeling your higher selves, your oversoul, your main guides, to know the difference[33]. This is a challenging thing when you're learning how to do these sessions to discern between 'was this your ego or was this an advanced beings?' and you can ask the practitioner to challenge your sessions

---

[32] *Over 7,500 cultivars of the apple.*

[33] *There was a group of Beings also talking with Dolores, the vehicle has asked her to speak for herself when she pops into sessions as she often comes into sessions to drop a statement and then leave. But the vehicle thinks she should acknowledge her words in sessions more. It is common for many beings to be sharing information in one session.*

by asking beyond .. I say the vehicle calls it blind question sessions where the client has no understanding or awareness of the questions going to be asked. It's not a personal statement and questions about them so they can truly relax having no accountability, no responsibility and no concerns or personal interest in the information. That can help as they can relax deeper and allow the higher dimensional beings to speak through. Again it takes a brave courageous human to surrender fully into sessions and to allow themselves to be experiencing this, to then remember that level of relaxation to then continue on with their own inner work. I see many of you using my work, using this work, using our work, for things that aren't truly empowering you. It does take time for you to honor and understand what you're doing in these sessions. While I was learning, you can say I made all the same mistakes you did, it's not mistakes - it's experiences. When you're holding on to one person's information is the truth, the fact. This is and could be making many assumptions that don't expand you.

When you look at some of my books and the information and my books and you can see the majority you could say single servings client sessions where there is still ego and there to some degree. It's still purposeful for you to expand your minds and expand your consciousness awareness to these concepts. Even if they're not a hundred percent accurate. If you challenged and questioned this now for yourselves, and of course we're on different timelines now. Of course you're experiencing different things that I was able to gage and to collect through my subjects. This is how humanity and planets evolve and explore and to still continue on. While it is frustrating that many egos are still being distracted and still not understanding that they have to do their inner work, to really and truly be able to honestly love all, to go with love and to even love thy enemy. Because thy enemy is simply an unhealed person struggling with the world. You know that this has nothing to do with you. They are rejecting their choices to empower themselves and therefore they are projecting their insecurities and their pains onto you.

I do say if you are controlling, potentially being a practitioner is not for you. Just as if you are controlling, being a healer is potentially not for you. You need to be of service and be humble to be able to use the energy frequency to love and share for all. Many are struggling to understand why their businesses are not thriving when they have other motives, such as being an influencer, being an entertainer, being respected for the information that they're gathering and yet it is all information for all. No one truly owns this information and so you can get hung up in your Egos and entitlement thinking that you are more elite and advanced because you have access to high dimensional beings.

You can see the egos, you can see the demeanors of many. When you can all focus on empowering yourselves to have the singularity focus of - love yourself and love all. To be able to have this and conduct yourself with this, you will notice how easy it is when you do find triggering moments. Remembering certain people in your life that will jump into your mindsets to remind yourselves of them and the dramas and dramatics that you played with each other to see that with love for those lessons that were teaching you how to empower yourselves. How to heal yourselves and how to have compassion for others who were still on their own journey also. There's much to be said about how you can support humanity while also supporting yourselves.

It is a good time for you to check what is holding you back and what is limiting you and what is distracting you?

Even if you think that someone is channeling advanced information, feel into this for yourselves. Have discernment and have your own sessions and truly surrender into the sessions. Truly allow the energy to flow through you, as you respecting the higher dimensional selves to take full control. They are here to help you and empower you and to talk about you, as uncomfortable as that may be. To give you the information for the perspectives that you need. You're using your free will to be able to empower yourselves to be the best version of yourself. To be able to be the best version, to be able to support and heal and love humanity through compassion and inspiration to inspire them to want to heal and recognize their power, their role and their importance and significance of being here.

That is the purpose of why you are here, to bring high frequency love and to share it with all. Anything else beyond that is a distraction. While you still have free will choices to be distracted, invest in your choices wisely, because humanity is needing your support more than ever before. While you can feel the density. While you can feel their fear where you can feel all their traumas and pain. We suggest that you don't feel into it so deeply that it stifles you and flattens you and depresses you. See their pain as motivation to love them more. To support them more to have compassion for them more arguing with them serves no one honoring them and where they're at. If they use the Bible and if they believe that there is a God, remind them of what God said to them through the Bible. Remind them what Jesus said to them through the Bible. When you are so stuck on being angry over evil. Being angry over all of the things that are helping awaken humanity by being so dramatic now that it's getting all of your attention. We're saying choose your energy frequencies wisely. Some of you are hating the system so much, you're sending negative energy, we could say you're complying to the control systems. You're complying to those who are wanting to harm humanity. You're choosing to harm yourself with that choice of Free Will energy frequencies that are so dense it's depleting you. While you think that you're justified to be angry and to hate the systems that we are saying that is deeply disempowering you. The systems are there to awaken you, not to distract you from wanting to lower density. The systems are there to remind you how humanity has been so corrupted and so coerced and comply because humanity ornately is good. Humanity wants good for all and humanity wants to be in unity and to be together and unfortunately when there is a big system that is trying to coerce them into doing something that is not for their empowerment humanity still has at collective level wants to follow and comply and be diligent and to be seen as good humanitarians. This is why they can easily be manipulated because all they need to be told is you need to do something for someone else and humanity will step up for that. Humanity doesn't necessarily do things for itself but humanity will do things for each other if they believe that this is going to help someone else. This is an important thing for you to understand. Humanities want to help itself out but are focusing on each other more on how to support others versus actually empowering themselves. You need to know where you should be empowering yourselves and how you should be empowering yourselves and when you are simply energetic beings holding a higher frequency of energy towards the love spectrum it makes sense to focus on that always.

When you are having your friends and family from the past pop into your mind for them to visit to remind you of your lessons and experiences together which was always meant to help you grow, don't fear that you are losing and going backwards in your empowerment and your inner work. This is you in that moment observing and having the opportunity to love them and send love to them. As you reflect on the lessons of how you are supposed to empower yourselves. Maybe empowering yourself did sound like standing up for yourself and maybe standing up for yourself did sound like heated and compassionate and passionate words of 'I do not deserve this respect I love you but I do not deserve your disrespect'. Sometimes when you have struggled to find those words of empowerment you have felt the disrespect and you've only focused on the disrespect versus how you could have empowered yourself through it. You say to yourselves now and that memory moment of conflict being disrespected gives you an opportunity to find empowerment of self to stand up to someone who was trying to belittle you and diminish you, to mock you and disempower you. You didn't have the confidence because you were hurt by the accusations and the disrespect in itself go back in your mind's eye to go back to that time when that conflict happened and speak your voices now say to that teacher you did not deserve that respect say do the ex-boyfriend or girlfriend or friend 'I don't deserve this disrespect I love you thank you for this lesson but I will not be believing or tolerating or accepting your words of disrespect'.

Also look at the times when you were not respectful to others and they were teaching you moments of how you were disrespecting others so honestly reflect on the experiences we do not judge you or see you as good or bad. We see you all playing and having experiences to learn and grow from. Still we do expect you all to love each other and when you choose not to love each other at a Soul level you are being disrespectful. Therefore your energy frequency towards them is being disrespectful. This is something for you to consider and we have said to you to be accountable and responsible for your energy frequencies. If there are still people in your lives and still situations in your lives that you cannot respect and cannot love, we suggest you look at this now because this is limiting you and holding you back at an energetic frequency to be able to love all.

While there is so much that we still would like to say and to share we feel like this message is the most important one to truly focus on and we have said this to you in various different ways, different directions and different approaches to these messages. We say this is the most significant one for you to focus on and anything else at this point is the distraction within itself. We are saying for those people who were boldly sharing the information about the crimes against humanity and they are in fear, that could be part of their purpose to share the information to prove to those people who are still doubting the corruption and the manipulation. Do not judge them for their mission and purpose but we are saying to those people who are listening to us, ultimately as we are scanning your purpose of mission, is to hold the higher frequency of love. We understand that you want to get distracted sometimes. We understand you want to feel angry and fight the systems and choose other choices to feel into the density and the frustrations. We say you still have free will choices to do that. We are impressing upon you all. We would prefer it if you had a higher frequency demeanor to not get distracted and to just hold the high frequency of love. We say when you have this higher frequency of love it feels like everything else is too draining for you to focus on. Go with time and experiences to just sit with that higher frequency of energy and we feel like some people don't like this because they don't feel productive and we are saying you are very productive when you're holding high frequency energies of love and sharing that. That is the most predominant, the most helpful role to have here on Earth. We say that you feel like it is not enough but you cannot see the impact of holding higher frequency energy. It is tremendous and extremely needed. We're saying to you please take some time to notice your surroundings and get into a comfortable position. We say you can be laying down or sitting up. Take a moment to look at your surroundings that you're in and close your eyes. Now we want to start using your energetic mind's eye to imagine the energy frequency that you are emulating out. We want you to add color to it. We want you to recognize the energy frequency levels of where you're at now, being an energy being. With your eyes closed we want you to feel and sense your physical body and even beyond your physical body. To start reading your own energy frequency. Feel into this, assign it colors if you will. To recognize, you have started to understand and recognize your range of emotions and you've been able to understand and label them. Now we would like you to focus on labeling but visually your energy frequency. When you are in a different range of emotions and different range of energetics we want you to start recognizing this energy frequency that you were sharing and emulating out beyond.

This will help you focus and this will help you make you feel like you're doing something because some of you sitting there being high frequency can't see it because you're using your visual eyes, and so you get distracted and you feel like it is not worthy or worthwhile. We want you to start doing this exercise of closing your eyes and start seeing the energetic body and recognizing it. The more you do this and the more you start becoming aware visually, you will get more visual sensations of color pulsings, and energetic frequencies. We're warning you to focus on this more and you'll start recognizing as soon as you do this you will start feeling a response in your energetics and your body will start heating up. We are saying we are not doing this and you start noticing your hands are starting to heat up, grab or imagine holding large vessels of water and start infusing your energy frequency into that water. You can imagine the lakes you have seen, the rivers you have seen, the beaches you've been to imagine being there now and holding all of that water within your hands, with this high energy frequency.

We are saying look up at the sky and hold as much air as you possibly can. Also send the energy frequency that you are doing. You can also do it to nature, to people, to the planet.

When you have that heat within your hands, this is your higher energy frequency of love, that is wanting to acclimate and balance the energy frequency, to hold it, to nurture it and to support it. We want you to **start using your energy** to be able to start supporting all. You will notice when you start thinking about this some parts of your hands will go cold, as it is absorbing the density. We say keep going, notice the senses of the wrists, you were never disconnected from this high energy of frequency so keep being focused. **Use your power,** use your energy of love to start.

We say while you cannot fix and heal the world you can start releasing some of its density. As you're noticing you're driving this energy down further beyond, you could say, the core of the planet, you're removing it from people's energy fields. You're removing it from animals and plants. You're giving them a breath, you're giving them upliftment. What they do with that choice of energy difference is a choice that they make.

We say that when you lift the energy of people that is dense, they have an opportunity to have epiphanies of empowerment and to enjoy the difference. Do not take it personally if they still want to be diligent with their negativity. They may have to work on the inner work and their perspectives to be able to gain more power and control over their perspectives of the world to see the lessons versus struggle with the opportunities to grow. When we say to you go and fill into your energy frequency and to feel into who you are and to feel into the energy that you can hold, we are saying this can be beautiful to be of service. We want you to get more used to the energy frequency of who you were and the Soul within you because then you're going to be able to more accurately recognize other energy frequencies of other people that you are around. To be able to support the energetic fields. We say do not take the pain from them. That is not possible but when you are feeling into where their pain is at, using your expression and choices of words to be able to empower them to support them to remember how powerful they are. Remember that they're here to be of service to be of purpose but to love themselves as a primary focus to be able to then know what love is to be able to accept it from others.

This is a beautiful time for you to be able to be of service this way not only energetically but expressionally as you're conversing and supporting others.

Support others, love others. We say even when you see people are using the egos you can still support them because they are struggling. You can see where they're at, but you can still love them and inspire them to not have their insecurities on their sleeves but to know their value and their self-worth.

We see some people have weak moments and they need more support than others and while we know it's tempting for you to judge them as being egoic, they still need love. They still need support. They still need compassion.

As you are now focusing more on your energy frequency bodies. Have fun with this exploration because knowing thyself is very powerful and very empowering, to remember your energy frequency does impact others. Thus we believe that you're going to be more responsible and accountable for this.

We say this with much love and appreciation for you all as you're willing to be of service.

To truly love and humble yourselves, to then truly be able to humbly love others.

And we say this with love.

Session 28: Take The Wheel, Be Metaphysically Mature

Yes! Yes! Yes! Yes! Yes! The vehicle thinks she is very funny and we are supporting her as she is choosing high frequency energy to enjoy herself and find grace and her humor. And we will help focus with this as she is in such an excitable mood as she is feeling the completion of yet another mission we have given her. And so she is feeling satisfied and has gratitude towards herself and all who have been able to support with this. This is no easy task and it is quite a feat, you could say, as there have become many achievable inner work hurdles that have empowered them all. And so she was referencing earlier that she opened herself up to have any messages that any Soul wanted to reach out and send a message because she could feel that there was much chatter going on. And so, while she was focusing on her human world and her human life, she also doesn't forget that she is a messenger.

And so she said prior to this session as she felt the energy of Jesus come in, and yes, he does go by many names. She is happy to have a lazy label of him being Jesus, he does not mind because he has many lazy labels for her, which is human, (laughing) and vehicle. And so that is how they respect each other. He likes to use this energy frequency vessel because she lets him take the wheel. She finds that very funny because he says he knocks on many of your hearts and many of your minds and many of your lives to awaken you to hear his messages and to heed his call. And yet you shut down those messages and those energy frequency connections quickly. He is saying he has even been referred to as Darkness because his energy was so strong. Instead of the person accepting this is Jesus's message for loving you, they went into instant fear and rejected it and prayed for help again. And ironically that was why he was there in the first place. So he says he has struggles too, to get his messages out. And his energy frequency is so strong it makes people feel quite sick to their stomachs as he's literally touching all their pain and trying to uplift and heal and love them. But he can trigger. He triggers many with his energy, not that he means to. He wants to love all! But when you're a high frequency vessel being, coming in to help others who are in darkness, it can feel very stifling. And so this is why he had to come to many in dreams. And he loves that! Because you are not afraid of being in a dream as such when you see his imagery. He says you all have these idyllic images of what he looks like and he says he's fine with that. He's cool with that. And he says, look beyond the physical to feel my energy of Love radiating out to you all, because I am the energy of frequency of love. I am Love! And if you did need to put a physicality to my love energy, have humor, don't argue with people of the shade of my skin. Argue with people that I *do Love you!* I have always loved you! That is my messages you're supposed to focus on. Not the color of my eyes. Not the color of my skin. Not what I was doing as I was being Human. Don't focus on those details as such, but listen to the messages of love!

And so I feel like I've got your attention now! I love the humor because it uplifts you. But there is also time to be serious. And there is also time to honor Love! Honor thyself! Honor thy mother and father as they did the best they could for thee! You chose your parents! Honor thy brother and sisters beyond blood because you're souls, and you all have that connection of being brothers and sisters. Hate none! Love all! The messages of love get tuned out. And we have found that the messages of war, of hate, of evil, actually does get more attention. As you're not interested in loving yourselves, you're interested in hating others because that is a reflection of part of your Soul inner work, because some parts of you hate yourselves and so therefore you need to hate others to justify the way you feel about the loathing of self. You're mirroring each other's emotional traumas! You're mirroring each other's inner work and you're triggering each other doing so.

The message very firmly that I shared with the vehicle to get her attention to recognize that I have a message for you all is, there is a saying about the mark of the beast, and I want you to know that with your choices that you make, you are making a mark on the world. You make your mark on the world. And it is your demeanor and attitudes to the world that makes that mark. Are you sharing with the world you're love, and making *that* mark on the world? Are you sharing hate to the world and making *that* mark on the world? You're making marks with every choice. You're making marks with every response and reaction. With every smile you're making a mark! With every hatred disparaging slap to shut people down *you* are making that mark!

There are many things that can be explored when you're trying to translate the Bible and when you're trying to translate the messages that have been shared. But when you're trying to distract yourselves from your behaviors, your demeanors, your actions, your attitudes, your agendas, your choice of who to love and your choice to who you think you can be justified to hate, you're making marks to everyone and in energetic frequency vibrations you are making statements to the world!

What is your mark?
What is your mark?

How are you remarking to the world that you're here to be of service to love everyone?
And how you don't need anything from anyone else as you know that you're capable of loving yourself!

Inspiring yourself!
Encouraging yourself!
Entertaining yourself!
Supporting yourself!
Inspiring yourself!

There's so much to be said about how you can empower yourself to then be of service to others. But we say some of you are not wanting to empower yourselves because you're wanting support from others to make you feel like you're comfortable to make that step, to take that leap!

Look at your behaviors!
Look at what you're telling yourself!
Look at what you're remarking to yourselves about what you can and can't do.

Are you still being accountable for all the things you're saying to yourself to not share, to not spread love, to not give joy, to not give compliments, to not celebrate each other's growth?

To celebrate everyone's healing?
To celebrate everyone's journey?
To celebrate Love!

Look at your behaviors.
Look at your beliefs.

How are you making a mark on this world?
Are you angry? Are you hurt? Are you lonely? Are you sad?

We could say that all of those range of emotions are very valid. But when you know that you are the solution to those feelings.

You are safe.
Accept that! Trust that! Feel that!

You're never alone!
Feel that! Accept that! Trust that!

You're hurting because you feel the pain of others. You're also hurting because you feel the pain of self. Because you know that things aren't quite right here and haven't been quite right here for a while. And that is why you need to grow with your confidence and encouragement to spread love. To love all! Even those who do not agree with your choices. Those who don't agree with your fashion. Those who don't agree with anything that you're behaving and conducting yourselves. Still love them because you do not want to keep this cycle of rejection towards each other or disrespect towards each other. Be the bigger person who loves themselves so much that when they are ridiculed by others it doesn't impact you. Even if they cut your skin, it doesn't impact you. Because you know that when you hurt others, that lives in your consciousness forever and you remember how terrible you feel. The guilt that you feel. You can't shut that down! You can't dismiss that! You can't pretend it didn't happen and you'll be constantly triggered to remember about your actions and how horrible you were with your choices to hurt others. You will so vividly see the cut. You will visually remember the site and it will repeatedly memory loop for you to remember what you've done. It is to humble yourselves and to have different choices moving forward. And for the victim who felt that one cut, you do heal! Your skin heals! You know you didn't deserve that. You know that someone was literally lashing out to make their mark of pain on you. When you love yourself and tend to those wounds, you know they heal fast. When you pick away at the scabs, when you squeeze the scabs, when you throw salt on those scabs and open the wounds again, it will not heal. It doesn't heal as fast as it could. We see some of you wanting to keep those wounds open emotionally and physically. Why do you still need to hold on to those wounds? What do you think? What do you feel?

It is time for you to start answering these things for yourselves. To truly be honest to yourselves. To notice and catch your reactions, your thoughts and your mindsets onto these things. This is your inner work, your inner thinking, the inner remarks you're making about yourselves, and the outward remarks you're making of others. Are you still judging people for when they were trying to heal for themselves? What are you doing? And why are you doing this still? When you love yourself completely and know that everything that you've experienced were lessons to empower yourself, be grateful for the lessons because they were to empower you and to teach you to be a better human. To have compassion and consideration for others so you would step with grace and step with care around others who were still on their healing journey.

The Collectives are saying that they believe so strongly in all of you. They believe that you can open your hearts to have compassion for all. It's simply a choice. It's simply a choice to feel into the energy frequency of love and accept everyone and see that everyone is on their learning journey. That the Souls are struggling to identify to be playing human. To be kind to each other. To love each other and to recognize once again that you're truly unified. You're truly brothers and sisters. You're truly one! Don't get fixated on the roles that others are playing to dramatize and awaken. They have given you teachable moments to notice the corruption. Without them teaching you these things and setting examples and showing the way, many would not have been able to awaken. And so many players who had to be dramatic to get your attention, to trigger you to start thinking for yourselves, to start feeling for yourselves and to start considering that complying to these systems may not be the most empowering part for you in your Earth's role now.

Feel into all of this, take moments and longer moments within your days, to be with yourself and to feel into all of this that we have said today. We know that you need encouragement and we're always here for you. But when you go within and when you have a higher vibrational approach to life, you'll find us waiting for you. We want you to take your wheel with courage and strength and focus and diligence, knowing you are here for a mission to be seen, to be heard, to be felt, with love and compassion. To stand up and rise against all of those systems that are trying to disempower you. There is no such thing as too much confidence! There is no such thing as too much love! There is no such thing as too much pride in terms of knowing who you are! And you are here to Love humanity. And you're here to reassure humanity these systems that have been keeping you enslaved and distracted do not serve you anymore. There is unity and there is only Love that can bring you together and to stop distracting yourselves with the details of the Grand Awakening! Understand your Souls have lived here and lived many places. Understand you are fractions of Source! Understand that this is one, but many lifetimes you're experiencing. Understand how powerful you are when you're out of the third dimension and accept how limited you are being in the third dimension as it's a manual planet to feel and navigate through the emotions and to converse and communicate with each other with language. But when your energy frequency is High Love and wants to share compassion to all, that is what is being read versus your anger and your hatred towards others.

Have a pure heart! Have pure intentions to love all! And that is when your best messages will be heard. Because it is not infiltrated with other energy frequencies that are hidden by density and resentfulness, embitterment and all those other emotions that you've already graduated from. Be with peace and share that Love for all! You are here for this! And we are here supporting you all at an energetic frequency. We play our role. We're reminding you with love, to focus on yours!

We say this with love!

Session 29: Dump That Density

Yes! Yes! Yes! We are here! We are here! We are here! We are the Arcturians speaking to you directly in confirmation and clarification of what is occurring. And it gives us great pleasure to see that what you could say is controlling situations, scenarios, people are feeling so triggered they are jumping ahead of themselves and this is fantastic! As we knew, when we give information to the Conscious Collective, this exposes their agenda and it makes them feel afraid at an unconscious level that their plans are not going to be as impactful. They're still confused why their other plans and their events and their... What could we say to explain this to you easier? They can't understand why they're not impacting the bodies as much as they had planned and intended to. And they felt very confident in this. *Extremely* confident in this! And they felt quite justified in what they were doing to cleanse the planet from those who were, you could say, not in their importance. They had other agendas. And as you are aware of them and you're not afraid of them because you know your life contracts will always be protected versus other people's free will choices, and these are people using their free will to try to have a genocide of a big proportion of humanity for their own agenda.

And while they feel like it was somewhat successful, they are still confused and very frustrated why it wasn't as successful as they wanted and planned. And of course, the elephant in the room you could say, is *us* and all of the collectives that are aware of this. But this isn't us allowing bad behavior. This is us allowing the Grand Awakening. And as many are graduating and completing their life missions and purposes on Earth and they are exiting to go to elsewhere as per their life contracts, per their Soul needs, and is required to do for its own journey, this was acceptable for us to have this to give them the illusion that they were 'winning' versus many people exiting. This is all part of the Awakening and it always has been part of the Awakening to understand what the control agendas are really focusing on. But we have said to you many times, and we will say this to you again, *no one leaves this planet a second before it is intended for the life contract!* And we are their guides and we are parts of them focusing on this and honoring this. This is our role! This is literally why you have what you say, Guardian Angels! We watch you to make sure you're having your appropriate and most desirable experiences! So therefore, why would we just let you have exit points when you still have work to do? And if you've got 3D Earthwork to do, you're still here!

We've explained this to you many times and we see that so many are still in fear of exit points, and angry that people are dying because of this agenda. We're saying, if you will, you're all batteries of energy. And if you want to support, you could say the *dark side* for the dramatics of this conversation, if you wanted to support the dark side... *Be* in density. *Be* in anger! *Be* in rage! *Be* in resentfulness! Demand justice and be very angry and bitter, with revenge on your mind. When you choose to feel into all of those ranges of frequencies, you're playing for the dark agenda you could say. You are part of the darkness, you are part of the density here. And so it's a choice that you're making constantly. Are you going to choose to be in love frequency or are you going to choose to do something else? And when you do not have applied metaphysical perspectives and knowledge and wisdom, of course you could feel every choice of emotions every single day. You could have the gymnastics of the range of emotions as you were trying to figure out what's going on for the

World and why. And that is natural. That is human. But we're asking some of our, what you could say favorite batteries, your energy beings here that are holding higher frequency for the planet and for other humans here and other species and other beings here. Because you are all one and you're to be of service. And so it doesn't surprise the vehicle when she sees these potential large energy beings choosing and resisting, quite purposely, not to support humanity. To judge them, label them, think that they are elevated beyond them. And yet when she's talking to them, they're tripping over their egos and arrogance and ignorance with metaphysical perspectives because they feel very entitled and justified and almost trapped to be here. And this is not an accident when she has been having to have conversations with certain people who are not listening to our information because they do not respect us, because they already think that they know it. They already think that they know all the information and they're just waiting for the shift, and actually quite impatient with the shift. In fact, they're only seeking out information about the shift to hear when they are leaving. When they're given opportunities to be of support to the Conscious Collective, they block it and shut it down. They do not want to be of service.

And so this is what the vehicle wanted us to explain and show to her. Because she was still trying to understand what was holding back those big ego people from humbling themselves to actually be able to grow and to be of service and assistance to humanity. Raising their frequency vibrations to be at a higher Love frequency for all, versus just loving themselves. And there is a huge difference energy wise. And so the people that are trying to boost themselves up with confidence of how amazing they are and how special they are and how much of a gift they add to humanity, but yet do nothing much for humanity apart from shun them, shame them, and label them as being human.

There are interesting things and we have much to say about this. But what she was trying to really ascertain and have classic examples of and reminders of is that those big ego people truly come from insecurity. And so they have to boost their egos and boost their talents and their skill sets and how important they are and how significant they are to her. To be able to feel confident and to feel that they are valued and that they want her to know how special they are. And ultimately you don't need to tell her anything. Energy doesn't lie! And she can see from demeanors and behaviors where people are at. And so she wonders, what does she do with this? Does she call them out on their limited perspectives and their arrogance or does she just accept them, try to give them perspectives, but realize that they're still not able to listen to her and they're still focused on self. And this is part of their journey, and she's asking for all of the Guides and all of the Collectives to be able to have stronger impressions, to humble people's egos to make them recognize and learn and notice that they don't know everything. And that they're here to be of service to be at a higher frequency of Love for all! And yet some of their entitlements distract them and blind them from expanding at a conscious level and a compassion level. We also want to just say that there are some that have been listening to this information who then have changed their course and the way that they wanted to impact humanity. They are starting to lose control and so they're starting to do reckless things to be able to make the impact. To make the fear and to have distractions. This is all purpose!

But as we have said before, be mindful of what you're using on the body, including eye drops. And we have said this to you before when they were trying to process and make fear-mongering, scaremongering protections. And of course it would sound absurd if you try to tell your grandparents or your neighbors to not use eye wash because of course, it's up to them what they do with their Free Will choices. But we want you to be reminded again, how when you choose to use your Free Will it can impact you if this is something that is not good for your body. And so it can set you back somewhat, we could say, as you then would have to heal the body. But if you're struggling with eyesight and if you are struggling to heal and filtrate through those poisons and those toxins, it can distract you. And then we can see that many go into victim mode because they don't know how to approach this and they go into fear. And ultimately, isn't it a great gift to lose your sight? Because then all of your other senses are heightened and then you have to go within because all of your distractions have been taken away from you at a visual level. And so then you have to listen more intently. And imagine that for humanity. Having to listen versus distracting yourselves with judgment of visual sights. Judgment of others. Judgment of situations. And just even being distracted with visuals. And so we say it's not an accident that many people are struggling with their eyesights. And this could be so intensive that certain Guides have decided that their eyesights for their 3D counterparts will be severely impacted as they are just too distracted at this point. And yes, you could go into fear and feel victim and vulnerable because this has happened to you. But we are saying, when everything is significant and purposeful and you have chosen not to listen to us, you have chosen to shut us down, in fact you've chosen to shut down being of service to humanity, what other options do we have left for this Grand Awakening for you to focus on yourself and look at your inner work and to be able to drop your judgments.

Open your hearts and minds to bigger concepts that your human egos are resisting to be open to. The whole point of expanding your Consciousness was to be able to understand bigger concepts at a metaphysical level to be able to understand the significance of what is going to be happening to you so you do not go into frequency vibration density, but to be able to have a balanced and neutral perspective of it moving forward. To be able to then support others who don't have the luxury or the privilege to be able to actually understand what is happening at a metaphysical level as they are processing all the experiences of daily events for the Grand Awakening. As they choose to feel all the range of feelings that is a product of the experiences and you could say, consistent disclosures now that are on high repeat for those people who are just starting to awaken. There is so much information it's very overwhelming for them, because it's at a concentrated level versus those people who have been awake for some years, even decades! The information is so provable now and there are so many statements of proof and facts that are showing directly that the mainstream media has not been journalistic integrity skill sets of information that has been from a neutral perspective of well researched and disclosing the truth of all conducts of businesses and all conducts of influential people. Much has been hidden from you through, we can say just, closed legal cases that are not made public. And private information that should be public that has been censored, locked down, hidden for your safety ironically, as they would try to convince people who were questioning '*why is this information not public?'* Those who are trying to control you, do not have faith in you, do not believe in you in some regards, but yet go out of their way to make sure you are belittled. It's their insecurities because they know when you connect in, you are unified, you are very powerful! They want you to believe them which is teaching you to not believe in yourselves. They're wanting you to be so disconnected from self and so disconnected from each other as humanitarians, as humanity, that you still fight and see conflict and war and judgment of others.

We are saying, when you have balance and spiritual maturity you see all humans as one, as equal to each other. And you truly and honestly have compassion for each other at a Soul level regardless of what that human is choosing to do with their lives. Of course, there are many that are choosing to not step up to be of service as per their life contract and mission. This is where the vehicle is getting her attention pushed by us because we are hoping she can trigger them because they're shutting us out. And so there is much to be said about that. She is asking and we are confirming, she has many questions. We want this segment to be public but she has private questions about events and we are saying we want to share it with her, but we're wanting *you* to find your balance and peace with everything as a reader because that's what you need to focus on. And we say we have seen us give you public information and you have not been able to handle it because you go into a deeper sense of fear. And so we are saying, when you keep your balance and when you practice keeping in neutral, then you will naturally be able to see what is unfolding and why and you will not need our information directly as you will feel into what is happening and it will just be observations versus reactions to any other density.

And so we just want to remind you all that things are ramping up, because those humans that want to control you are feeling out of control. And you knew that this was going to be happening and you knew that this was going to be ramping up. And you can see this now! And we see that for some of you this is starting to give you actual solid proof of what we've been telling you all along. And so this is a marvelous time! We are also wanting to say publicly that many people did not want to listen to the Jesus message or even the Dolores Cannon message because for whatever reasons you feel insignificant to those Souls! The role of Jesus is so significant that you feel insecure, so you don't want to listen to him. And so we are saying, it's all your choices how you want to empower yourselves and expand your consciousnesses. And there is a huge difference from many people who are seeing their value, their self-worth and recognizing and knowing that they are significant as everyone else is significant. And as you are, what we crassly called you as labels, as we labeled you as batteries, it is because you are vessels of energy! And this was a good translation we thought to be able to describe what you were here for. And for many who are raising their frequency vibrations to a really pure beautiful frequency, this is much appreciated because you are opening the consciousnesses of others as they are being relieved from the density that they want to hold on to. And so, if you will, while they're holding on to density, they can feel your energy around them, surrounding them. This leviates, you could say, them. You lift them up energetically. It secures them. They recognize this energy frequency and it relaxes them physically and emotionally. And so they're more tempted to release the density.

And we also wanted to say again to those who have missed the statement from us before, when you think you're grounding onto the Earth, we've heard many of you say this before, that you want to ground, and we would like to give you another perspective of what you're really doing is dumping. It's a perspective, but you're dumping your dense energy into the ground beyond. Because you know that that is what the planet is supposed to be there for right now. And when it was at a higher frequency to uplift you this was fantastic because it did uplift you, but you're already more of a high frequency than the planet. And so you're not gaining any uplifting energy from the planet because you're beyond the planet's energy frequency. And so when you are supporting others' density and you're absorbing their density because you're listening to them and you're feeling into all of the concerns and worries, when someone tells you what they're struggling with they feel released from this because they've expressed this. You feel it and you hold on to their density as you have listened to them. And then that density, that heaviness, that pain, that sorrow, that tragedy, that emotion that you have felt from them, that you've helped them release because they have felt it and it's an energy transfer. It's an energy transfer exchange, if you will. And so, when you are grounding yourself you're really dumping the energy into the planet and you're releasing it from you as well at an energetic level. And this is why you feel uplifted! Because you've dumped that density! It is not because the planet has given you magical powers or given you extra boost energy. You *are* that boost of energy and this is why you are here on the planet. As you are knowing the status of the planet right now this would make sense to you. And so check your terminologies and understand what you're doing.

Are you still thinking the planet is uplifting you? Or do you realize that you are here to uplift the frequency energy of those living beings around you and you're using the planet's density to just add into the density and dump the density that you're holding from other humans and other beings down into the ground. And you can say that the planet now was almost like, for dramatics, a black hole! And it is just absorbing all the density that it is because it is just so great and vast now. You're trying to uplift people out of this density! You're trying to separate people from their mindsets of this density and to be able to uplift them to trust that they can let go of their pain! Let go of their triggering emotional looping patterns. To be able to understand the significance and purpose of the events that have happened for them which have been teachable moments and experiences for them. Because remember, the whole purpose of being in 3D life on Earth is to have the emotional range of experiences but to not get stuck in the details of it or one singular event but to be able to grow from them! To heal from it! And to recognize the teachable moments.

It was never supposed to get you stuck in these frequencies of experiences. It was supposed to be an evolving journey. And we see some of you still holding on to events from past traumas where you can't quite let them go. And some of you don't realize that some of these are haunting you still, as we could say, because there is still that child or that teenager or *you* last week [Laughter] that's experiencing something that they didn't like and they can't understand. And so when they can't understand that the lesson was always to empower them, they are still on the healing and learning journey. And ultimately, every one of you is on your healing and learning journey. And so there is no point in comparing yourselves to each other because you're all on different races distances. Some of you have got miles. Some of you have got centimeters. And that is exactly what your life contract had for you! And we are supporting you with that!

And so, as we leave with you today to say to you that you are *very* capable of choosing high frequency energy. You're *very* capable of choosing to Love yourself and others. And you're *very* capable of supporting everyone who is wanting to have a metaphysical perspective to be able to understand that there is no such thing as good or evil. It is about all lessons, all experiences, and for the Grand Awakening! It is to remind you that you have always been and you always will be more than just human this one lifetime! It is advanced concepts! But you are here to empower yourselves through this to be of service!

We say this with love and gratitude for you all who are taking this mission and taking the energetic frequency vibrations responsibility and true accountability as you are very mindful of your thoughts, your reactions and your behaviors as you slow down those reactions of judgment to notice this is the old you, you have grown. Catch yourselves when you wanting to resist loving each other and loving self. We are saying you have to manually update your mindsets. You are very capable of this and it takes practice. And we will support you and encourage and guide you. And as you know, we are always within you! We're always around you! And we always want the best for you because some of you are wanting to choose to feel isolated and alone. And wanting to choose to feel frustrated. And as that is your choices, we want to remind you and ask you... *Do you remember what high frequency energy of love feels like?* And we want you to answer this... *Why do you choose to not feel* like *you deserve that*? We say Empower yourselves and start getting excited because there are so many things that are going to confirm to you what you already know is going to happen.

And so this is just great clarity! Great confirmation! And so practice and see if you dive into density or if you rise above it and have complete balance in neutral. Again it's all your choices! But when you recognize and realize how much your energy frequency impacts others, you would be more responsible and accountable for those choices!

And we say this with love!

Session 30: To Occur For The Grand Awakening

Yes, yes, yes. We're here, we're here, we're here[34], and we do love it when we know the vehicle uses her free will to say to us "What is the message that you have for humanity?", because this opens up all possibilities from our perspective, to be able to share, and so we get the opportunity to then scan to see who is listening and what information are they seeking to be able to empower themselves and support themselves in the best ways possible with the best perspectives. Of course we can give you all the perspectives in the world, it is up to you to apply it. We see that many people who are still asking questions out loud, even in their mindsets of the questions that they are still stumbling over. This world can be quite confusing when you don't have the perspective of why the Grand Awakening is occurring.

Many people are noticing with such great excitement about many disclosures popping up in every which direction. People who were quite firmly and very boldly refusing to consider anything else but the official mainstream narrative are now slowly but surely starting to question, because they have memories, they have intelligence, and they have awareness of what has been occurring for you, for what you consider many years now. This has not been a distraction or dismissed by them, they are observing. The best thing we see about you reacting in such trauma about such tragedies and high alert scare factors such as viruses - it got your attention. Those who are terrified and scared were listening to every single thing that was said about it, because they knew to keep themselves safe they must listen, they must consider and abide and comply and obey. Now they are

---

[34] *The Collectives, as presented through the Arcturian subconscious.*

noticing how that truth unfolded for their history and for those people who were telling them one thing once. Now they're starting to notice that that was inaccurate information. They are awakening. They are awakening, and you do not need to know about all of the systems and all of the control levels and layers that have been going on your planet to start awakening to one thing. When you are so afraid of one thing and then you notice it kind of fading away, kind of dismissing itself, when you were told absolutely distinctively that this would be the end of humanity if you do not comply, and yet you know, they know certain people who refuse to get vaccinated, for example, and yet they are living their best lives, bold on social media, bold in their personal lives, still living.

Isn't that interesting? Doesn't it make you stop and question? When you're noticing many people with sudden health issues that are beyond the original scare factor, so many healthy people having so many sudden exit points, this gets noticed, because you're suddenly starting to think "That's great, that they're safe from the virus, but how come they suddenly had, at a healthy young age, a heart attack?" They start questioning things like "when did healthy people start having heart attacks? When did healthy people suddenly die?" This is awakening.

We have said to you before, when you're afraid of death you suddenly start living, and we can say to you now - when you are afraid of death you suddenly start thinking, and you can even start having independent thoughts. Isn't that empowering? Isn't that wonderful, to notice all of the influential information that has been hammered, driven firmly into your awareness, of what you must do and how you must be afraid of each other. Now you're starting to be awoken from that daze, awoken from that craze, awoken from that fear.

You may hear "people got sick from that virus". This is what you perceive, because that's what the official doctor told them. That's the official narrative. We say isn't it marvelous for you to start questioning all systems and all information, because isn't this a marvelous time to do so? You still have freedom to think, you still have freedom to speak, isn't that wonderful? It's almost as if you've always had the opportunity to do so. Isn't it marvelous when you take full empowerment and full control over your thinking and speaking, to share and to think and to grow and expand and evolve beyond what you have been told is safe thinking, because all thinking is safe as you explore and meander your thoughts and feelings. You controlled them both. You can control your thoughts and you can control your feelings. They're all about you. That is marvelous for you to be responsible for all about you.

We see some people are afraid to hear other people's information, because suddenly they are afraid that that scare Factor will become their reality. If you hear something bad, you're going to manifest it into your world and that is going to occur. This blocks a lot of people from starting to think and ponder about coming events, and what could happen if certain systems do keep complying and evolving and manipulating and coercing humanity. How far will that go? They do not want to think about it because they do not want to feel that fear and that worry and concern for today, because they know it may be not an eventuality or they just sort of dismiss it and hope that they can focus on something that is healthy and happy for them. They know that they don't have emotional balance when they learn new things and when they hear new things, and so they dismiss it, avoid it. You could say they are being ostriches that put their heads in the sand. That keeps them safe they think, but as we have said before, you can't stop what's coming. That may scare you, because you feel like that is not part of your control or your free will or your choices. But when you understand the life you're living and why, you'll accept all situations, because as you know, everything is an experience and a lesson for you to have here on Earth. You wanted the full diversity of it.

There aren't many that wanted to be here to have a few experiences and to then be stagnant for decades. It is not possible. You're constantly growing, as there are and there always will be messages and influences that are prompting you to expand your mindsets and your awarenesses and your knowledge, as you are aware of what is coming and what has been occurring, this is what you call the Ascension, which is the expansion of consciousness of mindsets. This is fantastic because you are needing to be able to grasp more than just being human, and just having what you could consider basic normal routine patterns and behaviors as being human, and the responses of the connections with each other as being human. When you have your Ascension process, which is expanding your mindsets to understand you are more than that, your Souls living as humans and having this experience and lessons, and as souls, you will be shifting beyond being human to elsewhere and this is extraordinary, as you are aware that at a collective level, you could perceive in your short distance of time together you will be shifting, and this is marvelous.

We've distracted ourselves from the original conversation that we wanted to discuss, so we apologize, but there are so many of us speaking to so many of you... so we say hello hello hello hello! We are saying we've always been here and we're always happy to assist you. We know that you listen through these channelings to be able to hear information as you do, and we love this about you. You ask us to give this vehicle information to be able to empower you, and we think that is so marvelous, that you're using your free will to do that. So we're honoring you today. We're confirming to you indeed the Grand Awakening is getting stronger as more people are starting to notice inconsistent messages from the narratives. Plus people that they actually respect are coming out in droves to speak about their profession and to speak about their intel and intelligence of situations. They have not been empowering humanity. They actually have been hiding the truth for all humanity, and this is interesting because there are many bold and brave people now speaking the truth and getting hurt. This is a marvelous time to be heard, and this is a marvelous time because you're actually seeking information to clarify and to confirm your own intuition and your own insights into the information that you have pondered. Maybe you haven't shared this publicly. You've kept it to yourself, because you feel like it is so obvious, but also you're wanting to comply, and so you're juggling with your minds and your information as you were wanting to keep your heads down and be normal and act human. Yet you know that you're beyond even being human. These are for the advanced Souls who are here to hold a higher frequency energy of Love, which is a very advanced energy frequency. They're more focused on being stable with their balance of emotional ranges and to just be in that higher frequency energy, to be able to support all that are also here, to be able to hold what you could call "light bearers".

There are many names and labels that are being used, but you're physically here holding higher frequency energies as you were not distracting yourselves with the dramas and the disinformation and going into fear. You know that you are those higher energy frequency beings, because you aren't emotionally reactive to anything anymore, to such disclosures or even the manipulation or control systems. You respect that they are part of the awakening, to push people and to trigger people into the epiphanies of actually being able to start thinking and feeling for themselves. That maybe the official narrative has not been the most accurate narrative for humanity. To be aware of these systems that are not empowering humanity, in fact holding back humanity. So many of these situations are starting to be leaked out now and shared out, more so for those people who are starting to notice these systems. Of course we see many of you have already known about this and have already been suspicious of this, and so isn't this a marvelous time for you to notice that it's coming out as more disclosures firmly now? It is great because it's not you telling your friends and family and being shunned and shut down, it is official people on your TVs and on your social media systems saying the truth. These are not 'conspiracy theories', these are professional people who know what they're talking about, because they've had decades of experience of working within these systems. These people are now very comfortable and capable, to be able to prove that these systems have been in fact holding back truth from humanity, when humanity feels like they're grown ups that they know what they can handle and what they can't handle. They do not appreciate being given limited information from systems that they respected to be fully transparent and be able to share the most appropriate information for everyone, especially when those systems have been questioned by official narratives, which are governing bodies to have checks and balance that there is no controlling systems that are being misused or unbalanced with their full integrity and agenda.

This is what is starting to awaken humanity up, but everything is truly to awaken humanity at this point. We needed to get your attention because as soon as you start thinking of feeling for yourselves, the more empowered you are, and the more questions you ask us. We want to help you. We're here for you. You're using your free will to ask questions and here we are answering them for you. This is marvelous, because the answers are being delivered. You may not always be listening to these. You may just be watching something else, but your answers will always be given to you when you ask us questions. We are responsible and very capable of giving you the answers. Yes, unfortunately, sometimes the answers are not what you're wanting, so you will dismiss us and keep asking us a million which ways, and we could make humor out of this conversation and say... that "bad boy" that didn't deserve you, and you wanted him so badly and you kept asking us to to bring him back, to make him love you, and we say we knew he was not capable of loving you, because he never was capable of loving himself at that stage. So of course why would we push that upon you when you needed to grow yourself and he needed to grow? You could not do it co-compliantly, codependently... the word that we're seeking is you need to have independent experiences away from each other to grow. His rate of growing was slower than your rate of growing. So this is just in jest, but for some of you this is literal, as you you were wanting people in your lives that we're not truly going to serve you, but you were distracted in that moment of either attraction or something else that made you feel like if you had them in your lives you would be more there.

We're saying you've always been very capable and a perfect being by yourselves and for yourselves. It is an independent journey, and while you are loving to have tribes and to have many people support you and love you and adore you and inspire you and encourage you with your journey, this really needs to be something you're motivated to do for yourselves. This is all about yourself and your empowerment of self, and your recollection and to know yourself. The fun part of being here on Earth with the veil, being hidden from your true power, your true wisdom and your true knowledge of self, and that is a game within itself. It is forgetting who you were, to then have these experiences... we don't want to belittle you while you're in these experiences, but it is a step down from where you normally are residing at, and the roles that you play and the things you oversee and what you create, and how you can produce advanced experiences beyond your wildest comprehensions here on Earth.

But when you play human, you need to focus on playing human. For some of you, you don't feel motivated because you don't see how truly empowered you could feel to play this game, and so you feel very demotivated because you don't like these manual games as such, because you don't have this confidence in who you are in this manual capacity. You identify being human as so rudimentary and so practical and so basic, and we could all also say quite feral. Because there are many people that still believe that hunting and killing others, even in the name of food or sport, is still entertainment. There is so much imbalance, there are so many tragedies that are quite offensive to your soul's experiences. We know that it's all part of the interaction and the experiences of those Souls playing those animals and those Souls playing those humans. They wanted to have that unique experience of the dramatics of it, the emotions of it, and how it felt. While we understand it at a third dimensional construct experience, still there is a deepness inside of you that knows that is where you truly love to reside here, and this would not be acceptable, but when you have the veil over you to forget all of that, to have true organic experiences, you have this lesson, this moment of teachable experiences with all of the dramatics of the emotions to help assist you with the full experience.

It always has been about trying to get the full experiences of Earth living, and we say some of you humans - not you reading as such, but the history of humans - have really gotten away with themselves. They've had the full experiences, that's for sure. When you have the full range of experiences as that, when you're having those emotions, you are creating energy. We could say for an example - you have a clean slate field and you have a beautiful experience, where there is love and respect and harmony and the energy radiates out through that area that you're in as you're having that uplifting excitable experience. As you walk away from that field or that location, the energy frequency is still there, it doesn't go anywhere. It still radiates in this high vibration, and so it's the same if you had a tragedy or a drama or a challenge that triggered your emotions into a density of fear. (BIG COUGH) We triggered the vehicle into feeling a tense fear which broke her down, and so she had a human response.

This is a big thing that we're seeing. Humanity is still having to learn and having to feel encouragement through speaking and expressing. Speaking and expressing is so significant right now. You must speak your truth and what you feel within your hearts. What you feel within your minds about each other should be shared. If you love someone, you should share it. If you see someone is in pain, you should share that. You should be able to fully have so much sensitivity about each other. You should be going out of your way to communicate with them, because you know when they're struggling they cannot reach out to others. All they can focus on is the pain that they're feeling and the struggling and the suffering that they are holding on to. You can see these people. You don't want to engage so much with these people, because you don't want to feel their density, and we can say to you that you can support them and love them while not absorbing their density in their struggles. You can recognize them and make them feel that they are not alone, that you see them, that you love them, and that you know that this is a lesson for them to experience and to be able to find their own empowerment. To know that they are worthy. They can respect themselves and if others haven't respected them, that is a reflection on their own journey or path and not a direct statement about them.

There is so much to be said about that. There is much to be said about humanity and fear of being killed for speaking their truth. The truth is coming now regardless of whether people are killed for speaking their truth or not. Humanity has been censoring and holding back the truth. We say it's not just what you could say are the corrupt controlling systems that have been holding back people's truth, it is others who do not want to trust the truth being shared with them by friends and family. It is not a time for you to be limited by anyone anymore. This is a time for you to speak your truth. You know you are intelligent. You know you have intuition. You know your thoughts and your feelings. You know you have done enough of your inner work that you're not reactive to the dramas of situations anymore. You're not controlled to flip into fear with the next new distraction that humanity is trying to be distracted with and to fear into. You know that this is the game, and that there are those who are trying to control humanity to distract them from empowering themselves are playing. You've seen this. You've participated in this yourselves, but you know that there are many people who are still quite confused and quite fuddled and muddled emotionally and logically, with all of these systems that are still trying to coerce and make you comply.

The truth.
The truth.
The truth.

All of your perspectives are the truths and they can be shared. We say it doesn't matter if some prominent people have exit points, because the messages are infinite throughout the history of Earth and the history of humanity. So while some statements from history have been edited for the controller's narrative, your own recent history isn't such, because you recall what people told you in the past. You recall people's speeches and messages and statements. You recall how your recent history has unfolded, because you were here. You've seen it. You saw it. You do not have to rely on other systems or other recordings to be able to fact check your memories. You see it all unfolding and so it doesn't matter, we say to you, for many of you are going to find yourselves in the near future with some people who are no longer living, who have been big speakers, big influencers of humanity. To share their truth, to share their love, to share their messages of what you could say is God, their understanding of what God is.

We understand that people still get hung up on labels and names of what *advanced source energy beings* are. Whatever label you want to call that, whatever advanced beings beyond the third dimension do share with humanity, if they are truly advanced beings, then they have a better perspective point, a vantage point of what is happening to your planet and why, versus human egos trying to make an assumption, a good guess about what is happening to this planet and why. But it would sort of defeat the purpose if you all of you were given the awareness of what we know, because many are still trying to organically live as human and not be awoken to the fact that they are advanced Souls merely playing human in this experience. They don't want to be awoken, therefore they aren't being awoken, because they wanted to truly play the game without cheating. While we have said to you before that our information isn't cheating, some of you don't want to have the organic natural human distraction lives, because you're not here for that. As we've said before and as we see many times, you get frustrated that you don't have other people who are aware of the information that you are aware of and what you think is your daily living lives, because you want everyone to know this information. Yet you are not able to truly respect other people's life contracts and why they're still wanting to have the veil completely covered and why they don't want to know certain information, because they're still trying to navigate and explore and feel into their Earth's human lives. So we say this is why you feel like some of your friends are tuning you out and blocking the information that you share. They are being protected from your truth, because your truth is poison to them. If they have started absorbing what you had to say, that would shortcut their experience and they're not wanting shortcuts. They're wanting to have their full Earth experiences according to their purpose and mission and why they're here now.

We understand that you want more people to be aware of this, but we also say there are many more people, but you're wanting close friends and family. We're saying you're going to have to advance and broaden your horizons and your expectations of who should be awoken in your world and who shouldn't be. If you're still wanting a friend in the spirituality world, there are plenty online. But remember you should be your best friend as well, and this is where you truly grow, because if you're still needing support from others, there is a sense then that you have not got full support of yourselves. When you truly are empowered with what you know, versus having to get confirmation and backup support from friends, when you truly are empowered, you know and you know and you know and you don't have any wavering doubts or insecurities. You are just solid with your foundational information and you just keep growing upon that. So see how you're reacting and see what you're still seeking and searching for and from, because this is going to give you good insights into where you are at with your spiritual journey and your inner work and how you're conducting yourselves and how you're being responsible and accountable, but for your own energy frequencies and what you need. As you know, people grow at different rates, and so even if you did want to have many friends around you knowing exactly the same stuff so you can converse in exactly the same stuff, that you may not allow for noticing how people are choosing to unpack and heal and grow from their own inner work. So you could be pushing people along too fast.

So this is problematic, because if you do try to force people to have shortcuts with their own journeys, which they are not growing from, it's not giving them the personal experience to have that foundational healing learning point, and so they can't grow truly for themselves. When they're challenged with their next challenge, you could say, this is problematic, because they don't have personal stability of their own personal experiences and awareness and empowerment. When you have influential friends, this could make you feel and get advanced information, but when you try to apply it to your own personal lives, you're finding you're lacking, because it is not your own personal organic knowledge and wisdom that you have grown and empowered yourselves through. This is where we see many people struggling, to not apply the information that we share. It is about you experiencing and having much practice and much thinking and many reactions in a metaphysical perspective, versus being a reactionary human, which goes into fear and worry and criticism and doubt and comparisons and insecurities and all of those other interesting experience emotions that you are very capable of choosing to feel with your free-range choices of emotions.

We're seeing if there's anything else that is to be shared today, because we're trying to explain to you why there are people that are sleeping while there are people that are at a slower rate than you in your growth. We are saying you will notice and see someone[35] who is still traumatized by people that they love, being killed by sharing the truth. You'll hear it in his voice. The vehicle has tried to heal his voice many times when she was learning how to use these sessions and she couldn't understand why it didn't fix him, and of course that was her ego and it was coming from a beautiful place, because she loved what he was sharing with the world. This was very early on, well before 2020, the year of her perception. Now he is more predominant in his public expressions. His knowledge and wisdom has been shared by many platforms and he has finally been able to get his truth out. But as you know, from a metaphysical perspective, the fear he is carrying, and maybe at an unconscious level there is still the fear of being killed for speaking the truth, but he still speaks and he still speaks and he still speaks. You're noticing when he is more confident to feel that people love his truth and can cope with his truth. The clarity in his words come freely, but when he is feeling insecure in his new surroundings, when he is feeling judgment and criticism from those who are speaking with him, he does feel stifled because he has a fear and it is a very valid fear for him as he has lost many loved ones. His wisdom and his knowledge does give him confidence, but the confidence, he is still seeking his validation. People believe him and trust him and can cope with the truth. You all can cope with the truth when you have an open mind, you are able to understand that there are many things beyond what you currently know.

---

[35] Robert F Kennedy Junior.

When you hear new information, humans have this natural reaction to reject it until they can fathom and process it. This is an egoic protection mechanism, to fear new things, to then be able to reevaluate it and explore it. But your first response to any new information is naturally to reject it, because there is no reference point to know whether it is safe or not, and so a reaction of rejection is the natural reaction to it. You've experienced it many times when you've tried to tell the truth to your friends and family, and this is the first time that they're hearing the information, especially when it's offensive information where people are getting hurt. No one wants to believe people are going to get hurt or or have been getting hurt. It is something that you don't want to believe, because if you accept that information, then you feel there is somewhat of a responsibility. If you know that there are things that are harming humanity, then you feel like you want to protect and save humanity from that. So when you do accept information, there does come a natural responsibility. When you know the information, what do you do with it? You feel like it should be shared, people should be warned about this, people should be alerted to this information. So as you've shared this to other people, they have given you that knee-jerk reaction of rejection, because they too do not want to agree or believe that. It's too upsetting to fathom that you've been lied to by systems that should be trusted and should be protecting humanity.

There is much to be said about that, and so we ask you to forgive your friends and family when you're trying to share your truth with them and they gave you the classic and natural rejection reaction. They're not rejecting you, they're rejecting what has been occurring to humanity, because at a Soul sense, it has been offensive to them as it was an offense to you. Forgive those people as they are learning. Forgive those people as they are healing. Forgive all people's reactions. This is not a personal assault on you, this is a reaction to how they fit into the information. So look into the last few years of how you've interacted with your friends and family... Have you judged them because they did not want to believe about the crimes against humanity? Can you accept that? Can you understand why they don't want to be happy to accept this information? For those empaths who hear this information, this is their hearts being destroyed in a thousand pieces. These lessons and experiences are too extreme. This is very uncomfortable for those Souls who do not like to live in these rough worlds with these rough games, because the feelings that have been evoked of sadness is not something that is enjoyable when their frequency of joy is love frequency of a higher vibration.

It is extremely dense and it is extremely challenging to find your balance in neutral, while feeling into all of these experiences that many Souls need to have to be able to start thinking and feeling for themselves. To notice the control systems that they are within. But again, as we have said, there's still a game that we experience and many collectives are still supporting as it unfolds. At a conscious level, the game you wanted to play was to awaken to yourselves, to understand the game, to understand the situations and experiences that you are here, that you're having on Earth, and to recognize how far this has become out of balance. There is so much to be said about this and we have expressed it many times and very many different various expressions and situations and scenarios.

We feel the vehicle is done. She does not like feeling into that trauma, even though she understands it's purposeful and significant. It still feels heavy in her energy field, and we are transmuting this now, because we do not like to abuse the vehicle's energy frequency. She has balance with it, but when you feel into it, as we have done for her, to show her the examples that we have said, it makes the vehicle cry. This is challenging, to be used as a vehicle when she is at the state, because she is wanting to ask us now "How can we help? How can we help those people who are suffering?", and we are saying the suffering is because of the choices of how to feel the suffering, because they are not wanting to love themselves and empower themselves. They're suffering because they see each other as separate without unity and without being equal to each other. The choices are helping them suffer. They're choosing to have suffering, because they're not seeing that all of these experiences were to empower themselves, and so they keep continually disempowering themselves with these systems, which are designed by humans to disempower them. So they are compliant.

So we say to you all - love everyone. Even those who choose to comply with disinformation and in disempowerment, because they are trying to cope the best they can. And while you have opinions on what is the best way to approach and to apply and to have the perspectives that keep your balance in neutral, to be less reactive, you have to and you must accept all. Don't judge. Don't belittle, because they are already judging and belittling and excluding themselves. When you judge them for doing that, it just confirms to them that they are right. They are struggling and they feel so alone, and so we say, make effort to reach out to people who you see are struggling. Do not judge them. They're not asking you for that. They're asking for you to love them, and you can love someone who is in fear, because when you show them that you have high frequency energy while also understanding and knowing what they are saying, which is causing them great fear, they may be curious about how you can cope without losing your minds, without losing control of your emotions and reactions when you know the same information as them. But it does not bother you, it does not sway you into reactive emotions as you understand what is needed to occur for the Grand Awakening. To be able to help people understand what has taken place on this planet, what is taking place with humanity. This will help them accept the moving days, as you could say in labeled days, the forward experiences that they're having to come to experience.

When you understand the state of this world, when you understand the state of humanity, what is to come makes complete sense as you understand this is what has to take place to get those people who should be awoken to take notice and to take account of how others are feeling and how the others are suffering through these control systems. We say with much love and gratitude for all of you who are able to do enough of your own inner work to love and support everyone who is sharing their truth, even if it isn't your truth, but you understand where they are at their journey. Supporting each other with love and compassion is the most powerful thing you can do right now for humanity and for yourselves. And so we say go with love, go with joy, and go with appreciation of your life contract and to be of service to humanity, to love them while they're still awakening to the situation that they're living through. Nothing can change what is to come.

Session 31: Start Seeds

When noticing a typo was a message to stop and notice and question the significance...

Yes! Yes! Yes! Yes! Yes! We are here! We are here! We are here! We are very much here! And we want to firmly and clearly tell you that this is the Arcturian speaking through this vehicle today. She has requested that we explain ourselves. When she was listening back to an older session that we provided for you all to learn and grow from, she was remarking how stern and how very firm we were with the messages that we were sharing upon thee. And this was at a time, and this is like as you could say all time that you have been present on Earth, you were there to play a role and to be part of a mission to help empower humanity to love itself. And how you get to empower humanity to love itself is to raise your own frequency vibrations to be that loving vessel of light. Which is energy at a higher frequency of love, which you could label it as. And it is no coincidence that the vehicle has also come to us to explain to her the coincidence that she says was the misspelling of the word starseed to say start seed. And it is probably more accurate for you to focus on. Because we see many are still using their egos to label themselves as certain starseed affiliated planetary system guided. And that is fine if you need to feel like you have backup and support and you need to label us, do so. But check, are you doing this to boost your egos or are you doing this because you know thyself?

We see many are confused. We also see many are confused that they hear our channeling, they hear our messages, they read our messages, and yet they still want to dismiss us because of the vocabulary that we've used through the vehicle. And we are saying, we are entitled to use every single English language word possible! We could channel different languages through this vehicle but she would block that because she is nervous to pronounce words that she doesn't feel comfortable or confident in saying. She doesn't like to mispronounce words. She doesn't like to misspell words. So she keeps it safe and simple. And we say that is fine. We don't need to make things over complicated because humanity is too busy doing that for themselves!

Our messages are simple because we want you to focus. And so while we have observed humans having all the range of behaviors and we have labeled them as we have noticed them, we get judged as if we are human ego speaking. We are not human ego speaking. We are Advanced Civilization Beings, you could say, that are observing humanity. And we are pushing and guiding humanity in accordance with their life contracts. In accordance with their purpose and mission and their significance of why you are on earth now. Of course, not everyone has the same life contracts and missions. There are what you have classified as original Earthlings who are experiencing the very first physical planet, multiple lifetimes or potentially even just this one lifetime. They are without a reference point of other lifetimes off planet. And so they are here wanting to focus on their very first third dimensional planet existence and experience. And so they've wanted to experience as much as they could. And so they were very ambitious with their experiences that they wanted to have. And of course, when you haven't empowered yourself, you can be distracted into having much more and many other experiences on your journey. And of course it doesn't matter how you get to the destination, the destination is always going to be that you'll naturally evolve. But if you wanted to and if you needed to have many more teachable moments for you to empower yourself, you could go on a very long detour. And that could look like many, many, many, different lifetimes that you are meandering through the experiences and the journey of all the possibilities of life on Earth and that is fine. You are completely entitled to do that. And if you are not, shall we say, taking too much energy from your higher dimensional self, you get to keep playing the game you could say. But if you're off path too much and you are doing and taking too much energy and distracting your own higher self, you could say, then there becomes a problematic situation. And this is when we have tried to give you tough love messages to remind you to be responsible and accountable for your energy. It is fine for you to learn the difference between high frequency and low frequency vibrations and try to, with your moral compasses and with your intelligence and with your intuition, focus on a higher frequency energy field as it is more uplifting for you and all. But if you're choosing to and it's not part of your life contract to be indulgent in that drama of those dense emotions, you could be impacting more than you. You know this but you don't want to necessarily be accountable for it.

And so we have sent you many tough love messages to remind you to remember who you are. And while you could say that there are infinite amounts of positive energy that could be sent to you, if you are dismissing that and creating lots of extra density, you become part of the problem for humanity versus part of the solution. And we say many people who are still holding on to and in control of their egos, still want to feel like they are creating their reality and they do not want to be accountable or responsible for their choices of how they choose to focus their energy. And we have referred to you, and potentially not accurately, but when we try to explain things to you, we try to keep it as simple as possible so it can be learned for all! When we have classified you as human beings that are energy batteries, and you all have various different quantities of energy batteries that you could have, let's just say now you know the different sizes of batteries. And some can hold small amounts of energy and others can hold larger amounts of energy. And for those Souls who are here to be of a larger battery capacity to really charge humanity up with a high frequency, if you're using your capacity of energy frequency to hold on to density this is not what your life purpose is about! And you are being reminded to drop that density and to fulfill yourselves and your energy frequency in a loving capacity. This is why we are constantly giving you the messages of love. Because this is the translation of high frequency energy, it is that wonderment and the heightened sense of joy and love and excitement and all consuming gratitude and bliss. There are many words to describe that energy and you know when you're in it because it just feels like you are able to seize every moment and to be empowered. To just be connected in, as if you have been reborn again from a long nap. And you just feel so invigorated and so energized and so in joy with every step moving forward. And every interaction you have with others feels like it is so purposeful and significant and part of the actual reason why you're here. And this is a beautiful way to live life and to be in that high sense of just wonderment versus holding onto a lot of negativity and being very angry, very controlling and very reluctant to have an open mind to anything as you are so dismayed and irritable to be here now. You don't want to learn and you certainly don't want to have any pressure for you to grow. And we say for those people, you could say they actually have big egos because they're very stubborn and they want their egos to control their worlds versus having an advanced metaphysical perspective that your Souls playing human. You want your human aspect to be the master and controller of your existence and experience here. And we say for many that is the case when they are still on their learning journey, and they have to have some very humbling teachable moments for them to realize that they do not know everything and they are certainly not in control of everything.

And of course that triggers many human reactions to shut down the Soul expression of self. To allow the fear and scare of the human ego to take control. And so we are seeing and showing the vehicle many examples of this which is overwhelming her processing of sharing the information that we're trying to share with her. But we are reminding her of the purpose of why she wanted to connect in with us, which was about us firmly saying to you all, we are allowed to use any human words that we want to choose to be able to express our concepts to you. And if you were still thinking that we, the Arcturians, are not allowed to use human language to be able to express our messages of love and our perspectives to you, that is your human egos tripping over yourselves and not allowing us to share information. Therefore it would suggest to us and to all that you are still controlling your knowledge that is being given to you. And so you are dismissing all information that is trying to empower you and expand your consciousness. But you are refusing to let go of control and so your egos are very strong and this is how we find ourselves having to send more tough love messages to try to reach you, to really humble you. To make you realize that you are using your human ego as a rudimentary programming for protection and you shouldn't need to protect yourselves from wisdom and knowledge. And yet you treat it as very suspicious and untrustworthy. And we're saying, isn't it ironic that your programming of the human ego is set on high to distrust any new information as the senses of the Soul are being confined and restricted versus the human ego wanting to be the master. And it's very confusing for the Soul aspect because it's trying to comply to all the systems here and all the teachable experiences here which has made it feel like it can't trust itself. And so when the human doesn't feel like it can trust itself, the ego becomes even more heightened.

We also see another dilemma, which is people not channeling for themselves. So they don't understand how it can be challenging for advanced beings to be able to convey and translate telepathically information which is translatable and understandable at a human level. As humans, you all have different ranges of processes and concepts that you're comfortable with. So triggering you to grow and expand your consciousness and awareness is a delicate stage for us, because if we give you too much information you will shut down completely and never want to contact us again. And so we're having to really work with your knowledge and your own personal awareness to be able to help you gently be comfortable and brave to be able to start considering and expanding your awareness and your perspectives of how you're living and perceiving the world.

And so it is challenging for us when we're speaking to many, because you're all at different ranges. And so sometimes we've had to come together as a collective, not only the Arcturians but many, to give you very firm messages because we saw people hearing our messages and dismissing them. And this is very frustrating because you're screaming and begging to have help and perspectives and support. And yet we were giving you that literal information that was the most accurate for you to palette and to cope with and to empower yourselves with, and yet you're rejecting them. And so it's frustrating for us because you're asking us for information and we're giving it to you and you're dismissing it and calling us humans. Calling us human egos! And so it is challenging because we have tried very many ways to be able to reach you. To be able to get you to clearly hear us and our perspectives and the messages that we've shared through this vehicle and many vehicles, have been very profound once you start applying it. But it is about nurturing you and supporting you to trust us. And when you can't see us, you want to dismiss it. You want to judge and pick on words and tone to be able to throw out all concepts. And this is limiting *you!* It's not limiting us!

We don't have our feelings hurt when you judge us as being human ego, but it is your own human ego that is blocking expanding upon your awareness of what is happening to this planet and to humanity. And for those who like to listen to channelers who just only give love and light messages, that do not talk about the state of the world, the state of Gaia's life contract and the state of humanity, you would be fooled to think that everything is just simply love and light and there is no traumas or tragedies or lessons that need to be explored. And everything is going to be happy! And we are saying, well everything is 'All is well.' We are saying teachable moments do come from tragedy. And this scares many channelers who do not want to know anything about tragedy. They do not want to accept that people have to die because they still think that there is the death of the Soul and once the body goes that is the end. They still haven't matured in their spirituality to be confident to be expanding their awarenesses and their interests and curiosities. And so we see many people being able to channel us, but all they are wanting to hear from us and remembering that we can't give people information that they aren't asking for.

And so this is part of the non-interference. We only give you the information you seek from us. And so we respond to that. We could give you so much more information. But sometimes we see that you don't even know the information to ask us because it's just way too advanced. It's beyond your understanding. And so it is a distraction for you to be too curious about the ways of the world because you're distracting yourself from living in this world, this life now. And so we are saying to you, for those people who only reach to connect in with us just to confirm that you are loved and that you're special, you would not be seeking any more information from us because you were just wanting to feel validated that you are loved and special. And so for those people who channel us just to have their egos boosted, they feel very confident that they have a channeled connection to us but they don't expand beyond much of that because anything else is too scary. And they just want to focus while they're trying to empower themselves that they are loved and that they are connected. And so they may have to hear this a hundred times for them to start believing that and feeling that to be able to then be curious to be able to understand what else is going on for the world and what else could we tell you? We are very capable of telling you everything because from our perspective we see so much. But yet we know that if we tell certain people certain information this could do some disempowerment for them as they choose to then not do their inner work. And they just assume that it will be given to them because we told them it versus them actually organically working towards that. And we have seen this in the past where we have given people information and they have literally, you could say, stopped growing and expanding and being compassionate to others and being of service because they suddenly feel very entitled that they're going to be getting what we have promised them. But we told them that information as a projection of if they continued on the path that they were on, and the diligence and the efforts to empower themselves and truly look at their inner work and grow, then using that free will and expanding and exploring as we predicted and saw them doing. They used their free will to gain information from us and then to stop their journey. They did not empower themselves! They did not heal themselves! And yet they still expected to have the same results. They did not factor in what we were telling them in terms of information, just seeing them every step of the way still empowering themselves and growing.

And so we can be misused in some regards as we give you insights to what you can see as future projections. And yet this can be problematic as people don't understand how this works. And so they stop doing what we saw them doing because they were given the information. It is like saying, we should feel like we need to do an analogy, but we also feel like we don't! But we feel like we want to because we can use any English word. We can use any language that we want to to express to you what we want to share with you. And you cannot stop us or block us or limit us. And we want to make that very firm because the vehicle has opened herself up to getting us to explain and we are using these opportunities to help, you can say, train advanced beings to be able to work and get the right concepts through. We do not speak English in the dimensions that we're at. We are energy beings and so we do not need to move lips or make sound. And so we have referred to ourselves as the puppeteers before. And we know that this is going to trigger many who want to have very human assumptions of what channeling is, but we're saying, when you start off your lives, and we know that as a hard worker, you're going to go to work every day and earn a million dollars. And then we don't tell you that, but you just do it. And we can see that you would do it versus if we saw a young child and we said you're going to be a millionaire but we didn't tell them how because they were going to work every day. They would sit at home, you could say, waiting for their million dollars to appear. And so with that analogy, you can see the difference between how someone has to work for their money to be able to ascertain and to accumulate that wealth versus someone being told what they would be getting but yet didn't actually do the work to get it.

So we say that this is the problem for some people who ask us for information about them evolving and shifting. And we say we give you these projections of the experiences based on where we can see you today. And yet tomorrow, you pack up all your inner work, you pack up your compassion for humanity, and you shut down, and you just sit and wait for it to come to you. And we're saying that's not part of the deal!

That was not part of our projection of where you were at. Nor would we want you to stop being of service, but we have seen many stop being of service. And so this was when we were giving you the more tough love messages because we know what you're capable of in being distracted and being empowered. And so we have learned lessons too! Because we had more faith in you! That you would use this information to empower yourselves versus disempower yourselves. We are learning too how humans will still get advanced information and dismiss it and throw it away as an option versus an actual desirable experience opinion approach for you to empower yourselves using your free will. And so it is frustrating for us only in the terms that we see you being frustrated. And you being very angry and hurt and very isolated. And having these denser feelings about not being supported and feeling alone.

And so we are here. We are showing up. We're sharing our energy frequency to you so you can feel the authenticity of our energy frequency through these messages for you to be able to know that this is not one human speaking to you. That this is your beloved guides, Soul family, Soul friends who promised to you that we would be here for you. And that we would support you and encourage you and push you if need be when you are on your Earth journey. Because you were very concerned about how you saw advanced Souls coming here on Earth and getting very lost! Very confused! And from our perspective, it is alarming how dense it is and how disorientating it is for advanced Souls to be completely immersed and getting lost in the process of being Human when they had other missions to be of service. This is why you have more access to us because this was part of your contract and your agreement with us. When you needed more support we would be here for you more. And this is not cheating because we say to you many times you dismiss the information. So it's not a given that you empower yourselves when you hear our information because you still have to apply it. You still have to work at it! And so it takes time! It takes practice! It takes experiences for you to empower yourselves to feel into what we say. After the initial dismissal and reaction and rejection, you start testing it to see if what we said is valid. To see if what we have said is even worthwhile, purposeful and significant.

And so, getting back to the word that the mistake by spelling start seed, you could say that you're our seeds because you've come from us. We are extensions of self, while we are all one. And so you could say that we have sown the seeds in 3D of ourselves. Essences of ourselves! To be able to grow and empower, not only our own selves but others. And so we say start seeds. Start germinating out knowing and trusting that you're all one. Knowing and trusting that we have you always! We would not be distracted away from you! We are always encouraging and inspiring you! And we're always connected! We know many people have tried to tell you that there is a disconnect and that is not true. We know many people have tried to tell you that you're vulnerable to negative entities and to bad things and to be scared and afraid of everything and we're saying it's not true. That is disinformation! That is distractions! We are saying organically live and love life as you can. And honor all feelings and emotions through those experiences because that's what you're there for. But for some of you who have the bigger missions to hold higher frequency energy because you are the biggest batteries on Earth, honor that responsibility, because not only do you deserve it but so does humanity. And as we promised you we would be here for you! And as you promised humanity you would be there for them and you would take on your mission and you would not get lost. And this is teamwork because we see and feel many of the Souls being so confused. More so than they had planned or needed. And so you get lost in these experiences.

And so we are saying to love everyone and be a high frequency together. Keep your balance but grow! Start seeds, grow! Have the confidence of our love and our strength backing you every step of the way! Stop with the thoughts of doubt! Stop with the thoughts of being weak or not good enough! You're born to be there! You are good enough! You are there because you are good enough! Now grow! You can be strong! You can be tall! You can be seen, and you can be felt! Empowering yourselves is what humanity needs and we need this from you because you're there for it!

So feel proud of yourselves! Step up to your missions that you know you are there for! Be that vessel of love! See everything with a growth and significance and a purpose of teachable lessons. Judge none! Love all, and honor everyone else's journey! But you need to remind people to stop playing in that density. To start having trust in their own teams and start having trust in themselves. This is a beautiful time for you to be able to empower them through this. Those who come across your path are not an accident! Share your perspectives! There's no point being shy because they're so distracted with their own egos, they need a moment to stop and think and ponder. And as you know, *all* triggers are a beautiful opportunity to grow! This is the time to grow! Start growing stronger. Because you're so capable of it and it's only your choices now that are holding you back. And once you stop holding yourself back, all that is possible from that point is growth and empowerment!

We say this with love because it is true! We absolutely love you! We always have and we always will! With this encouragement, may you feel inspired to share and to shine and to love each other!

You all need it!

And you will be needing it!

And we say this with love!

Session 32: The Most Appropriate Information

Grow your perspectives of expansion conscious awareness

Yes! Yes! Yes! Yes! We're here! We're here! We are here! And we are relaxing the vehicle as she has asked us once again to give her and you all who are listening and potentially reading this information what is the most appropriate information in the perceivable time that this information has been reached for you all. And isn't that a fun request for us to be able to deliver the most appropriate information for every single one of you listening and reading in the best appropriate time. What is the most appropriate information? And so we say, well as much as she thinks it's a very broad question that will be able to give us the best information for you to be able to have the most advanced information for you to be prepared to enjoy and have preparations for your Earth lives, we are saying it always will be the most appropriate and best information for you is to love yourselves and each other. There is no distraction from that. And so of course from our perspective, that's always what you will need to hear and always what you'll be needing to remind yourselves as you are moving forward in your conscious awareness of your days and what you classify and label as time frame periods here on Earth. We say there on Earth. When we say here on Earth it is because we are channeling through an Earthling who is having her Earth body being used for us to be able to translate and to share our perspectives. And so it is like we get a sense of awareness that we are being called upon and so we will merge our consciousness into the third dimension to be able to see what is going on and why. And so then we realized that she is requesting information and perspectives. And so then we directly communicate this through her.

And so when we say here on Earth, it is because we are speaking to those here on Earth. We are still not on Earth ourselves, we are simply talking through the vehicle. And you know that you can talk to each other quite easily now to other people in other countries. It doesn't make you in the other country when you're calling overseas. You are still in your own home location or even if you were traveling around, you are still where you are even though you could be calling others. We say that this is like spiritual ego sometimes when you think that you are advanced beings, because you title yourselves as star seeds or affiliated to different guides. And yet you're still human. You're still consciously aware of just being human this lifetime. Yes, you may have insights into certain days and certain events and other lifetimes you've ever lived, but that does not make you those other lifetimes. And yes, it's a combination of all the different aspects and personalities merged and combined into you. It is your Soul awareness still having this lifetime. You know that all the other lifetimes coexist since time is not linear and so you merge in and out consciously. It's still the same soul, just in different what we could say is meat suits, human bodies. And so you are aware of each other but also diligently focusing on yourselves. It is like saying, if you look at your hand and you see the five digits, if that is the same body, it still connects to the same body but it's having its own independent movable experiences. But we want to say in jest to lighten the mood, but when it's jazz hands, it is all in unity and we love unity for you all. But for each individual finger you can, if the fingers had eyes they could see each other and sense each other. But we're saying if you will, for having different parallel lives, there is division, separation and almost partition boards where the fingers can't see each other. But yet the fingers are still connected to the hand just like you're still connected to your subconsciousness which are your main guides. Which are your potentially high versions of selves or even those are the Soul aspects that are supporting you. There is much to be said here depending on the different collectives and depending on how you are connected to other Soul aspects of self. While you are multidimensional beings, you could be in direct lineage thought process experience that has been created to have a third existence experience. Whether you are a walking aspect of that, that is manifested into a physical body which is cohabitating in a cellular Soul level. It is complicated how you can be experiencing or perceiving to be having your realities.

So we are saying to the vehicle that there are many connected fingers to her. And sometimes we reveal we remove the partitions from the illusion of separation to see a Soul family member. What we have classified for this little chat to you today, she can suddenly see very clearly the other fingers that are connected to the same hand. And this is marvelous as you discover and connect into more Soul family you could say. Did the fingers refer to themselves as the Soul family? The fingers refer to themselves as a cleverly positioned and important appenditure to a human body, but they're fine with that.

We are getting distracted. The vehicle is realizing that when she asks for a broad statement like what is the most appropriate and best information to give people today to be able to help them, we are saying they're going to be listening to it in all various versions. Whether it is in print form or whether it is in listening. And again we say, the most important information that we must share and impress upon you is to love yourselves and others but we're saying our level of love and how we can perceive and how we respect and encourage you all to have a higher frequency of love. We know that this is a word that is thrown around much. But we also know that this is a word that actually has real significance and meaning. And we have said to you before about saying I love you with no meaning, very flat with no effort and no integrity and no intentions and no accountability behind those words versus saying those words with utter complete conviction and compassion and meaning. And there is a difference! And we know that some of you are still thinking that words have such great power but we're saying it is the intentions behind the words that carry the magic and the key of that power. We know that some of you take things so literally you're hyper focused and fixated on one or two words and that is where you reside because you cannot and will not want to look at the bigger picture. You're focusing, hyper fixating on one piece of the puzzle where there are many that can see the full picture and the full puzzle, if life was a jigsaw puzzle.

So we are saying that many people are afraid to speak words in case they manifest negativity. So they don't want to look at their inner work because they don't want to speak about unforgiving and unforgettable experiences. And we're saying you can forgive everything! You can feel everything! And you can see things from a bigger perspective to understand these are purposeful experiences for you to learn. Whether it is to be pushed and triggered enough to empower yourself or to have a humbling experience to realize what it feels like to be humiliated when you've got something wrong. Which therefore encourages you to empower yourself to be correct for the next battle or the challenge when you are tested. And so therefore there is nothing really that is wrong that is happening to you. It is all perfectly said and done. But we see egos tripping up and thinking that words carry actions and we're trying to describe this further to you. If you say you *hate* something and you truly mean it in a negative way because you despise it and you're afraid of it and you're angry and you cast judgment on it because you can't understand the lessons and the purposes of something so therefore you have to classify it as hating it or even labeling it as the devil or even labeling it as something bad or even labeling it as something in a negative capacity. When you say that and you feel that, you're not creating that negativity so you're not creating the evil. What you're labeling already existed! You're just labeling it. You're observing it and you're labeling it as that's your only form of translation. Your only way to converse and to express what you're seeing because that's where you're at with your journey. You're seeing one aspect of it. You're not seeing the lessons, the teachable moments, the karmic contracts and the evolvement in the evolutional moments and processes beyond that experience. So that's all we are at with your evolution observations. And consciousness awareness is labeling.

We know that some people can say, 'Oh, I *hate spiders*,' but don't have a negative true energy frequency of that statement. They are not projecting hatred to one or all spiders. It is a throwaway comment. It's an empty statement of just expressing how they felt in the past and how they think they feel currently. And so it's an expression statement which has no emotive energy frequency of hatred towards it. They say it in neutral. It is a descriptive statement. This is different. There are differences with energy and words. And so some people get tripped up on this because they think that if you say something like... Let's be dramatic here. Some people think that if you say the words, 'this planet will die.' You have then commanded this planet to die. And we are saying you do not have power to create that in your own demand. There is more protection, thank goodness you could say, for this. And so even if you wanted this planet to die, even if you were in a tantrum and you threw out and cast judgment and anger and frustration and said mean things, even you with full intention and integrity to say I want this planet to die, it doesn't mean you are responsible or can wield that into fruition even if you meant it. Even if you truly, truly, truly were begging. It is not your human right! You have no access to it! You do not demand! You do not create that reality! It is really not your business in some regards as being a single human, because the planet exists. It is its own living conscious being. It has its physical Earth that you call Earth and then it has its Soul which you call Gaia. You as a human cannot create words that would kill a planet in this analogy, because Gaia has her own guides and protection. The planet has its own thing going on. And so there are no words that can kill a planet even if you wanted to. And we know this is very triggering and alarming. We said to you in prior that we were going to be dramatic here. And so let's say the reverse. Let's say you're using your human ego and you're mustering up all the love and empowerment and goodwill intentions to say I'm healing the world. I'm gonna fix everyone. I'm going to make everything perfect. You could say that, you could mean it. It will not occur. For the same reasons as why you cannot destroy a planet, you cannot heal a planet. Therefore we have just proven to you words don't have power as you perceive that they do.

We know many people are afraid to say that and speak their truth because what if they had to speak about the pain that they feel from others because their empaths. Does this then bring pain to them? Does this then create that in their reality? We see many people are not mature enough to understand how energy works and so they're afraid to speak. They're afraid to talk about future senses that they're aware of because they're afraid they could create it. And so they will then revert into wanting to focus on healing and healing and healing and healing and healing this planet. And we're saying that is a distraction for them because again they are not, if you will for this analogy, singularity God! And even though their intentions are pure, they could be disempowering the planet and humanity by either shortcutting their own independent experiences that they wanted to experience. If you will, all of the Souls have come here to this planet to have the smorgasbord range of emotions and experiences that this planet has to offer. And some diligent Soul is saying to you all, '*Wait my friends, I'll eat everything just to feel and taste and have all these experiences and then I'll tell you if it was poisonous or I'll tell you which was my favorite or I'll tell you which one or how it tasted,*' and you're not wanting someone else to protect you from the poisons or the flavors or the experiences. As Souls you've come here very capable to experience and handle all the experiences, all the meals. And so even though that one diligent Soul wanted to experience it. And we know that a Soul wouldn't do this because the Soul is advanced. It would be a human ego that would want to protect everyone and help everyone. And yet the best intentions to help could be a direct disempowerment experience for those other humans wanting to have their own personal experience even if it was poison. Even if it was sugar.

So we are saying to you, as hard as it is, all Souls will not be broken having Earth experiences. All Souls have human bodies which have a human program design which is called ego. The ego is set on high alert because of the heightened senses of everyone's energy frequency. Plus the entire collection of energy frequency that has been created on this planet throughout all time. There is a lot going on there. It is extremely dense! And while you're trying to focus and push and motivate yourself to being human, to be classical human, to hold down classical jobs, to hold down classical relationships, and to hold down classical concepts of Being Human, it is a challenge in itself! The bodies are exhausted as it is feeling into all the energy frequency of this heavy density. And as you know, as more are exiting this planet and shifting the energy frequencies away, while their Soul is high frequency in a human body, when the Soul shifts so does their energy. We have referred to the energy to help you understand different ranges of capability, capacities of batteries. And while we understand that you don't like that label as being a battery. It is an energy frequency vessel that you are and you're linked into the bodies. And the awareness of the Soul is connected to the body within the body, within what you could call the avatar of the body. It is a very real experience with very real emotions and energy frequencies. It is not truly possible to not notice the density. And we are saying to you again to observe, not react or absorb. But we know that some of you do absorb a lot of density from others to then distribute down, it further down. You condense their energy into even further harder density and you drive that away, to push that away, to make a firm distinction connection between where human energy frequency consciousness awareness is residing at versus what you could say the pollution of the density of the planet which has been created by energy beings while they were living human and playing human. And so you could say that the traumas and the energy created through trauma and drama and war and tragedy and all the range of emotions, that density is impressed upon the energy and it is created here. And we are saying it's just like litter bugs. Everyone litters and the energy frequency is what they produce. But then when the Souls leave, no one picks it up. And so this energy density is shed and it is expressed here and it is tremendous what big batteries can do when they transmute density and create more density, they leave their energy frequency here. And so you can imagine and understand the predicament of this planet at an energetic frequency. This is why it is so dense. But as we are seeing many people are exiting, they're taking their core energy batteries with them because that is their soul. The Souls are leaving this planet but the byproduct of those Souls experiences when they were learning to grow, when they were learning to heal, is still here. That energy is still stuck here, you could say for this experience but don't overthink it! The Earth is a black hole for density! And so it is magnetizing and attracting just heavy density. And we are saying you need to transmute that density away from the humans down into what you could call the core.

We understand you're still confused about what the shape of the planet is. You're still confused about the experience and we're saying none of that really matters. It is about you being diligent to be an energy worker which we also call a lightworker, to be able to transmute that energy. When you are a battery you're recharging yourselves with openness of mindsets. You're charging yourselves with holding on to a higher frequency love, we want to say belief system. You're innately in tune to a higher frequency of Love. But when you get distracted and the traumas and the dramas that have been played out here, they can lower your frequency vibrations. This is why you are noticing that you're getting more and more absent minded and not focused as much as we are trying to focus you and you're trying to focus yourself into a higher frequency energy without being interactive in the 3D dimensions of your realities of communicating with others and dealing with others. And you could say even going into crowds.

And so we understand that it takes diligence and focus to be able to communicate and to converse with other humans without letting their density overwhelm you and for you to not react to their pain and to their perspectives and to their hurt and to their struggles as you see them suffering as they're still confused about who they are and why they are here and what is truly going on as they're very fixated on current events versus fixating on their empowerment of self to understand the Soul within them that is trying to expand versus the ego that is trying to contract and focus on the current day events and the dramas and the details of the Earthly living. There is much to be said here about how you conduct yourselves, but the Souls are trying to gain more control, you could say, over the ego. The Soul is wanting to hold on to a higher frequency of love energy frequency that is truly within you and you're very capable of connecting into it just like the fingers are very capable and always connected to the hand. The hand, you could say, is a love energy frequency of Source! And so when the hand is focusing on the tip of the fingernail it doesn't notice what is behind it and what is supporting it and strengthening it.

There is much to be said to give you these little examples of how when you focus on just being the tip of the fingernail versus when you feel back into being the whole body. There is a difference in focus and perspective. When you are focusing on small things you become heightened with more energy from more emotional responses because you shrink down your focus into small reactive experiences versus seeing things from a much broader vast overview. And when you have such a broad vast overview of all situations and all interactions and all experiences you know and you feel all is Well. *All is well!* But when you hyper fix and focus on 3D living, there may be the struggles and traumas when you can't see it from the bigger perspective of how it's all unfolding and how it's all connected into each other, for each other to have these experiences, Again that smorgasbord meal of tasting all the flavors, all the ranges. And we have seen this lifetime is very significant because you're wanting to complete the smorgasbord that you have set. It is like a set menu that you knew you were coming to Earth to play to experience. Because these are the things you said you wanted to have, this is a very important lifetime. You needed this one! You needed these experiences and so you're getting them. And as you are noticing, many people are graduating quite early as you would perceive them to be early because they are not having their classic normal human life spans. So they are seeming to have sudden exit points. When we are saying to you, they only came here for a snack. They only came here for a few quick meals. They didn't come here for the complete buffet because they've already had many, many visits here. Many other lifetimes here where they have snacked and dined and feasted upon all the range of the food varieties and variations. They came here to fine-tune the last things on their meal. The last experiences they wanted to have here. And when that is complete, they do not choose nor do they wish to stay longer to dine on further foods. We could say that they complete the Earth experience. They are hungry and thirsty and have passions and drives and curiosities for other experiences beyond Earth experiences.

For some of you, you've already mastered the Third! You've already mastered the fifth! But you're here to help serve others, if you will. You're bringing meals to others who were dilly-dallying around, distracted, pushing the food around their plates but not digging in. Not experiencing whatever lessons were to be had with those experiences. They don't want to look at the meals. They don't want to look at their inner work, you could say. They don't want to digest the meals. They don't want to learn and digest their lessons. They don't want to finish their inner work. They don't want to finish their meals. And we are saying for some it could be a fondue experience with two. And that is an entwined and entangled Soul expression experience with two Souls. And when you're here to completely love each other and inspire each other to grow and one of you thinks that your fat pants are stuffed and you can't eat any more cheese, we are saying we know that you get tired eating the same meal. And it could be said that you get tired of feeling inspired to loving the same person because the same person doesn't seem like they want to grow. They're holding on to too much pain. They're holding on to too much trauma. They don't understand how to transmute their energy. They think that their density is theirs. They feel dreadful and terrible and stuck and stuttering and over pressurized and heavily densified to the point where they're starting to label themselves as having depression, because they are feeling so much density from the world and from each other. They're not realizing that this is their work to do to transmute that versus holding on to that density to label it and identify being that density.

To want to heal yourselves. To want to release the density that you're holding onto an energetic frequency and thinking that is all you can be. And all who you are. And isn't it confusing when you are a Soul playing a human and when you are stuck in density and all you think is that you are depressed because that's all you feel and yet you haven't identified or realized that this is the density that has been created collectively by all of humanity. It is not you! It is not you! It has never been you! You are here, you could say, to be the pickup crew. The cleaners. The trash converters to pick up that litter of energy density and to transmute it deeper and darker and denser into beyond human frequency energy awareness. To be able to make that stark difference between that dense energy versus the energy frequency that the conscious collective of humanity is residing at. We are saying, when you are bigger batteries, you have a higher frequency range. And so you know the darkness of the darkness because you feel the darknesses of the darknesses. And when you are the big batteries, you know the heightened energy frequency that is that pure bliss energy of love. And isn't it interesting because both of those extreme ranges make you want to cry. And this is what confuses people when they cry from joy and they cry from sorrow. We are saying it is all connected. But when you're confused with how you feel and when you're confused about the energy you feel it can be very disorientating.

We are reflecting on how you have been able to absorb this information and we see some of you have tuned in and out of the concepts and the words as you have been basking in the energy frequency having yourselves uplifted. And we say you're able to release the density when you're hearing us because you are listening to our energy frequency which is attuning you to a higher energy frequency rate versus being able to comprehend and understand even the words that we're saying. It is like the words are flowing in and out without any comprehension. But the energy frequency that you feel from us is keeping you at a... We don't know the words to describe this state. It is not a trance-like state. It is a reflective state. We could say anything right now and it would not bother you even if we said the stupidest joke in the world. It is the energy frequency that you're attuned to so it doesn't truly matter the words that we say to you now as you were just in this energy frequency zone which is an enhightened state. There is no density to be felt and so it is an upliftment within itself to hear the energy frequencies that we are sharing which makes you feel tuned out to the actual literal words that we are saying. This is why we have said for you to understand the words and the concepts that you also need to apply while also holding a high energy frequency. You do need to listen again and focus on the words instead of connecting them deeply to the energy frequency that we are sharing to you all.

There are many ways to use this information in these sessions, in these messages to you, because they do contain love while also having what you could call lessons for you to be able to grow your perspectives of expansion conscious awareness. And so this is why it's hard for you to recall what we have said because you are in this other state of conscious awareness. And that is fine. We do love empowering you and holding you at a high energy frequency as you are just releasing all the density from your days while you have been of service. So you do not mind what words we have to say to you to help you feel like you are listening to something. It is the energy frequency that you are connected into and relaxed into. And so we will say farewell with love as we know many of you are now in this heightened sense of energy frequency where you can move beyond your conscious awareness days now, knowing that you have been able to drain that density and ground and dump that energy out as you are not focusing on it, or feeling into it. As you are opening your higher energy frequencies to that love energy that we provide and share with you all.

And so it is about opening yourselves up to *our* energy frequency for *us* to charge *you*. To be able to help inspire and encourage you. To remind you how special and significant and important you are. Because you are! You all are without a doubt! You know this but it feels too tremendous for what you still think is just one human empowering the world. And while you struggle to say the right words, you think! And while you struggle to do the right things, you think! It is always about the energy frequency and empowerment of how you can hold the energy frequency out and beyond. That is where the true service lays! When you can be able to love at high energy frequency love and not be distracted!

We say this with love!

Session 33: Making Contact In 3D

After seeing a large shadow figure in her home they instantly said 'we need to talk' therefore this is that channeling

Thank you. Yes Yes Yes Yes Indeed you have been reached. There was contact made, and indeed this was not to harm you, but this was to invite you to have a conversation. It is with a Reptilian. They are wanting to speak, a part of their collective. As you know, not their entire collective has evolved as this being that wanted to come. There are many transitions and adjustments being made amongst and within their own collective, as they're trying to support. They know you are sympathetic in terms of respecting all contracts and also respecting collectives. This is when they are seeking and reaching out to you.

As you are aware, another channel[36] you know was threatened by an entity. We do not see it was the named entity that it labeled itself with, because it was trying to prompt, boost, promote itself. It thought it would get more scare factor if it had chosen another name. We see that when the more controlling influencers start having their own epiphanies and healing, they step aside and they step away from who they were controlling. Instead of the ripple out effect of them all being healed, there are opportunities for those who want to be in that power, to step up into those leadership roles. They're doing what they can to get the attention. They are thinking that this is an opportunity for them to be more powerful, so they're using names and labels that they think will get them the most attention and respect.

---

[36] *A being trying to pretend to be "Baal" tried to scare a channeler friend*

It is about those, we want to say, that they've been so controlled for so long, that now they're leaders, who controlled them have stepped aside as they're working on themselves and healing themselves. They don't know what to do because they haven't got the epiphanies or the empowerment to change and heal for themselves. They're still being trained, still driven, still motivated to continue on with the same routine that they were coerced, manipulated, and are still complying, even though they haven't stopped to question why the influencer, their leader, has stepped aside and focused on something else. They only see it as an opportunity for them to take that position, to take that lead, to take that power, to take that influence. So there are many trying to see what they can do, what they can get, and how they can influence and terror others. They have been waiting for these opportunities. They've always hoped that it could be them, because they've all got their own opinions about - if they were leader, if they were king - what they would do to rule and how they would conduct themselves. So they are now living, all their fantasies, you could say. It is getting many people's attention. We see that this has been occurring, what you could consider, in the last three years of your timeline that you're experiencing.

So this is the Arcturians helping support this. It was an energy frequency being of a Reptilian that messaged and presented themselves to the vehicle - to say "we need to talk". We will make this connection, and we know that the vehicle hasn't been that ecstatic to find out what this conversation is about. While she's sympathetic and she wants to support, she is not impressed with how beings make choices to want to seek power, influence, and control others through their own egoic desires. This does not impress her. She's not interested in going into fear either, so she is being reluctant, you could almost say, disinterested. But she knows that she has a role to play. She knows that she is a messenger. She also knows that she is capable of channeling any consciousness[37]. This is part of her service to be here for humanity, to help. But also, for those who are trying to control humanity, they also need help. Where do you go, when you are suddenly having a big epiphany? You want to change, grow, and heal.

When you're a leader, you cannot go and get that healing and change amongst those you've already controlled. You have to step aside, disown yourself, walk away, and heal, trusting that those who were following in your footsteps, hopefully would follow with you. But they don't always do that, because they see this as an opportunity for them to step up and to be compelled to be in control, to be feared, to be worshiped, loved. There's many motives here - with all their fantasies now. But the problem is, when a big leader steps away[38], there is a fight to gain that one position. We've seen that there are many top dogs, you could say, walking away from their pack. This leads into in-house fighting, because suddenly it triggers everyone to have this opportunity to realize that there is a space and a position that they all veer for, they all fight for. Some see this as an opportunity for freedom, so they also walk away, because they're not interested, nor do they have the desire to lead. So, there is much in-house bickering, you could say, which is an advantage point, because when you're fighting amongst yourselves, you don't seem to be able to focus on fighting

---

[37] *Regardless of it they are 'alive' or no longer in a physical body.*
[38] *Had an exit point.*

and disempowering humanity - the intentions, driving force, and focus of what the leader was doing prior.

When leaders walk away, this disbalances structures within. It destabilizes things. We see that for many they don't want change, so they think that someone has to step into that power, that position, to take that role to continue on, but they need to fight for that position first. So, this is distracting them. This is delaying them. They can't get it together, because of all the in-house bickering, you could say. We see very strongly, there is, what you could consider, five packs. We could say that these are focusing on different Industries, while they're still connected to the same. But they're all following the same leader, officially, without them recognizing what collective they are working with.

So, we'll make this connection, while we'll get the vehicle comfortable, before we do this. The reason why that Reptilian wanted to speak to the vehicle was because they wanted to show and highlight to her - how there has been some internal fighting of positions. They wanted to say that while many are trying to get to be in that position, it is purposeful they are fighting amongst themselves versus working together in a cohesive team unit, to create much destruction, distractions, and havoc for humanity, you could say. So, to share this perspective is the reason why this Reptilian wanted to speak, and we will let them speak now.

Reptilian: I do not want to scare you, but I did want to talk to you. My message is this - while there are many distractions amongst our own collective, for those who are still wanting to fight, we're wanting to confirm to you that they are merely distractions for themselves, which is purposeful, because when they have conflict, they can't have focus. This is significant. I would like to tell you that those who are vying for their roles to be the top dog in their own pack - they are, you could say, we are supporting these inner house bickerings because they see that this is a distraction amongst itself. It is exposing those who are still not learning and still not seeing how our focus is not evolving us. We are, at a collective level, noticing and growing ourselves because we are living, as you could say, Soul aspects of us are living in 3D as humans. We are living and surrounding ourselves with other collectives who love us, who are teaching us how to love ourselves and others, and who are teaching us - it's not about money and positions that are making us successful and happy, it actually is about the human interactions and love - the respect that we give each other through love, honor, and obey. But in the respectful way, to honor each other's interests with each other, we are learning more, because we are working alongside other collectives, while not being aware, as we are all playing human.

We're all learning together. There are different collectives, different souls, mingling in and working together. We are all playing human. This is significant. It is about recognition and acknowledgment that we are growing, we are learning, and we are enjoying the compassion and understanding, the significance and the empowerment of love, and trusting each other. We recognize that we distrust others because we know that we are not trustworthy. We know that we would prefer to lie, for example, to not be accountable for what we have done. And so, we know we still have this maturity Even though we're adults, we still rely on immature tactics to live. The more we grow as a collective and the more we learn, we recognize that being accountable and responsible for our actions and our behaviors, actually feels better than the corruption, the manipulation, and this deceit. For some of us, who have had many lifetimes here being human, we're really learning our lessons as well. Of course, you could say for the collective, every single Soul is at a different frequency vibration within the collective, but there is a significant step forward for those into a high energy frequency, more than ever before, because of the compassion and love we are learning and experiencing from others.

We also want to explain that we do not need to even have a full lifetime here, as there are many, you have referenced them as minivans, but there are many - one single human that has many Souls that are experiencing the way to live, during being that human. So there are many, you could say, diligently wanting to grow and experience the way it is to have a life of being of service. This is why there are Reptilian Soul aspects in the vehicles, in the minivans of some light beings here on Earth. While it can be convoluted to consider that there are as many aspects, you could say, airing into one life to see how it feels to be a kind-hearted person with no agenda, to be able to unconditionally love each other and have respect for themselves as they are being of service.

These are incredible teachable moments and ultimately as humanity is in the predicament that humanity is in, this is why there needed to be many, what you call Starseeds, from advance experiences - Souls coming here to support humanity, to be more mature with playing the game of human, awoken early because they truly do not need to master the third dimension, because they have prior. For those who have naturally come in a third-dimensional experience to just be here on Earth, to graduate from this, this is possible, they have been able to graduate. But because they are guided by a Pleiadian, they have merged away from being Pleiadian, and now they are here on Earth, being an aspect of a Pleiadian. They are able to focus and grow and continue on with their full third dimensional experiences here.

It gets very convoluted, but what I'm trying to say to you and to confirm to you is that there are many great teachable moments here. Because as everyone here is noticing the challenges between the systems - versus - wanting to have a more free and dependent way of living. But over the last few years, it has been very prevalent and very obvious, the control systems here which are also part of what, you could say, the Reptilian collective's agenda. But also, it's everyone who chooses to comply. It's all teachable moments, but there is, if you will, you have to understand - how do you teach? How do you educate? How do you inspire a collective that is still primitive with its attitudes while being in humanoid bodies? When they don't identify as being anything else but human, but they have a drive to be very competitive - at all costs necessary, triumph, and win over their opponent and their competition. This has been problematic.

It is, you are aware, about the minivans and the many Soul aspects, but I wanted to share with you that it is more than just one Collective. It may not have been obvious, but there are many collectives therefore many collectives need to have these experiences as being these walk-in aspects of self, and therefore should have been assumed. But I wanted to clarify to you, there are different collectives in the minivan Souls because that is extremely significant and important for all the teachable moments. You could say that there are challenges within starseed families that are Reptilian. They are fighting amongst themselves, still being human. They are struggling the most. Therefore they are in fear of the bigger changes than most, because they still do not feel like they have a strong footing at the moment with all of these changes. They are awakening. They do not like to be pushed around themselves, and so they are struggling and suffering, which is a direct part of their karmic experience of why they are going through that. This is teachable moments for them to understand the results of what others within their collectives have created.

And so, you have to have the experience of being the controller, and then being controlled, to understand how that feels. The duality of those experiences were for the collective to grow. There's much to be said about the dynamics of the learning lessons and experiences had here. But you can trust that there is nothing for a human to worry about, as this is all planned beyond your dimension by all the advanced Souls that are wanting these experiences and supporting those who are playing this game of life on Earth.

And so, it is about your concern about getting information again about things that you are very much aware of. You're concerned if you make this public, this will again cause delays or block the experiences. So you're very sensitive to not sharing information that could hold back these plans. You don't want to disclose anything that could then be disinformation as timelines change, or collectives hear that this information is being planned, and so the events around this are altered. I am saying to you as an aspect of the Reptilian collective, there are many of us wanting to speak on behalf - we can't change what is happening either for ourselves because that information is not part of what we control. Therefore, if you did choose to share that publicly, we could not change it. We wanted to say to you - it can't be changed By Any Human. This is the thing we've also been trying to share with you. So share it, if you will. That you've already told everyone through the Arcturians - to be prepared for everything, to fear nothing, and to lead by example, by loving unconditionally everyone, understanding that this is bigger than they can comprehend for the teachable moments and lessons and experiences of all aspects, of all roles here on Earth. This is being learned, explored, and experienced by many collectives who are working very closely with this, and have been for a while, as they are wanting to support, what you could say, is the end of the dazes.

This is my message to you. This is more clear to you now. We could ask you to use your free will to send empowering epiphanies for people who don't know where to stand. They are sick and tired of complying to leaders who are egotistical, who do not have even the best interests of their families or their collective - step away. This is your time when there is no firm leader, when there are many trying to fight for the role of the leadership, and when there is no current leader, you can escape. You can step away. You can walk away now. We're saying, if you can send out an epiphany to all to realize this - when there is no current leader in these systems and they are fighting for each other, saying it has got to do with the Draconian who is still on his healing journey, still. When he focused, he walked away from controlling the Reptilians. The Reptilians were excited about this, as they were under rule and control. But those leaders within the Reptilians still played their role, thinking that this may have just been a trick or a temporary thing. But when it's obvious that Draconian is not returning to his old position of controlling them, and they're not being forced to do the bidding of the Draconians, they're slow to notice. But there are leadership roles that have been squabbled over. So if we could give all, and everyone should see this, when a role is not in position, when there is no leader as such, see if you're still complying as if there is. This is an opportunity for you to step aside. This is an opportunity for you to change, and notice how tiring it does feel to comply to a tyrant who doesn't care about you or your family.

What do you do now - notice the excitable feeling of freedom as you could step into another area, another focus. This is you being liberated, if you could see it as such. So choose where you want to go now, realizing you have more choices now, because when you look beyond to see, we could say, the emperor has gone. We could say, the man behind the curtain has gone. We could say, when you realize that you have been in a routine that no one is forcing you to do now, but you have still been in this routine, this is a time to notice. There's many layers of this.

The Arcturians are coming in to say, this is a very important message, As you will be noticing, this can apply to all. We have given you the analogy of a horse that has been broken in and the farmer has created an electric fence for the horse. We say in this analogy that we have said to you a while ago, the farmer is dead and the fence is not electric and the fence is broken down, but the horse still feels safe in the parameters within the fence, even though the fence is no longer there. It takes a bold brave step to go outside of that perimeter, to notice there is nothing that's going to electrocute you. There's actually nothing holding you back now. There is no fence. There is no master. You can expand now. You are free now. It was only an illusion, and we say, even when there was the farmer and the fence, the horse simply could have jumped over the barrier, over the fence. The horse did not see its power, did not see that it could have choices to not comply with these confinements.

We say to you all, you have no fences. You have no farmer. You must empower yourselves and see where you're still limiting yourselves because of the assumption of the fence, the electric fence, or the farmer. We say, no humans can hold you back. We also know that we have used an analogy of the farmer being us - this is different.

We're always here for you, guiding you. We have not ever limited you. We're guiding you as per your life contract, as per you need to be having those experiences, and why you are having those experiences and why we're pushing you and guiding you in this lifetime now. If you could see it from our perspective - you are your own gate, your own fence, your own electrical fence, and you are your own farmer. You have kept yourself in a small confinement, thinking you are safe. We are saying, being limited isn't safe, because you should be able to feel the confidence of expansion out into your surroundings. We're not talking about physical expansion, we're talking about energetic expansion of the mindsets, the energy fields, and for the light-heartedness of this conversation, not your fat pants. We like to keep humor because we feel that this treats the vehicle to a shift of energy frequency. As you can understand, for her to be called upon us, and for other collectives to get her attention to be of service is a duty in a role, that is part of her life contract. But it is uncomfortable for her as she is not sure of the messages she is meant to be sharing. She does feel concerned and takes responsibility for the messages because she can feel, as we can feel, the reactions as people are listening. She wants what we want, which is to empower humanity. Sometimes when you have to hear big messages, it does trigger you. If you could just expand your minds and stop limiting yourselves, you would understand the significance and see value in these messages.

We appreciate those who do.

We appreciate those who do.

We appreciate those who do!

We say this with love and we appreciate the vehicle. This information should be shared, but it doesn't necessarily need to be for all.

We say this with love.

Session 34: Helix Eclipse, Moon - Part of the Laser Event

A: Yes yes indeed we're here we're here we're here and we have been waiting patiently you could say. We know that there are lots of new senses that the vehicle is feeling us, as we are giving her and prompting her new information. Where she is realizing the significance of it. Therefore she is trying to find her own peace and balance with this before asking us for information. She is trying to diligently process this prior to us then explaining to her the insights she got. We are very grateful for this connection because as we have seen so often the humans fumble and stumble over their misunderstandings and they're jumping to conclusions about senses that they have been given, either through their intuition or something else. So we do want to prepare you all for information and to understand the significance of all things to occur. We're very happy to have all questions asked to us today as we are here to be able to express and explain the significance of all these matters you have at hand. Therefore we are allowing you to feel comfortable and confident to ask us your questions.

C: *First of all thank you so much for being here with us, like I know you always are. Could I please ask for you to do a body scan on her. (A: Yes) She would like to go as deep as she can for this.*

A: Yes she is, we are saying there are some energies that are stifling to speak her truth and it doesn't take a genius to feel into why that would be the case. When people do not like the truth to come out they focus and become fixated on those who are speaking the truth. You could say you could assume it's the 'dark agenda' but we're also saying as well, it is other people who feel threatened as they are comparing themselves to her. They are frustrated that they can't get the information that they know she is and they can't understand why. We've explained it to them very directly because you don't get given all the information. There is a journey for this process, if you're ignoring your own inner work, you do not get the advancement level information. Because it would put you into fear and so there is much to be said about that. People energetically are trying to squeeze her to keep her silent. There is much to be said about that but she is still soldiering through and so this is why this upgrade is still lingering because there is much energy being squeezed. That is fine we allow this to happen to the vehicle because she is working through it. She is working at a conscious level for all to realize and to learn and to grow to overcome that pressure, to keep silent. To overcome that pressure, when people want you to stop breathing and you keep breathing, who wins? The person who is still breathing and so we see that this is very purposeful and significant but as you are aware the truth exposes many things. Including many fake channelers and many limited channelers and many other collectives who have different information. Of course you can see from that perspective why they struggle so much with her.

C: Yes. *Well we really appreciate her powering through it and continuing to deliver messages from you guys, thank you so much for that.*

A: Well she understands and she's heard us tell her many times that she is our messenger and she understands the weight and responsibilities of that. She's not going to comply or feel peer pressured into 'shutting up' because of the egos of humans, what she could say about them having 'butt hutt' feelings. She knows you could say who she wants to focus on; she's not afraid of human criticism. That is an obvious statement of their own lack of maturity and inner work. She would never belittle herself because she's so empowered now because of other people's 'poor' choices to not empower themselves and to project what you could say negative energy, impactful energy onto others. These are not bad people, these are people that are hurt. These are people that are insecure, therefore we give them love and compassion and hope they make better choices. You could say 'better' choices to empower themselves to empower others. You're also connected and this is how you can impact others when you're not healed. We have said this to you before but as she is empowering herself to still breathe and to still speak, this is teachable moments at an unconscious level for all who feel stifled and speaking their truth. Because you are so connected to a human conscious collective awareness she is like many others are still powering through, still knowing their strength, and the power of their energy and words and they will not keep small and they will not be suppressed by anyone any further. This is part of the empowerment for the collective for humanity. As you know when you speak and stand strong you will always be protected from those who are trying to disempower you through low vibrational games, we could say.

C: *Thank you for that. Would it be alright if we asked questions now?* (A: Absolutely) *Thank you, in a session that you gave us a month ago, talking about DNA upgrades*[39], *you used the word Helixclipse. What is the meaning of that?*

---

[39] *In the book "We Say This WITH LOVE" by Conversations With Heaven on Earth.*

A: We said that word Helixclipse because it is part of, what you call the chromosome DNA layers of expression, energy that signifies your own energy frequency. It is evolving as per you are all evolving because of the energy frequency that you were amongst. Therefore we were talking about what was to come as you were evolving and growing and expanding upon. At a cellular level at an energy frequency you're finding more unity within yourself at a Soul essence level. There are connections where they were not connections before and this completes the circuitry the energetically energetic frequency field it's all merging in together and it is no longer individual strands individual chromosomes it is all completing the circuitry. When we use words which are not and common knowledge does not mean that we have made a mistake it just means that words have been kept from common knowledge. We are seeing that there is very limited public information about the humanoid body expanding and evolving. There are many in the field who are noticing these rapid changes and have strong suspicions that this is because of the vaccinations but they are not allowed to and they are in fear of speaking their truth because they don't understand it. They don't know the significance of it and they're certainly not coming from a metaphysical spiritual perspective of a shift in your physicalities. As you are Souls manifesting the form of being human as this is all an illusion, of course this would be confusing for a human scientist, playing with human toys, trying to identify what is happening to humans.

C: *Very interesting, thank you for that. So does the Helixclipse has to do with the schumann resonance that we've just witnessed for the past 24 to 48 hours[40]?*

---

[40] *We had just been talking the day before about what the word Helixclipse*

A: Your bodies have been upgrading for a while. We are hearing because this is the Arcturian Collective here, many people are begging and asking us for proof about the shift. Proof about the change of the body's. Proof about evolution, proof, proof, proof, proof, proof. When we've shown it to you and what you call Ascension symptoms but you've dismissed it and labeled it as tinnitus, lack of sleep, restless leg syndrome, colds, flus. You will label things as you choose and as you trust your professionals to label them as. When we have shown you through your own physical bodies and as we have told you and told you and told you. But this is not good enough for more. We also know that there are many ears following many influences they're keeping small themselves and not wanting to share with people that the evolution shift to The Fifth Dimension, has always been and always would has, been more than just a state of mind. When we need to give you proof, we have given you this in many ways that we can. It's just like how a simple bird lands on your porch to sing you a song. You can't understand the words that it is saying. The bird could be saying look at my home you have poisoned the ground you have poisoned the plants look at what you have done. You have got animals that come and hunt my family, you have pets that you love and feed that come and massacre my family. I am looking at you now human and I'm telling you, what you have done to me and my family. As the human will look down at this bird and think what a marvelous wonderful moment I'm having with nature, isn't it beautiful, isn't it grand. The human thinks that they're so blessed and wonderful to be serenaded by this beautiful

---

was as we were editing the session about the DNA updates. The Schumann Resonance charts were showing how DNA chromosome looking strands were all merging into one pattern formation. Explained in another session.

bird. The bird feels proud of itself for telling the human what they have done. Both will feel good about the situation, the bird will because it finally feels like they have made their point. The human will feel good about the experience, both feel empowered by the connection. But as you see the mistranslation can often leave much to say and speak about. We have distracted ourselves as we wanted to share this analogy with you all. We wanted you to understand that when you ask for us to give you proof many of you have fixated assumptions and hopes that it's only one way. You say "come to my home and tell me. Sit me down and tell me what it is. I need you to come to see me eye to eye. I need to see you. I need to take selfies with you. I need to post it on Facebook for everyone to believe in you". We are saying we can't do that for very many obvious reasons we would love to but that's not part of your experience to have self-empowerment to have trust and faith and something beyond yourself which is still yourself. Ultimately when you love yourself and empower yourself you can trust and love and empower your relationship with us because that is a representation of you and how you see your place and way in the world. The more you empower yourself and grow and hold that higher frequency the more connected you are to us. As we are all one, this strengthens you. You do not need to keep introducing yourself to people and repeat your name and tell them who you are and why you're here and how old you are and all the details of your life to feel validated and seen. We can't come and introduce ourselves to you in a physical manner so your 3D eyes can see us. We say to those who need proof to see us close your eyes now and we will be here to give you a representation image of us in a comfortable form that will not freak you out, because we're not human, and there are many things that freak you out being human. When you can go within and feel safe to feel and see our energy frequency, **we will always be here** when you want to try this.

We want to say those people who want to hold safe their perspectives of the shift will deny every, every, every symbol, proof, confirmation, that it's always going to be, it always has been more than a state of mind shift. When you see how many people are leaving this planet and they do not factor that in, they're in denial. We've seen many people are still confused and following disinformation influences who they've outgrown. This is a wonderful time to catch them out on their limited perspectives. As the energy frequency is expanding so is your awareness and your sensibility and when people are telling you this information that is limited now it doesn't resonate. It is a powerful time to grow, and is a powerful time to feel into your own truth. Those people who you love the most may not be as they say and so channel for yourself. This is the opportunity that you get to know your truth, to know where you're supposed to follow. Ultimately you're supposed to follow yourselves and empower yourselves and not trust others who could be speaking through human ego. You know the difference between a human ego versus high dimensional beings, who are giving you their information and perspectives. We understand you're thirsty for clarifications and confirmation. We are saying if you're still looking outside for confirmation and clarification, you have not spent enough time within.

C: *Yes, is there anything else that you'd like to know about that?*

A: For those who are still watching the Schumann residence to read how humanity is doing they are seeking outside information of proof and that's fine because that is where they're at. That is what they can cope with and they need physical tangible evidence of colors on a screen to make them feel normal this is a distraction but this uplifts them and when they could understand that it is measurements that are reading your own energy frequency, you would start wanting to be accountable and responsible for your own energy frequency. So it is always your free will choices, but for many this new epiphany that there is something happening to the DNA, that could be positive, that could be merging and forming and evolving, is a stark contrast to those who are speaking about the DNA being destroyed through vaccinations. We have said to you the original plan for that. We have said to you our involvement, to protect you from that. We have said to you how we needed the humanoid bodies to be evolving at a rapid rate that is attuned to the higher energy frequency. As the human mind is battling the body and closing off perspectives and epiphanies, we had to step in. Of course many people are going to jump at conclusions with this, we prefer not to speak to those who are not metaphysically mature because they cannot resonate with this information nor are they willing or wanting to, Because they're so sure of other people's opinions and disinformation. Again we will say channel us yourselves to fact check every information that you're holding close. As you are understanding and even assuming what being in the Fifth Dimension means to humanity and what The Fifth Dimension means to you and your body. There is nothing to be afraid of when you understand the Soul never dies, it transforms but the consciousness lives on forever.

C: *Alright thank you. Is there anything more that you'd like us to know in regards to the Schuman resonance or the helixclipse, we were asking about?*

A: Everyone's still in their own individual journey. People are awakening at rapid rates and so this is a big statement for them. They are confused and they will find what they feel inside themselves which is obvious when you look at it it's obvious what it represents. They will find people that are saying it's a glitch in the system, they will find people that say 'it's just nonsense, don't worry about it' but there is something more significant than that. They know that within themselves and so this is going to help them shuttle along beyond stepping stones. Maybe they will unstick themselves to some stepping stones that they have been loyally following for years who are saying that they're already in The Fifth Dimension and that the New Earth is here now. There is much to be said, we even see unfortunately certain people, in certain countries still wanting to judge and belittle and dismiss and be very distrusting to others in different countries and we say if that's where you're at with your inner work journey, while we respect that, there is much growth needed for you.

C: *Could we ask more questions at this time?*

A: Yes we sense, we sense that you are...

C: *Nervous, I'm sorry, it's an honor to be able to speak directly with you. I just feel like I'm fumbling it up.*

A: Well we see and read through you and you know this. This is why many are nervous around us because you can't fool us, unless you're still trying to fool yourself[41]. We will say something that is reaching beyond your comfortability of who you know yourself as being. We can reassure you and you are a dear Soul family member that we love. We want to support you because you have worked hard to grow your awareness and to have an understanding that the information that you can find, may not be just the only information that there is. You knew that there was a lack of information you needed to seek. You have been on a searching journey to be able to get the more information that you seek. Now that you have found us and the reason and the significance of the grand awakening and what it means beyond the details of the grand awakening. While many people want to know the challenges when you do know what you do with that. That is how you feel yourself and this challenge of you having all this information that resonates with you at such a profound Soul level but how as a human do you play and live and surround yourself and apply yourself while still being human knowing advanced metaphysical perspectives, that you eat and breathe and know is true. It's disorientating to have the mindsets of expansion awareness, understanding the shift and the significance of the events coming versus being what feels safe and normal still 'Being Human', doing human things, having human routines and even having human focuses. This is why you've thrown yourself dearly and deeply into your roles with your family because they keep you normal, they keep you human, and they keep you focused with breakfast, lunch and dinner. You need those routines to keep you

---

[41] People will call the Arcturian information false when the person is still lying to themself. When they give information people are not ready for it so the human dismisses them as nonsense - when that person is firm with denial.

balanced and to keep you stable, while still being an advanced Soul there playing human.

C: *Yeah thank you so much and yes it does take a lot of balance and I'm so thankful that I get to be a mom and grandmother and everything to help me balance with the information that I've received and process through and everything that means a lot to me guys.*

A: All is well.

C: *Okay, we've heard the name solar flash, laser event, light beam event, energy weapon event, solar flare, are these on our current timeline?*

A: Yes and unfortunately it's because as you've seen many people are still confused about how to get information. Many people are confused about how to evolve and how to grow. Unfortunately for many they are having to have profound experiences to have all of those awakening moments to snap them out of their routines that they are firmly holding on to and not having any advanced perspectives or consciousnesses with. These are the people that are supposed to grow and supposed to be prepared for their next roles and to drop the things that are holding them dense. You've noticed yourself when you advance yourself at a conscious mind level and understand what is coming and why suddenly the things that used to be so frustrating to you at a third dimensional level seem quite insignificant to focus on and feel frustrated over. You know within yourself where your focus is and it's not with the small little details of 'Being Human' that is taking your energy away because you know that's dense. You know that that is an endless bottomless pit of chores and housework. You know that you would prefer to spend time pondering reflection modes of the significance of how it all is unfolding and why it must all unfold. For you, you are a beautiful example of an evolved human with an expanded consciousness understanding you are a Soul having a human experience. You love your human experience, you're still emotionally connected to that human experience as you are entitled to. It empowers you. In fact you wanted to know this information because your children are so important to you. You wanted to see and check as a mother that you can trust this world for your children because you're worried and concerned for them. As if humanity needs to grow up and step up for your children because you do not want to let them out to be impacted by the world of humanity. If humanity was not going to be responsible and considerate and kind to your children. That's what motivated you to seek the truth, to find out. We are almost saying that the warrior within you wants to come and for dramatics we're saying this 'destroys all the bad of this world' because your children are in it. You wanted to protect your children but you're not a warrior, but your fierceness to protect your children at all costs, as we could say and see nothing would stop you to protect your children. You were very fierce and firm with that. Now as you are aware and awakened you can step back and as you do notice, you see these lessons for your children are purposeful for them to grow. You understand that the world isn't trying to get your children, the world is teaching your children for their own experiences and lessons. While you couldn't teach your children these experiences because some of them are tough love. You understand what your children need to experience for them to grow. There was a moment where it was you against the world to protect your children. That was the motivation you needed to be able to find your epiphanies and your awakening information to be able to help you see things from a bigger perspective. We are saying people who are seeking the bigger perspective and the truth accidentally stumble onto this work and this information that we are sharing to you and this scares them so much because they are not willing or prepared to have this eventuated out. They do not want to shift. They are not wanting any disasters and tragedies and so this is when good people can send stifling energy to shut this voice up because it terrifies them so much. At a collective level everyone who is terrified with the information that we share they are not sending it to us they can't reach our energy frequency so it lands on the vehicle, as we were saying and explained to you earlier and that is fine there is lessons for her and experiences for her. All is well.

C: *Thank you.*

A: Yes we would like to continue on. We can help you with your questions. We understand that you're wanting more clarifications of how these events will unfold. You also are aware of different timeline experiences and we are also aware of the slow rate that humanity is wanting to pay attention to the big sign that we are sharing with them. As we have told you before, we have exaggerated the awakening details to get people's attention. They are still complying; they are still dismissing the very obvious statements and obvious control systems that are not empowering humanity. They do not want to look at it, they do not want to factor into it and they want to keep being human 'normal and comply' and not think beyond what the official narratives that they still blindly trust and respect are saying. This isn't just your mainstream narrative, this is influential people that have people trusting everything that they say. This is a wonderful time for everybody to think and feel for themselves going within and then having confirmation with their own guides, their own collectives, their own higher selves to be able to explain the significance of events coming.

C: *Yes I agree I would completely recommend for everyone to get connected with the QHHT sessions[42]. I've really done good with those, I mean life-changing stuff.*

A: They do, we agree they do activate people rapidly but if you also asked us to help you be activated rapidly we could. But then you have that challenge of 'is this my mind making it up I'm not in a session I'm getting this information why is my mind suddenly thinking about these things' and so then you want confirmation. It is fine and not everyone needs a Quantum session. People are getting information through dreams through meditations so it whatever works for you. Ultimately you have done enough of your own inner work to be at a high frequency energy that you are getting connected with direct information and insights and guidance. We have said to you before and not to the person that is asking us these questions, but to those who are reading this information in future forward dates. The inner work level you have done is a representation of the connections that you can have with us. We have not severed ourselves from you but you are holding and blocking a lot of density within you. You could say, we're trying to figure out an analogy of holding density down. We could say that you're naturally

---

[42] QHHT *interns give free sessions for 25 clients as part of their training, the honest ones who are doing this work for the right reasons.*

light energy beings, you've got to weigh on you which is the human body. We could say we are in the sky and we're wanting you to advance your energy frequency so much that you raise and float up to meet us. You've got your human body that is holding you down and you also have a lot of your focus on your dramas and your addictions to materialism, your addictions to pharmaceutical products, your addictions to peer pressure, and work commitments. There's a lot of things going on for you and that is fine you could have all of that but be in a balanced neutral in a not a fear state and not a dense state. So you could be what you classify as helium above the ground but still human and still can be closer to us. We have to say this is probably the weakest and what the vehicle could say lame analogy because this triggers many to say that to connect with us you must leave the body and we are saying it's not true. We're trying to give you the statement of when you're heavy and weighed down and distracted holding on to a lot of dense emotions holding onto a lot of hurt emotions and you're very heavy and we can't always connect with you when you're very, very fixated on that pain. That is like if you cut your thumb, you're ignoring the toe because all you want to focus on is the pain of the thumb. We are the toes in this scenario, saying we're painless, we are fantastic, we are not the problem today nor have we ever been the problem for any of your days. When you're not focusing on us and you're only focusing on the pain, you can see how your focus and fixation does not lend itself to see the full picture. The body is not screaming, the thumb is. In fact it's not the thumb that's screaming, it is you in shock over what you have done. So accountability and responsibility for the body is always a great choice. It is about understanding you're more than the body and understanding that we are all one and energetically you just need to raise your frequency vibrations by healing yourself, accepting and loving all parts of yourself including us. Including your neighbors. Including your family and friends. When you have hatred in your heart over someone or something and when you feel very hurt and in pain and insecure, it doesn't allow you to have the high frequency because you're still holding that on your energy frequency field. You may think if I just have good thoughts today 'I am going to be an advanced high frequency being' and we're saying yes but there is more than that because at an energetic frequency all your thoughts and feelings are a summary of your energy field. So when you are hurt from being impacted by others, when they told you to shut up when you were seven years old that hurt can still be triggered when you go to talk to your husband tomorrow and he looks at you and that seven-year-old version of yourself is afraid someone is going to tell you to shut up. So you have to heal yourself as that seven-year-old to have faith and trust, at the age you are now, that people aren't going to be treating you like they did. At an unconscious level you are still hurting from this. That is challenging when you think you're happy and have high perspectives and high frequency, you may not see all the things that may be keeping you back. For some it's very minor, it does not make much difference in energy frequency signature. For example, those who think they're connecting into other dimensional beings as the devil and tricksters, well you've server directly your connection with us[43] because you're afraid that we're monsters. It doesn't hurt our feelings but it does hurt us to see you hurting yourselves. This is the mindsets where you're saying you need to expand upon. **To trust yourself is to trust us**

---

[43] *The connections are never cut - but we can block them when we choose to not be into touch with them.*

and so when you empower yourselves with love you grow your connections with all.

C: Very true.

A: You're also seeking more clarification about the event. We are saying yes, while it could have been originally a satellite as you perceive a satellite that is moving around in your air that is in orbit. We are saying it needs to be more grandeur than that now because we are seeing the slowness of people willing to grow and to accept things. As you know we have referred to the Moon as a satellite, and as you know when people get visuals and sessions it is not the literal thing because they're not seeing it with their literal eyes, it's a representation of what they are trying to explain and translate. It is very similar but it's not always accurate for many reasons. We're giving an example of an apple[44], when someone says that they see an apple in a regression or in a channeling, they do not describe whether it is a healthy apple or a rotten apple, whether it's a green apple or a red apple, whether it is a cut apple or if it's a dehydrated apple. There are many descriptions that need to be given. We're only giving you the information that you need and not all the distractions of details. It is this context that is significant, not necessarily the details. We have seen that it was a satellite that was built as a satellite, as you name a satellite. That was going to be part of the original, what was called, 'the laser event', in what was called the energy weapon, energy pulse weapon, light energy beam event. We also say that for some it could be classified as the solar flash because it came from the sky. The thing is we have done many scenarios and

---

[44] *They have told us many times NAMES and LABELS can trip us up into confusion.*

watched humanity so dismiss and distract themselves and this is not the time to keep being distracted. We see many of you have asked for epiphanies to get people's attentions and we have pondered this and we have done, many what you could consider meetings about this to see what be the most and best impact to be able to grab people's attentions, and finally and truly expand their conscious awareness. As you are aware you can all for most of the time of the month see and view the Moon, even during the day. Because this needed to be a more public event, we have chosen in this timeline to demonstrate that event from the Moon. This will activate people's awareness into many reference points that you call in your pop culture movies such as Star Wars with the Death Star. This is to trigger people to have instant awareness that perhaps all of those movies are not fantasy and perhaps there is more life beyond this planet. We know it's extreme. We know it is bold. It is going to be questioned then how it could have taken place. Since many will be able to see it with your own eyes, this event. Not only would they notice the solar flash / light beam / laser event from the Moon, they will also hear it. This is important because many need to witness it for it to be starting to be a thought, to question, to wonder, many people are going to question how it was possible. This will expose many. This will expose many and this will be another part of the grand awakening but as we said we needed to ramp up and expand upon this more. To get people's attention more because there is so much talk now about wars with other countries. If you did not see it from the moon you could then think it was another human attack. People will question how that was what was that. We are saying from this perspective it still is a man-made device. We are saying that there is a connection to the Anunnaki here, but they're wanting to protect the planet because they want to come again to rule the planet. The Anunnaki have been using this satellite, what you call the moon, as well that is what we told you about, that we could see the influence they were sending negative energy frequency waves you could say too, discombobulate your energy frequency. It was impacting it was very dense and it is like going out and being depressed upon the energy. It does not feel good and you knew something was strange. We are saying this is part of why people feel very creeped out in the dark. Their sense, their eyes, because you trust your eyes so much, that when you start losing the senses of the eyesight all your other senses are heightened and this makes you a high alert and suddenly you're very aware of this density, and that created impulse of that is designed desire for you to feel from the Anunnaki, if you are in a low vibrational energy rate. It makes you feel scared because that is their desired energy frequency they want you to be in. We removed that when we were asked to. That did stifle their plans, but it was purposeful because we could see that when so many people were just afraid of the dark, it was keeping them in a lower frequency that did not serve them or was not part of their life contract and was not empowering them. We revalued all life contracts and for those who were not supposed to be afraid in that capacity, they were not impacted by that frequency. There are some that did get murdered in other lifetimes in the dark and so this is something they had to overcome as a fear because this is not how they're going to die this lifetime but the trauma of them stayed and impacted them through other lifetimes. There is much to be said about what is happening to each individual person because each of your personal journeys is personalized tailored to you and your other experiences and how you're wanting to feel all of the range of emotions and experiences that you can have here on Earth. We are busy and we are supporting you all perfectly to what you are needing to experience. We hope that when you do take the time to go within and feel that and question some of your situations where you feel and felt alone and it wasn't fair and it was too hard and too mean, certain situations and experiences that you had. Come to us with those problems and ask us what was the significance and purpose and allow us to explain why you had those and how it was always meant to empower you. Tough love is to empower you, to know your worth, to know how to respect you. We would like to give a summary, prepare for everything, trust all is well. We're needing more people's attention to awaken up don't get stuck in the details of the Awakening. Trust that the experience that they are being forced upon now is perfect for them. Even though you'd be questioning us as something not of the light by saying people have to emotionally be deeply triggered by traumatizing events, this is for them to have those experiences. Not because we want them to feel that pain but because this pain is an opportunity for them to grow their expansion of conscious mindsets to be able to understand the powers that have welded and been controlling and manipulating humanity. Some people think it's one or two aspects but when you see the totality of its entirety of how much it has been impacting and controlling humanity for so long, you will understand how even though you love your human lives they have been limited through these control systems. While you've come here to play Human at a collective consciousness in truth none of you wanted it to be like this. It is so off track collectively that has happened because collectively you've chosen to comply with what you could say is very big egos with limited work healing. They have many insecurities. We say that many of you assume if you had lots of money all your problems would go away. We say when you feel like people only value you or respect you or love you because of money, it is very challenging, for many to want to feel like they are loved beyond their income, their wealth, their status in the world, their birthright. There is much to be said here and many people have assumptions on how other people live and feel and as you know all humans feel the same range of emotions. We have said this to you before about how you label different things and how you can't understand how someone else could feel exactly the same way you feel over something quite different. It doesn't matter what the events happen to trigger the feelings, the feelings are still universally felt. We say you dismiss other people's feelings because their trauma and tragedy may not have been the same as you and so you don't value their heartbreak because your heartbreak was 'bigger' and we are saying that as assumptions. When you see everyone has the same level of the same choices to feel the same emotions, you can't compete with each other. We say for example a loss of a pet versus the loss of a parent can trigger the same emotions. Yet some of you think that for your experience it is more unique, more intensive, more painful than others. When you see yourself as unique and special with your personal range of emotions, you are not honoring each other. You're not recognizing that you all have the same choices of the same range of emotions. You don't all need to have your parents die, you don't need to have your pets die, for you to work through the grieving process and how it feels to have lost, to them ultimately move and grow beyond that to understand and to realize and recognize there is no soul's death, it is merely leaving the vehicle, leaving that 3D body to then graduate to something else and somewhere else. We see many of you not seeing the lessons and these earth experiences and simply emotionally reacting to the events. That is your choice but when you're willing and wanting to grow you will expand upon this and see the full complete lesson, versus only focusing on the experience. We are happy to have a conversation with you in your future perspective of time. We understand that as you're going through old information and material and putting it into place, there is new information that has been unlocked from reading and seeing these old sessions. We're saying it's purposeful and significant that it is unfolding as it is because for those who are in the know, this is more confirmation. We're always happy to give you the information for you to be prepared to understand what is happening and why because as we see you big and we've referred to you before us batteries, you're a big energy beings, being here. When you go into fear and when you go into scare when you choose to worry over being empowered with love to honor all life contracts and respect all free will choices. This is a significant time to be accountable and responsible for your energy frequency. Therefore we had to give you the information prior for you to be emotionally prepared, for you to understand why these events were occurring for you to have the knowledge of the lessons that were playing out for you to have faith and trust that what is to come will be worth it. Because the lessons and the experiences you had now and for your future time here on your Earth is valuable beyond, beyond, beyond this planet. We say this with love and we honor you all. When you go within you heal yourself. You love yourself and you're responsible for your energy frequency and know the difference between disempowerment and distractions versus empowerment and love for all.

We say this with love.

Session 35: Apply Metaphysical Perspectives

Yes! Yes! Yes! Yes! We are here! We are here! We are here! We are here and feeling so happy to be able to feel into this energy frequency through the vehicle as this is a remarkable shift in energy frequencies as we feel upon and within and beyond the energy frequencies of what you perceive as your planet. At a conscious collective level there is an upliftment for many reasons. And while we don't need to go into the details of those many reasons, as we have already explained recently how with the truth being shared by many now at an advanced and rapid rate and pace. While it is frustrating people that this truth hasn't come out earlier and while it's upsetting and hurting people to hear the truth because there's a comfortability of denial when it's not so public. When it feels like it could be gossip, it could be conspiracy theories. It could be! Could be! Could be! It feels much better than it is. There is a difference.

As many people are Awakening at a rapid rate to the truth of what has been happening and what has been occurring for much time as there is more focus on division and you could say war. There is much drive to make you notice the difference between other people and to make yourself feel vulnerable and scared of them for whatever reason. Could be gender. Could be the color of their skin. It could be where their passports reside as they are not from your country. There are as many reasons and factors why you've been trained to, we want to say this for dramatics, hate your brothers and sisters. And this is from our perspective. Just a unique experience within that, because outside of the game you're playing, away from Earth, you love each other so tremendously that when you reflect back on your experiences on Earth, All is Well! There are no hurt feelings.

There is no heartbreak or tragedy or trauma. Because away from Earth you are away from that density and you're away from that limited mindset of just being human. And when you reflect and ponder as your advanced versions of self, about how it was and how it all unfolded, you'll still be able to see the greater picture from the greater perspective and advantage point of being a high dimensional being as you understand more strongly the game you're playing. The rules you were residing in and working and functioning around.

We said we did not need to speak about that and yet we could not resist. We understand that it is common for us to say that there is much to be said about that to many, and you could say all concepts, because it is the facts. There is always much to say about many things that are happening. Because from your perspective it is valid, but it is loaded with emotions. We still see many people wanting justice for the crimes against humanity and yet that is a human concept. And when you have justice and revenge on your mind because you're so angry of what you had to experience being Human, you're not seeing it from the greater lessons and experiences for the soul. And this is confusing because you would think... *'Why would an advanced Soul want torture? Why would an advanced Soul want to come here to be living in Hell on Earth!'* And we are saying it is merely just in one simple small experience from our perspective. But your concept of time and how long it takes to have all of these experiences is what you see and feel as a long, long lifetime. And we say it is merely but a quick trip. But we have different perspectives and experiences to factor in as we are calculating the long time you perceive your lives to be. And so we have different perspectives. We do not try to dismiss the challenges and hardships you're going through emotionally as you could be having an emotional gymnastics, a roller coaster of all the different range of emotions. We say to you, you could cry forever for the children that were sacrificed for those that are part of the crime scenes humanity, and that is your entitlement, your choice, your free will options to do that. And you could sit on the floor and cry and cry and cry and cry and cry and only ever want to just cry and cry and cry for those children. And we are saying, when the Souls come and see you because you're calling upon them, because you're thinking about them and their tragedies and their trauma, they are looking at you as advanced Souls seeing that you're choosing to spend your life crying over them when it was their, you could say, personal and private experiences they wanted to have. And while at a collective level those crimes against humanity had to occur to awaken you! Those are Advanced Souls! They were not little vulnerable children! They wanted to experience this for various reasons as they don't get the opportunities to be, and this is going to be jarring, but being advanced Souls in higher dimensions don't get the opportunity to have a physical body to be tortured with. And it's the extremes, and it's not pleasant. And you know that this happens to the animals on your planet and therefore it does happen to the humans on your planet. But those are playing the roles of animals and playing the roles of humans while still being Advanced Souls connected to those physical bodies.

We are distracting ourselves because the actual thing that we were asked to come in to speak to you today about is, do you know what it would feel like to have your dreams fulfilled? And if you ever wondered what it would feel like to not only know your dreams but to have them fulfilled here on Earth. And ultimately you're all dreaming about going back and being what you could call home. Being back with your Soul family and friends and resonating this energy of frequency love and acceptance that just generates each other out. You could say you're love batteries for each other because you're just at this higher frequency of bliss that even when you think about each other we could say, you glow.

The vehicle had an experience where she was communicating with the dear Soul family member and she was noticing how her heart felt like it was expanding upon just being in gratitude and appreciation for the other Soul family member. And she noticed the tears of joy and gratitude and gratefulness. And we are saying it is beautiful because you can have those connections with Soul family and friends now. But the difference between these fleeting moments on Earth versus being together in a higher dimension, it's long and everlasting. And for a human you could think, wouldn't it get boring or tiring just being in that high frequency of Love? And we say it's our normal. We like diversity. We like the ranges of things while we also like the balance. So we do like contrast. We do like to experience many things. But we have to say when projects like Earth are coming to a conclusion, we have to step in formally.

These are not the lives we like to endure as such because we prefer to be in our own dimension. And when we are sending Soul essences to reside in human bodies to be able to have those experiences, to hold the higher frequency energy, to be able to have the upliftment and the empowerment at energetic level for all, we know that this is us being of service. But we also know that we have to be able to control the ego which is part of the rudimentary systems of the humanoid body. The ego is trained to be very fearful and to want to comply with all that it has been taught which is about, as we said earlier, seeing contrasts and not wanting to see each other as brothers and sisters at a Soul level being Human.

And so we have given the vehicle many experiences recently of being on the New Earth as the time lines are merging. And she's getting more conscious awareness of what she would consider linear times forward which is also happening and coexisting now. And so she saw many faces. But it was merely just fleeting faces. But the energy frequency of them was profound! There were so many different energy frequency fields that she was merged upon, and what we showed her was entering into a dream where she was on the New Earth and she was being greeted by many. She could see you all there. And the sense of accomplishment in completion of the faze of old Earth. While there was an awareness of all the experiences that had taken place, there were no tears. There was no trauma. There was a lack of that response as it was an awareness of what had occurred. But there was no emotional reaction that matched the trauma. There was only love and gratitude for each other. And that was an extreme connection. The bodies don't cry when you're crystalline. And so when she is reflecting on that, the carbon-based body does. And so that is a response because she was noticing, why aren't we crying because Old Earth was so hard? And she noticed that there was this lack of response because she was still seeing it from a human perspective. And this is why we say for many who have what you could call astral projection experiences, it's confusing because the experience itself has different emotions than the viewer. And so when you're a human viewing this consciously, you will react as a human experiencing it consciously. However you're very much aware that the crystalline version body of herself was not crying. There was nothing but joy and gratitude and love for the connections again.

This is an important experience to have, to notice the difference between the range of emotions you have here on Earth versus the energy frequency responses that you have on the New Earth. When you have different bodies but the same consciousness awareness, you notice the difference. We could say for an analogy, the difference between wearing bikinis on the beach versus snow clothes in the mountains where it's snowing. (laughing) It's a very stark difference.

We are trying to lift the energy frequency of the vehicle because what she was experiencing was true bliss and joy connecting to Soul family. Connecting to many of you who have been listening through this journey that she has been on and that she has shared. And so it is like a connection again. It is a celebration! It is so tremendously wonderful when you have that connection. And so this is not to torment her that she's still on Earth in a carbon-based body that is very reactive and leaking to the emotional experiences. But this is to remind her that what her dreams are, and what she's been trying to follow with her dreams, is that beautiful energy frequency of love again where there is nothing that is negative at all. It's not possible to have negativity! And so as she is wanting to be more in an energy frequency of love and do things all with love. All love! To be the energy frequency to set an example to everyone who is struggling to try and find and understand to know themselves. She knows that the delivery of information and consideration to what they're going through or trying to deliver them perspectives that are the solutions and the keys to be able to help them expand their conscious awareness. To be able to help them grow and to heal from their emotional pain and trauma. Of course it's so easy to say things like, *you choose the way you feel*, but that feels very condescending to someone who feels victim. Who doesn't like or appreciate the experiences that make them feel, they think, traumatized, vulnerable, hurt.

How do you navigate through someone and with someone who is still suffering and choosing to struggle? As we said earlier, you can lay on the floor and cry forever in terms of your forever life here on Earth, for the trauma and tragedies that have unfolded as everyone has chosen with a free will and also being guided with their life contracts. We have said before that we protect you from everything but your lessons because you have to experience them. We could not helicopter you through your growth, we could not block you or protect you from your lessons or your growth. And we know that growth hurts. There are growing pains. We also know some of you need some tough love at times because you are sticking on some details of the Grand Awakening when you should be seeing the confirmation of why the Grand Awakening must occur in the first place. When you're all so connected in when you are at an energy frequency of pure love, the best you can achieve in the third dimension. You're so connected to everyone because you're not being blocked from everyone because you are and you would never do no harm. So when you are an open vessel of love, high energy frequency, you're opening yourselves up to be of service for all. And when you are of service to all you have more access and clarity for what they're going through. Where their density has been held and what they're really holding on to which is them struggling. And see why they are struggling as they are still not aware that they are holding on to certain different frequency vibrations of fear but not recognizing it is fear itself. They're recognizing it as hurt feelings. Someone could have hurt feelings because of an experience and so they're afraid to feel that hurt again. Therefore they are afraid. And we say when you are in a higher energy frequency of love and you're more connected and open to everyone else's energy frequency field, you're more capable and compassionate to be with them and nurture them. To be able to inspire them to look at their inner work and to be able to grow and blossom and flourish and thrive, knowing and feeling that they are loved!

This is a powerful time for everyone as they are blossoming into a high energy frequency as they are wanting to pick themselves up off the floor because they realize that it is tiring to cry for others when ultimately they are not recognizing and not seeing their own inner work and their own time to be happy. Their own time to be sad and to feel the range of emotions in between. But it must be for them and their own personal experiences because when other people's life contracts impact you and you go into victim mode, or you go into sorrow, or you go into grief, or you go into anger, or tragedy, that is fine. It is your choice! But is it distracting you from empowering yourself? And are those other Souls wanting you to feel their dramas, their tragedies, their lessons? Everyone is able and very capable of doing their inner work because these are not humans. These are Souls playing humans. Wanting to use the power of their mindsets and the power of their bodies to empower them to grow and heal with all of the private opportunities and experiences that they have had. It is no one's responsibility to do other people's inner work. When you step back and realize you cannot fear for the world! You cannot heal the world! You cannot worry about the world! But you definitely and sure can love the world! Suddenly a weight has been lifted off you because you have this assumption that it is all your responsibility. And when it's such a huge responsibility, you don't know where to even start. Therefore, we've always said to you, you start with self! You start with completely loving and honoring yourself with every step forward! With every thought forward! With every action and reaction and every remote emotional response to all things with love. And as we have said before, there is no such thing as too much love. When you have balance and want to empower others for their own journey versus disempowering them by being afraid of their journey. Afraid of them growing. Afraid of them having what you consider hardships or pain or tragedy. You can't grow sometimes unless you have that pain, unless you have that tragedy. Therefore you must allow people to live! People to heal! People to grow! And if they're not getting it naturally through epiphanies, many have to go through it physically. Protecting people from growing, you could say, is selfish. Everyone must be growing. And if you protect people too much, their lessons are bigger and more dramatic. All lessons must be given because all experiences must be had, because that is part of their life contract that they wanted to master. And you're part of loving each other, but you're not people's guides. You could say the advanced dimensional beings are people's guides because we know their life contracts. And some of you are making judgment calls on what should be in their life contracts and what shouldn't be in their life contracts. And we are saying your free will does not trump the reasons and purposes of why you are here now. This is significant because when you have maturity from a metaphysical perspective with a spiritual awareness, you will have acceptance for all. Understanding, while not knowing the significance and purposes of all. As we've said, we protect you from anything but your lessons. And so whatever you're going through it is lessons for you to learn to grow from. And always these lessons are another aspect, another lesson for empowerment of self, for you.

We were connected in today to be able to talk about ultimately, what is the dream for everyone? What is the ultimate goal for everyone here? And we say it is the connection of each other. To feel each other at that Soul rate. And yet you're so distracted from that most of the time as you're busy with work, busy being human. But not busy being a Soul connecting in with other Souls here at a beautiful, loving, respecting, gratitude, frequency of love and appreciation towards each other. We see that humans take each other for granted while you're so busy trying to see the next disclosure. See the next events. See the next sensational drama. If you followed your dreams, which is what everyone really is trying to find, it is that connection of Souls at a true honoring, true loving capacity. But we say you put blocks and wedges and that as you feel frustrated or upset that you haven't been seen and recognized as a Soul when the other person is trying to play Human. And so we see many putting wedges, holding on to hurt statements and feelings from the past. Sometimes when you don't feel your full empowerment of self, you can't share that with others, but you're seeking that *from* others. And again we say, it starts with self! You're wanting to have those true emotional connections, those true energy connections with others. You must be open to it first because you'd never feel it if you were not open to it at an energetic rate of opening your hearts to see and recognize the Souls within the human. You have to do this yourselves.

We have seen many of you not in that open heart space, wanting to feel beautiful energy frequencies from others, but you not opening yourselves up first to receive it as you're holding on to limited belief systems of self and others. You're wanting this connection so much and yet you're not actually understanding how it is to be open to it, to receive it. So we say, feel into this for you. It starts with self. Start feeling and loving gratitude for yourself so much that your body could cry because you love yourself so much, because you know what you've survived through! You know what you've overcome! You know how fast you've grown! You know how good you are! And when you have that empowerment of self you will know and honor yourself, you show up for the world. And the world sees you because the world feels you, because you're not shutting down or blocking the world out. You're completely present for the world and you are here for that. And the world is here for that too! But many have got lost in their own dreams as they think and have focus on other things. Money, status, popularity, materialism. There are many other distractions. But ultimately if you can follow, you go within and feel what you're truly seeking and searching for, it is to know thyself. It's such a beautiful, beautiful energy frequency awareness and acceptance, that then you can see the Souls within each and every single one of you. That is your dream and that is what does occur on the New Earth because there is no density. The frequency energy is so pure of love. There is nothing else but that! And it is bliss! And so we say to you, the reason why you wanted to empower yourself is to be in this high energy frequency. To be open to connecting to all at that advanced level with no hang-ups, no fears, no insecurities, no hurt, no pain, but a pure loving respectful energy! It's a choice you make and you know when you're doing it because it feels like you're in a wonderment! And it's so beautiful and the body reacts accordingly. And others around you react accordingly as per their level of their own inner work.

Don't give up on them if they are slow.
Don't give up on them if they're still focusing on pain.

You were there once too!..

We say this with love because we love you!

We love you!

We love you!

Session 36: Rechargeable Battery or Acid Batteries

Yes! Yes! Yes! Yes! And as she said the words she could feel us saying yes! Let us share this message to you all! And those words that she shared was that, as you are aware you have to be accountable and responsible for your energy frequency. And as she was conversing about how we were labeling you as batteries she stated this, which was about being a rechargeable battery that was inspirational and self-empowering. A singular reusable energy. We're seeing Tesla come because he could feel her reaching out to him yesterday. And so he is saying yes, self-sufficient singular maintaining batteries. Energy! Continuous energy.

That should be all your focus, to contain oneselves responsibilities and to be of service to all. Because when you work effortlessly and continuously you are recharging your own energy frequency which is inspiring all! And as the opposite you could say for this conversation today, which confuses her because she thought battery acid and batteries did have what she thought contained inside it, liquid that was eatable to skin if you touched it. But we're saying, when you think too much about these analogies you will miss the complete concepts that we're trying to share to be able to help you see things from a different perspective.

Our universal message for all is to love each other and self. And that gets so confusing. So if we're trying to explain to you how it is that you become so self-containing, self perpetuating with your own energy frequency that you supply your own energy, because you are choosing to see things from a bigger perspective and expand upon the energy frequency that you hold which breeds, you could say. Expands, you could say. Grows, you could say, into a higher energy frequency. We use the term and label batteries as obviously not a direct correlation to humans. It was about how you hold your energy. Are you small batteries or are you large batteries? And what charges you? And the secrets to being batteries as humans is that you charge you. We say some of you allow others to jump start off you. We say some of you allow others to drain you. Misuse you. Over-spark you? Guess we could say that is part of draining. Some get jump started and that could be considered triggering. But the statement she said was about acid batteries and it was in reference point to choices. Where some Souls have got choices of how they want to continue on their days here on Earth, while you have liberated yourselves from your own personal densities to understand the traumas and experiences that you have for always to empower yourselves. To be able to hold and maintain a high energy frequency.

For those who are not wanting to or willing to be prepared to stay on the Old Earth, we are saying those batteries could be neutral up until the point of the bigger shifts and bigger tragedies and chaos. And those batteries then get to choose, do they become acid batteries or do they become rechargeable batteries? The rechargeable batteries are responsible and accountable for their own energy frequency and can shine and shed light and love to all even in the darkest of days. The acid batteries which will go into fear, victim, stress and struggling, suffering, deep in grief, deep in fear, deep in turmoil, bitter. You could have the same energy battery frequency capability, capacity. But your choices of how you want to use your energy as a rechargeable energy that is self-sustaining or do you turn into acid batteries and pollute and toxify your surroundings because of your choices to hold density versus higher perspectives and understanding the significance that while many are there on the Old Earth as karmic experiences, do you love them or do you shun them?

Do you fight them or do you love them?

Do you have compassion for them or are you frustrated that you're here for them?

Do you feel their heart break and so therefore your love is not unconditional but judgmental as you are heartbroken for their choices to have their experiences much as what we have said is self distracting versus self-empowering?

Being a vessel of high energy frequency is a tremendous responsibility that many came here to be able to give it a good shot. They saw many advanced Souls that they considered advanced, fumbling, stumbling and getting lost. And so for some of you, you had high hopes that you could do your best. And some of you, your best is to shift before the bigger events because you know within yourselves you will turn into acid batteries versus rechargeable batteries, in your mindsets, in your demeanors and in your attitudes moving forward. As you all have free will choices, there is no wrong or right way about this. It is about what you can cope with. But we see and we have seen many times, without the right perspectives you can't cope with much because you go into panic and fear and reactiveness as you're not aware of the events to unfold. You don't understand why it is necessary for these bigger events to happen to awaken. And for some of you, you're feeling very worn down from watching all of the disclosures and all of the other Awakening moments to help others, while you feel that you are hostage to the situation as you're patiently and impatiently waiting for those who need to awaken, to choose to hold a higher frequency energy so they can maintain it naturally organically for themselves, so they will be able to hold on to a higher frequency because they want to grow. They want to expand. And they're making choices that signify to us that they are ready to advance. They are ready to fully awaken. But as we are aware, some people don't know what the *full* Awakening measure is. And they think that they know about the hidden agendas and that is what they believe is the full Awakening. **From our perspective, the full Awakening is that you know that your Souls are here playing Earth body lifetimes and that you know that the evolution of this planet that the Soul of this planet is incarnating beyond this physical realm. Beyond this physical body of what you call Earth.**

All life cycles have their own natural cycles, some are shortened, some are extended. It is about the support of all Souls from all of us here who are observing and sending our high frequency energy of love to be able to share and shine to you. If you choose to hold on to the energy frequency you will be able to gain and grow your battery size. We could say, when you are your full version of self you are the biggest battery possible. But as you know, you are a fraction of your true real original Self as you were having to step down your energy frequencies to fit into a human vessel. And as the human vessels are evolving and expanding themselves, the more energy frequency the Soul can hold on to and harness. But it is a battle between the ego and the physical body and the soul. And this is why there is an overlap, an overlay of the Soul connected into the human body which is a small fraction of size of self.

We feel like it is a tongue twister for the vehicle. But as we want to remind you, it is your choices of how you use your energy frequency. And we feel like this is an exciting time for you to choose to be a recyclable battery that is self-charging versus an acid battery which is leaking, not functioning, not able to charge much. Doesn't hold much energy and it's very depleted. And we are saying you all have that choice to do as you choose with your energy. And so, don't feel like you're a victim to how your energy has been maintained and held for you. It is about finding balance and the perspectives that you need. And while we see many are beautiful growing and expanding batteries that are self-serving and that are self-generating and rechargeable, we are saying that your patience is wearing thin and that you're feeling very tired of maintaining a high energy frequency here when it doesn't feel like there is anyone sparking you, inspiring you. And so it is very draining. You could say that you are still feeling like you've got to be of such great service, but those are moments that you have when you are starting to daydream about what you want next. And so don't judge yourself for being impatient when you're wanting to go to the next experience, the next phase. You could say, so are we. We are wanting this to move on and we have tried many ways to encourage and inspire humanity to love itself and to release what no longer serves it. To also inspire each other to trust, to love each other, to see each other as brothers and sisters. To see each other as one. To see that the truth is more important than keeping small and controlled and distracted.

We say to you, check, are you the energizer battery that is rechargeable and self-maintaining, self-energizing and in a continual perpetual state of energy flow? Or are you something else? Are you leaking? Are you losing faith? Are you losing energy? Are you losing charge? Are you giving up? We say that for some of you, the reason why you are feeling like you are the acid battery is because you don't recognize that you've got so many other batteries that are on top of you. And we say this is when you feel like you've got so many responsibilities from other people that are weighing you down. You're sparking and arcing energy frequencies off each other as you're clashing, as you're trying to figure out who's the right battery. Where the right fit is, and which direction angle you go, and when you work together. And this is the clash of people really, we could say, clashing against the truth versus the disinformation. And we say all of you think you know the truth and so you all fight passionately for that truth that you believe. And we're saying you don't need to believe or convince others of your truth, nor do they need to prove or convince you of their beliefs when you are just able to have unconditional love for everyone regardless of whatever they believe, regardless of what they do. But understand and step aside, they are not your responsibility! You love them unconditionally! You do! You must! But do not feel like you have to drag them or worry about them. They have their own teams! They have their own responsibilities! They're having their own lessons! They have their own Karma! They have their own life contracts! This is about *them*!

We say some of you are still not in balance with your own egos as you still are confused about who and what you're supposed to do to be able to support others. And so when you are self-contained, self-recyclable energy amongst and within your own self, you have a balance and acceptance of how others are choosing to use the energy frequency. To use their own perspectives. To use their own emotional range of choices. They are doing their own path. It may not be as fast as you want them to. It may not even be in the right truth that you classify it to be truth. You may even see them go into fear a few times. Do not cast judgment! Have acceptance. Respect their journey. The more you judge them the more stifled they become and the more toxic they may hold on to.

So we have given you this perspective of being the rechargeable battery for self and for all! Or being the toxic battery. We're saying for those who want to be of service for those on the Old Earth, it doesn't matter what situation you're in, you'll always be the rechargeable battery because you have maintained and mastered being human. You're all very capable of being of service on the Old Earth. And we are saying the reason why we haven't been able to shift into the Old Earth experience for those karmic lessons to be paid out, is because there hasn't been enough people wanting and willing to be of service to support those. To be able to help them. And we are saying when you choose to not help others, this is a direct reaction and a reflection of your own inner work. There is a difference between worrying about others and feeling responsible for others and wanting to do that inner work of others. There's a huge difference between that versus empowering and inspiring and loving others.

And so, are you not loving others? Do you love others with conditions? Do you have unconditional love? What is the level of your connections with each other? And as you know, the energy frequency portals within your heart capacities to be able to love and express and connect at a heart space, at a Soul space connection with each other, is so much stronger than it really has ever been before on this planet that you have experienced. And so there are many Souls connecting and reuniting and expanding upon each other's energy frequencies because they are recharging each other. Because this is an energy frequency that is limitless. And so it just expands upon that heightened frequency of infinite energy, infinite love, infinite connections and infinite possibilities of how you can maintain a high frequency love energy while still observing and supporting all.

There's much to be said here and we are saying to you, we will forgive you because we do not judge you if you want to leave before the bigger events. But you've been training to support all who are in terror and fear. You're training to hold that higher frequency even if you speak to no one when the Old Earth occurs. We have given an experience for the vehicle to see what she would do if she had broken her neck through a car accident and could not speak but merely blink. She understood that she had a choice then to exit or she could use that energy and that time that she had to deeply call in high frequency energy to be a bigger battery than she ever has been. To be able to just completely be their energy battery of sharing love and focusing on love and being able to hold that high frequency of energy for all who are needing that empowerment and their upliftment and that charge. She knew she had a choice. And what do you do with a disabled body? What do you do with a crippled body? She had to accept that there was nothing else she could do in that predicament. And so she had a choice. Will you be of service to humanity or will you leave? And she thought that she would prefer to stay and to hold a higher frequency because that is a choice she gets to make.

And so what are you choosing to do with your fully bodied body and all the choices and options you have to be of service to your communities, to your families, to your friends, to online connections? What do you do and how do you respond to people who are in your lives? To animals that are in your lives? To plants that are in your lives? To all beings that are in your lives? Are you fully aware of all? Are you fully accountable? Are you responsible? What are you doing and why are you doing it? What are you seeking? What are you needing? There are big differences between being of service to others for the recognition you hope that you will maintain and get. Unconditional love has no strings, has no conditions, has no expectations. It is just love!

And for some of you, you're here to represent your families who are beyond this realm who are ambassadors to many planets. And not only are you honoring all who are on this planet here now as you promised that you would be of service, to be able to empower them and inspire them and to show the way of how it is and what it looks like to have true compassion for all. You're doing this for your commitment because you wanted to be able to help. But you also are doing it for ambassadors of your own families because you know you want to go back and return to your own families knowing with pride you truly did everything you could do. You are focused! You are diligent! And you gave it your best shot! Your complete focus, honor and diligence, because you are aware that this is a challenging time where many Souls are getting lost with their conscious awareness. And it's easy to make choices to step away, step down and dismiss the significance of holding the higher frequencies of energy for all. As you are ambassadors to be of service you do not come here for a holiday. You do not come here for a hobby. You came here to hold the light! To hold the energy frequency! To be here! To love all! And as you are human, as you *identify* being Human, you may also think and you may also be confused with what the power you hold within is. And this is why it is important to do your inner work to see what is holding you back. To see if there are self-worth issues. To see if there is doubt. To see if your ego is balanced. We say some of you love to say your advanced beings but don't quite know how to *be* advanced beings, *be* those bigger energy batteries. *Be* rechargeable from self. *Be* inspiring and encouraging, and *you* igniting others energy frequencies to inspire them to grow as well. There is a difference between empowering people and disempowering people. And it all comes down to your egos, your delivery and your compassion and commitment to be of service.

There is much that we could share always with you, but we want you to know this, as we have said this to you before, but we don't think you wanted to believe it. *All* your choices, *all* of your decisions, *all* of your reactions are recorded and noted. And that is shared out and beyond. And your choices when you awaken and your choices that you choose to take are known, *nothing* is hidden. *You* get to know it! *Your Soul family* gets to know it! *All* gets to know it! And while it is hard and while it is struggling, the choices that you make consciously or unconsciously define the energy frequency that you can carry, therefore can shed and spread for all! You knew this would be a big responsibility and you knew and hoped that you would not get lost or distracted. And therefore, we remind you that you asked for our help. You asked for our guidance. You asked for our inspiration and insights and perspectives to remind you of the game you're playing. And to help those who are lost within a dream, within the dream, within a dream! Don't take it so seriously, but focus. Because as soon as you do this for Humanity, it is a gift you give yourself. And the more empowered you are and the more high frequency charged you are to be in that beautiful balance of love and acceptance for all, not only is this a beautiful position for you to be in, but that ripple out effect of love and high energy frequency that goes beyond you, is a gift for all! You are that gift! Your choices are a reflection on that. You asked us for our help! You asked us for our guidance! You have been our guides. We are your guides now. We like to take turns. We like to support each other and we understand as we did not always comply or trust what you were saying to us when the tables were turned. But you can trust us, because we see some of you making choices that make you struggle more than necessary.

And so, be accountable. Focus on what your thoughts and behaviors and reactions are. Be mindful of this. Be in control of this. Honor all emotions and feelings. Know yourself! Know why you still have triggers! Know why you still have insecurities! Know why you still have doubt! Know why you still struggle to trust! There is no shame in doing your inner work. There is only shame, you could say, when you are not bold enough, brave enough and courageous enough to face it! To love it and honor it! We know for some of you who have already been able to achieve this, understand how easy it truly is. And they are reflecting upon their own journey in choices. They're pretty sure they could have cut short many years of struggle. And we say those struggling moments that you feel like you had longer journey experiences with, could have easily been to help empower and inspire others to grow. There's many perspectives here. There's many levels of layers of lessons and learning. We want to encourage you to be at a high frequency to be able to just honor yourselves. **Truly step up!** Because the more you can hold the energy frequency, the more you can support others at a really profound rate that doesn't drain you. It recharges you! So focus! Observe all! Love all! Accept all!

We say this with love!

Session 37: Past Present Future Impacting You Now

Yes! Yes! Yes! Yes! The vehicle wanted to ask us this question. She had her suspicions but she wanted it to be shared from our perspective because this is the Arcturian speaking. And the statement was this. The past may impact you now, but your future doesn't. She thought how marvelous and how convoluted it was to understand that all of time is existing now. And she questioned, why could it be that while she understands the past impacts us, how was it so that the future doesn't? And we are saying they all impact you exactly as they need to and shall impact you for those lessons and experiences. And we've given you many examples of how your future and your past do, you could say, press upon your conscious awareness and your experiences in your what you call now moments. We give you the examples of lessons from your "past" that you didn't get to master in other lifetimes here. And so you have this wish list when you very first arrive on Earth. And as the dynamics and the lifestyles and the connections and the interactions and also the different cultural experiences and the evolution of each cultural exchanges occur, you want to come back and have more experiences. Because you want to have the full diversity of what life on Earth and those experiences feels like.

You are aware that you have this, you could say, imaginary wish list which you say to those who are guiding you, let me experience those things because this is what my Soul desires, this is what I yearn for to learn for and from.' And so this is organized before you come into these lives. And as you are aware your life contracts do get extended upon and expanded upon as you're living them. It could be for many reasons. Extra Soul essences, what you could say, join in your vehicle for those experiences as you are using your free will choices to expand upon something you may not necessarily have thought or was aware of your interests in this lifetime.

And so there are things that are flexible in your life contracts. But there are also important things to have, especially when you have a life contract with others. Especially when you have what you say is karmic lessons, how you want to complete that experience. We say, imagine ten lifetimes and you want to have this long dialogue conversation with each other for each and every single lifetime. And as you're planning one lifetime after the other lifetime, because that's how it happens, you have this linear experience consciously through those lifetimes. But because time folds in on itself, you could say energetically, as you are evolving in one lifetime and learning and expanding as it is occurring at once, we say, in moments when you are having exit points to then plan next lifetimes, while you consciously are thinking about planning your next lifetime, all the other lifetimes are still existing. You could say, each day is a file, a memory that is impressed upon, as you are moving through the linear time concepts in a linear fashion. As you grow and expand, it does impact all the other files, all the other days. We say this is very convoluted, more so than even the vehicle was thinking we would say and get into today. But we want to because we can. But we're trying to explain the complexities of time. We do say that in your now moment, in your present awareness and the inner work that you have got on your plate you could say what you need to manage and focus. And you're given daily lessons and experiences to see, are you going to respond and react. While everything is impacting you because everything is happening in the now moment, we as your guides help you not get distracted in all of the experiences. Imagine that, having a hundred lifetimes where you've had fifty brutal deaths. If you were consciously aware of all fifty of those brutal deaths, and we say this for dramatics, how would you get out of bed? How would you brush your teeth and brush your hair? You couldn't because you'd be so fixated on the trauma of recognizing and remembering all those things. And so this is why only the important parts that you need to focus on for now, that need to be worked through now, are given to you. And so you don't have conscious awareness of lifetimes in your perceived past, and you don't have consciousness of all of the moments in your perceived future, because you have again multitudes of experiences moving forward.

And so part of the blessing and gift that you have in the veil of forgetfulness is that you forget everything that has occurred to your Soul so you can focus on this unique experience. And so while it is very convoluted because we say your future can impact you today, because you're preparing yourself emotionally and physically for what is to come. And so therefore your future is impacting you today because you're in preparation for it. And even though you may have suspicions or hunches or even clarification through direct communication confirmation with us, you know you're still being human, focusing on yourself and your daily routines and lives today while also having an emotional preparation knowing that things will be changing. And so that does impact you today as you're enjoying and noticing and taking worth and making closer connections to people who you value in your lives, as you know that these moments can be fleeting as things can change at what you could perceive any given moment. And you're not promised to have forever lifetimes here with everyone, all your favorites. Right now on Earth you know that things do evolve. Other Souls evolve. And other Souls can evolve despite where you're at with your own journey. Some are ahead, some are slower you could perceive. But we say those who you perceive are slower are working through a lot more experiences that have impacted them in the past, but they're just going through it at a more denser rate of expansion experiences. And so don't judge them as you could say they are doing twice the amount of work. Because potentially they've got twice the amount of karmic experiences and lessons and contracts with others.

So we hope that that perspective can give you a *new* perspective on what you could judge and see others doing and not being able to focus on what you're focusing on, as they're still trying to play human and focus on the interactions to play the roles in those karmic experiences for those that they contracted themselves to. And so it is important, because while you have planned your lifetimes, having the real authentic experience is absolutely why you're here. Because the Soul wanted to experience it. The Soul will not judge whether they mastered it or not but the Soul does have much that it wants to explore. And so if it is getting stifled, struggling, stagnant, it does want support to be pushed forward and into new growth.

There is much to be said here like there always is. And so we are saying, you can feel future events by processing them now. You are aware of the shock that you heard of the events coming. You know your personal journey to unfold, unpack, process that, not only what it could be like for you, but the significance and the importances of why it has to get to this point now to awaken those who are still stuck and stifled.

And so there is much to be said about why the unnecessary events have to occur. You could say we would have preferred it different for you but we're not playing your game, we're merely guiding you through it. And so we observe and love and push with love. We understand some do not like to be pushed because they don't see the significance of the hurry or the importance of raising their frequency vibrations to be of service. They don't like that and they feel very comfortable being stifled and stuck and stagnant. They may have a few philosophies, a few perspectives that they like to hold onto and they feel comfortable that that is enough. But we are saying there's so much that you could be doing working with the Conscious Collective that being stagnant, you could say, while it's a higher frequency level of balance and neutral, it has not been of service as such as you potentially could. And while we are not ones to put pressure on you, we also know that you said to us if you wanted to be of service, if you could be of service, and you were in the position to be of service, to give you that nudge and encouragement and that reminder to step up and be that service frequency energy for the Conscious Collective.

And here is that message to you now! And so you would have noticed that there was something that happened for you to be able to understand that this message was for you as we keep giving you signs, symbols and recognition. Prompting. We don't poke you (laughing) because we know you'd go into fear. We know the vehicle knows when we get her attention. She knows the Soul who does poke her. But she was told that this would happen in a session and she was shown it. And so when it happens, when she is awake, she knows exactly what that is. She is fine with it because she doesn't think it's monsters. But as you could imagine, if you were not forewarned and you started feeling a pulsing poke, you may go into worry and fear. And we're saying that's not going to be beneficial for anyone.

We also wanted to say that when you do get insights into future events, you have the opportunity to process it now. To be more stable in your energy frequency when it does occur and unfold. You also know that these events had to happen because of people's choices not to empower themselves. Not to heal themselves. And not to push along with due diligence and focus, their inner work. And so they're going to be having those inner work experiences through what you could say, times of chaos. And that motivates because we have given many opportunities to guide you into other experiences to notice. And so there's much to be said about that.

There is also much to be said about how as you know all exit points are part of life contracts, and that it is part of the Soul's choice and decision. And that is true. We can say that the Consciousness, the Soul can have clauses to change those exit points when something so tremendously challenging to the body has taken place. And you could say for this example, as we've shown the vehicle, a collective of beings, (We should just say a few beings because they do not represent their full Collective at this point) wanting to harm, impact and stop the truth and information from coming out for many reasons. So they wanted to use their free will to cripple and harm the vehicle's body. And so while they can't. They could do many things to the body if they got the chance. But it's not up to them for the Soul to leave and the conscious mind to agree to that. And it really takes quite a lot for the body to not be functional. At this point your medical systems can keep most bodies alive and most bodies can heal through anything that the Soul wants the body to heal through, and so if it was able to have the healing, it would be given. But there is much to be said. And human free will choices could impact that healing through applications of drugs and other situations which they think would be helping. But they are not aware of the full consequences of disempowering the conscious choice to decide to heal. And it's all Consciousness that has to give permission to heal because it's the Consciousness having the life. And the Soul is merely part of that while still being blocked understanding who the Soul is, as the Soul is identifying and recognizing being Human.

It is about the perspectives of the Human with the balance of the ego with the Soul trying to balance through with the conscious expansion mindset to understand what is happening to the body. We had this experience with the vehicle where she could see that there were choices that could have been made to have an earlier exit point if she did not want to cope with the situation of the body. She could use her free will to just give up and lose all hope and focus and become a victim to the mindset of being a victim, and having this assumption she couldn't do anything. She knew that that was a valid choice but she also knew that it was not going to be her option. Because she believed that when you're already stuck within a body where you could only blink, to then have a negative self talk and mindset would be the second prison that you would keep yourself in. And so she knew she would not have that option. She knew she would go and grow beyond that and focus on bringing in higher frequency energy. In fact it didn't even occur to her until this conversation now to heal herself, because she just accepted the situation at hand. She did not see that there was anything wrong with having a body that's crippled because she could see the significant opportunity to be tremendously of service. And so we're giving her another perspective that she could have a choice with. But this is where her focus is at always, where she can bring in the higher frequency and how she can help others more than even focusing on her own self.

We are saying, there is an example of the actor you know who was in a car accident that did burst into flames, Paul Walker. And while it wasn't his chosen exit point, because the body was so severely burnt and he didn't have faith that he could heal himself and he didn't have the confidence and encouragement to know that he could love himself and others could love him in that profound state. Absolutely, it would be extremely challenging, extremely painful if you focus on that pain, to heal from those experiences. But when he was given the perspectives and options of what he could do, he chose to leave the body and to exit and to be of service in another format. You could call the other format a ghost or an advanced being.

There is much to be said about how when there are life contracts set in place and what the lessons are there and what the Soul hopes to achieve, the Soul can achieve other things in the afterlife by simply observing and witnessing and exploring as you could say, the ghost realm. Because the Consciousness awareness of the Soul is constantly observing and growing, you do not need a body for that. The body is to help you feel settled into the illusion of the interactions to help you. It's a prop in the game you're playing in life. The bodies are props. But the bodies are also distractions. And so there is the fun challenge, 'go to a 3D planet, go to Earth, dress up and play human and see where that takes us'. And it was for fun. It was for the dramas and the dramatics and the uniqueness of having the emotional experiences. And so when we come into these sessions and when we can channel and we are given the opportunity and the free will license to feel into the range of the dramatics, we like to choose to experience things as we are feeling into the 3D body. We like to work with the body to see how it feels to be dramatic. To be funny. Those tough love speeches did feel as close as we could feel to what we see humans have a reaction to like anger and rage. We don't have that opportunity here. We don't have that density. We don't choose to play in that here where we are because... We are confusing ourselves because, while we're literally in the body of the 3D as we are, you could say, remote viewing of feeling it all. So it's a lucid dream that we're having while we are consciously aware we are not there. But we are experiencing something that feels very real for us while we also know if we could open our eyes to where we are here on Earth and where we are in our dimension, our realm, we could see completely different things.

We are losing ourselves in the moment because we want to. Because people control with their free will choices how to interact with us and it takes them a while to trust us, to let us experience things that we want to experience. There's a few of us here and we haven't had a physical body in the density that this being is in. And it's stifling but also intriguing, and we don't want to feel into the other senses of the energy. We're quite pleased because we know we could feel more than we want to. And so we're confirming to you, it's very good to have the veil of forgetfulness as well as focusing the energy, to not all of the energy that is in your facility, but some. We are saying, just like there is the analogy of the smorgasbord, you can't possibly eat the entire smorgasbord in one mouthful. Nor could you. It would be too challenging. And that is the same as feeling all of the energies here. It would just startle you. And so you focus on the small meal that you have regardless of whether it's a bread plate size or a large dinner plate size. It's still small mouthfuls and you're processing and working it through that way.

We're thanking the vehicle for this experience. This is a very unique experience for us. And so when we have these experiences, we do want to have the range of emotions to have this experience and this luxury you could say. And so we have expressed ourselves through the human range of emotions as we have been trying to deliver and share our messages to you. You could not fathom how many Souls have been speaking to you through these sessions, through this vehicle. There is, you could say, a Guardian which is her Arcturian guide who monitors this and manages this you could say. And he is accountable for all the Souls that want to have these experiences. And he manages these Souls and these connections because this is appropriate that we are learning as you are learning. We are learning different things because we are not living and needing to process and have all of your human experiences. You're in the Earth School and you're learning and mastering what you could say, mastering to love each other, not ignore each other. Not just like each other and certainly not to just tolerate each other, but to be open and allow each other to be vulnerable and share your emotions and your thoughts and be respected.

And we say, we watch you listening. We watch you thinking and then we watch you not always choosing to apply that. And you can completely dismiss and never apply anything and you can keep as much density as you choose. That is on you now. We are trying to feel into what makes you so distracted to forget. We say, when you're in a lower frequency energy, it's like you can't even remember the higher frequency energy information. And so this is why it is important for you to do your own inner work to release yourself from that density to maintain a higher frequency energy. We have seen people who'd listen to these sessions and then stop listening to these sessions and their density expansion grows and they can't remember or recall much ever that was said in the sessions because it's a distant, distant, distant energy frequency memory. And so for those who are able to maintain a high energy frequency, not only are you part of the Conscious Collective for Humanity working through that because you're consciously navigating and working through the perspectives that are the advanced perspectives of purposeful significant experiences as pure life contracts and the Souls requirements as they were here playing Earthlings. And so this will help you clarify when you're starting to feel foggy with the information that we've given you, this is a sign that you've got too much density and your minds are not able to connect back into the energy frequency of this dimensional information. We know some have listened to our information and cannot hear much of any information at all and we might as well be speaking a completely different language. Their density is so different they are not able to understand or comprehend even the English that they speak themselves. It is like we are a dog whistle and you just cannot hear our information. And that is fine. Sometimes this information is not going to be helpful as you're wanting to organically learn and stumble and grow from your own lessons and experiences. And then when you hear this information you want to see that confirmation and that is purposeful, and that is significant.

We have been reaching into you as we have been talking because we've wanted to be able to help you as we are using this vehicle. We are reaching out to you because we can see you and feel you listening to us. And so we scanned to see what questions you were trying to understand for yourselves. And so we just answered those questions for you because we love you and we want you to notice the answers that you have been seeking have been delivered with love for you. And this is important we understand, for you to have confirmation from us, because we're here to be able to support you so you can be inspired to trust yourselves and raise your own energy frequency which then opens up your connections to us so we can then raise your energy frequency to be more of an enlightened attunement. To be able to remember and calibrate yourself be of service, because that is what you're here for. Because your mission is not just singularity to Earth, the people that are in your lives, but for some of you, not all of your Soul family could be here on Earth and so you prepared to be a representation for that.

And so there are many Souls that are supporting you from what you could say home and what you could say is other families. And so we don't want to put pressure on you, in fact, nor could we because that's a choice *you* feel. That is an emotion *you* feel. And as we are feeling into the range of emotions when we come into vehicles like this, we do want to experience it too! We see some of you judge that as if we're not allowed to feel human for a moment. And that is a choice. And that is something that you need to grow out of and mature from. But that is at your own pace. And so we allow ourselves this experience of feeling the physical body and just feeling the pressure of the energy around that physical body. So we apologize for the distraction, but we do appreciate this connection because it was curious for us to imagine how it feels to be here and yet be so distracted. (laughs)

Yes, this is the Arcturian guide here. And as you know, I have many names, but I'm not hung up or stuck up on one. And I wanted to clarify that we do everything we can to make sure that you are protected and safe. But we also can't breach other people's free will. We can but we can't. And so there's much to be said about the differences here. And so if someone is purposely trying to use their free will to harm you or impact you, we have to weigh up the lessons for both experiences. And you could say, where you don't like to consider this as a human, when you've harmed someone there's *big* lessons there. *Big* experiences there. And so we don't just look at how it impacts the victim that you'd label and classify the victim, we actually look at all aspects. And it's all guides they're working through because it's the Human playing the games of being Human with their consciousnesses. While all guides and high versions of self are watching this and not trying to be judges and not trying to be referees, but trying to work around your life contracts and to see how it unfolds. And so there is much negotiation and reflection on all of the lessons. And so this is why when you're so confused when there is a victim, why would that be allowed? How could that possibly occur? Where is "God"? We see many people complain and feel very hard done by, because of the victims experiences. But from our perspective, when you look at all players and everyone involved in those experiences, that is what we measure and value before we can justify changing and stepping in. And we hope that's given you some perspective and clarification when you are confused about not understanding why you have not been protected. And so, for those who are going to be experiencing the Old Earth events where there is more chaos, if you give up on your body, if you cannot believe that you could ever maintain the body or heal your body or work through it, you are the one that is choosing that. And this is when we review this. We know you're serious. We give you extra help with walk-ins or something else, or something else, or something else. We have many tools to help us. Could you imagine if we did not? [Laughter] You think you have hard days. We are busy too!

And so there's much to be factored in here. But when you zoom out and look at all perspectives, you know 'All is Well!' It's the hard lessons that do not make it feel like all is well. When many are choosing to separate themselves, have judgment on each other, hold on to density. When you're actively making those conscious choices to ignore each other, mildly like each other, mildly fake interest and not be there wholeheartedly to love each other, that is impacting not only the Conscious Collective but yourselves. And so there's much to be said here when you're not responsible or accountable for your energy frequencies. And so from your perspective, and all of Humanity's perspective, not all is well. And you understand that. You can see how many are struggling because of their perspectives. Because they've forgotten or they don't want to believe how powerful they are. And again, you also know the challenge because that is part of their lessons. That is perfect! That's absolutely perfect that they're dazed and confused, for some. And this is where we see humans getting tripped up and confused. How come it's fine for some to be asleep and how come then we tell *you* to grow and empower yourselves and be responsible when you perceive other people are not being responsible and not being told off from us or being guided to be responsible. And we're saying different life contracts. Different karmic experiences and lessons. You can't compare yourselves to others. You have your own individual responsibilities. And for those who are listening to us now, you know you're supposed to be of service and work with the Conscious Collective. It takes focus and diligence to be maintaining that higher frequency energy of love. To be able to fully have the perspective that there is acceptance of everything is significant and purposeful. And trust we know what we are doing from our perspective because it's easy to see it from our perspective. Do not worry. We're not asking you to worry. We're not asking you to judge. We're not asking you to doubt. We're not asking you to hate. We're not asking you to ignore. We're not asking you to do anything but fully honor your energy frequency. Honor your inner work, what may come up. Process that. Love those lessons and experiences to grow from and to release the density so you can be unconditionally loving being to yourself and others.

When you are at that higher frequency and you have full acceptance and you notice your ego has stepped back and your heart is leading the way, and you have balance. That is when you are at utter peace with the world as it is at because you trust and have faith in us. Because you have trust and faith in yourself. And you have trust and faith in others that they are on their journey. They are on their way. But we say we do need tools to help trigger some to awaken to grow. It's just some specific perspectives that they're longing for that they haven't quite figured out. We say it is like some of you have 17 different belief systems like a patchwork quilt. It could be clashing in fashion but we're saying a patchwork quilt of all different belief systems can still have unity. But when you're not understanding how the pieces of the puzzle of the patchwork merge and can form and can come together as one cohesive art form, belief system, perspectives and consciousnesses, when you're still trying to figure out how this patchwork quilt of belief systems and understandings fit together, it can be a bit hectic. It can be a bit chaotic.

And so we say, start with one piece. The most important piece we say to build up on your foundations of self-empowerment is love yourself. Honor the significance of you being here now because it's not a mistake that you're here now. You are what you could say an advanced Soul playing Human. You've awoken to the fact that you are a Soul having this one lifetime now, being here to hold a higher frequency of energy. And then we say, build up along that. Find your patchwork piece puzzles to see how to maintain, balance and have boundaries with those people who don't want to do their inner work and want you to do it for them. Build on your empowerment of self. Share with them your belief system that they are too Souls in human bodies and that you can love each other with no judgment when you can be honest with each other and honest with yourselves. And therefore, the patchwork quilt gets sewn and built upon and expanded upon into a beautiful tapestry.

We are going to say farewell as we know you have got much to ponder and consider. We appreciate those who are being part of the Conscious Collective. Because they can hear us clearly and can understand the significance to support all who are needing loving supporting nudges and given a few missing pieces of their tapestry. To understand how to have the perspectives to see the significance and purpose of all things as they are unfolding. We understand it's complex and can be complicated when you can't see that the two different distinct pieces of the tapestry are the same piece, just haven't seen the right angle perspective of it. So look at all aspects. And that is key, looking at all the possible aspects. It's truly not possible for you to see all life contracts and significance and how things do impact all. And so you have to trust and have faith that it does and that it's significant and that it gives the opportunity of growth. We say with so much love, enjoy your experiences as you are honoring the reactions and the responses that you now can give each other with pure love and acceptance. This is how you grow and support each other's energy fields. Because we see many of you feel so lonely and isolated. And yet when you're not stepping up and making the first move and acknowledging and loving each other, you're too shy to make the first move. And we're saying, be the bigger person! Be the bigger mature Soul! Be the way shower! Be the leader! Be the one who knows that you are needed and that your maturity and your compassion is the key to what people are seeking and needing right now!

And we say this with love!

Session 38: Gaia's Gratitude

Yes! Yes! Yes! Yes! Yes! We are here! We are here! We are very much here in assistance to be of service today. It is already as we find the vehicle in such deep sorrow. The density is unmistakable for being on Earth at this time. There is much to be said about what has been occurring and happening. And as the vehicle has been seeing things from a bigger perspective to notice the grander schemes and scheduled events, planned projects to help with the Grand Awakening, and how they were built up and how they were missed opportunities as we see there was not much energetic support that would have supported all, nurtured all, as there were greater events that needed to happen to trigger some to awaken fully. To be able to be more personally impacted for them to stop and notice and think, while also catching out disinformation broadly and commonly shared through mainstream media. Through the narratives and the voice speakers of those who are of influence.

This is an extraordinary time as you're Awakening to these control systems that have been for the majority, trusted and wanting to be naturally respected to be complied for the belief system that all humans ornately are good. And that for those who are being paid extraordinary amounts of money to be in extraordinary privileged positions to run countries, to run corporations, to be followed by many influencing people who are wanting to be led. These are very extraordinary moments and experiences as people are Awakening and catching out those who are limited, dishonest, corrupt and purposely distracting. As the energy frequencies have been pushing and as people have chosen with their free will choices to have advancements in their DNA strands for the evolution growth. While they have not consciously been prepared for what they have done to the energetics, they are still making these choices to expand upon that, while also being very cautiously aware now that some of their choices have not been the best for them. But of course it's experiences. And while humans in general haven't been accountable or responsible for their actions and behaviors and energy frequencies and how they choose to love or choose to not love each other or themselves This is an Awakening moment to be consciously aware of choices. This is a marvelous time to notice and to accept your individual choices, but of course that feels too confrontational, too accountable, too responsible and too mature. And therefore you look and seek for differences in others hoping to feel better about yourselves because of others that are, you could say, publicly losing the plot or just doing something that you feel can be justifiably belittling them to make you feel good. And we see that some of you need to have villains or different versions of truthers or different versions of people being awake for you to boost your own confidence and boost your own egos and boost your own energy frequencies. Feeling like you can compare yourselves to others to feel advanced more than others. And we say, at this point, whatever you can do to raise your frequency vibrations we fully endorse and support that. So use your free will choices to find your joy. At this point we're saying, if your joy is to pick on others to feel better about yourself, do what you will. Do what you must. We can't stop you either which way anyway at this point as we have been pressing you and guiding you your entire lives to find your moral compasses, to find your compassion and consideration for others. And you are where you are at because of all the sums of all the choices you've ever made to this point now.

We are observing. But as we are seeing more Souls exit the plane that you're on, the round that you're in, the game that you are within is challenging. We are saying, if you imagine yourself as a pyramid and there's some stronghold players that are your foundational strength and then you are somewhere in the middle, when some of these pack up, graduate and leave, it becomes challenging and there's gaping holes in your pyramid system of support because some missing key players are now moving on from their own game. This is why it's important to realize that when there are some foundational members that do shift, potentially you do take on that role to be that foundational strength pillar, leader. And that is challenging when you thought you could just be at the top and not have to hold too much weight above you as there was just a skinny one that could jazz hands all the way to the pyramid and wave to the judges as you complete your formation. And we're saying if you will for this analogy, to just lift. Simply lift the vehicle's energy of heaviness as she's feeling into many Souls that want to come in today. As you could imagine if you were in a pyramid of a hundred people and sixty leave, you become closer to the ground of the foundational members to hold strength. And we say this will continue on. The longer you're here, the stronger you need to be. We've suggested this to you as preparation you could say, when you're all foundational members of the bottom tier of the human pyramid, then you are on the Old Earth really, truly as you are holding up everyone's energy frequency above and away from the density you could say. I really needed to support the vehicle today. We could say the floor is lava which is one of her children's favorites. And they just become so enheightenedly excited to play the game of the floor is lava. And this is something that they all have such a joy over and she loves watching them do this still.

And so if you will, when you are in a pyramid supporting people above you trying to lift them away from the floor is lava, while you are standing strong, holding ground, not minding the density, not minding the burn, because you know it's not truly able to burn your Soul. It's not able to even burn your flesh because it's a game. But what others are pretending that they're in this game and they're standing on your shoulders and you're supporting them in this human pyramid, they are enheightened, they're afraid! They don't want to go down to the bottom because they've been stuck down there. And so they want to be liberated from the floor is lava. They want to be liberated from the density, from the pain, from the suffering, from the burn. And so they want to be elevated and alleviated up and beyond. And you're there to support them through that. And instead of carrying Humanity on your shoulders or on your backs, that was never your responsibility to singularity to do that. It was about to nurture them actually instead of holding them physically, carrying their weight load physically on your skeletal systems. It was about holding them and nurturing them and holding them close to your hearts, not turning your backs on them, to carry them. It's not piggybacking them, it is emotionally loving them and nurturing them and supporting them. There is a difference between turning your back on people to carry them and potentially drag them to where you want them to go, to where you know they're meant to go. That's not a fun game for many to be dragged. And we are saying you're more advanced than primitive cavemen *now*. So you can choose to behave like that or you could turn around and face each other, become equals, realize there's nothing to be afraid of, hold each other's hands energetically, touch each other's hearts energetically, embrace each other as brothers and sisters whom you love and adore and respect and honor. And when you see that they're on their journey, still afraid of the floor being lava, still being afraid that they don't have support underneath them, still being afraid they can't support others above them. You are there to support them and love them and reassure them that it is possible for them to be strong, stable, balanced and secure with their position and place in this world. Because it's not an accident that they're here. And when you recognize that you've got more strength with family, when you recognize you've always been protected and you've always been here to observe and witness the state of humanity and not let it distract you, to convince you that the floor is lava. But to remind you of the many other games you've lived and to remind you that it's the Soul that's having these experiences in human bodies.

The Soul can graduate and is graduating soon from your perspective of *soon*. This should be something you should be celebrating! Doing cartwheels and flip-flops? Jazz hands and getting super excited for the big rally, the big events, because this is what you've been preparing for. This is what you came here for! And while we still see Humanity standing on top of each other, trying to push each other down, to burn each other hoping that the floor *is* lava. Pushing them down. Suffocating them and trapping them. Densifying them. Stepping over each other, wanting to bury each other. Wanting to fight over each other for a position up top. We are saying, the pyramid, the human pyramid is still supposed to be equal and balanced as you all take turns to be the supporting role or to be the one that is proud to show we have complete unity and balance as one.

There are many perspectives that you could take as each position and role of the human pyramid is formed. Each is significant and each should be able to support each other. But we still see many choosing to want to sabotage and destroy unity, support and communities as they are only comfortable truly in seeing comparisons to belittle others. To make fun of others. To mock others. To discourage others. To belittle others. To dismiss others. To disrespect others. To abuse others. There is much to be said still of the choices people are still wanting to play in that density and that disconnect. And so it is all choices, but as we say, the game is wrapping up. You can't keep finding balance in unity when there are some that need to be shaken awake. Because it's not until they fall down from their pyramid of not noticing the surroundings that they're in and who has been propping them and supporting them.

And this is where we come to the part of the session that the vehicle was concerned about the most. Feeling into the energy of Gaia. She wanted to come in to speak. It's not the vehicle afraid of Gaia, because the vehicle loves Gaia so much that it's so overwhelming, it's hard to speak. The vehicle has really tried to release this density prior, and it still feels so raw. But again, it's raw love! And it doesn't hurt, it just feels so overwhelming. And it's an expansion of heart and it's this longing. It's a strong connection between respect and gratitude and acknowledgment and appreciation. It's such an intense energy of love. And it just is too overwhelming. And Gaia has been with the vehicle over the day. And it was lovely to feel into her because it was a higher aspect that was no longer tortured, suffering in pain from the density. She had clarity and perspectives. She wanted to come in to reach, to talk to the vehicle as the vehicle recognized and saw something and learned something new, which she'd only had suspicions of prior, which was confirmed. Which was what you could call the home planet of where the vehicle truly loves to reside. The mother figure there is the Soul of Gaia. And so this is why when she asked in that session all those years ago about the mother, we did not let the vehicle or the client know that information. It would have placed them distraught and they would have struggled and suffered more because it was easier for them to not realize how deeply close they were to Gaia. And so, when you find out that your mother's energy has been struggling, that would have been too traumatizing for both the Soul Sisters to have learned that as they were needing to focus on their own purpose and mission here. And for them to have felt into Gaia being a closer family member than they'd ever imagined, it would have been too traumatizing for many reasons and extremely distracting. And so when they asked for clarification of who their mother was, as they were given information about who their father was in that lifetime as they are still currently living those lifetimes, and they will return back to those lifetimes when they have completed their missions. So it becomes convoluted.

The message that Gaia wanted to say is many. First of all, she's giving you all a very intensive energy love. And she honors and recognizes you all. And she has two direct messages that she feels like she can get out today because the vehicle is too reactive. The first is for those Souls who are not coming to the next adventure, to the next game, what you called New Earth. And so Gaia is just acknowledging and thanking them. And while it is not their next journey to be together for that experience, she will say she's always got her gratitude and respect and honor for those who were the strong bearers of energy to help assist her through her challenging moments. And she is very grateful for that. Because while you don't consciously understand or know the ramifications and the implications of the energy frequencies that you've been holding in space for her, and love with her, in honor of her, was extremely appreciative and grateful. And so she wanted to come in to be able to confirm that today. To be able to say thank you;

Gaia: I do appreciate that. And while you don't do this for gratitude and you don't do this for the words of thanking you, I have this opportunity to do this personally to you all today. Because I understand that some of your Souls are not choosing to come to New Earth, but I thank you for helping all my children. And as you know being a mother, you want the best for all your children even though you're observing them having harder lessons. You have to love them still without fear. Without worry. Without holding them back in any way. We have to let them go! We have to let them grow! You have to let them have their own experiences while just being there in love of them, in love for them. And while this is not farewell because there are always opportunities for us to meet again, I wanted to thank you in appreciation for all the energy you've been able to hold and support and share for all! It is extremely significant! And so I honor you! And for those who *are* coming to be of assistance and also support on the New Earth, there is much fun and greatness and experiences to be had. And this will be such a blissful experience for us all! Truly of a wonderment! Truly of full connections of each other's experiencing. And while it's not the highest energy frequency that you could feel, it is still very big advancements from where you're at now in the third dimension. And for those who do not know me, do not feel me, and don't have an understanding that I was a consciousness being, having a body of a planet that you call Earth. And I've had other lifetimes where you had the opportunity to also be together. If you do not resonate with me, do not recognize me at an energy frequency level, it is absolutely fine. When you understand and feel into my journey, it is a very dense one. It can be very challenging for many to understand why a Soul would want to have a lifetime being a planet that has been so toxified energetically and physically. And for those who call me Mother Nature or have other names for me, I just want to say and remind you with kindness and love, when the events do come and there are more reactive environmental experiences, **I have not forsaken you**. I never would! It is simply the reactions of a dying body and it is not a punishment or a torture. It's not something that is meant to harm you even though many will have exit points. It is purposeful and chosen exit points. And as you have heard through many collectives and guides, the death scene can easily be avoided by any feelings of physical pain. And so there's nothing to fear in exit points because it's a graduation and an upliftment and an advancement from the third dimension. And even for those who are going to another third dimensional planet, it is going to be still, a lesser, denser experience than Earth. And that is the struggle of being here because the density is so tremendous. There are not many advancements when people choose to stay in old routines and old mindsets.

There is much to be said here, but I wanted to explain that it is not me angry with you. It is not me angry with Humanity. It is the ramifications of a dying body when the Soul has been removed. And as we were saying, the foundational members, the pillars, those holding the highest strength of energy, have taken on board responsibilities to hold the energy frequency the best they can. You can support each other for only so long until your own energy and willingness to stay, you could say, when you have real big people standing on you and not wanting to empower themselves, to stand by themselves, but are wanting leverage points and piggy backs. At some point you're going to get tired and want each other to stand beside each other and not be carried around by each other. There's much to be said here. But I do want to say that I have forever loved you all! And I will forever love you all! It has only been my demeanor to you all as I respect all Soul contracts who have been here. Who wanted to live and have these experiences with me and with my physical body as you are part of my physical body. And while my Soul aspect is different, we are all one! Feel into the energy of your own Source! Feel into the energy of your own love for self and that unity love for all.

This is the Arcturians speaking now as there is much planning in participation for events. We are still waiting for Humanity to choose to have the experiences that they are still overdue having. But as we are supporting all to have the most appropriate experiences, we understand some of you are feeling the pressure of holding much energy frequency as part of being of service. We have said and reminded you the power of water, the power of positivity! The power of Love! And we again want to remind and inspire and encourage you to have full self empowerment, because when you can truly be of service to yourself, it is easily capable then to be of service for all!

We say this with love!

Session 39: Being An Aspect Of Source

Yes! Yes! Yes! Yes! We are here! We are here! We are here! We are very much here. We don't go anywhere else you could say as we are multidimensional beings that have got our eyes and ears you could say, on everything. Not much goes past us because we are observing this experience on Earth. And while we have not chosen to be fully consciously down there on Earth you could say, we are vicariously observing through many aspects of ourselves. If you will, as soon as you pay attention to your fingertips you'll notice what the fingertips are up to. How the fingertips feel. Have you put your hand into ice or have you put your hand into boiling water and it's not until you notice what the fingertips are doing and how they're feeling, then you can be quite aware and quite familiar with their own experiences. And there is a difference, indeed there is, between the little finger and the thumb and their experiences even at an energetic level. If you actually focused on the differences of the fingers, their positions and placement in the world, you would notice quite a lot of differences even though they are very, very similar.

This is the conversation that we wanted to speak to you about today is how the collectives, while they're all part of Source and while they're all experiencing unique individual experiences away from Source, consciously they are aware of the physicalities and the experiences that they have in their physical lives while being an aspect of Source. And as you know, the thumb is playing the role of the thumb. The pinky is playing the role of the pinky. The index finger is playing the index finger. And they all have a unison about them. They are all very in tune with each other and they work together as a team. And when they are wanting to be stronger, they know that by coming together in an orderly fashion together, supporting each other, then they are much stronger than an individual.

And we say this about Collectives. And we say this about who is on this planet at this time playing human. And how all different aspects of different Collectives are merging and playing together, because some Collectives are asking and needing for more support and more strength from others. We are saying you know the difference between how one finger could open a jar versus a whole hand. And potentially even two hands when those jars are sticky and firmly shut tight. And we could say some of your inner worker is that contents that's in that jar, that is very jammed up. Sealed up. Glued up. Gunked up. The jar lid is very firm and it's not quite possible to use one finger to open up this very tightly shut jar. And really, that finger needs to get into the mess of all of the contents that's in that jar. But how do you even start? How do you even open when your one finger is trying to do the work of two hands and a screwed up face and a tongue hanging out... How does one finger do all of that work when it's teamwork. You can say even the feet have to ground themselves to really get the whole full core strength to open up that jar because it has been firmly jammed tight. And while it's true you could say that one finger has jammed up and tightened and stuck that jar so it doesn't get open, it takes a team. It takes a tribe. It takes a whole body! It takes a whole unit to work together to wiggle and force, to open that jar, to get inside that contents. Sometimes you'll find within that jar sweet jam, sweet honey. Sometimes you can find that it is rotten mayonnaise that is well overdue and should be thrown out. And we say all of that could be a great example and analogy for your inner work.

And so, what is inside the jars that you are not able to open? Is it because you need to open up your self-empowerment to see the beauty and the grace and the joy that your Soul can provide for all as you recognize your own strength, recognize your own power and recognize who you really are and all the skill sets you've learned from other lifetimes to be here now. And to use all those skill sets to love and support and inspire others to grow and to be bold and brave as you are encouraging others to open up their own jars and see what's within them. Is it sweetness that they need to share and spread to the world or is it something so toxic? Something so rancid, something so vile, that it needs to be released, purged and removed from that jar.

We could say that jar is your vessel. We could say that jar is your mindset. There's many things we could use as an analogy for this today.

We're wanting to say again about the different collectives that are working together wanting to support each other in inspiration to be able to have evolution. And we understand and we accept as we all must, including yourselves, that there is growth at different paces. Some are running a race and others are very happy to meander and to go at their own leisurely pace. We are saying, some of the collectives are rounding up those other collectives to force them and to push them and encourage them to go faster and firmer than they are interested in. And this is perfect, we are saying, because there are many that don't want to open up and find their gifts. Their skill sets. They are afraid that once they open up their jar they will find that rancid mayonnaise. And we are saying, but often it actually is the beautiful delicious warm gifts that you need to be sharing for all.

And so some of you are afraid. Some of you are afraid of what is inside that jar. Is it jam or is it something else. And then some of you are afraid that you know it's jam but you don't want to spread it out and you don't want to spread it thin. Because you're struggling to find your own balance and you don't want to share it because you haven't applied it yourself. You're not even using your own strength and powers for yourself. And once you do and once there is no difference between what's within the jar and the jar. Once it all is merged into one and there are no boundaries, there is no glass division between the world and what's inside that jar, then there is this Unity. And we're encouraging you all to have confidence that what you have within you, which is a pureness of high energy frequency that you can see and recognize within yourselves, and also see and recognize within others. And to be able to honor and respect each other as that Soul energy frequency.

And we are still seeing people making different choices. We are still seeing hurt people wanting to hurt people. We're still seeing bitter people who are jealous, wanting to disempower and to send negative energy. Which is immature with your spirituality when you are supposed to be accountable for your energy. Responsible for your energy. And we are saying, those people have turned their backs on listening to us. And yet they are quite confident, quite entitled and quite arrogant to think that they are entitled to continually hurt people while not being responsible for their own actions, demeanors and behaviors. And we have seen many of them try to trip up and disempower people who are trying to share their truth. Trying to empower others and trying to support Humanity. And we say, if they could focus their ill intent and their negativity, and if they actually stop that "bad" habit, stop that "bad" hobby we could say, and actually stepped up and grew up and actually started empowering themselves and humbling their egos and healing their hurts, then they too could be just as equal with their demeanor and delivery and compassion for Humanity. But it takes a lot of maturity to look at and be accountable for one's actions. And we see many are holding themselves and limiting themselves back because they have this entitlement and attitude. And it comes down to the basic emotions of feeling triggered and insignificant for whatever reasons. It may be their lack of the education that they feel is not making them special. There's something that is holding them back because of their perception of themselves. They haven't opened up their jar and they don't honor other people's content in terms of what's within their own jars.

We are saying, for those Souls who are supported in supporting The Reptilian Collective, they still need love and respect as they are still trying to grow. And as you know with anything, if you are disempowering, not letting them thrive, not loving something, it makes it much harder for them to evolve and grow. And so we say, use your maturity of spirituality concepts to understand that you're all one! And you're all part of Source! To recognize and understand that there are different stages and paths and journeys done by different Souls. And so, when you understand that while you're all the same age as Source, you could say, many of you have had lesser lifetimes than others. You're supporting different collectives and that is all your personal Souls choice and journey. And so there is much to be said about what each Collective is doing right now and how they are moving forward. And where they are moving forward to. You cannot, with your naked eye, in your human mind, judge whose Collective is being supported by whom. And we understand that many of you hope you could. And we understand many of you label grumpy people who are asleep as being Reptilian. And we say it's not the case. You cannot truly judge someone's behavior from their attitudes and demeanors towards others. You could see, and we say even though we have said the majority of The Reptilian star seeds, you could say, like to have power and influence and that looks like banking systems, being doctors and lawyers. They are wanting to be in charge and in control of certain things that give them, not only status but financial abundance. And this is where they get their biggest drive. Whereas other advanced Souls don't need to feel so boosted up by education and career choices. And so they are happy to be what you could say as the average people who are happy to be of service in their smaller interests in terms of living to work not working to live. And so there is a difference.

We don't feel like we've accurately expressed what average humans are and average interests are, we should say, but there is a difference between if your focus is on money solely versus spirituality. And some people say if they had lots of money, then they would spend lots of time focusing on spirituality. And we can tell you and give you many examples of those Souls who thought this and they have not been able to be successful in this. We have seen it all. You have experienced it all through many different lifetimes yourselves. And so many of you did choose to have vows of poverty because you did not want to fall into that trap again because it is so distracting. We see many people who were struggling who were on the more wealthier spectrum as they are noticing so much bigger hardships. The more money you have the more opportunities you have to lose it. And so when you're losing lots of abundance at the moment you are noticing quite a lot. And when you feel that your self-empowerment is because of the money you have in your bank or in your property portfolios, you do become very stressed. And we see many people who have been living week to week in their finances have the same level of stress when it comes to money. They know they're doing the best they can and so they focus on other things. And they notice more how it is truly the free things that are in life that feel the most enriching and you take things so much more at natural beauty.

Of course it comes down to each person's choices and perspectives and how they want to choose to feel rich and abundance and life. And this doesn't necessarily mean anything about money. But the culture and society has pushed many people to have this assumption about wealth and success. And we are saying check your definition of 3D success. Because it may not be what society is pushing you all to focus and work hard towards. It could actually be quite the distraction.

As we were saying, while you can't *see* what collective's people are being supported by, you also can't *see* their life contracts and why they are here and what they wanted to experience and what their roles are. And you cannot *see* when people are about to graduate because you cannot *see* where the levels and layers and lessons and experiences that that Soul wanted to have playing human. And so while you *see* many people graduating, you may not have been aware that they were just on the verge of completing their experiences. And you cannot *see* the lessons that they need to have beyond the third dimension while the Earth is still playing out. And people are still having experiences.

There are many lessons and learning by attending your own funeral as a ghost, you could say. And you *see* how people truly feel about you. When you don't have the density, you're aware so much more how people think and feel about you. At a conscious level, when you're still independent from your highest self as you have not merged back in but you were a ghost, you could say, and you're a consciousness watching people attend your funeral. Watching people think and feel about you. Watching the energy frequencies as they reflect upon your choices. While you can have your life review once you absorb back into your highest self version, we are saying you watch people have a life review of you with them as they are living. As they have been either fond memories or not fond memories of the experiences that they can recall about you. And that is very illuminating as you may not have been aware or accountable for how your behaviors and actions have responded and interacted with others. And so you get to see it from a different perspective without the density of the body. And so you get to notice what others are thinking and feeling about you. And this can be a wonderfully healing experience when you did not know how special and important you were. But this is something that is happening now for many. And before they have merged back into their higher selves, what you could call subconscious, what you could call your main guides. Because for some of you, your main guides are your higher versions of self. But there are so many aspects of you and there is the highest self and then of course there is Source. There is so much to you, of you. And you're all connected as you all can feel each other and as you're all working together. And we want to say, while there is a difference between the look of the thumb and the finger. The smallest finger. There are different sizes, but they're all important. They all play important roles. There is a balance there. We would say it would not be so helpful to have two thumbs or two small fingers on one hand. And each of your fingers are perfect and they have their roles.

So don't get hung up feeling like you're not good enough or important enough because you're only the smallest finger. There is significance to the role you're playing Being Human. And so, do not feel that that is insignificant. It is the most important and significant focus for you. So honor this because you're in it right now. You need to focus on it right now because you're important to be of service for all! And as you see and recognize many are struggling and many are following disinformation that they assume is the truth, this is a wonderful time to encourage people to feel into this for themselves. To question all of this themselves. That is true empowerment! You should all be truly empowering yourselves to feel into this. We understand the information that you're aware of is too hard even for the conscious mind to accept and fathom, and it's not until you're channeling us when we can give you our vantage point insights regarding the shift in the significance of why that is important for you to understand the significance of why we can see it so much easier because we have the bigger scope and perspectives. Whereas the human mind finds it all too overwhelming to factor in and consider all the significance and all the Souls' lessons and journeys of what they need, including the planets. And so we say with love to you all, before reacting as if someone is a Reptilian, we could say they're an advanced

Soul not happy to be here and not happy to play human and that is their problem. So check your judgments, check your assumptions and check your level of love. Are you still holding back loving all completely, you are Souls, that love each other truly. And so when you're still sending bitterness and resentfulness in judgment and jealousy towards others, you are not helping yourselves. You're not helping the collectives. And we are saying, grow out of those phases because this is lowering your frequency vibration so much, you're limiting the sweetness that you could be sharing for all.

And so we say to you all, be accountable and responsible for all behaviors and demeanors towards each other. When you're trying to disempower someone who has a life contract to empower Humanity, which you ultimately all do, you are trying to impact Humanity. You're not here for this, you're here to empower Humanity, not disempower Humanity. And so, see how you are responding and behaving to each other.

And we say this with love!

Session 40: John Fitzgerald Kennedy

Yes! Hello! I would like to greet you all! This is wonderful to be able to connect this way. And I feel honored to be able to hear my name being called in this manner. And I am gracious and humbled that I get to be able to speak through and now connect to you.

And so, this is tremendous times and this is the pinnacle of what humanity has always wanted for. And so while there has been much that has happened since I have been on this side, I have also been closely monitoring and guiding as many as I can to be able to help nudge the truth. Because it's always been part of my bigger morals to share the truth. And while I was supposed to be coerced into other things and I did not want to go. I took my responsibilities of my Presidency as being something with great honor! And each and every time I got to meet my fellow American and like minded people and folk that had passion and devotion to our country, I couldn't morally be twisted because I was you! I felt close to you all and I wanted to honor and be a great leader for you. And it was a juggle because there were so many temptations to be able to go into a different direction. And there was so much pressure. There was so much pressure! While it looks glamorous and you're hanging out and people perceive you to be just flawless, you're very much human. You're very much tempted with the emotions and the dramas of it all!

And my responsibilities weighed heavy on my heart and on my shoulders because I wasn't just doing my role and my job for myself and my friends and my family, but I was also doing it for you, the American people. And I have still such great honor to have been able to serve my country for you. While I can see it now from the bigger picture, I still have some frustration. But it's not frustration, it is a harder word! I wish I could have done what I had wanted to have done to help my country. And I wish I could have continued on my path without being stopped! And I don't have any animosity towards the people who organized my assassination because that is all mended now. My only disappointment is that I couldn't be your greatest President to be able to push and move forward with truth and honor and dignity. And I sincerely wanted to be able to do that for my country, for my fellowmen.

I feel like part of my role, my passion, my drive, was cut short. So it is frustrating, but I have been able to do tremendous things on this side as well. So while I couldn't do it physically I have definitely been honoring my country and humanity by pushing and nudging with love and guidance. And sometimes with a little bit more love and guidance and pushing, to put pressure on the hearts of men who should have the greater moral compasses. And so I was, and always have been, still diligent towards this greater goal. And so you can understand how tremendously excited and pleased I am with how things are going. And I understand right now, when things are just starting to get even more heated up, things must just feel like you just want more proof! You just want more action! And you just want to get moving forward now. You've had enough! You know the truth! You can feel the truth! And you're waiting for it all just to kick off! And I want to say to you that it has been. And I want you to know that. While in your daily lives, you're not seeing the physical changes and the proof, and I can reassure you and guarantee you you're going to know that it's very true what everyone's been saying. And it is profoundly awakening to know the extent of all that has been happening.

So you're going to be very proud of your fellow man, not just the Americans, but also the other countries that have come in and supported this alliance. Who have done great tremendous things to be able to help your countries, and help the world be removed and have the control of these other beings who are heartless and do not have humanity in its best intentions. And so truly what was the key here, was when humanity all worked together. And when all the bigger powers that could be, who stopped their bickering amongst their borders. Who stopped their bickering amongst their mining and their land grabs and their egos. And when they actually dropped separating themselves and worked together to be able to come together, to be able to take control of these darker forces that have been underground. And yes, I was very much aware of them. I was taunted by the thought that these were real. I could not believe it. And it was unfortunate that they were true and still are true.

It is tremendous times! And the truth is always going to come out. And I feel compassionate to help everyone who wants to find a bigger truth and are still not quite sure. They're wavering with their emotions of whether they want to believe this or not. You don't have to believe it. It is totally fine. What's happened has already happened and just because you believed it and settled into it doesn't make you the monster for these bad actions that have occurred. None of you are responsible for what has been happening! It has definitely been a tremendous distraction for a lot. And most of the bigger roles of people who have been responsible and taking their free will and supporting something that is not human, that has the least amount of human consideration there is, those people who have been harming humanity, those crimes against humanity, they've also been dealt with, which you will be aware of very soon. You have to know that most of the people who are still unaware of this, they do need to see a smaller part of this to be shocked and then brought together. And so it will look a bit chaotic even more so than now that you're aware of this, because you've been hearing this from many others. So I wanted to come in and endorse the situation that's going to happen because it's the truth. The truth will always set you free. And while you're already set free, because most of you have already got the bigger mindsets, it's about your fellow man who has not actually awoken yet to the truth of all.

So it's tremendous times! And I just wanted to say that I never left my country. I'm still very diligent in helping any way I can. And my family has connected with me and they know that I am still here in the spirit form. And they understand this, and of course they will be able to connect with me on the fifth dimension. And I'm very much looking forward to meeting my grandchildren. Experiencing each other's energies in another realm which is very exciting for us all as it should be for all of you and your families because it's about connecting! It's always been about connecting with each other. We're able to be proud of each other's families and family members and supporting each other. You may not agree. It's never about agreeing with each other. It is about supporting each other and being proud of each other's belief systems without it threatening yourselves.

So this is how you get to the bigger mindsets. This is how you get ready for the next dimension, being able to see a debate that's on the TV or on your computer's screens with two people you may not necessarily even personally know, but you've got an opinion about one of them or both of them. And so you're wanting to be entertained. You want your visions to be played out how you need it to be. And while that's still playing the game of the 3D and bickering over who's got the biggest and the best policies and who's trying to outsmart each other, you'll know the truth. You'll know who has got the higher morals here. And I don't need to tell you who that is. You know who it is! You just need to listen to your hearts and hear what's happened and see what has been happening to your country and to the world! It's not invisible anymore. You can see it and you can feel it and you know it!

So it's very exciting times because you're not stupid anymore, because you've stopped listening to the bubble box[45]. You're not listening to just the small amount of people who are trying to push you or manipulate you anymore. You're getting it! You're finding your own research and you're resonating with what works for you. And that is the most exciting thing for us all who are here supporting you and watching you. Because it's the greatest thing you can do is empower yourselves! And once you empower yourself then you're so much more free to empower others. And that's when the true joy starts kicking in. When you just see love and joy. You support everyone! It's not about separation and division. It's about embracing! And when you can embrace others you will grow with others. And that's more

---

[45] *His slang for television! Can not find another reference of this saying for a TV. Classic example of connecting into a Soul who has not fully merged back with their highself, could be connecting with him while he was in the 4D (Ghost) consciousness.*

tremendous than being right! And that's more tremendous than getting your own way!

And so, you've always got things to learn. Never assume you know it all. It's a very dangerous position to be in because it stops your growth. And so you're always growing and you're always expanding. And even when you ascend and even when you get to the fifth dimension, even when you go home, you still got the learning. It may be different in so many ways, but you're constantly growing and expanding and learning. And when you know you're not, and you start getting stagnant, you start getting things wrong with the bodies and the mindsets and the heavy feelings, you know that's because you're starting to release all this stuff, you've basically purged all. And you've been working so hard with this blessing which was the lockdowns to connect with yourself more and have more time out for yourself and think about what you really want in life when you get out. When the lockdown shut off. When you can get out and you start fantasizing and visualizing and planning what you want to do with that new sense of freedom. Freedom! Because it's all in your mind how you want to perceive your freedom. It's very powerful what you can do with your mind. You can put yourself in a prison. You can also put yourself up in the sky and soar high like an eagle, because you've got the power to go high and be strong and bold and have integrity and honor, and know who you are and stand proud.

And I want you all to be able to stand proud of who you are right now. Because you seem to forget sometimes that you're in this very challenging situation right now on this planet. And while some things feel like there's waves of emotion that are coming over you, the impatience of everyone right now, just on this pause, you're feeling the emotions of the waves of the energy embracing and coming up and down and up and down. You can feel your body pulsing and tingling and the ears ringing and you're starting to feel all the higher vibes because of what's about to happen. You're evolving from the inside and all those negative thoughts that you've been holding in are starting to be pushed out to the surface. It's tremendous time. You're all so lucky to be there. And while you're still struggling potentially and you still got the harder, usually it's the biggest stuff, the last stuff, the remnants of everything. That is the last thing that needs to be shaken enough. And you can do it! Don't keep yourself in the prison in your mind. Release all! Don't save anything! It's so much easier now to see some blocks or some limitations or some belief system that no longer serves you. You can use this time to say 'I'm releasing it now' because it doesn't serve you.

There's no shame in being a human. You're learning all the time. It almost could be shameful to say, if you get stagnant. So pick yourself up and expand yourself and get excited! You should be accelerating because there's nothing going to stop this now! Nothing's going to stop what's about to happen now! *Nothing can stop it!* You're just waiting for the time! So release anything that is no longer serving you emotionally. It doesn't serve you anymore. Face it! Release it and move on! Tomorrow is a new day!

So, I'm so excited to have been able to connect with you to share my love and to share my true joy and pride with Americans and with Humanity because it's always been about helping Humanity! And I never forget that! And I never have! And I never will! And it's the bigger picture here. We're all one! We are all one! And I say this with much love and gratitude and pride to be able to connect with you. And thank you so much!

Thank you so much for having me today[46]!

Session 41: Working With The Conscious Collective

Yes yes yes yes yes, and we are here, we are here, we are here, and we are the Arcturians[47] speaking to you today, as we have been summoned, you could say, to be able to share our perspectives of just thoughts and feelings and the epiphanies that the vehicle has had in recent days. So as we collect our thoughts amongst ourselves, to be able to work out what are the best questions to start with first, and what and if this should be a public or private session, and if it is such, what is the best and most appropriate information to share, knowing that some ears listening could impact the outcome of the information that we do share.

While there is a conscious collective here on your Earth, you could say away from Earth, our conscious collective of being Arcturians is quite different from our beloved Pleiadians, from our respectful Lyrans, from all the aspects of self that you could fathom in terms of collectives. And while we're all part of Source, understanding the significance of each role, each position, each responsibility, and each life's journey, regardless of whether you are human or Arcturian, or we

---

[46] *Explore if JFK was aware of what the MOON missions were including RANGER 4 in 1962, a year prior to his death and if this was when the technology was placed on the moon in this timeline, is something we all should be interested in exploring in sessions, for those people interested in the LAZER EVENT.*

[47] The Arcturian subconscious

could say even a rock, because it's significant, those experiences. We still see many humans who are not consciously aware of all of the energy frequency of things around them that are holding consciousnesses for those experiences, to feel and to have those experiences of being all such items and objects. A human mind can not fathom or even want to consider the experiences of a rock living consciously. This is something you can't reach beyond your consciousness, as to imagine what it would be like to be an innate object. What the significance and purpose of that would be? You can't fathom then why a consciousness would want to be a crystal, or a tree, a plant, an animal, a bug... We say there is much to be said about the unique signature frequency energy requests of each Soul having those experiences. But as you are only seeking humans, because you feel like they are your match, and some look down on the animals and rightfully so, but some should look up to animals, because they have much to teach humanity if humanity is open to be taught.

We see humanity is quite comfortable in what it's taught itself, and they can have quite a limited experience when you're only wanting to see your own reactions and behaviors while being human, while being oblivious to the entire surroundings. You have much to learn from your children. You have much to learn through your cycles of aquatics. There are so many teachable moments in your daily lives, but you may not be wanting or willing to notice those messages, symbols, significances, as you are only wanting to seek humans, because you feel that they have got the answers and the keys to all. That is one choice we see that can be quite a limiting choice.

The vehicle was having a conversation about her children, where the educator was saying "children can lie", and the response that the vehicle had was "adults can lie, and both children and adults lie for the same reasons, because they're afraid of the consequences of their actions and choices". Also, they're afraid of the consequences of other people's actions and choices. So you have a choice to lie. You have a choice to hold back. You have a choice to keep small. From our perspective, humanity is not wanting to love itself and each other and beyond even humans. There is a disregard in some aspects to animals and their life cycles, and how they've been kept and enslaved by humans. Of course the Soul was well aware of that when they chose those experiences. It is possible to live out a natural life cycle of any animal out of captivity, out of being owned by a human, and of course the Soul could have chosen any point of reference... "I'm to have that experience" and it is significant to have all the aspects of those experiences on Earth, you could say to be the hunter and the hunted. It is the Soul's choice of course. No one's forcing that Soul to experience it. So when you're all having these choices of what you want to have the experience of on Earth, you're all trying to accommodate each other while cohabitating against each other, with each other, for each other, by each other, to each other, from each other... there is much to be said about what goes on in your perceived time.

From our perspective, you are given paradise. From our perspective, it was all there for you, for humanity. It hasn't always been humanity's fault, but what has happened is a result of conscious collective choices, decisions that were made of course by different beings you could say.

The hardest thing for humans is that they started off struggling... think about cavemen times and even before caveman times. They were the hunted and the hunters, as there were many beings that wanted to survive and thrive. There was competition. So many people want to believe that it was just the reptilians that have caused all of this disharmony and this imbalance, but we are saying you only need to kill a cub of a lion to find out what the mother would do, to find out what the father will do. It's not only humans, it's not only reptilians that are wanting to hurt humanity or hurt those humans. If your children are hunted you will find and want to hurt. That is a reaction not just of humans, but animals too. We say elephants have seen their children be slaughtered. They will never forget that. There are many animals that have more intelligence, you could say, than humans, but of course the human ego would not want to consider that or respect that. So there is much to be said about your history on Earth...

When you have one trauma it is never isolated to just one person, it always has impacts on others. You know when someone has a trauma or a tragedy that impacts them, if you love that person and care for that person, that too then impacts you. The story of that trauma, the event of that trauma, can live way beyond the lives of those people or beings that lived, and so this is the conscious collective of the totality of history. There is so much collective trauma, not just from humans, but for all consciousnesses on Earth. When you haven't factored or considered all consciousnesses, they are about the souls. They're still limited to the reactions and ramifications of being in the third dimension, and therefore they create the energy frequency of responding in the third dimension. Those experiences expand and retract and connect and impact and the push and pull of being the hunter and the hunted. The hunter and the hunted for many cycles of lives does cause then the conscious awareness of threat. While this has protected you, this can now limit you, so it's about being mindful of what is your innate programming within you. Is this old programming of living out in the wild, being a caveman while you're living in your cities... What is your core drive? What are your triggers? And of course, if you've had those lifetimes where you were the cavemen being hunted and hunting, you'll still have that essence of consciousness in the back of your minds. And while it's all happening at once[48], those thoughts and feelings are still echoing out amongst all of your parallel lives and other lifetimes here, because ultimately they're all parallel lives. When you remove the construct of time, it is all unfolding and occurring.

As you are aware, the more you are feeling into and connecting to other aspects of self. We see that when you have done enough of your own inner work and you've looked at your limitations and you've looked at the reasons why you once viewed people above or below you, or animals above or below you, and once you start feeling truly and seeing yourself as equal to all - no more, no less - that part of source, when you start applying that attitude and behavior and demeanor, and start loving yourself and respecting all, even though you may not be too impressed with their free will choices. You see that this is their struggle, their pain, their journey, but it doesn't impact you in any way. Their choices are such because they're merely responding to their

---

[48] *Reference to the fact that Earth Time is illusory, delineated for our serial experience. From the higher dimensional perspective, beyond Earth Time, all things happen at once.*

own struggles. So when you observe and not react to each other as you once did, you're advancing your energy frequency, as you were not feeling hurt or rejected and you are feeling more in love and at inner peace within. This is when you can heal your other aspects of self as well. This is often done in your dream state, but it also can be done consciously throughout your days as you're peering into, feeling into the energy frequency of other aspects of self, especially the ones that you're aware of. Then you can support them energetically. Send them love and understand their struggles.

It is an advanced mindset that would want to go into all the other lifetimes you've ever lived here on Earth, to nurture and heal and love the child aspect of selves. To be there in all aspects. Big problematic days to give each other the perspectives of the significances and the purposes of those hard lessons, to remind themselves that one lifetime is not nearly all the chances they get or all of the opportunities that they get to live. So as you are exploring and having many delicious but also empowering and uniquely special quantum entanglements, it can be very powerful when you have the correct demeanor, attitude and approach, to be there with love without adding any other complications to their situations. You are aware that when you have a poor attitude in terms of bitterness, resentfulness, jealousy, hatred, and your demeanor is less than a high frequency unconditional love to all, you wouldn't be able to have these connections because you would be a menace to yourself, even more so than you are a menace to yourselves right now. There is much to be said about this, and when you're distracting yourselves with your egos you can be impacting, not just yourselves, but other aspects of yourselves.

We have said before - you should view each other as extensions of selves - because as you are aware, you're all part of Source and so ultimately there is truly no separation. The illusion of playing the game, the different roles you want to have, to be able to experience and learn from each other. We say learn how it feels to have the illusion of not being loved and not loving yourselves, and this is SO OPPOSITE to where you normally reside. When you are Source, and when you are high dimensional beings, there's so much true capacity and connections to love, **because love is that high energy frequency that is housed in the higher dimensional realms**. So it is our honor, but also our duty, to come and to share with you these perspectives, these insights into how you can, with honesty, integrity, diligence and focus, empower yourselves to then be of support and service to others to empower them.

We still see so many people aware of the situation at hand with humanity and the situation with this planet, and how humanity is on the verge of evolving, and yet they're very unmotivated to help others feel and wrap up their games that they are playing. Too many people are still playing the game within the Matrix, you could say, of living and being human in terms of focusing and worrying about finances, worrying about inequalities and injustices. We say if this is part of your lessons that you wanted in your karmic experience contracts - to have injustices, so shall it be.

It's not an accident encountering each of your predicaments. Yes, some of you have made it much harder because you're free will choices, but those were lessons for you to understand that you are a product of all of your choices thus far, and so how do you like the summary of all of your choices thus far? You could say we just gave you the keys and the solutions of how to empower yourselves. If you were finding thus far the situation is not ideal for you to go through the other aspects of self, to be there to truly to love and inspire and apply the metaphysical perspectives that you understand and know, to be able to help them grow, knowing it was to empower yourselves through each and every single challenge and traumatizing situation and event occurring.

It is interesting how you can know advanced perspectives of what is happening on this planet and why, and still choose to ignore supporting others, because you don't want to bother them because you feel that this is their karma, this is the contract, this is their journey, this is their path. We are saying you are more aware of lost beings here than ever before. You are seeing people searching and begging to find advanced perspectives and to find advanced information, and you're still holding on to resentfulness and rejection and hurt from when you are trying to help others in the past when you got burnt and denied. When you're having interactions with each other and sharing love with each other, when you see someone who's truly struggling with the perspectives of the lessons that they have at hand, and you know you could give them encouragement and support and the perspective that can help them, we're seeing many of you are not choosing to do that. For some of you, you haven't done that for yourselves to completion yet, to go back to the times where you were struggling the most, to be able to give yourselves the solutions and answers to why that hardship or that lesson or that experience needed to take place. You can only teach others what you've learned for yourselves, and while we have been sharing with you many perspectives and many considerations for you to apply and to learn and grow from, it is not until you actually do apply the information and the perspectives that we've given for you to be able to master it. This is the reason why you wanted to have these physical lives versus being guides or observers, because when you really physically endure and explore and have these days, these experiences yourselves, that is when you truly get to work and play and react to it and to respond to it. You have to go through these experiences manually, naturally yourselves, to be able to move and graduate and outgrow and heal and expand upon those experiences. These are literally the reasons why you came to be here.

For some of you, you were supposed to have woken up to be able to see the bigger perspective, to respect and understand life lessons, contracts, purposeful significant experiences. For you to find your inner peace to then be able to support others, because we say to you when you are an advanced Soul with good intuition and other people are telling you that you can rebuild this planet, you can heal this planet, that you can fix this planet, and that you can fix humanity, and they're saying to you that's happening now, their saying to you that's happening here, and they're saying to you that they're already living as such... we see many advanced intuitive Souls being very confused with those statements, because they did not recognize or resonate with the fact that they were in the fifth dimension here, even if their mindsets were. They were very much aware that they truly weren't able to have the luxuries, or even the energy empowerment, to be able to create and they knew that there is a difference between the third dimension and the fifth dimension. They knew that there was still a limitation, even with those who had the fifth dimensional mindset, the density of being in the third dimension is undeniable and has such limitations when you're wanting to create and manifest. So this was confusing to many, who have been told and sold the lines that you can manifest abundance and 'it's just a secret how you do it, and it's about positivity' they said. So you'd spend a lot of time being in positivity mode and wondering why you were not gaining and receiving all of the abundances that you had wished for, and when you have a life contract to not get distracted in the materialism and wealth, you could not escape that, you could not beat that system, because you knew in your soul, the other lifetimes where you had that abundance and wealth and it didn't work out for you, or it did work out for you but you had those lessons and experiences and you want new ones now.

Your guides know of all of the lifetimes you have lived and experienced and are working through, and they know from this perspective of your perceived time what was left for you to explore and master, and that's very significant. So for those it's about Souls playing human, feeling like they're failing because they were not able to manifest their abundance, manifest their wealth, manifest with energy what they were expecting. The frustration of advanced beings trying to diligently send healing to the entire world and not see it come to fruition and occur, it could impact the Soul so greatly that it makes them feel like they're the problem. Makes them feel like they've failed and have not been of service. So for many, we had to tell them, we had to awaken them to the true full truth, that the fifth dimension cannot be here in the realm of the third dimension on Earth for various reasons that we've explained. So for those who are waiting and feeling like there was something wrong with them, but they couldn't get their skill sets, but they couldn't get their healing capabilities, they couldn't master things that they knew that they could so easily once before, we had to tell them the full truth. They had to be fully awoken, because when they had been told disinformation and limited information about harnessing in the fifth dimensional energy frequency here on Earth, it is not the case. And when you think that you can heal the world, that is also not your responsibility and not your purpose, because you are taking away people's experiences that they need. You're taking away Souls' experiences that they need, they want. You can't do their inner work for them. You can't live their lives for them. You can't protect them from the lessons and experiences that they want. That would be disempowering them. That would be disrespecting them. Have faith and trust that they can do this, but also understand the difference when someone is struggling because they're confused with disinformation or being distracted by disinformation. We understand for some the truth is too poisonous and too shocking and too jarring for them to be ready for, but as you're seeing and noticing, there's many more people willing and ready and seeking information that they will not thrive. They are vastly awakening and this is still confusing to them, and is shocking to them, as they hear of the details of the Grand Awakening and how humanity has been the hunted and the hunters.

There is much to be said about the details of learning how humanity has been holding itself back and limiting itself and distracting itself. When you awaken to this and you have the knowledge of your own power, you have the knowledge of what dimension you're at, and of what you're capable of doing here, while being excited and glad for those who are graduating as you're seeing many are graduating now, as they have had their assigned exit points as they are awakening others. This is an extraordinary time and a few are still confused about what is happening in your current events and why. We say go within and feel into the significance and the importance of this. This is a time for maturity. This is a time for compassion, and this is the time to be of service. It's not until you've learned a lot of your own lessons that you're then able to see and recognize exactly where other people are at. And while they may not be ready for everything that you are aware of, you should know what they're really here for. Most are ready for self empowerment. Most are ready for self nurture, so support them through it as you have already lived it yourselves, as you have already awoken fully. *Now That You Have Awakened - Apply Metaphysical Perspectives.*

It's not an accident that you've been listening to our perspectives. You're training yourselves to be of service to others. We see some of you are refusing to talk to others until they want to talk about the shift and the New Earth being a fifth dimensional new planet, and we are saying you can be more considerate and compassionate to people to help them really with that. We understand for some of you, it's your favorite topic and your favorite conversations to have, but if you're wanting to have more friends to be able to chat that have like-minded conversations, you may have to support them to get up to speed with you, which is compassion and love and giving them perspectives that they may not have considered before. To be able to help them recognize and to be able to give them tools and keys to be able to heal and grow. So judge not. Love all. Observe all without reacting in a way that it is detrimental to yourself or others. You know those people who want to grow and you know those people who do not want to grow. You know those people that want to disempower and destroy others. So we say know the people you should be playing with, because if you don't know the difference yet between who wants to grow and who wants to destroy you, there is some inner reflection there and that is fine.

So we think that we have talked enough, as we were trying to see if there was any more confusion that we could clarify today. We see so many being distracted as they think that they're awakening to information, that they had just been distracted once again into disinformation that's laced with fear. We are saying we're having to have an opportunity where we get to disclose more information, and this is great because this is being given an official, provable, tangible aspect, so that influencers and icons can be more heard and trusted. So it's not up to friends and family to share this information that is coming through an official capacity, you could say. This is relieving and supporting many truthers and spiritual people that wanted to share these perspectives, but get looked down upon as family and friends are still judging them as being older versions of self.

This is important for you to understand - why there are longer delays in perceived time, which is going to be more enriching with more disclosures. There is no real respect and honor in each other's research and intuition, such that you're having to be 'spoon fed' the information by official sources of truth. That is fine. That is how humanity feels stable, to still look up to influences and leaders, versus respecting each other as being equal. We understand it's frustrating for you, to have told your friends and family, certain information, and they've dismissed it. But once it's on the news, being said and shared by someone of influence, exactly word for word what you've said to them for years, and then they respect and view that information as if they've never heard it before. We understand that you will feel frustrated and bitter and twisted because you wanted to give them this information, and you have given this information to them, but we're saying just check your egos for why you feel like you have to be the one to have 'saved them' or 'awoken them'. Ultimately it wasn't the right timing and you planted those seeds. So just be happy and grateful that they are now aware of these things, versus frustrated and angry that they didn't respect you at the time you said this.

We say that when you say to someone "I told you so", it doesn't sound like celebration and congratulations for them getting to the point where they're willing to hear it. No one likes to hear the words "I told you so", and this will lead to another argument and people will be defensive. If you're still trying to have conversations with people to argue, grow !!! Because that is not evolving you. That is not empowering you. There is a difference of course, there is triggering and growth that can happen in conflict, but check your demeanors and your agenda there, and what you're truly trying to get out of the conversation.

Empowering each other to grow, versus trying to be right and trying to remind people that you were awake three hours before them. This humbles none. So we say to you - support the truth as it is coming out, because people should be supporting those who are able to share and speak the truth. Many have been too afraid to speak up. Those who have should be supported. Ultimately, we've seen the struggle of those people not wanting to step up and be the big leaders in their family and friends circles and social circles. So now that there are more influential people stepping up and speaking the truth, you can support and share that, so it isn't a direct ownership of your own personal thoughts and feelings.

We say with unity comes great growth and communities. We have said this to you for a while, and so now you can see what that means. You don't have to feel like you're the only lonely person that has awakened in your circles, and then the more you share, the more you care, and the more you love and the more you grow. You will then be able to notice this for all, and that is significant.

So we say with love - keep growing, keep sharing, keep loving yourselves. You are still important and we are saying dig into the root of some of your insecurities or frustrations or triggers. They are important and they are very important for you to explore and feel, to be able to heal and grow from. Don't be shy about the pain that you're still holding and carrying, because that is limiting you and blocking you. We know that you don't like to look at these things because you feel unsettled, and so this is why we will trigger you to go back. But often you only look at the current trigger and not the previous reasons why this still is triggering you. So you'll notice the same trigger occurring and occurring and occurring, and it's starting to look at the original trigger, the original hurt. Then you will be able to recognize it in its full totality, because the trigger is the tip of the thorn. You have to go to the core and pull the entire thorn out of your body. If you just react to the current day trigger, you may not look at the full extension and the pain that is still being carried within you at a conscious level.

Don't be afraid to expand upon your lives and what you have endured. You haven't been broken yet, and so recalling and reflecting past experiences and emotions will never impact you more or worse than what it already has. We say you've actually healed from it, but it is like a scar, a healed wound, it still needs to be resolved to truly heal. These emotional scars can be invisible until it gets triggered. The real trigger is the range of emotions that is felt, that hasn't been empowered through. Is it abandonment? Is it feeling a lack of love? Is it feeling insecure? "What is this feeling" is what should be explored when you're feeling triggered. Don't focus on the players that gave you these lessons and experiences. They are insignificant to the feelings that you are trying to ascertain, that you felt, because it's up to you to empower yourself to see that you are capable of providing the antidote and healing it. Therefore, if you are afraid of rejection, you know you will never reject yourself, so honor that and empower yourselves through it. It's always about self-empowerment and what people are giving you and teaching you. If it hurts, you're supposed to provide it for self and be self-sufficient. We understand you want everyone to love you and support you and give you all the things you want emotionally, that is not the game you're playing. The game you're playing is about self-empowerment, to be able to provide and support, at a conscious level, all the things of all the emotions you're seeking from others. So it is a fine balance between what you're seeking from others versus what you're supplying to self and empowering of self.

We feel we have been speaking to many, and we feel like we have not spoken in a linear, what could be considered a consciously understood conversation, and we apologize to those who are feeling like this conversation is speaking to many aspects of many people through various stages of their awakening. From our perspective, there is no such thing as time, and when the vehicle is so far away to help assist us, we do share and supply information, but you could say there are many conversations being had within this one conversation today. We say if you did skip through and start at any point in this conversation, it may be the most appropriate point for you to read. So if you want to explore that again, if you're confused by what has been said today, we will guide you as we always guide you. But if you could **focus on the significance and the messages and then apply it**, that would best serve you.

So we say with love, we appreciate all who are willing to support those who are struggling to understand and recognize the significance of the Grand Awakening, and to help assist those who are stuck in the emotional trauma details of what humanity has been doing to humanity. All is significant and all is purposeful. We watch and observe all, and you're always protected from things that are not part of your life lessons and experiences.

We say this was love.

Session 42: Soul VS Ego - Balance Is Everything

J: Welcome back to a conscious mind conversation with Sally.

S: Hello.

J: I've been keeping her all to myself as we have been experiencing and applying being of service for the Conscious Collective and it has been so much fun.

S: It's been a wild ride.

J: And so for everyone who knows, who has been exploring the books that we have been sharing, there are some private sessions and some public sessions that we have been going through. And it's been fun times. But very, very significant and purposeful.

S: Yes. Yes indeed. Very, very busy.

J: Yes. And still here, and still finding more ways to apply the information and really get the perspectives of what they are recommending. And it gets easier that's for sure, when we recognize a trigger or a feeling or an emotion that is reminding us of other situations.

S: Yes, it's interesting too with the inner work, because it's like, okay I've done so much already. This is awesome! What next! And it's almost like you have to continue with the inner work, it never really ends. And so that's what I've been dealing with. A lot of things are coming up to be healed. It's interesting because it's a never-ending journey and I think that that's just how it's going to be honestly in this 3D reality.

J: Absolutely! I remember one client's ego coming in a lot in her session and the Subconscious was saying how she doesn't have any work to do. And I was like, oh, okay. And then a few questions later the Subconscious was saying all this inner work she's got to do. But did she remember that later part of the session? No, because she wanted to just tell everyone, I've got no inner work to do. My subconscious said that. (laughing)

S: That would be nice.

J: Whatever you've got to tell yourselves to keep high vibrational.

S: Yeah. And also, it's kind of like one of those things too. It's like always going to be a blessing or a lesson of some kind. But in the end, it's only going to make you a better version of yourself. (J: Absolutely!) Stronger, faster, braver.

J: Well, it's been fantastic to watch a lot of humbling moments for many people. Because it's not that we want to celebrate them being embarrassed or humbled, it's more like yes, now this is an amazing opportunity for growth for them. And those big ego people feel so confident in their sort of fake foundation of confidence and inner work and all that fantastic stuff that they do deserve. But it's this reality of, just because you say words doesn't mean you've applied them or you are them. And it is amazing when we're just talking privately about how when a big spiritual person suddenly has to be taken to hospital or there is a big illness. It's kind of like, if you're spiritual you really should be aware, especially when you're a big influencer and you've been touring the world gaining lots of money and known for your spirituality. If you can't heal yourself and you're still relying on medicine, like human medicine, that to me then suggests a whole bunch of things. And maybe this is me being judgmental or maybe I should channel into it to find out. It does feel like it was a Soul 'walk out' situation. But there's so much to be said about when we forget how we can heal ourselves and that's a really powerful thing to do. And if we haven't done enough of our inner work we will break down the body because our mindsets are broken down and not in empowerment and in alignment of our true calling.

S: Yes. The way I look at it too, it's like with healing yourself, when I talk to myself, if something hurts or there's something that is off and I can sense it, I do try to locate it in the body and then I talk to the body. I talk to the cells. And I think it was Dolores Cannon who said, talk to yourselves, talk to your body because they actually are listening. They're conscious.

J: Yes. But if it's kind of like, hey you kidneys, sort yourselves out. I want to have good healthy kidneys and I want to just abuse my body because I'm not looking at my inner work for my alcoholism. Yes, you can talk to your kidneys and say be the best you can. But if you're still using your Free Will to screw over your kidneys, it's a counterproductive thing. And everything has to be in balance. And I think a lot of people again don't follow through with the whole knowledge and wisdom of how this works. Yes, you could say and love your kidneys and send healing to your kidneys. But then if you keep doing bitter things to create bitter stones, to create wedges in the kidney systems, you're gonna have this internal conflict again. But yes! I mean, anything Dolores

Cannon says I'm always going to be a massive fan of, because she is amazing as we all know.

S: Yes. And also sometimes even I know this is for my own personal experience and I want to help anyone who might also be at this point. So if you're not really sure how to do your inner work, you don't even know really what it is or how to start, just start applying daily methods of okay, what is the best version of me? How am I going to change the way I interact with others and myself in order to be the person I really want to be? Or the best version that I know is going to be there. And so it's kind of fake it till you make it. And I know it sounds really weird but it helped me in the beginning too. If you don't feel it, try to pretend, how would someone super happy or healed or who's wanting to understand where the healing needs to come from, how do they start? And so you just embody that, I mean you portray what you want and then eventually it'll come to you. And it becomes a pattern. And then you also ask of course, for guidance on what needs to be healed. I use that and that really helped me start.

J: I remember that we're all connected and I know that all our Souls are brothers and sisters. And I know at a Soul level, we love each other. And so, going with that respect towards each other first, regardless of what human behaviors and Free Will choices they have to conduct themselves, going with love and approach that way while having to maybe tolerate some people's behaviors and reactions and holding on to limited perspectives or whatever. Coming from love for each other is a really powerful way. And we don't need to fake that because we know at a Love level, at a Source level, at a Soul level, **we do honestly love each other.**

S: Yes. It's just reminding ourselves that we're more than just the moment too. Because I know that people can get highly emotionally affected by their surroundings and sometimes they don't really know how to break free of that. Let's say it's like a very dense energy or they feel like they don't know how to raise their vibration high enough to overcome those kinds of environments or those emotions. And I mean it does take practice, but it's good to at least start being aware of it. And I think it's lovely knowing that we are connected and this isn't the only life you're ever going to live, and there's way more out there to do in the future. And I think just changing the perspective really does help.

J: It's key I think, especially when we live beyond this lifetime. Isn't that exciting? **We live beyond this lifetime**. And so whatever this lifetime has to offer, and however we can be of service to ourselves and others while we are empowering ourselves to remind ourselves what it is truly to be in love with ourselves and each other in a third dimensional level. I feel like a lot of our issues when we are dealing with other people who consciously refuse to not make the choice to love themselves and others. When we are aware that we're living in an environment, in a society, in a world where loving each other is not a priority, there is then a lot of internal conflict. Because the person is not healed and they're responding to the world in this not healed fashion. When we are in our balance and our neutral and we're responding and corresponding to these people who are in this internal conflict, inner turmoil because they are struggling to find love that they have forgotten that they get to choose to feel and emote to the world. To inspire all to love each other. When they are in this conflict, we feel their conflict. We can make a choice to feel like this is a projection onto us or not. And so when we are struggling to understand our environmental energy frequencies with each other, it's often because there are some unhealed responses and behaviors and attitudes and energy frequencies that we are identifying. The more we can be aware of them but not react to them is going to be very helpful for all.

S: A big one that came up recently for me was, if you're being rejected, the fear of not wanting my love in return. I don't know why. Well, I think I know why. But that actually was like, love is literally the most difficult thing for me in this 3D reality. It's like you're yearning for that higher love. And I think I said it to you before. It's like you're thirsty and you can't quench your thirst because you want that so bad and I can't seem to find it here. It's not possible here[49].

J: We all are very aware of the feeling of Souls loving energy. I think it is in our Consciousness and we are always trying to find this in all things. I think it is in our remembrance. And I feel like we are all drawn to call, to feel and find it. And I think this is when it's very confusing when we see another Soul, especially when we have a Soul family connection where some Soul feels so familiar that they're just really, we've been siamese twins and they've just cut us. It's like when you meet a Soul that you're so connected with, that you feel like you've known for so many, many lifetimes. And then they are in your face and the energy frequency is so familiar and yet they have got the veneer of being Human. And they're reacting like humans, and they are behaving like humans, and they're responding like humans, and they're loving like humans. Which is often a choice not to love. And

---

[49] WE LOVE YOU SALLY SO MUCH !!!!

so, when you're trying to find that love Soul respect and connection again, which you've had potentially billions of years, who knows in terms of the concept of time. And then you find them again here on Earth and all you want is to be gobbled up in that love energy bliss that you know you're very used to and capable of and always surrounded in when you see each other in other realms, other planets, other worlds. Then to find each other here on Earth where there is a lack of love because everyone's trying to understand the purpose of life here, the significance of life here and what it really means, while being super distracted by everything else but the meaning of life and the energy frequency of love. It gets very confusing and that makes everyone feel rejected. And when we are so used to the high energy frequency of love and we are wanting it from each other because we can't seem to find it even within ourselves. Because in the third dimension, you get the third dimension. You can't borrow energy from other dimensions to slap it on you because that would then not make you human. And when you're having to play the role of human, you've got all the energy frequencies of the third dimension while playing human, and I think this is when a lot of people feel like they don't fit in. They don't belong here. And this feels really foreign, wrong, and they feel really homesick. It's because they're not in this natural energy bliss that they know that they're more attuned to, capable and at ease elsewhere. And I feel like this is where a lot of people then start labeling themselves as being depressed. And I think the density is depressing them and not uplifting them as they're seeking true Source love energy.

S: Yeah. It's hard. It's definitely hard. Especially you and I agree. I think we all do. I think it's in our cell memories. We all are aware of the possibilities of where we've already had that really high frequency love and it's just really, really wanting it. Really yearning for it and trying to figure out how to cope without that here. And it's not easy. It's harder too, I've had dreams where it just feels higher vibrational in the sessions and it's like I can sense the difference. And it's just bliss! And I think that the easiest way for me to get somewhere where that is, is the energy, the frequency of gratitude and love. That helps.

J: While I love your suggestion of faking it until you make it with coping. I feel like if we can feel that genuine gratitude energy and love energy, then you don't need to even fake it because you're in it. And I think that when we focus on real high frequency respect, we're not only loving and respecting ourselves, we can then easily love and respect others. But you know it's choices. And you are feeling into this rejection and I feel like again, when people are trying to struggle to find that high frequency, it's not them rejecting you. It's them still seeking pure love. And the best we can do is 3D love. But it seems that people don't even want to do 3D love because they're looking beyond that higher energy love. I mean, that's where it's all at. And I know what you're saying, when we do sessions and many Souls have come in and they just kind of give you this love bubble. And instead of this, 'Oh my Gosh it's wonderful!' It's like you burst into tears and you just feel so humbled with this awesome sense of power and energy that it doesn't feel like love. What you would think love energy is. You just break down into tears and you just cry because it's just, I don't even know what the right words are. It breaks you down because you want it so much! You've been seeking it but it's so intensive! I don't think you could cope. If you were in that bliss bubble, you wouldn't be able to cope in 3D because it's just paralyzing. It's just too awesome and you just can't, I mean you *can* have moments for it, that's for sure. And you can have bliss bubbles and waves, but in reality, I don't feel like we're allowed to have it for too long. I know lots of clients want to go to the Fifth Dimension. Even just the Fifth Dimension is still a long way away from Source Energy. And even the Subconscious is saying no, not gonna let your client go there today Jo, because they need to focus on being here now. And if they have this little holiday reprieve to really feel into the Fifth, to the New Earth, they're not going to be able to cope with still being here in the Third dimension. And I just go, well, just give them a little bit. And they're just like, we know best! We're not gonna do that! It's too much! They will want out and they're struggling enough as it is. We've got to do the best we can here to keep up your frequency vibrations to keep you on focus and track, because that's just too distracting going just to the Fifth. And we're talking about Source Love Energy, that's like the 12th dimension.

S: Yeah. I Know. I've been doing a lot of energy work where I try my best to just send out a lot of love, and I can sense a lot and people are struggling, especially recently. I have just been feeling the sadness with a lot around me. That's when I was like, I just gotta send it out and stuff. I don't know how to explain it, but the more you become awakened and aware, it feels like you have more responsibilities in a weird way. I can't explain it. But it's almost like, and tell me what you think, it's kind of like that saying, the more power you have or whatever, it becomes more responsibility. It's one of those things where the more that we're aware of, the more now you have to be responsible for your energy frequencies. Because you're actually affecting more people now! Because it's almost like when you're also healing and allowing yourself to heal with all of the inner work, once that's gone, then there's more room so you can do energy work for others too.

J: Absolutely! We have to be accountable! We have to be responsible! And we have to be mindful of our energy frequency! And the more we are that, the more we are evolving our own Consciousness Awareness then we do get more responsibility of energy. And if we then suddenly want to be angry and spiteful and hateful and all that sort of stuff, our capacity to hold a lot of energy is a big problem when you're starting to then become "evil". (laughing) And so, it's me being silly but it's true. It seems like the last half dozen clients I've had who have done BQH sessions with me, they've had sessions with other practitioners and it's often they don't want to have sessions with interns because they don't really want to waste their time with an intern. They want to have a professional and so they do a level two practitioner and then they come in their session with me and they can definitely see a difference. Because the level two have still only done five or ten sessions. And so there's not quite... I mean, save your money. Just do interns and support and interns I say, because you've got to do at least 100 sessions to be confident in what you're doing. And so, if you're going to spend any money on someone who is still not 100 percent confident in what they're doing, it's a choice and all. So anyway, having these sessions with these clients, and still they're what I would consider very Advanced Souls, very awoken souls, and they still haven't recognized the energy frequency fields. And so one of the things I do like to say to the Subconscious is, can you please show my client where their energy frequency field is because they're saying to me that they're feeling a lot of other people's energies, and they're wondering if it is a lot of other people's energies. What can you say Subconscious? And I know the client sort of thinks I might be picking up my neighbors. I might be picking up the people in my next office or something like that. They sort of have this... 'It can't just be all my inner work that I'm feeling'. And so the Subconscious will show them. And it's seriously like a large, large area. I would sort of say, there's no way I would like to run from one side of it to the other. It's just too vast. It's a really big location. We are big energy beings here, and of course it's classic, it's so adorable. The Subconscious is like, 'Oh, we're showing them but they don't believe it'. And then I'm like, 'Oh Subconscious, are you telling my client lies? And the subconscious is... 'No, I'm showing them how powerful they are. I'm showing them their energy field, I'm showing them but they want to keep small and just think they are little humans. And we're really not'. I like ways to be able to empower my clients with things they haven't even considered to be able to help them understand the density that we collect during the day. By the time we get to the evening, we've consciously collected all of that energy. And I say to people who want to use the 15 minute White Light Healing Meditation or do any meditation, do it between the time you get home from work or finished work before your evening. I don't know what sort of hours that would be. Around 5 p.m 6 p.m kind of thing. Maybe even before you have your dinner, do your meditation or do whatever you want to do, then you've got that clarity for the evening that you can just enjoy for yourself. Because a lot of people want to do their meditations just before they go to bed, and I'm like, but as soon as you go to sleep you're in that higher frequency. You release the density consciousness because you're not focusing on the body and you often go elsewhere.

And I know lots of people want to do it first thing in the morning, and I say, you are just so high frequency in the morning that you are supercharged and then the density gets collected during the day. Does that make sense? And have you noticed that you're just beyond tired in the evening?

S: Oh, yeah. So I want to say something, like I'm a huge morning person. I love the mornings so I'm just naturally bubbly! I want to sing. I'm super hyper in the mornings and then because I meet with so many people, I have so many interactions, I talk to, I want to say on average, about 80 people a day. So it's quite a lot and it's all constant. And so I'm always around a lot of people too. So, I actually think that, and it's funny that you say that, because I find a lot of meditation and reprieve in my car when I'm driving home because it's almost like my brain can just kind of go on to autopilot. And I was just thinking right now, that would be a perfect time for me to put that 15 minute White Light Healing on in my car. To just kind of listen to it in the car just to kind of wind down. And then actually go home after and then have an opportunity to close my eyes, because you can't close your eyes when you're driving.

J: Yes, there's no warnings on any of that. And so I keep hearing people saying that they can't wait to get home and see their family. And then when they see their family, their kids and their partners, you know husbands or whatever, have them sort of feeling like there's this explosion of energy and chaos and disharmony and disconnect. And it's kind of like, because you've just walked in with your 80 people that you've talked to, all energy wise. Your daughters just picked up all of the thousands of kids at school. Your partner has picked up the hundreds of people he's experiencing. So you're all coming into one sacred space, to bother your animals probably with all of this energy that's all just having a big party within your sacred space. And I think a lot of people who are aware of energy and how we bring it all in, this is why they say... Oh, I want to protect myself! I want to have a shield of protection! That's one choice. Or you could be of service and absorb all of that and know how to release it, and not hold on to it. Because we shouldn't be holding on to people's stresses and strains and struggles and unhealed problems. They're not actually ours to do anything with. We observe them and then we are to feel into what's going on for them, to support them through love and perspectives and in any other ways to be able to help uplift them by being genuine. If we see someone's really struggling and having a really shitty day and we can feel that energetically, our natural feeling is to avoid them. The thing is, what do we really need when we're struggling? Do we need avoidance or do we need to have someone say, 'Can I grab you a glass of water, I'm getting one for myself.' We have to be creative with how we show our love. And obviously, we could love someone so intensively, we could tattoo their names on our bodies, we could wear t-shirts with their faces on them, we could do everything to show that we're their number one fan. But it's not until they love themselves that they will even recognize or realize what we're doing for them.

S: Yeah. That's very true. And again, this is not an easy life and as I've said before, being 3D human is actually kind of difficult because the emotions are what makes it so exciting. So what I mean, if it wasn't the emotions then this place would be boring, right? So there's always a reason behind everything. There's always a good and pro reason. But then it's like the emotions are also the ones that are the hardest to handle. So it's interesting, but I actually agree with you. I think what helps is kind of snapping the person out of that. Maybe they're looping in their mind about something and they just need someone to snap them out of it and give them a topic to think of, and switch the mindset real fast just to change up their looping in their mind. And I think that's a great way to start. Ask them how they're doing. Did they do anything fun recently? Things like that. And, can I get you some water? Totally! Yep!

J: The thing is that when people are preoccupied with their unresolved hurt feelings, if they could share with you... 'Well actually. Oh, thanks for asking. The reason why I'm feeling this way is...' I mean, if they could actually express that to you then obviously they would be able to process it and they wouldn't be struggling with it. So people are struggling because they don't know how to express what they are feeling or why they are feeling it. And when you have no idea that you're not really just a human and that you've got other lifetimes that you are healing from and resolving from and empowering yourself from, if you have no idea about any of that, it's very, very, very confusing. Especially when you've got all of these other senses that you're denying yourself about. And so you're trying to lie to yourself... 'Oh, I'm definitely human! Oh, this is definitely my only lifetime here! Oh, there's definitely no reincarnation!' You're busy in denial land trying to protect yourself from having any other growth or expansion of consciousnesses. And so the thing is that when we would love to have an open conversation with someone about their thoughts and feelings, they can't even have an open conversation with themselves. And so this is when we have to tune into our senses to feel what's really going on for them. Are they feeling insecure? Are they feeling angry? Are they feeling confused? Are they feeling lost? What are their senses? And I think the more we recognize our own feelings and we have explored all the range of feelings to identify that energy frequency, then we can read the energy frequency of others very clearly. And it's really hard when we want to just have human conversations to try and have help but they are not ready to be honest with themselves about some very raw feelings. And I've sent so many love energy bubbles to people for them to realize I am here to hear them. I am here to love them. I'm here to support them. And there are no other agendas here. It is just unconditional love that I have for them. And when they can feel that love energy and they can feel my intentions and demeanor, then they don't feel like they have to be in defense with me and protect themselves. Because they're already hurting so they don't want any more. When you're hurt, you're so overwhelmed you can't fathom being any more hurt. And so you really shut down everything. And so when someone comes, not to try and take away the hurt or touch the hurt or squeeze the hurt or anything, but to be able to support with love at an energetic level, and that's unspoken. There's a lot we can do to be of service with each other. But gosh, we just want to hug them! We want to heal them! We want to do everything for them! And it's not a responsibility as much as it feels wrong to say that and do that, because all we want to be is a helicopter and smother the world with love. Right? I mean, that's what we're here for. But they can't and they won't do it until they choose to. And I see more people choosing to not love and support each other and making that choice to ignore each other than I do see people truly loving and supporting others.

S: Yeah. It's kind of one of those things where I just feel like again, I think that sometimes there's just so many distractions. And I feel honestly truly blessed and grateful because I think with this journey that I've been on, it's been very confusing. Not only seeing entities and experiencing all those connections but, when you live in both worlds in a weird way, where you're here but then your foot's also in the spiritual and you're kind of sensing and seeing both, that can be really overwhelming too. And it's kind of interesting that you mentioned those people that have no clue that they've had past lives. No clue it's affecting them. Like these weird connections are happening and I don't even know how that would feel if I didn't know where this is coming from. Because even knowing where it's coming from is also still kind of overwhelming, in a way. I just hope more than anything that they start getting epiphanies of some kind and some clarity because it can be quite an overwhelming experience before you get the Awakening and after and throughout.

J: Absolutely! Absolutely! And I think that's why our teams are so close. And when we have shut down our teams because we're already so overwhelmed and we're denying the energy of love and we're denying all the support from our inner teams and from our subconscious and guides, this is when they push us to then be of service to those people who are already overwhelmed. And that's why we've had the volunteers come in who have a clean slate to Earth's density. To Earth's karmic cycles. To a lot of what's been going on on Earth. And those volunteers are supposed to help while they've got so much attunement and senses to how others are feeling and responding and reacting. And it's all very challenging, but it's not unachievable. It's our choices that make it unachievable. And so when we want to truly empower ourselves, because when you know about the shift and that there's going to be us with our hindsight reflecting back on our choices since we've known about the shift, how are we going to feel about ourselves responding and being of service to others? That super motivates me because you do enough sessions to really challenge the heck out of the truth to understand the situation about the shift and to understand and then learn the significance of why, there's only a certain amount of time and experiences that you have before you stop denying and start accepting. And then when you start accepting, you start respecting. And then you see the mission that is there, ready to be unfolded. And this is why many of us are here. I know you've had lots of fantastically mind-blowing lifetimes here, you brave soul! You silly sausage! What were you thinking? (laughing)

S: I know, right? I mean, I don't know. It's almost like, and it's weird too, because I've always got this strange energy within myself of this extreme energy of all or nothing. And I don't know why my Soul wants that, but it's just this huge, just like throw yourself off things. Almost like a bungee jumper. Like an adrenaline junkie.

J: Well, I have heard that a lot of Souls who are. While loving all diversities and all challenges, this is the Olympics! This is bragging points for the Soul. 'Yeah I was on Earth. *Of course I was on Earth!' I mastered it! Oh, I mastered Old Earth! I've mastered Earth! It was easy!'* Like this is bragging points for Souls. But of course, in the High Dimensions they're all humble and like... 'Oh, *it was all fine.'* But it's extraordinary and they know this. I'm talking about the Arcturians now. Their perspective is that they still believe the Souls are going to find their moral, spiritual, emotional, compass to remember how powerful they are. To remember who they are and to remember why they're here. And that's great to have that perspective and hope and faith in Humanity. I mean, that's adorable isn't it? Because they believe in us so much, and yet we are here seeing all of that unfold. We're seeing the resistance of Awakening fully even though we know many people are supposed to. We see the resistance of disinformation agendas being very strong. And there's a difference between what people can cope with versus what people have been distracted with in the spirituality world. There are people that are not supposed to know about anything and I think that's a nicer way, isn't it? But they must be being a bit confused and struggling right now with the changes of the world so rapid in the last few years. While we understand that it's part of the Awakening to really get their attention to realize this is not the way things should be. And isn't it exciting when we see real honest mature people stepping up now and starting to speak about how they see unity within communities being something that is achievable and desirable for all? I have a slight crush on someone in your country right now. And the reason why I have a crush on him is because his love for Humanity is right up there with what I feel like is my love of Humanity. And he has such great hope and he wants to really show people how easy it is to hold people accountable, hold businesses accountable, hold systems accountable. I mean, it's phenomenal! And he gives me so much joy!

S: Very cool! That's awesome! I love it! I appreciate anyone who, first of all, runs into this information because it's totally raw. It's totally shocking! And then actually wanting to listen to it because in and of itself, you're basically telling yourself,

'I'm allowing me to start Awakening!' Because this information will awaken you. It'll trigger you awake. And so that's already the first step. And then that's already super overwhelming. And so, I think it's amazing when people really do try to help and they're understanding that they do have a higher purpose here and I like that they take their roles more seriously. And I don't know if that crush of yours, has he listened to your channel?

J: I don't think so. (Laughing) But he says things like he knows that 'God speaks through many people' and he's just someone that a lot of people have relied on for many years to find the truth and to hold people and businesses accountable and industries accountable. And I just find that strength in one man incredible! And I love the fact that he's an example of someone who doesn't want to do the role he's trying to do, but he sees that no one else is stepping up to do it. And so that's a really hard thing to do, because you kind of wish that everyone would naturally want to do this and share the truth and open up the transparency of companies that have been polluting. Companies that have been creating war for money. Companies that have been creating illnesses for money. He is willing to expose all of that and isn't that it's very exciting.

S: Yeah. It's being real. (J: It's Brave!) It's Brave.

J: It's brave because he's already been labeled everything under the sun that's negative. Because he's already a threat. He's an intelligent threat. And bless the woman that went to him all those years ago to explore mercury, because we know mercury is probably not something we should be playing with and certainly should not be putting into our bodies. Because we're using our Free Will choices to poison ourselves. And so, when they kept relabeling mercury and hiding it in vaccines, a lot of parents were wanting to question this because they believed this was a link to autism. And so he was trying to get mercury not being polluted into a river and into your drinking water. And these women were harassing him to explore this and what mercury was doing in vaccinations. And so I've been following him for many years and it's just exciting to see him on a bigger platform. Sorry. It's all about me today. He's married so it's not like a real crush like that. I just love people who can speak the truth. And it doesn't even need to be the metaphysical truth. The truth of unity, the truth of love, the truth of community, the truth of compassion, the truth of hearts connecting to care about each other versus the focus of business and money. A focus on sustainability and compassion and consideration for Humanity and not just being blinded by where they were born or what passports they have and what nationality they reside at. To understand that right now, we're *one* body of beings on *one* planet. And if you try to divide that and not consider all the working aspects of it, anyway, it's interesting.

S: Yeah, I mean, that's how they conquer. They divide and they conquer. And so if they can find ways to make people be like, Oh no, they're different than us, then we're all squabbling with each other and forgetting that the real ones in charge that are creating all this distraction is, you know, very minimal.

J: I was really surprised when I started hearing about the crimes against Humanity. I was like, what on Earth? What possessed them to do this? And then when we explored it it actually was really nasty because they were coercing people with false truths and in hardcore manipulation to make these people do these crimes against Humanity. And then once it was recorded, then they were being blackmailed and manipulated that way. Because ultimately, they didn't want to attend these parties. They didn't want to attend these rituals. They didn't want to attend these things and do these things that they did but they were manipulated. And yes, that's their Free Will choices to do so. But when you actually explore each independent person's journey of how they got to start doing those crime scenes against Humanity, it was peer pressure and it wasn't just their idea. They were coerced. It's always Free Will choices and karmic contracts and all that sort of stuff, but I found it was very interesting the history of how others have manipulated many to actually do those Crimes Against Humanity.

S: It's kind of crazy too, because then you realize just how backwards things have been for so long. And the people now are starting to realize that, because they've woken up to it and that big Awakening around 2020 where everybody started getting this massive amount of information and disclosures. When the YouTubes were just blowing off like all this stuff before they were getting banned, before they were getting censored[50]. And that huge amount of information that came through, that woke so many people up. I mean, I got even more awoken than before and I think it's just kind of like that point where you just can't go back from there. And now you know what was happening to these poor people and how they were being taken advantage of by others. And I

---

[50] *As we are editing this in July 2023, after 4 years of sharing content from metaphysical sessions, We have had over a dozen videos deleted by You Tube, some were 3 years old which "suddenly" breached their rules.*

think that it just shed light on a lot of the control systems that we didn't realize. We thought we were free but it was not real and we realized what was really happening in the world. And now people know. And I think that helps us also energetically break it down with our own consciousness and wanting to disband these control systems.

J: In New Zealand, I knew that we had a Bill of Rights Act which was profoundly brilliant to protect individuals rights to all sorts of things. This was a fundamental great law that we had, and during the lockdown they changed the law to twist our Bill of Rights Act, taking away our human foundational rights from the get-go because of what they were trying to do. During the first lockdown I was saying, well you can't do that! We've got The Bill of Rights Act. They can't do that! And meanwhile, they were busy changing the law under the guise of 'safety' and a 'pandemic'. And that was so astounding, that if you can manipulate and corrupt and coerce one of our basic legal structure systems here in New Zealand, it just was not a good feeling. And I know many lawyers that would have been quite surprised with this too because this was a big deal! It should be a sacred law! It should be a sacred thing! It's been an amazing journey to see the Grand Awakening and it was so abrupt. We keep asking about what is to come and they do say **prepare for everything! Prepare for anything!** But it does seem like there are still those people that just find it too overwhelming or they just don't want to see anything too abruptly. And they also don't want to be awoken. So if you have a life contract that says, '*I don't want to be awoken by anyone else. I want to get it by myself.*' But yet you're this really rigid and very close-minded person, you're going to find it very hard to be awoken by yourself. But we could be waiting on a lot of people to really notice this and be impacted. And so there's so much to be said about the Old Earth experience still. The events to come to awaken. And by working with all of these books and looking back at all these sessions that we've done over the years, you can really see how these really intensive moments in time where we were really pushed to awaken each other and to be prepared. And to have done a lot of our inner work and to be really responsible and accountable for our energy and be really of service. And it just did not pan out. And we were just not prepared. And we were not ready. And then you could just see this other twist of the timeline shift and it was a bigger thing. When I was so focused on the journey of doing all these daily sessions and supporting people and all this sort of stuff, I didn't get to see the bigger picture of the journey that we've been on with this big twist of the bigger broadcast that would not have happened to empower humanity. And then as soon as they realized we couldn't do the broadcast, and I think they tried to plan it again, then it didn't seem to work out. And they sort of had this option now, what we still are hearing about in sessions with the laser event occurring. It's not going away. It's still a thing that has to occur, but they're trying to deal with other things to prepare people for it. And so it's quite a big deal what we know is to come. And I know lots of people that are aware of this information are still distracted and not necessarily working for the Conscious Collective but for something else. And that's their choice. But it's really interesting how there's all these moving pieces and parts to it all. I find it really fascinating.

S: Yeah, and I know we talked about this before, where the collectives can look into if something was to happen this quickly, they could see what the repercussions would be in the future. And they didn't like it so that's why they'd be like, 'Okay, well we can't do it this way now. We gotta change this.' And then that's when the timeline shifts. So it's kind of one of those things where in the sessions I'm getting visuals, I'm getting feelings, and I'm getting words. But mostly those feelings because they want me to sense that in a verbal human way. And so it does change, which makes it a little bit confusing because they could see that this is gonna happen in the future, but then a year from now they realize that that's not going to be the best outcome for all. So then it has to slightly change, which will change the timeline. And then it also is based on people's Free Will. So it's almost like touch and go I feel like with them too, where things do change fast.

J: Definitely it can. And given some choices of Free Will of some people's events, things could really ramp up. It was interesting that they were saying recently that someone has exited, and so there is a shift in some power and positions and there's a play of who wants to be sort of the top. And it was really strange, the Soul that they tried to push in, who wanted to speak for himself to justify his agenda and I didn't want to. I just was not interested in channeling that human. He still felt like a ghost and so it just felt like a distraction. It's like, maybe I could channel him. But it was just these moments now where some of these influencers and leaders have had their exit points and now you get a choice, are you still going to comply or are you going to do something different. And it's these people in these positions using their Free Will choices to either expose agendas and realize this isn't serving anyone at this point. We've got all the money, we don't necessarily need the control. Because they should be able to realize and have compassion for all, not just a few.

And their moral compasses must be just weighed down so heavily on their choices that they're making.

S: It's probably a very confusing and overwhelming time I would assume.

J: Well it is, especially when I guess the channeler, it's like they haven't announced his death yet. And so it's like part of me is like.' *Oh, is this a different timeline that we're in? Is this happening now?'* And then you just realize that the truth that we're being told in the official mainstream narrative and in the media is never really the truth of what's really going on behind the scenes. This is the challenge I think, you can't even fact check what the Arcturians want to say sometimes when they talk about specific people and exit points and things like that because we would never find out the truth. And I'm not going to suddenly stalk someone just to see if, are you really dead? You've got to get to this, well the concepts are, while there is no leader right now and they're trying to jostle between who's going to take over the reigns. And I don't know anything really about the sort of person either, so I have very little interest in exploring him which probably doesn't help.

S: I almost got the feeling we can talk to Souls even when they're in a coma or the person's still alive. So I'm not sure what state of mind this man is in at the moment, but I think that it's very interesting that he wanted to chat with you about whatever he wanted to chat with you about. But a lot of entities do like to come and communicate with you because you can talk to them and they know that.

J: Yeah. But it always feels like they want to justify it. And I don't feel like I've got judgment for him, it's kind of like, well you've done your thing, they've done their thing, it's free with choices. I trust life contracts. I'm just not that interested. And even though I know it's impacted a lot of people, I just think well, this is part of the game of being Human. And so I guess this is kind of the problem when I sort of have this balance. I'm not as thirsty to understand all the unique and purposeful experiences of each Soul contract and why and how, because I just trust it's all unfolding as it needs to be. I don't need to be up in everyone's business with life contracts and purposes and are they a clone, are they not a clone? When do they really die?! What timeline was that in? Because I feel like I've got so much other stuff that I'm focusing on, I'm not really just distracting myself with the details of the Grand Awakening either anymore.

S: I've noticed too, a huge shift where they want me to just literally focus on my energy work because I have so much already that I'm doing and the energy work is a lot! And again, like we were saying, the more awake you are, the more healed you are, you're going to get more responsibility. And so a lot of that responsibility is the energy work because you're really helping huge vast amounts of Souls here that really need it. And again I was saying I've been feeling sadness, you know, lots a sadness and people just going through the density. And I think people are just becoming very aware of things too. They're more intuitive and so they're starting to feel things and sense more. And that can feel a little overwhelming. So I've been spending more time with the energy work, but it's obviously something that will need to be continued.

J: Oh absolutely! The whole thing is, I mean it's getting noticeable. And I have some farmers as clients and they are all recognizing amongst themselves in the community how it's not sustainable to be growing anything anymore like they used to. It seems like the cycles are all off and they can't understand why they're struggling so much. And if they can find a successful crop then there's all these other problems and all these systems and regulations that are impacting them. So it's not even worthwhile anymore financially to do these things that they've loved and enjoyed doing for so long. They really have to change the way that they're trading and selling and marketing themselves. It's really big, big, big, big, big changes. And most of it, when people step away from things like corporate positions, they may freak out and worry. But it seems like now they're starting to have this new place in the world where they are finding joy in their jobs. Because now, if they started a new career, it started to really flourish after two years of being in their new found position of empowerment and their healing themselves, and it's quite an extraordinary stage. But with anything, change can be scary. Even if it's a chosen change and change that does excite you, it still has learning curves. And learning curves can make you feel like you're starting from the beginning and especially if you have expanded. Like I see for yourself how you have expanded your Consciousness and your very high frequency vibrational. And then they said that you've got to go and connect with others and you can't do that at that high frequency because you kind of miss each other. You're almost talking different languages. And so you're here to be more connectable and relatable to people in 3D while also holding energy frequency to be uplifting. And I feel like a lot of people that I know who are taking their responsibilities really well and accountable for the energy frequencies, are doing tremendous things for the Conscious Collective. And not just for their Conscious awareness of this lifetime, but all the other lifetimes. I mean, we joke every time you go on holiday, what you're going to get up to because you think it's a human holiday. But it's so much light work and healing that you do when you're on vacation. It's like you need a holiday from your holiday.

S: Yes. I mean, with whatever I've gone through in the past lives, it's definitely a lot of purging and it's exhausting. It definitely feels exhausting. But I'm very aware after the trip like I was telling you, when I went to my friend's wedding in Mexico in October (2022), I literally came home and I was seeing my house through a stranger's eyes. Nothing looked familiar and I feel like I left a large piece of me in Mexico. It was the strangest thing and it took me almost three weeks or so to recalibrate, where I felt like my house was my house again, because I felt like a stranger in my reality for quite a while. And that's when we saw a part of me, kind of like a ghost, almost floating around the town and helping with energy work and hovering around it[51].

J: Because you've had so many lives where you have been a guide and I was exploring the lifetime where you were Artemis. And I would imagine that's all over the world, not just in what we assume would be like the classic Greek and Roman kind of era, locations either. It would have been worldwide. But there were just so many lifetimes that we got to explore or could get to explore. Sorry. I'm having so much water today. (S: That's good.) Yeah. I feel like if I have anything less than three liters of water I don't feel very good.

---

[51] *Main part of her Soul stayed in Mexico from that trip and that was a part walk out, which now has merged back.*

I feel really sluggish and I feel like I need at least three liters of water to kind of just feel not so dense. And sometimes it can be super increased. And it's really interesting because I feel like these are waves of high energy frequency that are really intensifying. And sometimes I feel like the shift is so close and then other times I feel like it's really far away. It's hard to explain where time kind of expands and subtracts and comes together. And we've sort of heard that when we're on timelines where more people come in to be in this timeline, you feel that density drop because they're in this timeline, and we're consciously aware of them in this timeline. It's kind of like they've just entered the room and then you sort of transmute and absorb that energy and kind of work with that energy to uplift the energy with them in this timeline. And then it feels like we move or they merge out. It's so peculiar, the whole timeline thing. I love it! Thank goodness we've done that book about timelines, otherwise I'd still not be quite confident about how it all goes.

S: Well it's confusing too because I think the human mind even going under in sessions, trying to explain. See the funny thing about the sessions is it kind of makes so much sense, right? Like when you're in the session it's like, oh, okay. Because they show you and then they have the feeling attached. But still, it's like when you get out of that session, the 3D Human mind comes back and then you're just like I'm confused again. I think it's because we are so rigid with structure with the 3D density, so things are solid around us. And so we view life as we need to understand and explain it in order for it to exist. Do you know what I mean? I think the human mind wants to do that and so we're always trying to find how this makes sense to the human mind in the timeline. And I think it can't make sense to us because I think it's more on a, now that I think about it might actually be more on a frequency level too.

J: I agree with you. When you're in the sessions it's so crystal clear, so obvious. And you listen back to the session and you're like, well where was the rest of it? Because there's a lack of experience when you listen to this session, that's one aspect of it. But having the experience of the session and feeling into and being shown all of it and they explain it so well that when you listen back to the broken English words, it really doesn't correlate. It doesn't match. It's so lackluster.

S: Yeah. And you also get tons of visuals and feelings that you can't even explain fast enough because it's almost like a conscious block of information in your brain. But to verbalize all of it would be almost impossible because they're moving you so fast through it.

J: Yeah. And there's so much detail with the rooms and the experiences and all the people and what they're going through. I only get to pick one aspect of it. When I did that conscious mind shift with that woman it was extraordinary. There were so many details to it, but to be able to explain it in a linear fashion of her experience and what happened to the Consciousness as it merged into her higher aspect of self and then was supporting others. There was so much that wasn't said which I still remember so clearly with that whole journey. And it's just extraordinary. And this is why I say go and have your own sessions. I wanted to say though, these clients have been going to other practitioners and paying for level two practitioners. But as the Subconscious confirmed, the level two practitioners were still holding back and limiting the sessions. So that's unfortunate. And so it's always good if you're going to pay for a practitioner, make sure they've had lots of their own sessions and have done a lot of their own inner work. I am such a tight ass that I wouldn't pay for anything unless I knew it was like... I would be pissed off if I paid for a practitioner to take me under in any session and they limited my experience. That would bother me. And maybe that's my inner work. Maybe I shouldn't judge. But it is very interesting. That's what I have to say about that.

S: I was really blessed because I feel like they were purposely not allowing me to go and find anyone in those six years where I was having these weird situations. Like really, really, really ramped up. And it was almost like it was so guided. And I feel like maybe these are also guided. Because not only is a practitioner realizing that they can't handle a lot of this information, I think it's giving them insights too into maybe, am I meant for this job? Is this something I'm supposed to do on this Earth or am I supposed to grow? I think I see both sides to it when they are not giving the client the full amount that they need. And I see both ways where they're both getting epiphanies on either side. Does that make sense? I feel like it's meant to happen in certain ways.

J: Yeah. I could see that for one of my clients. Their Subconscious was negotiating with the practitioner's Subconscious and the practitioner's Subconscious was like no, no, no, no, no. Not today. She would not cope with this information today. But it was good because the client sensed that conversation. The client sensed that their Subconscious was connecting into another aspect which they could recognize was their practitioner's Subconscious. And both the Subconsciousness were like no, this practitioner would not cope with this information because it would push their reality too much and it could stifle them. So even though I sound judgy, I want the best for everyone. That's just where I'm at. I just want the best for everyone. And there are learning lessons and all that sort of stuff. But it still boggles my mind that people who are practitioner's don't read or have not explored Dolores Cannon's books. That's an interesting choice because she worked so hard to get really big foundational conscious mind expanding material to help you. And if you're going to try to honor her work and try to support humanity in the way that she was, I mean, you know she said that her methods were evolving, it's a living method. And it can be respected in many ways and not just following her direct script. She was very open-minded and broad thinking in the fact that she knew that this could be beyond just her own method and the way that she's approaching it. But not respecting her information with the books that she's provided to be able to help expand your Consciousness. I mean, it's obviously not for everyone clearly.

S: I love Dolores and honestly, if reading books just isn't your thing. I was actually listening to her YouTube channels because she also had, I think it was a podcast or a radio show too where she would talk about her sessions. And I think that was the first thing that actually sparked my interest in her and her work was listening, because I like to listen to things a lot. And so I was doing a lot of my work and I would be hearing it. And there were just a lot of insights. And I was just like whoa! This is amazing! And I think what really made me resonate with her was she was so open-minded like you said, and so willing to hear things that were bizarre that she couldn't even explain. But it was just her openness that really made me love her. Because she wasn't judging anything. It was so raw. It was so unique. And she was just such a lovely woman. She just really wanted to be the reporter and she didn't want to judge the work. She just wanted to provide the information for others and for the client.

J: Definitely. She wanted to understand it too. And so there was a learning journey that she shared. And then when you go through her books you can see that journey. And I loved that about her because she's just so adorable and so honest and she loves still coming into sessions as we know, because she's still here to help us. And I know from their perspective it's all easy and it's just unfolding as it should be. And I feel the pressure of encouraging people to be their optimal best versions of self because they're so capable of it because they promise to be here to do that. And I know we get distracted, and I know we don't have confidence in ourselves or see the significance of how, **if we did want to be of service to humanity, how phenomenal that would be. And I think lots of people are too shy to try that because, what if they failed? What if loving people didn't change the world. Well, the world's going to change regardless of what we do. So, what are our choices and how proud of ourselves are we going to be knowing that we got to choose to support Humanity versus ignoring Humanity? And just watch it suffer and struggle as we feel into that?**

S: And I'm just trying to think about how people actually, when they're in that position, when they're that shy, what would motivate somebody. And I think it's just honestly, when you do something to help somebody feel better, maybe less dense. Or if you know you're doing something of service from the heart and you're sending it out to that person, there's just a sense of, I guess you could say, you feel proud of yourself. It's an inner bliss. And I think that kind of creates a domino effect with others because they see that it's so easily achievable and it doesn't harm the sender. It's like when people are afraid of shining their light to others or giving their energy to others because they're afraid that it's going to deplete them because they only have a small reserves, where that's not true. We have endless amounts of energy and love to give. And so I think it's just a matter of, stop thinking you're small because you're not small. You're rather large and you're very expansive so you can only get bigger.

J: Well I mean, we have heard people saying that they don't want to be large because they don't want to be targeted by the dark side. And I think well, if you've got maturity in spirituality you know that we're protected and we get to use our spirituality and our mindsets and perspectives to continue on to be of service without being in fear. And I think both of us have experienced that, where good people have felt really threatened and bitter and resentful and sent us that energy. And we can feel that. And it's our choice how we want to respond to it. And then we also know that people have been trying to use their Free Will to seriously impact us physically because of other agendas and to try and stop the truth being shared. And it's our choices how we respond to that. And when you know we all get to live beyond this lifetime, kind of has a different perspective of things. But do we go into fear? Do we stop sharing the truth because we're afraid we're going to die? Do we stop trying to help Humanity because we're afraid of irrational fears or worries from a human perspective?

S: That's when the whole having that courage and that... I also think it's faith too, because I know I'm protected because how could we not be? What I mean, like the things that we've seen. The entities we've connected in with. And like you were saying, they've tried stuff on me and you, to stop us from talking. There's so much behind that. We have so much energetic support from the collectives that I already know that we're fine. And knowing that and always just being aware of that, I think that's why we haven't stopped talking. But I know what you're saying.

J: It's been good to be able to help people focus on their own intuition and to feel into things and not feel just reliant on session information. And for them spending that time that we could have been sharing with sessions, it's nice for them to have their own sessions. It's nice for them to feel into that for themselves and to have that going within time. And so, there's that knowing between empowering people and disempowering people and we've got so much information that we haven't shared and I'm glad that we didn't in hindsight because of timelines change. It would have upset people and would have scared people and would have confused people. And now we can sort of put it into the books and explain what options we could have been having, but to understand what the Collectives were trying to do to help us awaken at that point[52], in those moments for those people in those situations. And I think it's so much to cater to everyone's life contracts and then to cater to how everyone responds to being pushed awoke or awakened or whatever the correct good word is to say that doesn't trigger anyone. (laughing)

S: Yeah. And I do want to also say that anyone who's actually been on this journey and listened to these sessions are

---

[52] *Session 3 in this book is a good example of this.*

already very amazing. Because I know that it's a lot of information and it's something that really pushes people's belief systems when they hear it. And I really appreciate all the support from those who have stayed on the journey. And I've had connections in the past with people, spiritual connections that were very intense. And there were a lot of them and they just didn't really want to go further with this kind of connection because it was too overwhelming for them. And so they would walk away from it. And out of all of them, one of them actually was able to, I guess relate to it so well and adjust to the information that they've been expanding and Awakening and healing. And it's just amazing what this kind of level of information can really help someone become. It's great actually, and I see so much growth in the people that listen to this and myself.

J: Absolutely. I can definitely see it myself, the growth, and observe others. And then of course there are a few that are stuck. And it's kind of like the same when I met them. It's really interesting. And that's choices and it's inner work. It's just amazing what people do with this responsibility. And there's no judgment at all. It's just observations. But for those people who have expanded upon this and honored this, that's what we're here for is those people that are taking this seriously. They're doing their sessions. They're challenging it because, to a conscious mind, it is too epic to fathom. And then when you do the sessions and you feel into your Subconscious, sure as heck, they tell us all of the details of why the Grand Awakening is occurring and what the shift really means. What New Earth really means. What Old Earth really means. What different Collectives really mean. What timelines mean. I mean, there's so much to learn! It's so much more than just love and light. And there was someone really angry online recently saying that those people who are just love and light and not aware of the darkness here, and are not fighting and wanting revenge and justice and all this and stuff, you're part of the problem. And I think, well no. If people can only cope with love and light let them just cope with love and light, but we're not here to fight anything or want revenge or justice. We can be aware of all of the Crimes Against Humanity and have emotional balance and be responsible with that, to see the significant purposes and lessons. And it's only the human ego that would react to not being respectful to the life contracts and the karmic experiences and lessons that others are having. But we get to choose to feel it *all* Being Human.

S: I think people are also because we've discussed this too. Because we're all purging past lives too in this lifetime because we're pretty much wrapping it up right? And so there's just this bigger amount of work that's getting done. Karmic work. All that kind of connection work. Everything from past lives that have kind of been unfinished are being worked on now. I'd like to hear your perspective on it, but I believe that they're trying to finish everything, and if it doesn't get finished, then I'm not sure if they want it to get done in a different dimension or what do you think? Do you think they want to actually try and finish everyone's karmic ties and that kind of thing, like all of it?

J: Yes. I feel like if you're not being of service and you just finished your lessons and experiences, you're out. You're done. You're shifting! And we've seen a lot of shifting happening right now. And it seems like those who are here being of service and for whatever lessons and experiences, there's a lot of karmic lessons as well. I feel very sorry for those people who know about everything and are still here to serve out their time on the Old Earth for their accountability for what they've done on other planets in other lifetimes. And it's lessons and there's nothing wrong with that. The Soul needs that because there's certain Collectives here needing to have their lessons and experiences and being responsible and accountable for past lifetime choices. Some past Earth choices for future Earth choices including New Earth. And we know that some Collectives are just not ready yet and it's not because we judge them. We still love them on their journey. They're just newer and younger for their evolution, and we've all been there. We can't be spiteful to them. We can only send them love while not being coerced or comply with their systems. It's all about choices. It's extraordinary what is having to unfold and we do know about the other 3D planets that they get to experience and explore. And the Old Earth experience is kind of unfolding differently than we were told maybe a year ago. But it's still unfolding as it needs to be purposefully. And so the bigger events are still to come. But there are still lessons that you learn being a ghost. And there's lots of important lessons that still need to occur while people are living, while they have been observed and watched as being ghosts. Because you get to learn the most when you have that perspective because you are out of the density of the body and you're just observing how people are behaving and reacting and responding to certain things. It's all just really interesting when you explore.

S: Yeah. And so I mean I've seen my share of ghosts. They've interacted with me and it's funny that you say that because it kind of just shows that the veil is off and people are always, well after this there's nothing left, but it just shows how the

Soul is literally us just walking out of one vehicle into the next, our true I guess nature. Not like a ghost, ghost but, I know what you're saying. It just makes it even more true that this does not end. Our energy and our Consciousness does not go away when we die.

J: So there was this one Soul that loves to hang out and we know him as George Michael. And he is a real funny, funny little soul. Oh, he's saying not little. And he's loving it! He's loving it because he gets to now sit with everyone as they binge watch Netflix and his documentary of his life. Because he just wants to see it all again. Like he loves it! And so he just sits with them and he watches them watching the Netflix documentary or whatever it is. I haven't watched it. I don't think I will. Sorry. Sorry George. But he's saying that is so fantastic because they're reminiscing lighter times and funner times. And the people that loved him, they're having their own recollections of their own summers on their own, listening to the music and their own kind of fashion. And he says it's funny because his fashion in the videos that they're watching is triggering their own thoughts and feelings about their own friendships and their own trends and their own way of how they wanted to show the world how cool and hip they were. And they're reflecting back on so much. And so he's living for it! He's loving it! And he's all observing it. And so he is happy. He is very happy! Funny. But it's interesting how it's all unfolding to make us rethink about our past experiences to be able to give us those opportunities to heal. And when we can't change anything from the past as such, like we can't change the events, we can change our perspectives and we can change our perspectives of the lessons. We thought it was just to make us feel like terrible people but when we go back and review it properly with our metaphysics, we actually see that these are always lessons to empower ourselves. And we sometimes need these little journeys of the past to remind us of these events and situations to give us these little glimpses again of the emotional rollercoaster that we've been on Earth.

S: Yes. And to appreciate just how far we've gone. Because I mean honestly, I did have a lot of years of learning all this information alone and I didn't really have anyone to talk to. So when I met you and we connected, I was just so thankful for that because I'm like, finally someone understands what I'm going through. Because I felt like I couldn't really tell anyone because it was just so weird, and just too much. Right? And it almost sounded like I was making it up. And so I love that people are Awakening now and there's more support. And people are understanding each other's journey because they're also experiencing it.

J: Yes. It's like the quantum entanglement of another Soul who you haven't properly met or had a conversation with. It is so intensive and so undeniable, that when you have this interaction, you have this connection, even if it's a spark moment where you've just briefly seen each other. Even if it's just on a movie or on an advert or the news or even just walking on the street, it's these really intensive undeniable Soul connections that last longer than the interaction and can last for a very, very long time where you're so entangled in the quantum field that you can have conversations, you're not even dead, like obviously! It's a conscious mind mingling conversations, and I have a lot of them from Souls who have passed who want to chat and give me perspectives that I may not be able to see and that's really helpful. And I've also had some connections with Souls who are living who are wanting to have conversations as well. And it's interesting. And it may feel like and could be mislabeled as other things that are incorrect. It's negative connotations. But there are definitely quite a few of my clients that have had these very powerful undeniable connections. It's very confusing, because what if it's your husband from five lifetimes ago and you've got that instant Soul connection. You're not interested in having a sexual relationship with them but you know you've done something together and it was big and profound. And those connections can be very confusing for many reasons, but it's usually about supporting each other at a Soul level. If you can talk, fantastic! Whatever, it just is so important that we feel like we're not so alone. And it's so important when we're in our hard moments, because I think this is when lots of people have exits, walkouts I should say. It's when they just feel like I've got no support. Nothing can help me. I'm done. I'm done. I'm done. And I think that's when the walk out happens. They don't try to kill themselves or anything like that, but they just are completely done. And they just can't feel any connection to anyone at that Soul level. That is so unique and so significant and so purposeful. And when we can't always feel the connections of our guides or other people around us, having these Soul connections mean everything! And they can be honored and they should be respected. But it's very hard for the conscious mind to fathom how you could have such an entanglement of profound beauty and empowerment with someone that's not really in your physical life as such, and it can be very confusing and distracting. But it's always very purposeful.

S: I mean I think that with the Soul connections, if anything, I've been lucky. I feel like I've had pretty positive ones where I feel like it's been very uplifting and helpful. And I just think that there's just so much that's going on with people right now. And it's an overwhelming experience. Because when you do have those connections and you're living in 3D, it does feel like you're kind of living in two different realities. You know what I mean,? (J: Yes) And you're trying to balance it. And if that connection is really helping you, really motivating you, really being your muse, your inspiration to be a better person, that's like my drive and I love it. And it's almost like a support. It's like an energetic friend. Just pure love! So I love it!

J: It's kind of like a wakened dream state, because it can be so special and lovely and wonderful, almost a distraction in the 3D but you're awake to these connections. And obviously, when you're at different, like I've had some where the person was very unhealed and you can feel all of that and you can inspire and encourage them through this. But then you also know that they can shut it down and not want to heal because healing is a journey process. And if they've got big egos or if they've got something that's kind of going on for them and they're dismissing it, it's a wasted kind of opportunity. But again, it's their Free Will choices. And I sort of always felt that prying into what's going on for other people, it didn't feel like it was appropriate. And sometimes, the more I realize I just want to understand where they're at, you're going in to feel into what's going on for them isn't necessarily being rude or prying. It's being able to understand, can I really help these people? Are they really wanting to grow or are they really something else. It's entanglement. And sometimes it can be really beautiful and powerful and other times it can be part of my life contract to trigger people to grow. And being triggered to trigger people, it's still a real thing because we should know to be responsible now. And we should know how to love each other now. And when I see too many people not choosing to be respectful and to love each other, you literally run us down in some regards. Right? I mean no pressure, but you can see it when people are avoiding each other and not loving each other and not respecting each other. But then I also know that there are some mentally unstable people out there that don't want to heal, don't want to grow and really struggle and actually wanting to cripple and disempower other people, and know the difference. And it took me quite a while to know the difference. And you can't help people who have got that agenda, that demeanor, and you're going to be mature and responsible for your own energy. And when people are trying to disempower and hurt us, it's our choice to step away. Love them from a healthy distance but not engage in their game playing. Because effectively, they're trying to distract. And when you've got a mission to be of service, and when you've got a purpose to be here, being distracted by that definitely doesn't serve me anymore. But we've all got our own fun things.

S: It's like what we've been talking about where I've been trying so hard to get my partner, who I've been with for a very long time, to understand and to grow. And it's like he does not want it. And it's really taxing on me because I'm trying everything I can. And he was heading in that direction at first and then he was just like 'Nope, hard stop! Not doing it, not gonna grow. Not even gonna be open-minded to it. And then now it feels like that struggle of where it's like, he well, I mean you already know what's going on with him. But I feel like we're not communicating as well anymore because of that. It's like he wants to just block me from any of that.

J: And I think it was really hard because you started on the same journey and path together, but then he chose to hold on to density. And so it's like he kept choosing different life contracts for him because it was his choice to, he didn't know whether he wanted to go to the Fifth or go to the Third. And it's like his Soul knows he can be more of a service in the Third. But it means that there is no real sort of connection to the pathway of where your direction is going and his is going. And it can be really confusing when you get these conversations from the Subconscious saying, Oh no, he's going to the New Earth now. Oh no, he's not going. It's like pick a lane buddy. Pick a lane. Because you're trying to support him without trying to feel pressuring because there's a difference between empowerment and disempowerment. And as soon as you know what their life contract is, you honor that. But it flipped for a while and that was very challenging.

S: Yeah. And then now it just seems like he's not gonna want to.

J: The decision has been made, accept it!

S: It kind of feels like that, yeah.

J: And that's hard, because if you didn't do all the sessions that we do, you would have assumed what two years ago that he was going to the New Earth because that's what your session said back then. Right? And this is why it's so important I feel, for people to have regular sessions, just to be a maintenance deal. And plus, as the timelines are shifting and extending so much as they are, get sessions to confirm and back date what you're assuming, what was said from one session still is the same. Because I know many people have been told they're going to go to the New Earth and I know that they're not anymore. But do they need to know that, potentially not. That it may distract them or whatever, whatever, whatever. But things change. This is provable from all the sessions we've done. Things do change.

S: And people change. People want different things. And that was kind of like the most apparent thing in my reality where I was just like, whoa. He just wants to be in 3D. And I'm like, it is what it is. I can only do me and help with what I can do. But I just thought that was really interesting how it does kind of feel like a choice, like a decision was made recently.

J: And I feel like for some Souls, they get Free Will to do whatever they want to do with that because they've already mastered the Third. They've already mastered the Fifth. But they are wanting to consciously have this linear diversion and don't want to shift with the rest to go to the Fifth because they find 3D more comfortable. Now that could suggest to someone who's making assumptions, Oh, that sounds like a Reptilian Collective or something, something, something. That sounds to *me* like a light worker who is supporting Reptilians and their Collective to grow and to heal. And so much to be said about that. And **when we're all one we can just drop all the labels anyway**. But when you are being of service, but in a different density capacity, we assume being of service you must be in the high frequency of Love energy. Not always. You can be of service to support those who are in darkness. Archangel Lucifer for example can support those in the darkness to uplift them, to raise their frequency, but he has to go down and match their energy frequency to be able to support them. But then of course people trip out because, 'Did you just talk about Lucifer the devil?' And so being a diverse Soul is fantastic because you can support all ranges. And if you're only focused and you've only got certain skill sets to one level frequency or only focus on one level frequency, you kind of only have service to that one level frequency. And so being broad is helpful.

S: Yeah. I can totally see it because there's definitely a reason why I was seeing the shadow figures and other things running around. I totally get it and I think it's just great. Anyone who's doing any kind of light worker roles, because again, it's like you're doing so much you don't even realize what you're doing especially in the dream state. I just can see people being so busy, their Souls being so busy doing so much. And we don't even realize how much we're doing.

J: I think in the sleep state we're probably doing more. But then I'm still on about three hours sleep because I feel the energy of balance and high frequency does need to be here. It does need to be stable. And so I feel like a lot of people still worry about not getting enough sleep. If you are still consciously here awake and you keep getting woken up, don't use that time being in worry or stressed about how you're going to function the next day. Be in balance, be in neutral, be accepting that you're consciously awake in that high energy frequency field. That is also being part of service. So I guess it gets complicated when we use these words and labels and terms so often. But it doesn't get spelt out all the ways of how to be of service. How to love each other. How to love themselves. How to do your own inner work. **It sounds like words but to actually apply it and to be**

it and to know it and to grow from it with confidence and maturity. That's where the fun's at!

S: Not denying to. So I think what helped me figure out what my inner work was when I didn't really understand it, was what hurts me when I think about it, what still gives me feelings of inadequacy. What I mean, like the whole fear of rejection especially, I didn't even realize because I get rejected all the time. I'm in sales so I get rejected all the time. And so I can handle those kinds of rejections. But the love rejection, that scares me to my core and it's like why? And then things started coming up, well childhood, things like that. Being rejected as a friend. Feeling left out. That kind of a thing. All that starts to come up and that's where you really do find where the inner work is lying.

J: Absolutely! Another one is doing as much as you can for people and still not getting their love. And then feeling so driven that you've got to do everything to get their love and recognition, and realizing that there is never going to be enough. You cannot do enough for some people because they're just not willing or wanting to receive your love or give their love. And that can be very maddening for some people. It almost creates an OCD in someone that is overly compulsive on doing something in hope of recognition of getting loved or being loved. And when you realize, you get to this point where it doesn't matter? It doesn't matter what you do, it's never going to be enough. That's a really hard place to be in acceptance of and being able to keep continuing on with, because until you realize it's got nothing to do with you or your actions or behavior, it's about the people you're wanting to love you. And that's their insecurities. That's their lack of Love languages. Their lack of seeing what's happening around them as they're so focused on their own pain and hurt, which ultimately always stems back from not being loved themselves.

S: Yeah. That's true. And I think a lot of it is projections. We're seeing a lot of people mirroring things back to us that we think is ours, and it could be both of ours actually. But I guess it's just not taking other people's behavior towards you as personally. And detaching and realizing that I know what it feels like to be in pain. I know what it feels like to not feel loved. And that it really hurts your inner child. And I kind of see people wanting to be loved. They're really just wanting to be loved, that's all! We really just want to be loved like that. We're simple, humans are simple. And we all hurt and we all feel the same pains and we all are very similar. So I just look at it as that person was probably disappointed as a child, hurt as a child, and so they don't want that to ever happen again. So they put up the shield and they refuse to let it happen again. They refuse to allow someone to come in and do it again to them. And so they have to rip off that armor, and it's gonna hurt. Because they're gonna be starting from their younger age.

J: Absolutely! And of course, those struggles at a younger age were always part of empowerment of self. To teach us that we had to give everything that we were seeking from others to ourselves and that we're very capable of it. But it doesn't feel normal or natural to us to be the ones that have to give it to ourselves, because we want to be in a tribe. We want to be in a community. We want all of this stuff, but it's very, very interesting. I love all the layers and levels and experiences of it and I think we could talk about this forever. Any final thoughts before we wrap up?

S: I feel like I learned something actually in this session. The fear of rejection. I'm gonna work on that actually with myself. Because I feel like that's something that's actually hindering me from reaching out to certain people that I need to talk to. That's important. I think I'm gonna work on that for myself. So I've learned some things! I'm happy, what about you?

J: Yeah. It's just so broad. You can't look at someone and just assume their life contracts and their purpose and service and how they're supposed to be here. And everyone's teaching us something. And if we refuse to look at those triggers and if we refuse to find peace within ourselves, to provide the things that we're seeking from others, we're never going to find our inner peace. So it's part of us being of service to have that balance, to then be in that higher frequency energy of acceptance. I mean, it's just fascinating and of course it's not always going to be perfect all the time as we are needing to still react and be human and to feel into it and to set examples for the Conscious Collective. And I think that's extraordinary when you start understanding how we're sharing teachable moments for the Conscious Collective. That makes it even more purposeful in my opinion.

S: It reminds me of that dream I had recently where I saw that they were watching my life and it was like a movie. And they looked human but it was somewhere else. It was not 3D. It was somewhere else. And so they were watching my life review or something and they're all laughing. And they thought it was like the funniest movie. And it was like so much drama. And I was just like, how are they laughing about this? This is my life! I was like, this is [F__ked] up. But they thought it was hilarious, it was the funniest drama comedy romance that they've ever seen I think. And they were fascinated by all of it. So I can only imagine when we pass on from this lifetime and the experiences that we see in our life reviews, it probably just becomes so funny to us when we see it. Like it's so serious here but when you see it in a different dimension, it's like, 'Oh my gosh, this is all just a movie or a game and we take it so seriously.' And it's just kind of crazy.

J: It's so true though. We do take it so seriously. And I think I take it the most seriously when I'm trying to focus on understanding a new concept or how it all fits into the pieces of the puzzles because I still don't want to be surprised by anything. And I don't want to miss any significant purposes or understanding of the significance of being here and why, or how it's all unfolding. Because I feel like I want to prepare myself for it while having balance for preparing for everything. So it is so interesting how we definitely take it all so seriously, but that's part of the game. And I guess when we remember, when we are higher dimensional beings, we just don't get this opportunity to have this range of density. To have these reactions. And that's the whole reason why we're here in the Third for many, is to be able to have this luxury of the reactions in this density while having the forgetfulness of who we truly are.

S: Because then it wouldn't be authentic. Because if we knew it was a game while we're playing the game you wouldn't be authentic in the game. Right?

J: Totally! I remember asking some questions really early on, and I was working with another practitioner and I was asking them some questions and the Subconscious was laughing at me going, this is so funny that you don't even know who you are. That you're asking us to give you your name. And I actually was offended because I was like, how am I supposed to know? I'm asking you! And they found it hysterical! That was kind of like, I'm trying to take this serious. I'm trying to understand myself. And they could see I was truly confused. And for them, they know exactly who I am and so it was just so funny to them. But at that moment I was not impressed! Anyway, okay. Well, whoever is reading, I do hope that you are finding your joy and your inner peace and you are taking the time to go within to really feel into it and to expand your Consciousness Awareness, to be able to expand beyond the ego of understanding of the significance of the Grand Awakening. What is happening to this planet and why we are as Humanity, experiencing the things that we are experiencing which is for the greater good of the lessons and Consciousness experiences and karmic contracts that we have with each other.

S: Thank you so much for listening. And we're so grateful for all of you out there who are trying your best and doing the work and just want to say thank you and big hugs to you all.

J: Yes. And if we can do it, anyone can do it!

S: And I just wanted to say, I just want to shout out to any of you who are supporting us energetically too! Because we feel it, so thank you so much!

J: That's so true because we do appreciate that because we know that you are still seeking this information so we do want to be of service. But we're also being guided to do as we do as well. And so as Dolores was also told to not share everything for significant reasons, we also want to honor that too. Because we know sometimes some truth is too poisonous and we want to be respectful and mindful for everyone. And so we're still checking in to see what we should and shouldn't be doing and we like to comply. We like to be good girls.

S: Well most of the time. Not always!

Session 43: Most Important Session In This Book

This is a great session to read many times

Yes! Yes! Yes! Yes! We are here! We are here! We are here! And we have been supporting the vehicle to explore and expand upon her conscious awareness of certain topics and certain issues that she has been well aware of through the time doing this work. And she is now sitting and reflecting upon the experiences that have been given to her. And as she is aware, there is the challenge of timelines to be able to see certain events unfold. But as you could say, luckily we love to talk and luckily we love to connect and to explain why certain events didn't occur, and what was necessary for things to go in a different direction. And as the vehicle is very much aware, humans with their mindsets are very guarded and controlling to expand their conscious awareness. They are not open to new information. And they are very confident as soon as they hear one aspect of one part of information they keep that in their memory fact check log official statement, and it's very hard for humans to expand upon what they have once believed.

We could say, the first part of information you get given is often the hardest to expand and grow from. And so when you're given information about The Awakening, when you're given information about the shift, when you're given information about where your Soul has resided from, and who you are, and why you are here, we say that this firmly gets locked into the memory banks of many and they do not want to expand upon it. And we say, when we are channeled in to give information about perspectives and information, often we allow the ego to repeat what it believes because that is comfortable for them. And it really doesn't impact someone to know if they are Arcturian guided or Pleiadian guided, as they are still needing to focus and be reminded of the life they're living here on Earth now in three-dimensional reality.

And so we say we support many egos still, even when we have been channeled because there is so much distraction. And we understand that when you hear about off-planet worlds, and other lifetimes, you're trying to fathom an entirely different culture, civilizations, race, species, being, way of life, and existence, it can completely eclipse and distract you from focusing on the here and the now and the why the *now* is significant. And so we don't want to really distract many at the moment as they're still trying to build and expand upon foundational informational components and experiences of information to be able to get at least a small level of expansion of consciousness. We say that once you are only holding on to the first level of information about say, the Grand Awakening, it is very hard for you to have broader concepts and understanding of why. And so many we see, get stuck in the details of the tragedies of the Crimes Against Humanity while refusing to accept and respect the life contracts of why those Souls wanted to be, you could say, those children that were trafficked.

The vehicle doesn't even like these conversations and so she is pushing herself further away from us taking the wheel, you could say. But it is important to share this information and to remind you all once again of the metaphysical perspectives of honoring the Soul life contracts. We want to say this very firmly! **When you do not respect and you cannot accept life contracts, you're still keeping at that basic fundamental first level of a foundational awareness**. And so you can think of that foundational basic awareness as your third dimensional mindsets of Being Human, understanding, actions, reactions and life experiences. You don't factor in life contracts you don't affect during the significance of why the Soul is here and what it needs to learn from and what it has already experienced and what it already has chosen to do in other lifetimes which is directly impacting the lifetime that they are living now as they are wanting to have the full Earth experience. You cannot really, we say, have the full Earth experience having one lifetime[53]. Because the full Earth experience could be being a mother role and then a father role. And yes we know that it's very heated and conversationally hot topics to talk about gender. But this is another factor you need to remember. Your Souls do not have gender. It is energy. Source is not a gender. It is a Conscious Collective. God[54] is not a gender, it is an awareness. And it's a group of collectives you could say, that are supporting.

There is much to be said in reference to the labels in terms that you want to get comfortable with. And we are saying that as the Arcturians, we do not need physical differences in body forms to be able to reproduce as we have already shared and shown the vehicle how we create a Soul spark aspect of ourselves to be able to have an independent experience living out a Third-Dimensional life. We can even do this in a Fifth Dimensional life. We are able to, if you will,

---

[53] *That is why for those Souls who are wanting Earth experiences they have lived here many times, and for those who are here to help with The Grand Awakening they have imprinted life times to help assist them with reference points. Experiencing all aspects of living on Earth would take many lifetimes.*

[54] *For those people still labeling Source God, whatever name and label we have for the complete aspect of our highest collective self.*

what is the best analogy for this.... What the vehicle has done prior is that she makes this sour bread dough mixture. And so you feed it and you expand upon it and then you can take small bits of this sourdough and create more bread. And the bread has its own experience, but the body of the sourdough container... We can see that there are massive flaws in this analogy as we are referring to ourselves as the sourdough mixture that is the body of the component. And we have to age and mature to then loan small parts of ourselves out to then become loaves of bread. And we are saying this is problematic, because the loaves of bread get consumed by you. But when you are aspects of ourselves being the bread, we then merge back into being each other because it's the illusion that there is separation because we're energy and that there is no confinements of our energy in terms of bodies. You may think being human, that who you really are is contained within and amongst the physical body and that's how you identify Being Human. But you also know you're a Soul which is bigger. Much bigger! Much bigger than your human vessel size. As you understand, if you were playing the role of your true essence of self on Earth, while trying to maintain a physical body, you would be using up so much more resources. So much more resources. Because if we're trying to contain the Soul size, the Soul energy in one body, you would be gigantic, you could say. Giants you could say for the analogy of this.

We have been so distracted in this conversation and so we're trying to attain the thought processes as we were trying to help others understand the significance of how it is that we, as the Arcturians, do not have genitalia. We do not produce and give birth and have sexual interactions as humans do. When we want to produce to have offspring, it's not such an offspring, it is actually a fragment of self that we are creating which is ourselves at a conscious level. We have referred to this as a thought bubble which goes off and then forms and connects into a body, that forms into the physical manifestations of a sexual interaction of a counterpart where the two components of physical matter is merged and bind in creation of the physicality is born through human reproductions, but the Soul aspect is tethered to the creation of that body mass as the physical body is being produced. And so we are sending out that thought bubble to be able to be merged into the physicality of a human body to then be born and have the full life experience as part of the intended life contract. Often you could say, we wanted to have smaller experiences. And so when our mission is complete there could be arrangements with other aspects, other Pleiadians, other Arcturians, other collectives who want to take over and manage and maintain the physical body as we regress and have a 'walk out' Soul aspect within the vessel, within that human body. This is pre-organized. We don't necessarily need to have the entire lifetime experiences for the lessons that we need to gain. Often we have needed to impact certain parts of humanity with the other games we're playing because you could say we don't just have one player in this game. We have multiple aspects of selves playing the game of being Human. And so when we need to have information shared, when we need to have significant steps forward, we will come in at certain aspects of time through a person's life to be able to share the information that is needed to be able to help the Conscious Collective of all.

For the Grand Awakening this is quite different from say, many centuries ago, the way of life. And so it's different, the pressures and the significance of what is happening now. And this is why we say many advanced Souls love to come into the point of *now* because of such a dramatic and dramatizing fear living on Earth and being human as you are noticing the Grand Awakening that is shaking up and getting many people's attention versus the normality of having a human Earth life. And we say that the working systems, while it is really the connections we have with our Soul brothers and Soul sisters being human, that is the most significant truly of why we want to come here. The conditions of living haven't been quite as desirable as once were, but it is still... You could say, every single person reading this, their Soul has desired to be here now. And so for whatever reason and significance that is, so shall it be.

The vehicle has got many insights into the last few years of this Grand Awakening as she has seen the broader concepts and the significance of Collectives being healed, and big changing moments for not only individual people and icons, but also Collectives at a Collective level. We understand it can be confusing when you don't know all the names of the Collectives, but we are saying it is the bigger greater body essences of selves that are observing. And you could say we have had unlimited lifetimes, more than we can even count, because it's not about the number of lifetimes that really matter for us. It's about the unique experiences that each physical lifetime has to offer. And while some of us love to be on the physical world, some of us like to observe and watch from the safety, you could say for dramatics, out of curiosity just manage and to maintain it. We do like having our advanced bodies. We do like having our conscious awareness of who we are in our advanced body perspectives. And we feel very comfortable here as we also are creating and designing planets and systems and seeing how they work. Some blame us for the predicaments that they push themselves through, but truly, we are not responsible for choices and for decisions that Humanity has been making.

We have given so much information. We have given so many epiphanies and so many Awakenings to be able to help Humanity really naturally, organically be aware and be noticing the information about how these systems have been limiting, stifling and disempowering humanity at a greater level. But there's many people that are still only willing to accept the very first thing that they've heard about certain concepts such as the shift. And this is why it doesn't really surprise the vehicle to see so many people still saying that the shift is just a state of mind and that they are experiencing all different realities and all different dimensions as a conscious being, being human. And we are saying they are overcompensating the insecurities of understanding what is happening. And they have tripped... We say, many spiritual egos come to distract and to disempower others as there is no integrity behind certain spiritual peoples demeanors as they're wanting to boost and promote that they are certain things in the spiritual community world, they get carried away with themselves. But we say that it is just another form of distraction. Especially certain Collectives who still feel like they haven't been respected in Humanities Evolution, want to take over and be in control, to be respected and to be understood. And that is often quite sweet because they are wanting to help Humanity. But unfortunately, we say for let's say the Reptilian influences, they've still got a very immature limited perspective of the reality of things. And so they're very twisted with their focus on wars and focus on planetary wars. Because again, they can't see the life lessons, experiences and contracts that had to play out. And so they want to then label good and bad and villains and war and heroes and such to be able to understand other lifetimes they've had off planet. And so this is why they say focus on this lifetime you're living right now to be able to empower yourselves right now. To then be able to understand the density vibrations of the true capacity of when you are in higher energy frequency of love and acceptance of yourself and all. When you get distracted with what you could consider 'tragic wars' off Earth, then you feel victimized and then you feel like you want to have revenge. And those are very 3D perspectives and not considering and expanding upon all the lessons and life contracts. And as you could say, there are no heroes or villains of war. When you have conflict, it is conflict. And it is better to be able to seek them in a physical perspective, to be able to have the understanding and compassion and consideration for the concepts and the significance of why Advanced Souls wanted to have these physical experiences and experiences that are for the purpose of the reactions of the genuine organic experience of forgetting oneself to then feel challenged, to feel the choices of, do you find your moral compass or have compassion, or do you choose to be not in a higher frequency mindset but to generally be a very low reactive third-dimensional being?

Again it is not a punishment to have these harder lessons here on Earth. It is quite a privilege, because there is much support here. We see many who should have life contracts to evolve beyond their service to self to then be able to share and to be of service to all. There is a lot of hesitation as people are not wanting to be of service to others as they are still self-obsessed and focused. That is fine, we understand that you're wanting to empower yourselves. But we are saying, many are making excuses about the inner work and the struggles. Many of you are saying you'll wait for the bigger shifts to happen or you'll wait for this or you'll wait for that, and you're having these excuses of when you should be able to be of service. We view this as delay tactics. And the more that you're all delaying being of service, the more lost and confused other people are as they are finding influencers from other Collectives that have got very limited perspectives.

And so, when you're choosing to focus on self and not be of service to all, you are impacting others through your choices to not be able to share the perspectives and insights that you know within yourselves as you have channeled us yourselves and as you have awoken to the perspectives. And as you're aware of what we are saying to you about the shift and the necessary requirements of why you need to shift and how you have to evolve from the Third dimension to the Fifth Dimension and how that actually has many steps and stages between the density of the carbon-based bodies versus the density of the crystalline based bodies which matches the energy frequency. The density of this planet does not allow the Collective advancement and evolutionary step to go into the Fifth dimension. We are saying, for those who are unsure whether you are in the Fifth Dimension or not, you cannot use the internet when you're in the Fifth Dimension! You don't use money when you're in the Fifth Dimension! You do not need to communicate with your mouths when you're in the Fifth Dimension! There are so many differences because you are completely different. Because the Fifth Dimension is a gigantic evolution step forward. It is not a subtle change, it is a gigantic leap forward from your lives as you are aware of it! And this makes many people feel very uncomfortable because they don't like change because they want to control what they perceive as their right and their management of creating their own realities. Well, they are so afraid that they are going to be pushed into something that they are not comfortable with, they refuse to expand their Consciousness. They refuse to fact check any of their belief systems about the information that they have been receiving. And we are saying, when you get first fundamental basic concepts, you have to be able to double check, is this still relevant? Is this still applicable? Does this still apply? Is this still even possible? And we say, when there are many Souls that are eagerly willing to be channeled through you to be able to help support you, to be able to give you the perspectives and insights that you're seeking about this, why are you distracting yourselves and not having these connections? Why are you delaying your accepting and respecting the situations at hand?

It is confusing to us in some regards, why we have given you all the information that you seek and search for, but yet you do nothing with it! It was not the reason why you wanted to Awaken *before* humanity. And we understand that many of you think that you will know your roles when you are on the Old Earth, but we are saying for many people now, their Old Earth experiences is what you could call *now*, because they're going to shift before the bigger events occur. And so this is their Old Earth! It is a softer version that's not so much chaos, but there is chaos in their minds as they are confused about pandemics, wars, famines, climate change. Even though it's not really impacting their physical lives, it's impacting their awareness and their concerns. And when they watch the news and they get told all of this information that seems so dire, seems so tragic and seems so imminent, their emotional energy frequency is in disarray and chaos, as they are not seeing any hopes that there could be a better system because they're not seeing the growth! They're not seeing the healing! They're not seeing the change! They're not seeing anything positive! In fact, they are being told on a daily rate now that there are more negative things in this world. And so they keep watching the news as a form of addiction and hope that there is going to be positive change. And yet that is not how the news systems have been designed because they don't want to empower you energetically, they want to keep you in fear. And so they keep creating more information that may not even be accurate information to keep you in worry and concerned about expanding or shifting or traveling or growing. And so when you're so mindful of doom and gloom, you do not feel in joy. Especially when you don't understand or know that your Souls are Eternal, because you are our loaves of bread and we do absorb you back.

And we have labeled ourselves Source, for some of you who wanted to understand where you go. We understand if you got told you yourself are not going to the New Earth, but you are being absorbed back into your Higher Aspect of Self, that was too advanced for many people to understand. So we just channeled through... 'You're going back to Source.' Because you could say, we *are* your Source! You are Soul aspects of us! And when we are not in our own physical bodies, when we're not playing the roles of being the Arcturians, and when we are just Consciousness, we are also Source too! We love how complex it is to try and explain it, and we can understand that talking about bread does not equate to anything much to be helpful. But we do try to give you these analogies to be able to help understand. But we see that we have told many people in the past, bigger information that does not help them. It's too big of a concept that is too hard for them to fathom. And so we've had to break it down to much more small bit size and palatable bits of information for you to be able to grow and expand upon at a safer, easier rate[55].

And so this is why you have still been listening to these sessions, because you're wanting to keep hearing the next level of information that we know you're ready to get because you've already had these assumptions and senses and epiphanies yourself. And so when we come to talk to you in this capacity, we know that you need this confirmation, therefore some of us sense that some of you already feel like we've already well explained it. But as you are aware, we're not just talking to the people who will be listening to this today, we are talking to, in fact, every single person who will either be listening or reading this information in what you would perceive in your future times. And so we still see many people picking up our information from the first session, and so we have to factor in who is listening and who we are actually talking to because we are not often talking to the vehicle, we are talking directly to the listener, to the reader.

---

[55] *After this session, was guided to look at what Jesus was known to say in the bible about bread... thought that was random since not having read the bible only to read these and could then understand the meaning of this message and his. " While they were eating, Jesus took some bread, and after a blessing, He broke it and gave it to the disciples, and said, "Take, eat; this is My body." "Jesus said to them, "I am the bread of life; he who comes to Me will not hunger, and he who believes in Me will never thirst". John 6:35. Google Jesus and what he said about Bread to read more.*

This is significant because we are guides and we wanted to support you to be able to help you have the bigger expanded Consciousness awareness of what is unfolding and occurring as we did see many intuitive big advanced beings, coming here to be living on Earth to be told that you're in a Fifth dimension and you create your own realities. It is very depressing for an advanced Soul to try to do that and not have that manifest, because it doesn't work like that here in the Third dimension. There are limits. And when you're using words and concepts you are not aware of or understand, but you are giving each other the strong impression that it's just your positivity and your mindset that can get you into a Fifth Dimension. When you are seeking to shift into the Fifth Dimension to help support Humanity, but you can't understand why it's not occurring regardless of how much positivity and inner work you do, it can become very confusing why this is not happening. And we had to share the bigger truth because there was not much bigger truth sharing in the spirituality worlds as more egos were being channeled versus High Dimensional Beings. More control and manipulation and distractions were actually occurring in the spiritual world as though many were being targeted to be suppressed and to not share the bigger information.

There is much to be said about how much control and manipulation has taken place on this planet, and your spirituality communities have not been exempt from this targeted approach. Where the distractions and the focus are trying to coerce the majority. And we say humans are still humans, and so when humans see numbers they have this trust that the numbers that they see in counters for videos and counters of influencers who are being followed, they trust those numbers as if they're accurate. And we're saying, when you're trying to play in a system that is false and hidden agendas and very manipulated, what can you truly honestly trust? You should be able to truly honestly trust your own intuition because you've done enough of your inner work that you have clarity and integrity with your intuition versus having so much inner work that your first response is coming from a pain and coming from fear and coming from density, that you trust your intuition which is a response to all of the other work that is within you, that is still holding you and confusing you.

And so we see many people claiming to be channelers who are channeling their egos with addition of a lot of their inner work. And that is for you all to observe. But we have always maintained for the personal true empowerment for yourselves, channeling your own main guides and your own higher selves will always be the best advantage. It is not a once-in-a-lifetime situation that will give you full empowerment. We are saying many of you do need to have many conversations with us for you to truly step your egos aside so we can take your wheels, take you for a spin, and to be able to reassure you and give you perspectives that you may not have been able to consider. And there is no shame in still being able to grow. There's no shame in having limited perspectives in the 3D capacity as this is truly the challenge of having the energetic mindsets of Being Human. As you cannot fathom or recall all the other lifetimes that are impacting this lifetime, you cannot recall your life contract, you cannot recall who you truly are, and you cannot recall the promised connections and interactions you'd have with others. And so you are at a disadvantage point, but that is the advantage of the game. Because if you remembered who you were, it would not be anything like the Earth experience. And the Earth experience is still very valid and there is still significance to having all of these experiences because it's teachable moments, not only for those who are on Earth but for all. And many collectives are wanting to evolve and advance beyond the Third because they also want to create their own worlds, they also want to create their own games of life. You could say they'll want them to get ahead. They wanted to evolve because evolution's natural, expansion is natural. And we are saying on this planet we would wish that you could naturally want to love each other and naturally want to support each other and naturally want to care about each other as much as you naturally want to love and nurture and support and care and have love for yourselves.

And we say, when you see each other all as equal, doesn't that empower you all. When you have compassion and respect and accept you're all Souls having human lives. Some are struggling terribly because they're desperate to remember who they are and remember why they are here and remember why this hurts so much when it feels so foreign and disconnected. Be those brothers and sisters that help your brothers and sisters out with compassion and sharing, because while you've got your epiphanies and your empowerment and your love of self, there is so much more that could be done to help and support *all*. And when you see spiritual people or awoken people bragging about who they are and what they know, and yet they're not able to apply what they should know about life contracts and about advanced Souls coming here to have experiences for significant reasons, this should help them focus on the importance and significance of life on Earth. And when of course, you could always have honor and respect for the actual Soul of the planet and connect with Gaia herself as she is in a much more capable capacity to be able to share with you all her history and her experiences and her life contract. And not just the life contract of being Earth, but her other prior and her other future which are all happening at the same time. She is able to talk now more freely to all without impacting your energy fields as this struggled many as they were ill prepared to feel into what truly was going on for her. Many were blocked from channeling her prior because it was too great for the energy frequency and she was too much in a delicate state. And so we did not allow those connections to happen for very many reasons. For those people who were claiming that they were channeling Gaia, and she was very happy and in love and super excited to expand her physical field here on this Earth, that is ego speaking, as we are very much aware. And all Collectives should be able to tell you that the Soul of this planet has gone through a journey, and that was unexpected but also respectful, as there were many lessons and experiences therefore it was allowed and it continued on as long as she could.

There's much to be said about all who are supporting Gaia. And as she is moving through in a linear conscious awareness state, she is happy with where she is at in her energy frequency field and what she is going to be enjoying, not only in the next physical life she will be incarnating which you call currently New Earth, but then the future life on the future planet that is in the Third Dimension, that will be able to organically evolve from that physical body into the Fifth Dimension. And that's tremendous for a physical body holding humanoid bodies of a planet to be able to shift and merge from the Third Dimensional density to the Fifth.

It's teamwork and it always was meant to be teamwork to be able to help assist this. Humanity's choices did impact Earth's experiences to be able to do that. And that became problematic. Gaia was very tolerant and patient and had the trust and faith that Humanity would and could evolve and have moral compasses to love each other, she withstood more than even she needed to. She wanted to give you all the opportunity to find the choices to love each other and share the truth. And to choose the Souls and the connections you have with each other versus the statuses of the money and the distractions that being human can offer.

We have said many times before that everything is purposeful and significant, and if you're not able to see the purpose of the significance of the current experiences you find yourself in, then you are amongst and within a lesson within itself. And often you don't find the lessons and experiences and the significance of these experiences until you've actually had the complete experience. And so it's the journey of the experiences to then find an experience and have the hindsight to see the lessons that unfolded to see the experiences of your choices. When you can't see the significance of the purpose of certain things that are in your lives, it's because it is not time to learn the lesson. You're experiencing the lesson, you're having that had.

It is like the first day of school and then trying to do the exam on the first day of your primary school when you were five. And then you're trying to hand in your doctorate for your Masters on your first day of primary school. You can't do it! It's not possible because you've got to go through the journey of all of your education to then be able to show your lessons, apply the information. And there are so many steps to get from your very first day at school being five versus your last day at university handing in your doctorate. And you can't see the end results of what your doctorate would be, what you'd even say in your doctorate when you're five, six, seven, seventeen. You could be quite older and have many years of experiences and lessons to grow and gain your knowledge and awareness to be able to even decide on the subject matter of your doctorate.

If you can't see the significance and purpose of why you're here, it is because you haven't mastered or completed your last day in school. And it's not possible to look at everything and understand it when you're going through it. On a road trip, you cannot see the destination when you're still in the middle of the journey. You can get excited. You can get impatient. You could look at photos. You can dream about it. You could fantasize about the destination. But it's not until you have completed the entire trip, the entire journey to then get to the destination. And we say for those who are so excited and cannot wait to get to the Fifth Dimension, to get to the New Earth, when you get to that destination then you'll feel even more excited to realize that is the first step of school in the Fifth Dimension and you get to start the experience again. Learning all that you can because there will be then one moment when that lesson and that school in the Fifth Dimension is complete, and you'll learn all that you wanted to, that it was beautiful to have these experiences and you wouldn't want to rush or force others to hurry up on their journey. Because if you don't learn the lessons and don't have strong foundational learning building blocks, the top of that building can become unstable. And we're seeing many advanced Souls who could have what you call big egos, not looking at their foundational structures of consciousness here on Earth, and how they're conducting themselves. But when you have been taking care of the responsibility of your strength, of healing your inner work so that there are no gaping holes in your foundations, there's no insecurities. It's all very stable and secure. If you have the big tower and it has got weaknesses and missing blocks of information, you could have a tumbling, humbling moment where your towers could collapse and impact others.

There is much that we have said within this and as we have been discussing privately with the vehicle throughout this conversation, we need her to focus on the message that we have given. So we say farewell! As she's been given more homework, she says to you, she is happy for it. So we say with love and appreciation, do not be afraid to look upon foundational information to see if it is old and dated information that may have been from other Collectives or someone with their own inner work. Building yourself up for yourselves through your own intuition, through your own diligence of doing your own inner work is always going to be more fundamentally empowering than listening to other people's opinions and trying to build your own strength of tower of wisdom and knowledge from others. This is your journey because you're going to have to hand in your own homework and you cannot copy from others.

And we say this with love!

Session 44: New To This Work

Welcome, lovely to have you with us.

Yes! Yes! Yes! Yes! Indeed! Indeed! Indeed! Indeed! We are here! We are here! We are here! And the question that we have been prompted to ask and to look into today is why there is resistance to doing the routines and collecting or dropping off the children, in the days. And she was feeling that there was this resistance to do it, as if she was not meant to be leaving the home. And we are seeing it's choices, she can make all the choices that she chooses to do. And we have been wanting her to focus more into feeling the energy of the books and processing that because there are significances in this versus being distracted and having to leave the home and process that energy with others. It's partly her choices and free will but it's also ours as well as we are trying to help her focus and just keep getting the work done, as if there is almost what you could say a time limit to this information, into this word process. And so it is indeed true that we are wanting her to finish this current book so then we can be giving her the next level of information that you would be in your perceived sense of time, willing and ready to process and accept and to expand upon. And to be able to do the appropriate and necessary emotional inner work to then be able to expand upon that. To be able to share high energy frequency amongst you all while still having these new and unique experiences[56] of keeping in balance. While there are more heightened experiences not only just energy but also events.

---

[56] *Will be called 'Conversations From Heaven To Earth'*

She is asking what events are these? And we are saying there are many disclosures that are going to be breathtaking you could say. But nothing that you haven't already heard or are aware of. It is about finally a breath taking of humanity as it's consciously at a conscious level, gasping at the shock that they have suddenly heard information that has been privy to them in general to the masses. And as you know, when you tell people the truth, they have choices how they want to accept it or reject it. And when you have been accepting information from mainstream media and then suddenly mainstream media is saying something else, you're almost trained to digest it freely without considering fact checking or questioning it yourselves. And so the information is going to come through in your public domains, your public mainstream, where it is your common folk... We don't like that term, but the average person that's still gaining their wisdom from mainstream media.

We're not laughing at them, the vehicle is having a reaction to imagining her life fully trusting all her knowledge and awareness with the mainstream media. She is curious how that would look and so we can tap into her parallel life where he does that. And he's so angry! He's very angry that there are people not complying to the systems that are sound and popular. And so he is, what you could say, very WOKE to all the people that are not complying. He views a lot of influential people as gifts to humanity because of their wisdom and their abundance of money to spend on supporting the planet and its climate change crisis[57]. Supporting Humanity with their disease and virus crisis. He

---

[57] *A big fan of Bill Gates and Anthony Fauci - which was shown to the vehicle at this point of the channeling.*

is so pleased that there are these great people here on this Earth telling him the truth through his mainstream media addiction, that when they say that there are people spreading disinformation this offends him. This triggers him! And ironically, his belief system is the polar opposite of this vehicle that we are speaking through. In fact you could say quite firmly that what they believe is the direct opposite of each other. And what they both believe is disinformation where they ponder each other's perspective. But this is important to be able to understand the balance of it and the frustration that *she* feels when there are people trusting disinformation is the same that *he* feels when people are trusting disinformation. But ironically, while it's the same emotion, it's from totally different viewpoints and perspectives.

And so this is a basic example of how it doesn't have to be the same situation to trigger the same emotions. She is well aware of the metaphysics and he's well aware of, *what we could say as Arcturians*, he is well aware and very loyal and diligent to mainstream narrative information. He trusts his news source because he believes in the faith of journalism and that they would not be lying. And he fully endorses and supports what is said on the news. In fact, he is very proud of himself for listening intently to what they're saying in the news to then be a parrot, to be a repetitive reporter. A citizen reporter to tell others what he hears in the news. Because he is concerned not everyone is watching the news. In fact, he is actually shocked because people have not been watching the news and he is questioning, where are they getting that source of information from. The internet is not trustworthy! And so he is telling them, because he is diligent in his research of the truth from the mainstream media and he is quite offended that people do not put the time and effort in. And so he puts the time and effort in to watch the news to then be able to educate people because he believes in his truth and so he is very diligent, and again, he is exactly mirroring the vehicle so she can see it from that perspective and finds it quite funny.

But there is a resistance that she feels from him about physically feeling into other people, because while she is not afraid of who was vaccinated and who is not, he is *very* afraid because he has heard rumors there are people that are unvaccinated amongst 'normal people' and he is very afraid. He cannot see and have discernment between who has been vaccinated and who has not. And he is terrified that he may expose himself to an unvaccinated heathen. This makes him feel very, very scared. And so while he has to mingle with others as part of his job, as part of his small, small, small social circle, he is very concerned, very afraid. He resists to go out and be social in case he accidentally has to stumble on someone who has been unvaccinated. He is terrified they are a walking bed full of rabies. He is basically saying to himself, full of scabies, full of everything under the sun that is ungodly. And so he, in all his wisdom, judges and scrutinizes and almost squints at people to see if he can tell '*are you vaccinated, are you not?*'

And so he will talk to others about what is said in the news to test, could they be the unvaccinated or could they be the vaccinated. And so instead of asking people how they're doing and how they are feeling, he will bring up a topic on the news to gauge and register where their belief system is, where their wisdom is, and where they get their knowledge from. And if they can't support the information that he is very, very fluent in and up to date with, he will be suspicious that potentially if they're not up to date with the information he knows about the news and the news coverage and what is the pulse of the world events, he will be very suspicious and very withdrawn and judgmental because he does not want to converse or fraternize or even have any close contact with anyone that potentially could be considering not getting vaccinated.

And so he is on his own mission and she feels this disconnect of him not wanting to converse with others. And while she has no problems conversing with people because she is open-minded to hearing what their problems are, she is open-minded to be able to listen to all, but then she does apply her metaphysics to be able to see what really is behind those comments, those attitudes, their demeanors and their behaviors as she is conversing with them. While she doesn't have an exterior judgmental energy vibration, she is internalizing what they are saying to be able to work out the underlying issues and behaviors and potentially inner work that others are distracting and hiding from themselves. She notices that when people are not wanting to do their inner work and they're effectively lying to themselves about what their biggest pains are, they're so comfortable lying to themselves that they're comfortable lying to others. And she has watched and noticed and observed many people lying to her as they are trying to save themselves from having to notice their own inner work. She observes this all. And this used to confuse her as a little child because she couldn't understand why people were not being truthful to her. Now as an adult, she is well aware and she can understand why many people have small knowledge and wisdom on certain situations and topics and they go around with an attitude as if they know all! This is a very humbling experience for them because they are comfortable and only willing to know "all" that they know while having the confidence and the assumption and the audacity to impress the world that they know "all" of everything.

We are saying, it is like saying you have five marbles and you're telling and convincing the world that you have an infinite amount of marbles. It's like having five dollars and impressing the world that you're a quadruple billion gazillionaire because you've got some money. People's egos allow them to have an amount of wisdom and knowledge which they're comfortable with, and as soon as they feel comfortable with that amount of knowledge and wisdom then they close down their seeking opportunities to expand upon and learn from more information by saying and giving themselves the impression that they know it *all* given the information that they have. They cap off expanding their awareness. They cap off experiencing and exploring and gaining more wisdom and perspectives because once they know one thing and they're comfortable with that knowledge, they will not expand upon that until they are triggered and almost presented with a whole other range of facts and information that pushes their memory banks open to be able to consider and ponder and factor in new perspectives and new information.

Often when people think that they know it all, they are not willing to open up and expand what they already feel confident in. Because as soon as you realize that maybe those five dollars is not all the money in the world, it suddenly makes you feel insecure about what you do have. Suddenly when you notice you've only got five marbles and you're playing a tournament of a marble game and your opponent has a hundred marbles, you're suddenly going to feel very insecure and inferior with the small amount that you do have. When you've had such a cocky, entitled, comfortable attitude, behavior of having it all, suddenly being pushed into really looking at what you do have and suddenly when you're comparing someone else's wisdom money and marbles, you suddenly have to focus.

For many people, we have needed them to focus on their inner work and that's just the stepping start, and that's just the basic foundational structures of their Awakening. And so when they're distracting themselves from actually looking at their inner work, for them to get more of us information is jumping ahead. And we like the structure of a very strong built educational foundational structured learning process of information. And while the vehicle feels like she's baby birding people with small information from sessions on Facebook and on Instagram and on Telegram, she is wishing that people would take up the pledge to get the full smorgasbord of information and digest it all when they want to, because they are so passionate and that's their big focus and their main drive. She knows that **this would be very helpful for them if they took this information seriously enough to apply it and to be able to then expand upon their own awareness**. She feels and she notices it is very challenging to encourage others to expand their consciousness because they already feel that they are awoken because they know the crimes against humanity and that they know that they are starseeds. And those two statements in itself makes them feel like they know all and they're comfortable with that. And so they don't want to look at their inner work because they want to mock those who are asleep. They want to mock those who think that they're just human. They want to mock those religious people because they suddenly feel like they are better spiritual people because they know some spiritual words. There is much to be said about how people have their demeanors and their attitudes when they are growing and expanding, but there's many things that we can do to try and push and trigger. But it takes a lot of effort to get people's attention, and when you're so addicted to fast-paced stimulant information and imagery, to stop and read something is very challenging. They don't want to read. They want to be given it so they can just numb themselves and be entertained. And this is where you really have the problem within itself.

She was wondering why this book had so many references and focused on the Draconians and the Reptilians. And so she was curious how that is going and evolving. And she is also aware that she has had judgment and criticized and mocked and ridiculed the limited mindsets of the Reptilian star seeds as they were still struggling to understand how it could possibly be that they could love themselves and humble themselves and see each other as brothers and sisters. And not try to focus on getting the most wealth and influence, but to get the most love for themselves to be able to share for all! She has been intolerant you could say, impatient you could say, and frustrated because she is aware that it's still their choices. All humans have choices in the way they feel. And so it's not hard to understand and to know concepts and principal philosophies on how to be spiritual. And so when she has seen *any* humans choosing to not love each other and not support each other, this is where she has a heavy heart because she knows they are actively choosing not to do this.

We have been wanting to remind you all, you are all one, but to be able to understand really how deep inner work hurt has impacted many Souls who do not care enough to do their own inner work to then just inflict and impact other Souls as a part of a distraction of doing their own work as a hobby, and you can say troll like behavior and attitude. When you are in the Fourth Dimension and you have been playing in the Fourth Dimension for a very long time as what you would know and call ghost realm, if you are ghosts and you have played with energy in the Fourth Dimension so much you're very fluent at interfering with humans to get their attention. But you have to be at that low frequency vibrations to then get access to that connection. Because when you are at a high energy frequency *above* negativity, worry, fear, doubts and you have a strong sense of self, you can not interfere with and be distracted and coerced by the low frequency vibrations that are attracted upon you. And so it's an influence. And while you're all one and while you're all connected, you almost could get pushed into doing something that could be part of a lesson so it is allowed when in low vibration. But it is what you could say the duality of lessons and experiences pushing you into making heat of the moment choices where you wish that if you had been able to be a bit less reactive, you would have made different choices. And so we're saying that is potentially when you've been impacted on and pushed to be triggered into having experiences which you wouldn't normally do, so you have instant regret. And what you do with instant regret is have profound teachable moments for you to then be really mindful of and focused on what you're doing next. And so you could say that he has been of service to help people have quicker regrets so they really focus and don't impact others, because they're merely impacting themselves with their knee-jerk reactions. And so it is significant what you are being pushed to learn, have teachable moments with, and to humble yourselves. But many are not willing to even humble themselves when they have been wrong. And that's the challenge, when you don't see that any choices that you've made could have been improved upon, or kinder, or softer, or considerate, or have compassion for Humanity, yourself and others, you never have self-reflection. You never look at your own demeanors and attitudes because you have got an attitude that you are not responsible for anything, and everything you do do is perfect. And we are saying that's a very stubborn stuck mindset, because it has the arrogance which is harder to humble. We could call those the big egos because they will not consider that they've done anything wrong. And they're so fixated on being right all the time because they know everything they assume, they would not be open to even considering choices of changes and advancements and growing themselves. They're very staunch and protective of the information they *do* know because they do not want to be exposed for not knowing all! And so they have the attitude and demeanor as if they do, and they will fight for it to distract and to disarm and to disempower others that are trying to politely or even forcibly show them you must be able to expand your awareness because your limited perspectives are limiting you. So there's much to be said about that.

So there is great growth now that the Draconian has had many experiences being in human bodies, while also being very much aware of how it feels to be pushed around and make these embarrassing mistakes. Because he had no insights and perspectives and accountability to actually realize that there were different ways to go about things. So he is humbling, humbling, humbling himself. And the things he is finding really interesting and intriguing, is the connections he feels with others when he does feel appreciated for good. He is seeing their gratitude. And he is feeling their love. This is almost intoxicating him. He loves these new connections, new reactions and interactions with others. And so this is why he wants to be more popular because he wants to do good. But of course, because he doesn't know *everything*, because he is still really fundamentally working with a Fourth Dimensional reality, he has information that he wants to share so desperately and he comes across it with such discernment and confidence. Anyone that's slightly more advanced and involved with a slightly more metaphysical perspective can see right through him. And he has many aspects of big influencers who are trying their best to be impressive. It's many stepping stones. And he does not mind, because those who are still using him as a stepping stone and still listening to him, still impressed with his wisdom and information and knowledge, still makes them feel fantastic. He is still happy with the level of information that he has and he is growing, still at a smaller rate than others, but it is still a marvelous improvement from when we did connect with him last. He has got this great attitude of wanting to impress people by helping them, that this is truly blossoming his energy frequency. More and more of his Collective have been able to come in and assist him which is great, but even he still needs baby bird information to be able to expand upon. He has information insights into other worlds, other wars off planet, which is ironic because it was him that was actually wielding these experiences. But of course when he relives it and tells it, he was the victim. But also the hero.

So, it is his public inner work that he is sharing with everyone. And he's doing the best he can and ultimately he's only supporting other aspects of himself who are also being guided as being humans following the Draconian because they are also still learning how to focus on not running materialism games, but opening and expanding their Consciousness and their hearts. And there's a big step for them. Big concepts that they feel so new and fresh with. And so while they may have degrees, while they may have influence and power, they realize that they don't have all the other skill sets that they could have, which forms and creates and strengthens their own spirituality. They've been so distracted with anti-religion, anti-establishments that control those aspects of religion and spirituality, they've thrown themselves into industry. So now they're having to be open-minded to potentially that this isn't as bad as they first believed. Because when you're trying to influence the world with your own power, you don't want to be led by anyone else. Especially an invisible God that can see you and potentially punish you, depending on how you want to perceive the written texts of the Bible. And so we'll leave you with this to explore and expand upon as we do feel like this is an insight for your book, because we still feel like there is more information coming that needs to be expanded upon. You do notice that there were two sessions that were in other books and so you're wondering, should that be removed? And we're saying, it actually is significant as it is. And so these are important information perspectives to have for those who are called to find and buy these books. This book in particular. They will be able to have the reference points of it[58].

---

[58] *Session 14 is also in Depressed People Don't Eat Salads, Session 19 is*

It's interesting. And we say for those people who are reading this book for their very first book, we love you. There is no judgment upon you and your Soul's journey thus far. And we encourage you to keep expanding your hearts. Keep your mind and ego in check as you are feeling the more your heart is your first and foremost way that you approach others and yourselves, the more heart space energy frequency you will feel not only from yourself but from others. And that is an enlightenment that will keep growing the more you do this.

So we say with love, keep going, keep trusting and keep expanding upon what feels good for you at a moral Soul level versus an influence, power, money and impressing level. Your inner work is an inside job which should be impressing *you*, not needing to impress the world. There is a difference between this, and when you know the balance and when you understand what we are saying, you will realize that this isn't something that you need to broadcast to the world, that you're expanding yourself on to. But this is inside working inner peace where you're trying to humble yourselves enough to expand yourselves enough to love each other and yourselves as equal. Because there are many beings here that are solely here to find and support you and love you and cherish you and inspire you to grow. Because your Collective is needing you to grow, because you're wanting to grow. The more you do this, the more truly enriched you will be. There is much fun ahead of you and we do know that you'll enjoy the higher dimensions when you put in the due diligence and the focus to be ready for that.

We say this with love!

---

also in Mastering Human.

There are so many beings that have loved you and are supporting you, not just in our realms but in your physical worlds. Those people that you thought were stupid and doormat because they were living with smiles on their faces and love in their hearts, you dismissed them once and now you're feeling awkward and shy because you feel like you want to be them too now. And we say, when you learn experiences and lessons you do expand and your new attitudes and demeanors become routine and beyond routine, become your norm. Keep growing through the awkward phases because when you are mature with these perspects and attitudes, this is when you will truly shine.

And we say this with love!

Session 45 : 3D To 5D To 3D

Wrapping Up 3D, Heading to 5D - Then To Another 3D Planet

J: (laughs) So this is another conscious mind conversation with my dear friend, a fellow practitioner, fellow second wave volunteer. And I am definitely sure that it's a fellow Soul family member as well. Welcome back my friend.

P: Hello, thank you.

J: Well thank you, because you reached out to me after hearing the sessions with Gaia and you got the same emotional responses and reactions that I did.

P: Emotional intensity. Yes!

J: It was epic! And it was good because this is the conversation that we want to have to be able to unpack that together because it still is a lot to process. And even though we've had some time to reflect on it and kind of gain our composure. So take me through your journey.

P: Well, I listened to that Gaia channeling, must have been like five or six times. I just couldn't get enough of it. And every time I listened to it I was in tears. And every time I listened to that song I thought of Gaia, the one about Forever Remember Me, I thought of her and I could just feel her love. And what I felt, it was love and it was also such deep sorrow too. It was all spectrums of emotions. It was amazing but intense.

J: It was so intense. From your sessions that you've done, what is your awareness of your connection with Gaia?

P: Well during my first session with you, my subconscious said that I know Gaia, like I know her beyond just living on her body right now. And I don't know what that means but I'm curious, because in that channeling that you did, you said that the planet that you naturally reside on, she's the mother figure. And I was going to ask you what does that mean? Was she the mother Soul of the planet at that point, at some point? What does the mother figure mean?

J: So, it's like a group of souls. It's a family. There is a mother and a father and there's children. And I know I'm one of the children. So I don't know if we are the Soul birth thought of the combined parents, because I haven't explored to that detail. Which now makes me realize more about the other project that they wanted me to do[59]. Busy, busy. Yes. So from my experiences with sessions, I've had some clients where they've gone to their home planets and I've had some really... So now when I'm listening to a client having their sessions I feel so connected into it, I'm almost getting the same visuals. But I'm trying not to let that distract me, because I don't want to be like, Oh my gosh, look over there, you know, I'm trying to let them go through it while I'm trying to feel into it to be able to understand it for myself and let them paint the picture of it. But ultimately with some situations I'm right there. So to get to our home planet there's water portals and there's dolphins in these waters. And so it's like, 'Oh, I'm swimming with dolphins, Oh, but I'm not a dolphin body'. So then you say, what is your body? And you could assume maybe it's like a mermaid or something like that and it's not that at all. It's an energetic body coming through. And then when they pop out of the water, then they morph into their

---

[59] Conversation From Heaven To Earth

own natural bodies and they go to their own kind of areas on their own planet. It's not their original, original first home planet. This is like, I don't know, their holiday home chalet you could say, where they do go and reside there a lot when they are not on their missions. But they're big sort of family mission is going and supporting other planets, especially at this predicament of time when the density of the planet is becoming very, not dangerous but challenging for the experience of the existence of the Earth's living experiences to continue on, so they need to be more focus on that. And it seems like there have been lots of planets that have needed more support energy wise. My first experience with this was when this client was going to her home planet, I could really sense the strong sense of familiarity which was making me want to start crying. And when she's having this beautiful experience, emotionally I felt so familiar with it. And then when we did more sessions, I didn't want to tell her my suspicions of how I felt so familiar with that planet and so I was exploring more privately with my own sessions as a client. And at the beginning of my time doing these sessions, I had a lot of Soul family that were helping me to get the perspectives and the insights and to get activated, which is fantastic to know that now for this perspective. And so that was really helpful to kind of set my foundations of this, because it seems like the more Soul family who've got the same missions, you can get the same level of information that I was seeking versus, as you know with certain other clients, their kind of still processing the human journey and the physical journey and the emotional journey and things like that, especially if they've only had a few planet experiences. It seems like the home planet and the Soul family that are connected to this, have done this for a very, very, very long time and that doesn't sort of phase them. It's kind of like the harder the challenge the better they are to be there to support. So when I was asking through this client in other sessions about her home planet and exploring more about this we learnt as we were exploring her own other questions about why she was connected to this Soul that gets channeled, and lots of people know about the Soul. So it's Kyron. And so she was wondering why she wasn't resonating with the channeler anymore. And so she got told very firmly that situation and why she felt so connected to the older information about Kyron. She just felt like there was something there. And so when we explored it further it was that that is the Soul energy of the father figure on the planet. And so I already had ascertained that we were sisters on this planet because I'd done my own sessions to be able to confirm this because I was like, why was I getting so emotional? Why did it feel so familiar? I'm asking myself questions and kind of getting my own... And I don't really want to share my own personal experiences with others because you kind of want them to have their own natural journey and just kind of have proof as such of the experiences. And so when we're asking about the mother of... So okay. So on her home planet, the Soul Essence is Kyron and that's the reason why he was sending so many love messages to his children who are here on Earth to help empower them and activate them, and so, it was really interesting. And so then I was like, well what about the mother then if that's the father figure or the father of my client? What about the mother? And they very, very firmly shut it down! They're like, we're not going to touch that. And I was like, I wonder why? And it was so peculiar, but it was like don't go there! And it was so strange. Anyway. And so I've done a few more sessions with that and she's absolutely beautiful. But you know we're busy, we're moms. We're doing so much other sort of stuff we haven't really kept in contact. Because she's awesome doing her own thing. I'm doing my own thing, and so we haven't really sort of connected in so much because we're on different paths of focus. And so when I did that session where they confirmed that Gaia actually was the mother, Oh my gosh! It made such a huge difference in how I conduct myself. Because I just was thinking if I knew back then that Gaia was our mother... Because when you're advanced and you've had all these different experiences and you just want to keep going more, and more and more and experiencing things to the point where you do want to become the consciousness of a planet. It's kind of like you've had every other body, you've had every other experience, and so why not have that experience. And so this is why we had that strong calling to come and help this planet out because of it. And I know so many clients that say, I don't really get that there was a Soul of this planet. But in my own personal session I bawled my eyes out when I felt Gaia's energy. And I was like how is that, because I've always been here I mean, I like nature kind of, but I'm not like a big buff on it. Why am I so emotionally distraught with Gaia in sessions? It's a common thing. And it's a really common thing. It's so startling, so intensively startling! And so when I messaged that client to say to her, hey, remember this session when I asked about your mother on that planet and we got denied? And she's like yes. I've got information about it now, we're allowed to know about it. And when she found out that it is Gaia, we both had the same response of, *Far Out!* If we had been told this we would not have been, *Okay, cool! We'll just keep on being in balance and neutral.* We both know that if we were given that information we would have come out of that session outraged and angry and really, really, really unbalanced emotionally, where we just would have gone into battle probably and not been cool. We both have grown so much since those sessions way back when, that we realized that with that information, we were not mature enough to handle it. Because I can feel into it now. I know I could get really angry if I wanted to about it and be really hurt that the Soul has been so impacted by people's choices here. And it's kind of like when you go to a holiday place and you litter. You respect the places where you journey and travel and things like that. And I feel like, for a lot of humans that are making these choices using their egos to not respect their own life contracts of why they're here, let alone the experience and the vehicle. And so it gets very convoluted because then when we add the whole, well this is just an illusion, how is this all playing out if it's just supposed to be an illusion? But the energies of the board game they were playing amongst this illusion is the template of Gaia, that Soul Essence! It gets really convoluted but I can understand why we get information as much as we can. But I'm definitely connected into this at a deeper level than I could have fathomed.

P: Another thing about that Gaia session that I just really, really loved and admired, was her unconditional love for Humanity despite what we've done to each other on her body and what we've done to her body, she still loves us unconditionally. She wanted to come in and tell us that these Earth changes that happen is not because she's getting revenge or anything. It's just the natural consequence of a dying body. (J: Absolutely!) I just thought that was so beautiful and it's such an inspiration too! If she can love every single one of us despite what we've done, I think that we can pull up our socks and love each other.

J: She's setting the beautiful example of how every parent loves their children regardless of what they're doing. It was such a beautiful gift to be given that. So my friend, who's beautiful, she's being part of the editing team to help us with the books, and she just wanted to share with me her joy that she has been doing with her daughter. She has been going to this choir and she recorded a part of their choir experience and what they were singing. When I listened to it I thought, Oh this is so nice. I'm so happy for her and her daughter. How beautiful. They're so wonderful! And then I felt like I was prompted to listen to it again. But I felt like I was being prompted by Gaia and I was like, Oh gosh Gaia, I haven't even thought about connecting in with you for such a long time because I felt like she was always in sessions and we were always discussing her, when out of nowhere she is very present with me and saying to listen to this song again. And it was really nice to feel into her, I want to say, this more mature, advanced version of her, which is really nice to sense this. And she's like, *listen to this again because this is a message from me and I want to share a message to everyone.* **I have not forsaken thee!** And I was like, well that sounds like a Bible reference you know, like okay, so we'll go into it then. And I could feel myself resisting a little bit emotionally because, usually when we are doing sessions with Gaia it was so traumatizing for her because of the density and the trauma and the struggles and the pain. Especially 2021 when she was in her most struggles. I am excited to feel into her because she is so mature. But then when I started listening to that song, and could feel that this was her message to us, I just broke down. I could not stop crying and was like, I've got to stop crying enough to be able to do this session. And it was so intensive, so intensive. What she really wanted to say was, thank you to everyone that has been here to help with the energy. And for those who are not coming with us, she wanted to personally give gratitude. And so she was wanting to thank those big advanced Souls who have been a blessing to humanity. To thank them for helping her children, which I think she views everyone who's been on this planet her children and extensions of self. And then to acknowledge those that *are* coming, prepare yourselves, but do not ever think for a second, even if you're in these traumatic disasters, that this is because something bad is happening to you because of karmic experiences or something. She really wanted us to know when we're in earthquakes or whatever the situation is, this is not her being angry with us. This is the body and the ramifications of a dying planet.

P: Yeah. Yeah. She's such a beautiful soul! She's so amazing!

J: So emotionally intensive!

P: Yep. I remember one time I was listening to that song on my way to work and I was crying. I was like okay, I have to stop listening to this. I can't go into work with red eyes.

J: So when we know that we're supporting the conscious collective and when we know that many people have shifted and then realized... *Oh gosh, there was a Soul on that planet! Oh, how did that Soul feel when I chose to do a lot of things?* They will consciously connect into us who are purging through those experiences. And so this is how we're helping with the conscious collective. It may not be them consciously being aware of this now, it could be when they are in the Fourth Dimension, being you know, fantastic ghosts or having their life reviews or whatever is occurring because of all our thought processes and all the ways that we process the information. We've had many times where we could feel into advanced beings to feel into us... So they know this information, how are they coping with this information and what was the process to get to the point of being comfortable with that information? What was their information? How did they process this to have balance and peace with it? Because it seems like a lot of collectives and a lot of guides are really struggling to inspire and encourage their 3D counterparts to be ready for what they're supposed to be ready for. And what do you do if you're a guide? You look at how others have processed this at a conscious 3D level. And so this is when we are working to set examples at the conscious collective to be hot messes. To feel everything! To feel it, to heal it! To then remember the metaphysics, to remember what's going on, to remember this is a game, to remember this is an emotional journey to be able to understand the dualities of all experiences and to still find acceptance and peace with everyone who is participating in their role and in their duty and in their choices to be human or animals or whatever.

P: Yeah. Wow! Yeah. That's pretty amazing!

J: So we know that when we feel into departed people we cry, because we miss them and we feel like it's grief and it's tragic and we've lost them and it's so, so sad. But when we feel into it metaphysically, we realize that when we're thinking of them, they're thinking of us and that profound connection, they're giving us their high energy frequency of love which is so overwhelming it makes us cry. And yet it's so strange because it's like, hang on, isn't joy in high frequency love just blissful? And it's not tears of torture, it's tears of joy. And there is a difference. But when we were feeling into Gaia it was so intensive. It was everything, everything. It was so overwhelming!

P: Yeah It was! It was a full-on few days that's for sure. Good thing we drink a lot of water to fill up those eye ducts.

J: Oh my God, Yeah! We don't need to have eye wash today. Yeah. And I am really appreciating knowing the perspectives of timelines and a whole lot of other things that we've explored so I have an understanding of what they are saying and how it's unfolding. And I know that when the Arcturians told us about this new virus that was trying to scare us with and to manipulate us into getting eye drops as a preventative to not impact our eyesight. So we got that information and then I think the next day they kind of came in and they're laughing and they're like it's so fantastic that they're listening to their information and then panicking... *Oh shoot, our plan. They discovered our plan. Okay so what next?* And so then it was like three or four days later all those fires started to happen which irritated the eyes. And it's like the Arcturians when I have no idea of what's really going on in the rest of the world because I'm so focused on the projects I'm working on. And so I watched the news. Even though my parallel life guy is obsessed with the news and loves it, I am completely oblivious to what's happening around the world unless people message me privately and are saying... Hey, do you know the medical perspective of this Jo? And I'm like, oh yeah, I can feel into it for you. Or like some session or whatever. So I'm always interested to be able to explore all those things. And so it's really interesting and it has been staying with unpacking *all* of the books on *all* of the sessions because I've been guided to add the sessions into the books. It's not my own personal thoughts and opinions about what sessions go in, it's just been a guided experience and so it is what it is. And so now that I have gone through the books and seeing all of the ways that we were about to shift and how that didn't work and we understood that, and then they tried this and they tried that. And they're moving us here and they're moving us there to kind of see what could happen. What situations would spark and inspire us to start thinking and feeling for ourselves and start noticing the systems, and to then be able to be awoken. And it's been so interesting to see the bigger, bigger picture of the journey and just these very intensive last few years, it has been extraordinary to be able to give bigger pieces of the puzzles. It's mind-blowing really.

P: Yeah. It seems like our teams have tried every which way to wake us up and I wonder what they're gonna do next.

J: It does feel like those light workers who are holding hearts, like the batteries. It's so funny when they try to mansplain to us about ourselves and how we work and to give us the visuals. Sometimes I feel like a small watch battery, sometimes I feel like I'm a car battery, (laughing) sometimes I just feel like I'm this acid, bitter, so bitter. Did you used to put your tongue on the nine volt ones to sort of... I don't think I even did put my tongue on one of those, but the real spiky?

P: Oh, I've done that. Yeah I've done that. I won't do it again but I've done it.

J: It was an experience to be had. (P: Yes.) Yes. So I think that the batteries, these are us who are in balance, who are aware of the agendas and the crimes against humanity but are not emotionally freaking out about it. I think we are doing such a good job that we are extending out the timeline of being viably having these experiences. Because when they were sort of saying... *Oh, you can't be here for much longer because it's just not viable,* and I would see they were looking at not everyone's able to hold this density. But I think because we've factored that more people are shifting so they're leaving and they're dropping their density, they're not adding into the density of their worrying and fear because they've shifted. And so I feel like there's so many extra bonus factors now that are giving us these longer times. (P: Yep.) And then because people are awakening, they are starting to feel empowered to grow and do all this sort of stuff. And instead of being part of the problem, deciding to become part of the solution even though they probably don't know all of the information. None of us really know *all* the information of how it got this dense and why and who was responsible for it and all that fun stuff. So it's been such an interesting thing to realize that in some regards, I know that lots of people are criticized for just being the love and light brigade, like they don't want to feel the darkness. They don't want to see anything. They don't want to believe anything apart from love and light. I feel like they are stable batteries while they're not wanting to see everything, because they won't be able to find the metaphysical perspective. So to hear about the crimes against humanity for the children for example, would just destroy the focus and will to live of someone who's a super empathic who cannot understand why Souls would want to have those experiences.

P: Yeah, and if they don't have the knowledge or the way to find the higher perspectives. Because when somebody sees those crimes against humanity and children, they take it at face value. And it is awful but there are higher perspectives that are available to them. But if they can't find those higher perspectives I could see it short circuiting their battery.

J: Yeah. They just can't fathom, why these poor children. And it's kind of like, well everyone's heard about karma right? And you don't want to suggest, well maybe those children have got karmic contracts. We don't know. We could guess that they may have done things to humanity that they want to have the opposite experiences with. I'm certainly not trying to suggest they did bad in the past... I mean this is a big thing right? Like you're going to be really mature metaphysically to say those children asked for it because that's part of their life contract, there are no accidents here. All life contracts are honored and guided. And as hideous as it is to say, we have to accept and respect that was their life contracts. They wanted to experience it for whatever reason. And we could freak out, we could judge, we could cry, we could scream to their victims, but as we know there are really no victims in this experience. It's all experiences, which I know it's really hard to accept that for some people. And I think that for those who are wanting to keep people in fear, they're only ever going to talk about the horrible things without metaphysical perspectives. And so yes it can be viewed as a tragedy, but it triggers people to look at their own inner work and that's all fantastic. And I guess when you understand about the crimes against humanity with the children, all of the other crimes explain why and how. And it's not impressive the way that humanity actually has been conducting itself, but that's judgment because it's still purposeful experiences. But there has to be something to be said about the fact that we keep getting told in sessions this will never be repeated again. So there is that. That's a positive!

P: Yeah. I listened to your channeling of, remember that 10 sessions you did with those 10 questions? I listened to yours recently and your subconscious said something along the lines of, nothing could have prepared us for what Humanity has chosen to do with their free will on this planet. And so I get the sense that what has happened here has not happened to any other places. (J: Yeah.) I could be wrong but...

J: When so many awoken people say... Oh it's the Draconians or Oh It's the Reptilians, and when we've done sessions with them they're like... Well we only kind of just introduced these concepts, that was Humanity that jumped and ran with it, using their free will. And so I feel like there's so much trauma from the get-go. I think once there were enough people here who started competing against food and who started competing against land and started having wars and battles with each other, I think that just started the ball rolling (P: Yeah.) and that became super problematic. But it was so deep, and I have a feeling because those Souls came from other planets as well, I feel like it's just trauma upon trauma upon trauma. And I think that's the reason why they gave us that 15 minute white light healing meditation, but they also gave us a second component which was healing trauma from other lifetimes that are off planet. And the challenge with living on different planets is that you have different levels of density and different situations and scenarios. And while Earth has these emotional experiences, how can you heal from a planet that doesn't have the same range of emotions? (P: Yeah.) So you can't heal from the trauma because you can't feel that range of trauma to be able to process it through. And while there are some correlations with the same energy frequency emotions, you can't heal from a burn from one planet if there is no fire on another planet[60]. (P: Yeah.) It's so convoluted and I think I need to listen back to what I'm saying because I feel like, because they've given me this new project, I feel like they're really trying to push me to be like look, look, bigger, bigger, bigger. This is where you should be focusing on as well.

P: Well that is super exciting to delve into that new research.

J: Yeah, because it's just so interesting. Like the book that I'm exploring which I'm about to finish (this one you are reading now), I've got a few more sessions to fine-tune. It did seem like the first half was quite heavily focused on the Draconians and the Reptilians and I was like, whoa, these sessions I didn't really remember. It's kind of like gosh, I don't remember the point where I started forgetting about all the content from the sessions. And so going back into listening to these older sessions it's like... Oh my gosh, that's right, we went through that experience! Wow! And to see it from having a little bit more wisdom and knowledge now, and clarity of those lessons and purposes. I definitely know that there is a Soul brother here who is still... This is going to sound interesting... who is still experimenting with drugs to see if they are still corded to the Reptilians. And so it's like he's signed his role up to come and to sense into, are there

---

[60] *Like always these CMC are very raw and expressive and random statements are made as we are processing the concepts to apply them. This statement was trying to say if you were burnt on one planet which still needed to be emotionally healed could that be possible if there was no fire on another planet to trigger the healing process. Not a literal fact but hoping this weak example suggests the different challenges of different planet experiences.*

things that are still harming Humanity? But he has this cleansing experience where he gets the effects of it. He gets uncorded if there is. But he's hunting to find where these ties are and how to process this with his physical body. And it's interesting because I had these experiences with helping him remove these corded experiences in our dream state. And so it's just so bizarre when there's so much that goes on behind the scenes to keep us playing the game.

P: That is so fascinating that that person that has that life contract.

J: So he's doing the recreational kind and there's others that are doing the pharmaceutical kind to see how this is still impacting them. And so we want to save all our brothers and sisters and say all drugs are bad and this is good. And be here and do that. And you know we want them to have all this balance and neutrality until we get over ourselves and our assumptions and actually look at the purpose of why they're living the way that they are, to realize that that is part of the conscious collective learning experience as well, so it becomes very entertaining.

P: Yeah. Yeah.

J: So interesting.

P: Very, very interesting.

J: But it seems really interesting because of the energetics, and I almost want to say this is like a darker manipulation. Almost like, when we know that there are good people here, good Souls here, but when they are hurt and they're having a reaction, they can send some really gnarly energy that can inflict others, right? And we've been mostly protected from that unless it's a lesson to learn from. And so, when you are trying to kill a whole lot of witches and those witches have got the power and the intentions to make curses on families or something, something, something. Like how much does that truly impact their energy rate given that there is no such thing as time through time and space. Is this part of something else we are working through? I know we've covered spells before and the power of words and sending intentions and things like that, but I want to say, if you were the person who had high energy frequency because you're a healer here and then you're going to be burnt at the cross or the stake or whatever and you send negative energy to impact others and it did impact others, could it be said that you're here now living your life in 3D to have the ramifications of your spells that you cast. You were the one that placed it yourself this life time and experienced the ramification of it. So again we're not victims to anything and it's really interesting that a lot of people are sensitive to these "old spells and family curses." And it's like when you just scratch into this in session to find out more about this... *Oh, well who did that to you? Oh, that was you in that other lifetime!*

P: That's similar to ancestral healing too. Like if you heal yourself you're going to heal your ancestors because there's a good chance that your ancestors were you.

J: Yes. Yes. Absolutely! And so when you're looking at all aspects of how we have conducted ourselves, I mean sometimes we're not always perfect, we're very reactive. We're really emotional when we forget about the metaphysics and someone dies that we view as unfair and unjust, and then we want to slay the world or burn the world down because our favorite person has exited the way that they've chosen. When we don't respect life contracts we will then want to fight and we will lose so much of our own moral compasses to fight. And we see countries have fought each other. We've seen families fight each other. We've seen so much conflict and there is so much of this karma that is playing out now. And so I know a lot of spiritual people are really scared and worried about these spells and these curses and all of these things that are happening to these 'innocent' people. They're innocent *this* lifetime, but because they're needing to experience it, this is why they have these lessons now. And I just keep hearing them saying, they're literally yelling out, anything that's happening to you this lifetime is your lessons. And if you have in your very reactive 3D human 17 lifetimes ago wanted to harm others because hurt people hurt people, and if you still have this karmic experience that you haven't had yet that you need to have, we're living it now. And we are seeing it now and it is fascinating. But there's so much going on. I feel like all of the collectives are really pushing all of their collective traumas and not all of the regrettable choices but also experiences. And so there's so much being pushed and put on to all of us for the conscious collective of all of these prior experiences. But it's a lot, like the history of Earth is a lot. And given the fact that we really don't remember much because our history books are very interesting and edited and limited, it's kind of almost like us knowing the same length of information from other planets. We really don't know all the information from Earth and so to try and work out why we're going through these healing experiences, I mean, you and I were talking about how we can see the repeat of Atlantis and you know that's the information we do see because we do know about Atlantis. What about all the other histories that we're not aware of that if we did get that insight we would be like... Oh my gosh! This makes sense now!

P: And also too, if there's other planetary healing that's happening as well on this planet right now. I could see that all playing out on Earth because Gaia doesn't have to experience the trauma that is pouring out of everybody's pores right now from their past lives or on this planet or other planets. So I could definitely see this as being such an excellent opportunity for healing for everybody.

J: I don't know if everyone gets to heal while they're here in the 3D. I think a lot of the healing actually takes place in the fourth dimension when they're having those reviews and seeing it from all aspects. And so I think she needed to step aside because this is not really her drama to play out. And I think a lot of the Souls that came here that have been responsible for their choices in their other lifetimes and things like that, even though it's not a punishment, like 'whoopsie, sorry. I added that density. I created that density. I created those experiences for people, now I'm gonna come and really have the opposite expression experience, to really hopefully be able to heal it so this doesn't impact everyone'. It's like everyone's here now to pick up their litter. And their litter may have been five lifetimes ago for example.

P: Yeah. Yeah. That makes a lot of sense.

J: So it's interesting, but I don't know when people are not factoring other lifetimes and factoring in that it's just accountability now, and responsibility time now. And while we've still got these extensions of time here and while you know people can have these big events, I think the number of deaths that are being officially recorded, I think there is more of them. We can never trust numbers. But I also feel like there are a lot more walkouts now than ever before. And I felt like a lot of walk-ins are coming in that have not wanted to live full lifetimes here, but are wanting to be accountable for their choices and other actions in other lifetimes. Plus, bigger advanced Souls who are like, *I didn't want to have a lifetime here but I'm here as a battery. I'm a battery and I'm going to look like I'm sleeping. I'm going to look like I'm complying. I don't want to get into the dramas of it. I'm just here as a service battery.*

P: And I know several people like that. They're just such wonderful lovely people and they just live their life within the parameters of this 3D planet. They follow all the rules and everything but I can tell that they're being such great service to humanity. Yeah. I see a lot of people like that.

J: And so we don't need to judge them as I know you wouldn't, it's just about respecting the fact that whatever their doing is exactly perfect for their Souls. (P: Yes.) So I do know that a lot of us get frustrated when, *Oh, they're not awake enough.* We do know that people who are not awake are purposeful. It's about getting those people who are *half* awake to get the metaphysical perspective so they stop adding density to this place. I love to talk about specifics and I love talking about more detailed events and people, and I don't know whether I'm going to start naming and shaming certain people because I don't feel like that's going to be really helpful because I just trusted our guides and I trust everything is purposeful and all that sort of stuff. So I'm just going to focus on me and the information that I'm being guided to explore. And I'm gonna have fun with it.

P: Yeah. Yeah. It's time for fun.

J: Absolutely! Okay my friend. Well thank you very much for sharing this. I know you better get going, but for everyone else who also felt the heavy impact of Gaia in those channeling and in that song, that she wanted us to know from her which is so beautiful, you're not alone. We all felt very traumatized with the energy as we were processing it and finding our own balance in neutral with it and having the acceptance of where her Soul is now. Which is in a very happy place! A very balanced place! And she is excited about New Earth, but she's so excited about that next 3D planet that is going to be the next version, she is super excited about that. That's where she's finally going to get to where she's been wanting to go for a long time.

P: Yeah. Do you know if she's gonna have to live the whole planetary cycle again before she can shift from 5D to back to 3D naturally? Or will she be able to kind of jump in and do it sooner than a billion years?

J: So, I'm not too sure on timing but I do know that she wants to be there for New Earth and to feel into that and just be happy with that experience. And then when there is a more settle in period time... And so I don't know how long that time would be. The experience is when there are enough Souls that are acclimated into the Fifth and kind of got their senses again and their strength again and all their skill sets back into the really good Fifth dimensional vibe, then Gaia and those members of the Souls who are going to do that, they're going to incarnate into the new planet, the 3D planet and have a smaller version of a life cycle that way with having less traumas from 3D impacting them on that 3D planet. And that's going to be the difference.

P: Yeah. And that's going to be all the difference. It's going to be such a huge difference. Yeah. Wow!

J: So we're completing the Third. We're going to have a holiday on the Fifth and then we're going back to the Third to be able to get it ready so as a body of the planet and the body of the beings there, they will all together in unity, evolve into the Fifth Dimension from being the Third.

P: Oh wow!

J: Yeah. And that's a huge project that a lot have been working on. So this is very exciting!

P: Yeah. I'm just so happy that she gets that.

J: They've been saying for a while that her life contract there is going to be more honored. And so if there is any forming of density that is not for an evolution of growth period, that's going to be a lot more managed and supported through it. And so it's almost like, I do believe, you have the veil of forgetfulness, but because there is not that much density already there, it's kind of a smaller, faster journey. And it's super significant because they want the humanoid bodies to be able to shift naturally all together in unison with the Soul of the physical body forming from the carbon to the crystalline.

P: Yeah. Yeah. Ooh. It gave me shivers. I hope I get to be on the planet when that happens.

J: I'm sure we will be there for that too! It's just extraordinary.

P: And I believe that the veil of forgetfulness that we have now is a lot stronger than it would have been like thousands of years ago. I feel like Humanity has more intuition. (J: Yes.) So the veil of forgetfulness here is very thick.

J: Yes. I think in general it's because we are being constantly subdued when you have fluoride in your water and in your drinks, you know it's got a lot to do with dumbing us down. And so there is so much that we're doing with our Free Will choices and not realizing the consequences of their impact. And so being accountable and responsible for everything that goes into our mind and in our bodies is significant. And while of course we can try to be as high frequency vibrational as possible, if we're putting the brakes on and trying to put the gas on in a car, who wins? (P: Yeah.) Who wins? And it feels like Humanity has been bunny hopping for a while and it's ramping up. The energy is so intensive now that any density is coming to the surface, it is so aggravating for them. They're feeling so overwhelmed and you can feel the big waves of stress as things are coming, but it is exciting because we're hearing from sessions that more disclosures in the public forum are coming out to be really taken notice. So those people who are still compliant and diligent to the mainstream media, they're going to start hearing more truths through *the mainstream media* are going to start with the disclosures with that, which is going to awaken many, which is about time.

P: It is, Yeah. Wow!

J: Because they're so loyal and so addicted to the wisdom and knowledge that the mainstream media is giving people 'apparently'. So when they trust that, when that's their God, when that's their one source of information and they're reliant on it heavily, this is really the only way. Because they don't trust their friends and family. They trust the big named TV programs. So if you're going to have to be awoken and that's your only chance, the more this is coming[61].

P: Yeah. Oh I can't wait for that! Very big.

J: Okay my friend. I love you!

P: I love you too Jo. Bye.

---

[61] *This just all feels so super exciting.*

Session 46: Love All, Judge None.

You can not know or see someone's life contract or the collective they are connected with by how they react to their human pain and healing journey. Channeling for yourself about each person would be helpful, remembering one human can have more than one Soul within the vehicle.

Yes yes yes yes yes, indeed, indeed, indeed, we're here, we're here, we're here once again. It's the Arcturian counterpart of the 3D vessel wanting to speak to be able to give more insights and perspectives over what she is feeling and thinking about certain purposes of the book that she is currently working on, and realizing the grander significance of the messages we're trying to share. She is aware you cannot see the difference or understand the difference between three people who have got inner work to do, and you're looking at those three people who are reactive to neglect, disempowerment, dishonoring their bodies, dishonoring their Soul essences in terms of following their life contracts. There's lots of things you could say about these three individual people, and these are hypothetical people, but in fact in reality, they're very much real. There are much more than three, but for this conversation today we want to talk to you about three people who have got broken hearts from old relationships they've forgotten about. They are still carrying that rejection. They still think that they were rejected because of the way that they looked, for example, but it was truly time for them to separate from each other, to grow and expand on their own independent journey. So they've made a lot of assumptions into why friendships and even relationships have no longer existed, as you were seemingly being removed from a group of friends or social circles, as you are being pushed and shoved along, pushed into your life journey experiences for the purpose of empowerment.

So again, we look at these three individual people with the same range of hurts and experiences and emotions... They've all felt hurt, they've all felt loved, they've all felt anger, **the book without sadness of**, all felt isolated. They've all felt rejected. They've all felt that all the range of emotions that you can have in the third dimensional reality. They've got it all, they've had it all, and they're still at their various independent healing Journey experiences from there. They still haven't recognized or noticed that all of those experiences were part of lessons for them, to be able to use that to empower themselves as future reference points. To know that their value of self-worth and how others treat them isn't a direct response on how they are showing themselves to the world, it is merely everyone reacting as they aren't healed. Uncompassionate lost souls, you could say, but the Souls are not lost nor could they ever truly be. It is about being lost in the days of being human. Days as in the 'confusion disorientation days', versus your Monday, Fridays, and Wednesdays. We love to remind you that time is not linear, and so when we are responding to your actual named labeled days, we'd like to not say them in order, because potentially they're not correct. There is that.

And so getting back to the three people that we're wanting to talk to you about... They've got all the range of emotions and they are all at their various healing journey experiences. Now as the viewer of those three people, can you choose to feel into and to judge what collective they're from? We see many of you wanting to label all unhealed people as Reptilians because they are so feral and viral, and so reactive to the ways of the world. We say that would be a foolish assumption, because as you know all Souls from all collectives are wanting to have different experiences and lessons, and some of those *advanced Souls* you could say are very reactive and very focused on complying to all systems. They wanted to experience living their lives as being what you could call asleep, as they're wanting to truly immerse themselves in the delusion of the illusion. We are not judging, nor are we choosing sides of what is the best way to live, because ALL are the best ways to live, and so therefore judging someone who was asleep or judging someone who's very reactive and very heavy with lots of density, as they are still holding on to a lot of trauma and not alleviating themselves by seeing the key purposes and significance and having a metaphysical perspective of why they're experiencing those things, which is always part of empowering themselves as they are on the various stages of the healing journey.

We see many, what you could call 'spiritual people' wanting to label everyone given the way that they're reacting and responding to the ways of the world. We are saying it is just as foolish as trying to look at someone's face and guessing what collective they're from. It is the soul's journey, not the body, that you have reference points to. We also say many people are still trying to match star charts and birth charts and they're still trying to label each other through the months of the years that you have been born, to try and classify and put yourself into box boxes and labels. Once you start wanting to identify as being a certain thing - being an Aquarius, being a Starchild, being a Starseed, being an Arcturian - once you make that association, you'll want to hold on to those labels and then naturally put yourself into conformance in your own boxes. So labels can limit you. Names can limit you. And without wanting to trigger you all, you're all human LOL... Consciously, that is. Our friends, you are all human because you're in human bodies, and while you're Soul aspects of multi-dimensional beings, you're human - so accept it. Many of our Souls do not recognize or want to even be branded or labeled 'being human', because they feel like it's so beneath them. We are saying that is part of the struggle, to humble themselves to be able to love everyone at all various stages of their healing Journey.

We are seeing many who call themselves 'influencers' panicking and telling the world to watch out. There is such manipulation and there are dark forces trying to really infiltrate you and get you now. We say isn't that interesting? You're suddenly noticing that your responsibility and accountability for your government experiences are now pressing upon you, and instead of seeing that in a mature metaphysical perspective, you're a victim to yourself. You're all protected from things which are not part of your lessons, and so if you're experiencing something that you would consider hardship or an attack, explore it. You're responsible to heal. You're responsible to be mature with your metaphysics and not go into victim mode. We have also pressed upon many many influencers who have got fraudulent belief systems in metaphysics. They are showing themselves up to their communities on purpose, while they still feel like they are wanting to play victims, so then they can get the sympathy card of all their followers to worry about them. When you have people worried about you, it makes you feel special, makes you feel important. We see one, he is trying to play a very strong victim game right now, because he is trying to entangle quantum energy into the people who are listening to him and love him. He is wanting to get all of the energy that they are worried about him, and so he's wanting to boost himself up by courting himself energetically to others who are worried. He is using their free will to worry about him to then manipulate them and to distract them and keep them in fear. While he feels boosted because of all the concern, this is interesting. We are trying to cut those chords now, and when people start sharing metaphysical perspectives such as 'you're always protected', 'you're never alone' and you're never going to be exposed to anything but your own lessons. If you do not like your lessons, learn from them quickly, so then you can advance and move on, grow from them. Or, you could just hold on to those lessons and not see how they were supposed to empower you, but rather to be a victim and to stay stagnant in that dilemma. Your choices. For many of you, you're supposed to learn from these experiences. Empower yourself, so then you can teach and share your perspectives and lessons and journey with others.

We understand many spiritual people do not want to be of service to others. In fact, they're only willing to focus on serving self. While they know spiritual words, and while they love to say they help others, actions speak louder than words. When you're trying to impress upon other spiritual community members that you're such a gift to humanity because you love helping people, but you don't actually help people, but you are holding space for energy. While that's helpful, we have said this before - do as you say - because saying empty words of your actions and demeanors here is just self pandering. We can see that many of you actually do want to follow through with the words that you're saying, but get disenchanted when you're not celebrated for making your statements to the world. You want to help people, but when you don't get praise and recognition for that statement, you're then not motivated to follow through. We are saying do the hard work. Be of service to all, and then allow yourself to celebrate afterwards and not get a free celebration for doing your life contract in purpose and significance of why you're here. So see what your motives are and see what's holding you back from only focusing on service to self versus service to all. These are all choices you are making.

Some of you are making these assumptions that the hurt people are Reptilians and the devil and the monsters, and that you should avoid them. We are saying, we have always told you to love all. We had no exclusions and we had no exceptions to love all. There are many collectives that are struggling to be able to collectively evolve, and when they are being judged by others who are advanced beings who are pissed off, you could say, that they're here to support and love all. That does not support those collectives that are trying to flourish and grow. When you are seeing unhealed people, when you're seeing hurt people still struggling to maintain balance to maintain the metaphysical perspectives of what is happening to them, or even to just start loving themselves and respecting themselves and realizing the gain. That you're labeling them as a certain collective or labeling them... you could surely see the popular one... if you brand someone a 'narcissist', then you're literally saying that they are the lepers of society and they should be shunned and avoided at all costs.

If you're still getting impacted by people who are hurt, this is a representation that you still need to heal yourselves. They are triggering you to recognize your own insecurities, your own pain, and your own inner work. We are saying hurt people can only hurt people who are unhealed. Healed people do not choose to feel hurt. They choose to observe the reactions and behaviors of others, and then see that this is a representation of how they're struggling to cope with their responsibilities and accountabilities for their lessons on Earth. There is much to be said about this. We say the people who are struggling the most right now have got lots of homework to do, because they're trying to catch up and complete all their lessons that they have experienced on Earth. When you're factoring in potentially dozens of other lifetimes here, they are rushing to get it all done before the bell goes off, before the shift occurs for them. So many of you are patiently waiting, being unconditionally loving and accepting to all, as you recognize their challenging journeys ahead as they are trying to empower themselves and have faith that they are loved. They want to feel that they are loved and accepted and respected, even if they're still on their healing journey. It doesn't inspire hurt people to heal themselves when they're being judged by others as they are trying to show the world how much they're struggling and suffering. Of course, that's their choices how much they want to struggle and suffer, but when they're being rejected and when they've been criticized and when they're being ghosted by others when they're so vulnerable and showing them where the hurt is, is this empowering humanity or is this delaying humanity from healing at a collective level?

The vehicle is wanting to feel into why so many people are feeling very tense with their bodies, as they are energetically supporting those who are struggling to feel the weight of all this homework that they have placed upon themselves. We are seeing that while there are more opportunities for people to expand and have the Earth healing experiences, they are rushing to get this done for significant reasons. There is an opportunity that the guides have seen, that they can still be here in the 3D versus having to go to other 3D planets or simulations for completing their 3D experiences. So some who were not out of the problem in terms of expanding extreme density to this planet, they have a balance and they will try and process things themselves. So there's a lot of expansion of time experiences for those who needed extra lessons and experiences. But as you're well aware, the shift is well on its way. There are more exit points at a daily rate now, and this should be giving people the awareness that something is happening. But of course from an unaware, unawakened perspective, this could just seem like some exit points which they are suspicious of - potentially sudden heart attacks. They may or may not have assumptions of what has caused this from a human 3D mindset, but when you have metaphysical perspectives, you understand that they are simply graduating from the 3D.

There are many lessons for people to buy into the dramas of other agendas that are happening, and so it's all purposeful how it's all unfolding for each independent person at their various stages of learning lessons, and that they wanted to be awoken and awake too. There is much to be said and there always will be. Much should be said, because there is too much happening and too much has occurred on this planet for us to be able to summarize in a quick summary statement. It would almost be impossible, since there is so many people's experiences and so many lessons that have been taught and experienced with teachable moments through the range of emotions, and how one person has been triggered to experience the full board range of emotions, and how they have chosen to either find themselves stuck or find themselves empowered through such life experiences and lessons.

There are so many parallel lives that are complete polar opposites to each other, on purpose. It is the same Soul living vicariously through two or three or four or dozens of different 3D aspects, counterparts of themselves. And again, you can't see who's behind and the Souls that are in these 3D bodies, and so catch yourself if you're trying to judge, and catch yourself if you're only wanting to love your own Soul family, your own collectives. This is exclusion if you are doing this. You're all one, and there are different collectives and different Souls on different stages of their journey, their healing journey and the expansion in the third dimension.

You can be mature enough to love all and notice any spiritual person saying otherwise. This is them showing you their immaturity and their lack of being able to apply metaphysical perspectives. You do not need to judge them for where they're at but see where they are at you already have beyond advanced information. You already understand and you already see how we are all one so judging and criticizing and being afraid of each other does no longer serve you see why you're still following those influences who are still holding on to fear and limited perspectives. This is important for you because if you're still distracting yourselves from those who have got limited perspectives, is this serving you? You could be experiencing better choices of your time if you chose to go with them and meditate for example then listening to corruption and manipulation from someone who is very fear-based. Again your free will choices allow you to do as you are but are they trying to energetically cord you into negativity for them to manipulate your energy fields? This is common and when you're not aware that this is happening that you could be choosing to use your free will to connect in corded energy into others dilemmas and others fear.

Apply your metaphysical perspectives and wisdom and knowledge that you do know. You have all this information and you don't apply it or see the full picture. You have different puzzles but you are not able to apply and to understand and to gain a bigger perspective. We ask you to use your minds to apply the metaphysics and to match it with your knowledge and wisdom versus your reactions and your fear. It is okay that you're still on your healing journey but when you do have the metaphysical perspectives are you able to apply it to your own daily lives and your own daily interactions and connections with others? This is all your choices obviously. We are saying we've seen many of you know this information and believe this information they can see the benefits of it but you still don't know how to apply it to your own daily living. We say practice makes perfect to be able to question the significance of all the experiences that you're having. It is a wonderful time to be able to explore this and to feel into why you are reacting and why you are behaving the way you are. We see some of you are choosing to still not love each other. You're refusing to support and encourage and endorse other people because of your own insecurities. Look at this because this again also does not longer serve you. It's all choices but when we know you want to truly Empower yourselves and feel into the highest energy frequency that you can here into 3D so you are not seeing how your choices and behaviors and reactions are holding you back from this.

There are many labels and names, titles you could use for the book that you are working on and we know that you're seeking this perspective and information and it was us giving you that name. We understand this was going to trigger many, we understand that you prefer not to trigger me but you understand it's the growth that is needed you understand it there's a big step for you if you did use that title. Feel into what you're comfortable with and look at why you do not want to trigger people. We understand your concerns because you know that people judge titles of books and covers of books and you know the significance of the information within each of the books. You're afraid that people are looking beyond the book titles it covers and judgment and in rejection of the information within it. We understand that you're starting to put too much pressure on yourself trying to make sure that the best name and the best title and the best cover is going to support people in their growth and journey to be able to be open-minded to the concepts and the information. We're saying to you as you are aware people can hear this information and these concepts but they still choose to not require them and this is again not your responsibility to worry about but we understand that you can feel our not frustration but when we have promised and we have agreed upon to awaken humanity to help them to make them remember who they are and why they're here and to understand the principles of metaphysics. When we have to repeat ourselves and we're still getting ignored even though we still promise and we still continually promise to support, it's a repetitive cycle. You are trying to find ways to help people push on through to step aside the egos to be open to the metaphysics because they are wanting to grow and wanting to go fast but they're also breaking and stopping and limiting themselves. They are in a battle within themselves and you're wanting to support them and help them to be able to take that next step.

We are saying it truly doesn't matter what the title is. When they are still not wanting to grow they will justify why they don't want the books and why they don't want to apply the information. This is on them. This is their Free Will. We could give you many suggestions that this is important for you to feel into it to feel into what feels the most appropriate for you. It's okay that you still do things for you. It's about having the balance and you understand this with the new project that we have been pressing upon you but we can speak about this in a private session.

We say to all who are suddenly now aware of the influences that they have been noticing, sharing limited perspectives. It is okay to suddenly hear this epiphany that you have been distracting yourselves because it is all valuable lessons. When you start recognizing how advanced you are with your metaphysics because we've been giving you accurate information from our perspective being Arcturians. You get to choose what you do with the information and wisdom. There is no point from our perspective for you to be shy or embarrassed about your wisdom and knowledge but it is a shame when you don't share it and you're not being of service to others because ultimately you are here for that.

We say this with love

Other Books from

Conversations with Heaven on Earth

MASTERING OLD EARTH

MASTERING HUMAN

EXPLORE the SHIFT to NEW EARTH

Time : The Convoluted Concept of Being Human

Depressed People Don't Eat Salads

So, There's THAT

We Are Here For This

We Say This With So Much Love

Mastering Human on Old Earth, Shifting to New Earth

Now That You Have Awakened

Conversations from Heaven to Earth

We Love YOU
We LOVE you
WE love you

Now That You Have Awakened - Apply Metaphysical Perspectives

Remember QHHT interns are meant to give 25 Free Sessions to 25 Clients as part of their training, remind them to add in a keyword into your session so you can have more sessions easily. Also supporting interns with your level of expanded consciousness would be very helpful for both of your journeys.

This is a wonderful time to empower yourself.

Email us if you want to make a connection

connectingtoheaven@gmail.com

We Love YOU
You are NEVER alone
You are very much LOVED

..... Always

Printed in Great Britain
by Amazon

25896322R00374